Persuasion

Second Edition

CURRENT COMMUNICATION
AN ADVANCED TEXT SERIES

Series Editor

Jesse G. Delia   *University of Illinois*

CURRENT COMMUNICATION is a series of advanced texts spanning the full range of the communication curriculum and including all the core ideas of the field. Each volume in the series is a substantive, lucidly written book appropriate for use in advanced undergraduate and beginning graduate level courses. All the volumes survey current theories and concepts, research and critical literatures, and scholarly methods, but each does this within a distinctive and original framework that makes the material accessible to students while enhancing and shaping understanding of its area for professionals.

Persuasion
Theory & Research
Second Edition

DANIEL J. O'KEEFE
University of Illinois at Urbana-Champaign

Sage Publications
International Educational and Professional Publisher
Thousand Oaks ■ London ■ New Delhi

For information:

Sage Publications, Inc.
2455 Teller Road
Thousand Oaks, California 91320
E-mail: order@sagepub.com

Sage Publications Ltd.
6 Bonhill Street
London EC2A 4PU
United Kingdom

Sage Publications India Pvt. Ltd.
M-32 Market
Greater Kailash I
New Delhi 110 048 India

Printed in the United States of America

Library of Congress Cataloging-in-Publication Data

O'Keefe, Daniel J., 1950–
    Persuasion: Theory and research / Daniel J. O'Keefe.— 2nd ed.
        p. cm. (Current communication, an advanced text series; v. 2)
    Includes bibliographical references and index.
    ISBN 0-7619-2200-8 — ISBN 0-7619-2539-2 (pbk.)
    1. Persuasion (Psychology) I. Title. II. Series
    BF637.P4 O54 2002
    153.8'52—dc21   2001005182

01 02 03 04 05 10 9 8 7 6 5 4 3 2 1

Acquiring Editor:	Margaret H. Seawell
Editorial Assistant:	Alicia Carter
Production Editor:	Claudia A. Hoffman
Copy Editor:	Alison Binder
Typesetter/Designer:	Tina Hill
Cover Designer:	Michelle Lee

Brief Contents

443948

Detailed Contents

Preface

This preface is intended to provide a general framing of this book and is particularly directed to those who already have some familiarity with the subject matter. Such readers will be able to tell at a glance that this book is in many ways quite conventional (in the general plan of the work, the topics taken up, and so forth) and will come to see the inevitable over-simplifications, bypassed subtleties, elided details, and suchlike. Because this book is pitched at roughly the level of a graduate-undergraduate course, it is likely to be defective both by having sections that are too shallow or general for some and by having segments that are too detailed or technical for others; the hope is that complaints are not too badly maldistributed across these two categories. Readers acquainted with the first edition will notice the omission of chapters concerning social judgment theory and persuasive message production research and the addition of discussion of functional attitude views and the theory of planned behavior.

Adding material is an easy decision; omitting material is not, because one fears encouraging the loss of good (if imperfect) ideas. Someone somewhere once pointed out that in the social and behavioral sciences, findings and theories often seem to just fade away, not because of any decisive criticisms or counterarguments but rather because they seem to be "too old to be true" (information about this forgotten source will be gratefully received). This apt observation seems to me to identify one barrier to social-scientific research synthesis, namely, that useful results and concepts somehow do not endure but rather disappear—making it impossible for subsequent work to exploit them.

As an example: If assimilation and contrast effects are genuine and have consequences for messages' persuasive effects, then—although there is little research attention being given to the theoretical framework within which such phenomena were first clearly conceptualized (social judgment theory; C. W. Sherif, Sherif, & Nebergall, 1965; M. Sherif & Hovland, 1961)—we need somehow to ensure that our knowledge of these phenomena does not evaporate. As another example, consider that although selective exposure is not at present a topic of compelling research interest, it is plainly valuable to keep track of what factors have been found to influence voluntary information exposure. Similarly, although it has been some time since substantial work was done on the question of the dimensions underlying credibility judgments, the results of those investigations (the dimensions identified in those studies) should not thereby fail to be mentioned in discussions of credibility research.

To sharpen the point here: It has been many years since the islets of Langerhans (masses of endocrine cells in the pancreas) were first noticed, but medical textbooks do not thereby ignore this biological structure. Indeed, it would be inconceivable to discuss (for example) mechanisms of insulin secretion without mentioning these structures. Now I do not mean to say that social-scientific phenomena such as assimilation and contrast effects are on all fours with the islets of Langerhans, but I do want to suggest that premature disappearance of social-scientific concepts and findings seems to happen all too easily. In the field of social psychology, one can from time to time hear complaints that "this allegedly new idea actually just represents a revival of so-and-so's ideas from the 1950s (or 1930s or 1970s)" or "this new phenomenon is just another name for something that used to be called X" (e.g., N. Miller & Pedersen, 1999). Without endorsing any particular such complaint, and without forgetting how grumpy old researchers can sometimes view genuinely new developments, still one can see in such remarks the real possibility that "old" knowledge has somehow become lost, misplaced, insufficiently understood, unappreciated, or overlooked.

It is certainly the case that the sheer amount of social-scientific research output makes it difficult to keep up with current research across a number of topics, let alone hold on to whatever accumulated information there might be. In the specific case of persuasion research—which has seen an explosion of interest in recent years—the problem is not made any easier by the relevant literature's dispersal across a variety of academic locales. Yet somehow the insights available from this research and theorizing must not be lost.

Unfortunately, there are not appealing shortcuts. No one exposed to Stephen Jay Gould's campaign against textbook copying can, with an easy mind, simply reproduce others' citations or research descriptions (Gould, 1991, pp. 155-167; Gould, 1993, pp. 103-105; for other examples of the perils of such copying, see Tufte, 1997, p. 71). (One hopes that it would be unnecessary to say that as in the previous edition, I have read everything I cite. I might inadvertently misrepresent or misunderstand, but at least such flaws will be of my own hand.)

Moreover, customary ways of drawing general conclusions about persuasive effects can be seen to have some important shortcomings. One source of difficulty here is a reliance on research designs using few persuasive messages, a matter addressed in Chapter 7. Here I will point out only the curiosity that generalizations about persuasive message effects—generalizations intended to be general across both persons and messages—have commonly been offered on the basis of data from scores or hundreds of human respondents but from only one or two messages. One who is willing to entertain seriously the possibility that the same manipulation may have different effects in different messages should, with such data in hand, be rather cautious.

Another source of difficulty has been the widespread misunderstandings embedded in common ways of interpreting and integrating research findings in the persuasion literature. To illuminate the relevant point, consider the following hypothetical puzzle:

> Suppose there have been two studies of the effect on persuasive outcomes of having a concluding metaphor (versus having an ordinary conclusion that does not contain a metaphor) in one's message, but with inconsistent results. In Study A, conclusion type made a statistically significant difference (such that greater effectiveness is associated with the metaphorical conclusion), but Study B failed to replicate this result.
>
> In Study A, the participants were female high school students who read a written communication arguing that most persons need from 7 to 9 hours of sleep each night. The message was attributed to a professor at the Harvard Medical School; the communicator's identification, including a photograph of the professor (an attractive, youthful-looking man), was provided on a cover sheet immediately preceding the message. The effect of conclusion type on persuasive outcome was significant, $t(60) = 2.35$, $p < .05$: Messages with a concluding metaphor were significantly more effective than messages with an ordinary (nonmetaphorical) conclusion.
>
> In Study B, the participants were male college undergraduates who listened to an audio message that used a male voice. The message advocated

substantial tuition increases (of roughly 50% to 60%) at the students' university and presented five arguments to show the necessity of such increases. The communicator was described as a senior at the university, majoring in education. Although the means were ordered as in Study A, conclusion type did not significantly affect persuasive outcome, $t(21) = 1.39$, *ns*.

Why the inconsistency (the failure to replicate)?

A typical inclination has been to entertain possible explanatory stories based on such differences as the receivers' sex ("Women are more influenced by the presence of a metaphorical conclusion than are men"), the medium ("Metaphorical conclusions make more difference in written messages than in oral messages"), or the advocated position ("Metaphorical conclusions are helpful in proattitudinal messages but not in counterattitudinal ones"), and so on. But for this hypothetical example, those sorts of explanatory stories are misplaced. Not only is the direction of effect identical in Study A and Study B (each finds that the concluding-metaphor message is more effective), but also the size of the advantage enjoyed by the concluding-metaphor message is the same in the two studies (expressed as a correlation, the effect size is .29). The difference in the level of statistical significance achieved is a function of the difference in sample size, not any difference in effect size.

Happily, recent years have seen some progress in the diffusion of more careful understandings of statistical significance, effect sizes, statistical power, and related matters. (With the hope of encouraging greater sensitivity concerning specifically the magnitude of effects likely to be found in persuasion research, I have tried to include mention of average effect sizes where appropriate and available.) Even so, we are still not in a position to do full justice to the issues engaged by the extensive research literature in persuasion, given the relative paucity of—and uncertainties and difficulties in doing—relevant, careful, reflective research reviews. All these considerations conspire to encourage a rather conservative approach to the persuasion literature (conservative in the sense of exemplifying prudence with respect to generalization), and that has been the aim in this treatment.

Of course, one cannot hope to survey the range of work covered here without errors, oversights, and unclarities. These have been reduced by advice and assistance from a number of quarters. Students in my persuasion classes have helped make my lectures—and so this book—clearer than otherwise might have been the case. Dale Brashers provided especially helpful commentary on drafts of this edition's chapters. And I thank Barbara O'Keefe for both useful commentary and an unceasingly interesting life.

Persuasion, Attitudes, and Actions

1

This book surveys social-scientific theory and research concerning persuasive communication. The relevant work, as will become apparent, is scattered across the academic landscape—in communication, psychology, advertising, marketing, political science, law, and so on. Although the breadth and depth of this literature rule out a completely comprehensive and detailed treatment, the main lines of work are at least sketched here.

This introductory chapter begins, naturally enough, with a discussion of the concept of persuasion. But because social-scientific treatments of persuasion have closely linked persuasion and attitude change, the concept of attitude is discussed as well, some common attitude assessment procedures are described, and the relationship of attitudes and behavior is considered; a concluding section discusses the assessment of persuasive effects.

THE CONCEPT OF PERSUASION

About Definitions

A common way to clarify a concept is to provide a definition of the concept, because a definition specifies some set of instances to which the concept applies. A definition of persuasion can illuminate the concept of persuasion by specifying some delimited set of cases that are to be labeled "persuasion." So, for instance, a definition of persuasion that characterizes persuasion as "human communication designed to influence others by modifying their beliefs, values, or attitudes" (Simons, 1976, p. 21) implicitly identifies certain instances of communication as persuasion (while excluding other cases from the category of persuasion).

But definitions can be troublesome things, precisely because they commonly are treated as providing sharp-edged distinctions, as somehow drawing sharp lines (between what is and is not persuasion, in the case of definitions of persuasion). What is troublesome about such sharp lines is that no matter where they are drawn, it is possible to sustain objections to their location. Thus one definition might be deemed unsatisfactory because it is too broad (it includes cases that it should not), whereas another is deemed unsatisfactory because it is too narrow (it excludes instances that it should include).

Fuzzy Edges and Paradigm Cases

Definitions are almost inevitably open to such criticisms, no matter where the definitional lines are drawn, because most concepts have fuzzy edges, that is, gray areas in which application of the concept is arguable. For any concept, there are some cases that virtually everyone agrees *are* cases of the concept (few would deny that a chair is an instance of the category "furniture"), and there are some cases that virtually everyone agrees *are not* cases of the concept (a pencil is not an instance of furniture)—but there are also some cases that fall in a gray area and can give rise to disagreements (is a television set a piece of furniture? or perhaps is it an appliance?). No matter how the line is drawn, some objection is possible. If furniture is defined to include televisions, those who believe that televisions are not furniture will object; if the definition of furniture excludes televisions, those who believe that televisions are furniture will object.

So, for example, if one defines persuasion in such a way as to distinguish cases of persuasion from cases of manipulation by requiring that in genuine instances of persuasion, the persuader "acts in good faith" (as do Burnell & Reeve, 1984), then some will object that the definition is too narrow; after all, such a definition almost certainly excludes at least some instances of advertising. But including manipulation as instances of persuasion will meet objections from those who think it important to exclude instances of sheer manipulation from the definition of persuasion.

Happily, it is possible to clarify a concept without having to be committed to a sharp-edged definition of the concept (and thus without having to settle such border disputes). Such clarification can be obtained by focusing on the shared features of paradigm cases of the concept. Paradigm cases of a concept are the sorts of instances that nearly everyone would agree were instances of the concept in question; they are straightforward, uncontroversial examples. By identifying the common features of paradigm cases, one can get a sense of the concept's ordinary central application, without having to draw sharp-edged definitional lines.

The Common Features of Paradigm Cases of Persuasion

Consider, then: What is ordinarily involved when we say that someone (a persuader) has persuaded someone else (a persuadee)? In such straightforward applications of the concept of persuasion, what sorts of shared features can be observed? (For an alternative to the following analysis, see Simons, 1986.)

First, when we say that one person persuaded another, we ordinarily identify a successful attempt to influence. That is, the notion of success is embedded in the concept of persuasion. For instance, it does not make sense to say, "I persuaded him but failed." One can say, "I *tried* to persuade him but failed," but to say simply "I persuaded him" is to imply a successful attempt to influence.[1]

Recognition that persuasion is connected to the notion of success leads directly to the next two features of paradigm cases of persuasion: the presence of some criterion or goal and the existence of some intent to reach that goal. To speak of success is to imply some standard of success, some goal, some criterion (one cannot, for instance, win a race without a finish line). In the case of persuasion, the usual implication drawn from the invocation of the concept is that the persuader had some intention of achieving the persuasive goal. For example, if I say, "I persuaded Sally to vote for Jones," you are likely to infer that I intended to obtain that effect. For just that reason, it is entirely understandable that someone might say, "I accidentally persuaded Mary to vote for Brown" precisely in the circumstance in which the speaker does not want a hearer to draw the usual inference of intent; absent such mention of accident, the ordinary inference will be that the suasion was purposeful.

A fourth feature shared by paradigm cases of persuasion is some measure of freedom (free will, free choice, voluntary action) on the persuadee's part. Consider, for example, a circumstance in which a person is knocked unconscious by a robber, who then takes the victim's money; one would not (except humorously) say that the victim had been "persuaded" to give the money. By contrast, being induced by a television ad to make a donation to a charitable cause is obviously an instance of persuasion.

When the persuadee's freedom is minimized or questionable, it becomes correspondingly questionable whether persuasion is genuinely involved; one no longer has a straightforward exemplary case of persuasion. Suppose a robber threatens to shoot the victim if the money is not forthcoming, and the victim complies: Is this an instance of persuasion? We need not settle this question here; settling this question requires some sharp line that distinguishes persuasion and nonpersuasion (and that sharp line is not sought here). It is enough to notice that such cases are borderline instances of persuasion, precisely because the persuadee's freedom is not so clear-cut as in paradigm instances.

Fifth, paradigm cases of persuasion are ones in which the effects are achieved through communication (and perhaps especially through the medium of language). That is, persuasion is something achieved through one person's communicating with another. My physically lifting you and throwing you off the roof of a building is something quite different from my talking you into jumping off the same roof; the latter might possibly be a case of persuasion (depending on the circumstances, exactly what I have said to you, and so on), but the former is certainly not. What distinguishes these two instances is that communication is involved in the latter case but not in the former.

Finally, paradigm cases of persuasion involve a change in the mental state of the persuadee (principally as a precursor to a change in behavior). Some ordinary instances of persuasion may be described as involving *only* a change in mental state (as in "I persuaded Joe that the United States should refuse to recognize the authority of the World Court"). But even when behavioral change is involved (as in "I persuaded Charlie to take piano lessons"), there is ordinarily presumed to be some underlying change in mental state that gave rise to the behavioral change; in learning that Charlie was persuaded to take piano lessons, we might plausibly presume (depending on the circumstances) any number of appropriate underlying changes in mental state (Charlie came to believe that his piano skills were poor, that his skills could be improved by taking lessons, etc.). Thus even when a persuader's eventual aim is to influence what people *do* (to influence, say, how people vote or what products they buy), at least in paradigm cases of persuasion that aim is ordinarily seen to be accomplished by changing what people *think* (for instance, what people think of the political candidate or of the product). That is, persuasion is ordinarily conceived of as involving influencing others by influencing their mental states (rather than by somehow influencing their conduct directly).

In persuasion theory and research, the relevant mental state has most commonly been characterized as an attitude (and thus the concept of attitude receives direct discussion later in this chapter). Descriptions of the relationship between persuasion and attitude change vary. For instance, sometimes attitude change is treated as a necessary aspect of persuasion (for example, in the claim that "persuasion inherently has attitude change as its goal"; Beisecker & Parson, 1972, p. 5); sometimes persuasion is defined as one species of attitude change (for example, as "a modification in one's attitude that is the consequence of exposure to a communication"; Levy, Collins, & Nail, 1998, p. 732); and sometimes persuasion is simply treated as identical with attitude change generally, no matter how such change arises (e.g., Chaiken, Wood, & Eagly, 1996, p. 702). Whatever the particular characterization of the relationship, however, persuasion and attitude change have long been seen as closely linked. Even when a persuader's ultimate goal is the modification of another's behavior, that goal is typically seen to be achieved through a process of attitude change—the presumption being that attitudes are "precursors of behavior" (A. R. Cohen, 1964, p. 138), that "attitude change is a principal determinant of behavioral change" (Beisecker & Parson, 1972, p. 5).

A Definition After All?

These shared features of exemplary cases of persuasion can be strung together into something that looks like a definition of persuasion: a successful intentional effort at influencing another's mental state through communication in a circumstance in which the persuadee has some measure of freedom. But it should be apparent that constructing such a definition would not eliminate the fuzzy edges of the concept of persuasion. Such a definition leaves open to dispute just how much success is required, just how intentional the effort must be, and so on.

Hence by recognizing these shared features of paradigm cases of persuasion, one can get a sense of the central core of the concept of persuasion, but one need not draw sharp definitional boundaries around that concept. Indeed, these paradigm case features permit one to see clearly just how definitional disputes can arise—for instance, disputes about the issue of just how much, and what sorts, of freedom the persuadee must have before an instance qualifies as an instance of persuasion. It is also easy to see that there can be no satisfactory definitive solution to these disputes, given the fuzzy edges that the concept of persuasion naturally has. Definitions of persuasion can serve useful functions, but a clear sense of the concept of persuasion can be had without resorting to a hard-edged definition.

▨ THE CONCEPT OF ATTITUDE

As mentioned above, the mental state that has been seen (in theory and re-search) to be most centrally implicated in persuasion is that of attitude. The concept of attitude has a long history (see D. Fleming, 1967). Early uses of the term "attitude" referred to posture or physical arrangement (as in someone's being in "the attitude of prayer"), uses that can be seen today in descriptions of dance or airplane orientation. Gradually, however, attitudes came to be seen as "orientations of mind" rather than of body, as internal states that exerted influence on overt behavior.

Perhaps it was inevitable, thus, that in the early part of the 20th century, the emerging field of social psychology should have seized on the concept of attitude as an important one. Attitude offered to social psychologists a distinctive psychological mechanism for understanding and explaining in-dividual variation in social conduct. Indeed, by 1935, Allport could de-clare attitude to be *the* central concept in social psychology. Understand-ably, then, it has been within social psychology that the greatest amount of conceptual attention has been given to attitude. This extensive atten-tion did not produce any immediate agreement on a definition or con-ception of attitude, however. The range of diverse views on offer can be seen in a number of extant discussions of the varieties of attitude definition and of the issues surrounding that task (e.g., Audi, 1972; Breckler & Wiggins, 1989; Eagly & Chaiken, 1993, pp. 1-21; McGuire, 1969, 1985, 1986).

If there is a predominant theme in treatment of attitudes, however, it is the view that an attitude is a person's general evaluation of an object (where "object" is understood in a broad sense, as encompassing persons, events, products, policies, institutions, and so on). The notion of an attitude as an evaluative judgment of (reaction to) an object is a common theme in defi-nitions of attitude and (as made clear by Fishbein & Ajzen, 1975, pp. 59-89) is also implicit in traditional attitude assessment techniques.

▨ ATTITUDE MEASUREMENT TECHNIQUES

If persuasion is conceived of as fundamentally involving attitude change, then the systematic study of persuasion requires means of assessing per-sons' attitudes: Without procedures for measuring attitudes, one cannot tell (for example) whether a given persuasive effort has induced any atti-tude change.

As it happens, the assessment of attitudes is itself a substantial research area. A great many attitude measurement techniques have been proposed, and a large literature is relevant to the use of attitude measures in specific circumstances such as public opinion polling and survey research. The intention here is to give a brief treatment of some exemplary attitude measurement techniques; more detailed information can be obtained from the reviews of Dawes and Smith (1985), Himmelfarb (1993), and W. A. Scott (1969).

Attitude assessment procedures can be usefully distinguished by the degree of directness with which they assess the respondent's evaluation of the attitude object. Some techniques directly obtain an evaluative judgment; others do so in more roundabout ways.

Direct Techniques

Direct attitude measurement techniques directly ask the respondent for an evaluative judgment of the attitude object. Two commonly employed direct assessment procedures are semantic differential evaluative scales and single-item attitude questions.

Semantic Differential Evaluative Scales. One popular means of directly assessing attitude is to employ the evaluative scales from the semantic differential scale of Osgood, Suci, and Tannenbaum (1957). In this procedure, respondents rate the attitude object on a number of (typically) 7-point bipolar scales that are end-anchored by evaluative adjective pairs (such as good-bad, desirable-undesirable, and so forth). For example, a measure of attitude toward the United Nations might be presented as follows.

The United Nations

good	___	___	___	___	___	___	___	bad
undesirable	___	___	___	___	___	___	___	desirable
positive	___	___	___	___	___	___	___	negative
harmful	___	___	___	___	___	___	___	beneficial

The accompanying instructions ask the respondent to place a check mark at the point on the scale that best represents the respondent's judgment. The investigator can straightforwardly assign numerical values to the scale points (say, +3 for the extreme positive point, through 0 for the midpoint, to −3 for the extreme negative end) and then sum each person's responses to obtain an indication of the person's attitude toward (general evaluative judgment of) the object.

Single-Item Attitude Measures. Another direct means of assessing attitude is simply to have the respondent complete a single questionnaire item that asks for the relevant judgment. For example:

> To what extent do you consider yourself to be
> favorable or unfavorable toward the United Nations?

extremely   ____   ____   ____   ____   ____   ____   ____   extremely
favorable   unfavorable

There are, of course, various ways of wording the question and of anchoring the scale (e.g., "In general, how much do you like the United Nations?" with end anchors "very much" and "not at all"), and it is possible to vary the number of scale points, but the basic procedure is the same. A single-item attitude measure familiar to U.S. survey researchers is the "feeling thermometer," which asks respondents to report their evaluation on a scale akin to a Fahrenheit thermometer; the endpoints of the scale are zero degrees (very "cold" or unfavorable feelings) and 100 degrees (very "warm" or favorable feelings; see, e.g., Alwin, 1997).

A single-item attitude measure is an understandably attractive technique for circumstances such as public opinion polling. The attitude assessment can be undertaken orally (as in telephone surveys or face-to-face interviewing); the question is typically straightforward and easily comprehended by the respondent; the question can be asked (and answered) in a short time.

The central drawback of single-item assessments of attitude is potentially weak reliability. That is, a person's response to a single attitude question may not be as dependable an indicator of attitude as the person's response to three or four items all getting at roughly the same thing.

Features of Direct Techniques. Direct attitude measurement techniques obviously offer the advantage of being simple and straightforward, easy to administer, and so forth. Another advantage of these techniques is that they are relatively easy to construct. For instance, a public opinion survey of attitudes toward possible presidential candidates can easily accommodate some new possible candidate: The surveyor simply asks the standard question but inserts the name of the new candidate. General evaluative scales from the semantic differential can obviously be used for rating all sorts of attitude objects (consumer products, political candidates, government policies, etc.); to assess attitudes toward Crest toothpaste rather than toward the United Nations, one simply makes the appropriate substitution above the rating scales. (This may be a false economy, however: For arguments emphasizing the importance of customizing semantic differential evaluative scales for each different attitude object, see Fishbein & Ajzen, 1975, pp. 77-78; Valois & Godin, 1991.)

One salient disadvantage of these direct techniques is that because they are so direct, they yield an estimate *only* of the respondent's attitude. Of course, this is not a drawback if all the researcher wants to know is the respondent's attitude. But investigators will often want other information as well (about, for example, beliefs that might lie behind the attitude), and in such circumstances, direct attitude assessment techniques will need to be supplemented or replaced by other procedures.

Quasi-Direct Techniques

Quasi-direct attitude measurement techniques assess attitude not by directly eliciting an evaluative judgment of the attitude object but by eliciting information that is obviously attitude-relevant and that offers a straightforward basis for attitude assessment. For example, paired-comparison procedures and ranking techniques (see, e.g., Hughes, 1971, pp. 103-105) do not ask directly for an evaluation of any single attitude object but ask for comparative judgments of several objects. In a paired-comparison technique, the respondent is asked a series of questions about the relative evaluation of each of a number of pairs of objects (e.g., "Which candidate do you prefer, Archer or Barker? Archer or Cooper? Barker or Cooper?"); in a ranking procedure, the respondent ranks a set of attitude objects (e.g., "Rank order these various leisure activities, from your most favorite to your least favorite"). The obtained responses obviously permit an investigator to draw some conclusions about the respondent's evaluation of a given object. Similarly, some attitude measurement procedures ask the respondent to indicate separately the degree or amount of positive feeling and negative feeling toward the attitude object (see, e.g., Kaplan, 1972; Lull & Cappella, 1981); these can then be combined to give an index of overall evaluation (and, not incidentally, can also be used to assess the degree of attitudinal ambivalence, that is, the degree to which the attitude is based on a mixture of positive and negative elements; see Breckler, 1994; Priester & Petty, 1996; M. M. Thompson, Zanna, & Griffin, 1995).

The two most common and well known quasi-direct attitude measurement procedures, however, are those devised by Louis Thurstone and by Rensis Likert. In these procedures, the respondent's attitude is inferred from judgments of (or reactions to) statements that are rather obviously attitude-relevant. The attitude assessment instrument, then, consists of statements to which the respondent reacts (say, by agreeing or disagreeing with each statement), and the respondent's attitude is inferred from the pattern of responses.

Obviously, however, if a researcher is going to gauge respondents' attitudes by examining respondents' reactions to a set of statements, not just any statements will do; for example, one is not likely to learn much about attitudes toward the United Nations by assessing persons' agreement with a statement such as "Baseball is a better game than football." Thus the task faced in constructing a Thurstone or Likert attitude scale is the task of selecting items (statements) that appear to serve as suitable indicators of attitude. One may start with a large pool of statements that might possibly be included on a final attitude instrument, but the problem is to somehow winnow that pool down. Thurstone and Likert proposed different methods for doing so, with corresponding differences in the nature of their attitude scales.

Thurstone Attitude Scales. The idea that one might obtain information about a person's attitude by examining the person's reactions to attitude-relevant statements was the basis for one of the earliest attitude assessment procedures, that developed by Thurstone (1931; Thurstone & Chave, 1929). Following is a brief and abstracted description of Thurstone's procedures (for details, see Green, 1954).

The investigator begins by assembling a pool of about a hundred possible items, opinion statements that may indicate something about a person's attitude toward the object under investigation. For example, if the topic of investigation concerns attitudes toward the First Federal Bank, the initial pool might include statements such as these: "This bank is reliable," "This bank is inefficient," "I prefer not to do business with this bank," "This bank is old-fashioned," "This bank has unfriendly personnel," "This bank is trustworthy," "This bank is not dynamic," and so on.

Then a hundred or so people are asked to serve as "judges" of these items. The judges are asked to indicate the degree of favorableness or unfavorableness toward the attitude object that would be implied by agreement with each item. Concretely, the judges are asked to sort the items into 11 categories, equally spaced along the evaluative dimension; category 1 is to contain statements indicating the most extreme negative attitude toward the object, category 11 is for statements indicating the most extreme positive attitude toward the object, category 6 is for statements that indicate a neutral attitude, and so on.

Items on which the judges disagree widely are discarded. Thurstone's procedure is aimed at identifying statements such that one can dependably tell something about a person's attitude from whether the person agrees with a given statement. Hence if a statement is not consistently seen (by the judges) as indicating a given attitude, the statement is a poor candidate for inclusion in the final attitude scale. For instance, the item "This bank is old-fashioned" as a possible item for assessing attitude toward a given bank might engender such disagreement; some judges might think agreement with this item indicated a positive attitude (where "old-fashioned" was taken to indicate solidity, reliability, and the like), whereas other judges might think agreement indicated a negative attitude (where "old-fashioned" was taken to mean stodgy, behind the times, and so forth). If this item were to appear in the final attitude scale, one would not be able to make sound inferences about the attitude of a respondent who agreed with the statement; hence the item is discarded.

The final attitude scale is composed of approximately 20 items selected from among those still remaining in the pool. The investigator computes the average scale value for each of the remaining items (that is, the average across the judges' ratings) and then selects about 20 items such that they are equally spaced along the evaluative dimension. For instance, an investigator might ideally try to obtain items with scale values of 1.0, 1.5, 2.0, 2.5, . . . 10.0, 10.5, and 11.0.

When this attitude scale is administered, respondents are instructed to check all the items with which they agree. A respondent's attitude score consists of the average scale value of the items that are endorsed. A respondent who agreed with items that had scale values of 9.3, 10.0, and 10.7 would have an attitude score of 10.0 (a strongly positive attitude, reflecting the respondent's agreement with three highly positive items).

Two possible problems with Thurstone's method of attitude scale construction have been noted. The first is that the attitudes of the judges may influence their placement of items along the evaluative dimension, thus biasing the scale; the empirical evidence, however, suggests that any changes in scale values are likely to be small (see M. Sherif & Hovland, 1961), and in any event, the judges should be representative of the population to be studied. The other potential difficulty is that judges may not clearly understand the task they are asked to perform (Romer, 1983), but careful instructions may minimize this problem.

Likert Attitude Scales. The attitude measurement technique developed by Likert (1932), like Thurstone's technique, draws inferences about a respondent's attitude from the respondent's agreement or disagreement with attitude-relevant statements. As in the case of Thurstone scales, constructing a Likert attitude scale begins with assembling a large number of attitude-relevant statements as an initial pool from which the scale items will be selected. But Likert's procedure differs from Thurstone's in the manner of selecting items from the pool and in the sort of response that respondents are asked to give. The following is a brief description of Likert's procedures (for details, see Likert, 1932, or Green, 1954).

The investigator begins by discarding any neutral or ambiguous statements from the initial item pool. One then has test respondents react to each of the remaining statements. These test respondents are asked to indicate the extent of their agreement or disagreement with each item, commonly on a 5-point scale. For example:

This bank is reliable

strongly agree   _____   _____   _____   _____   _____   strongly disagree

Each response is then scored from 1 to 5, with 5 representing the most favorable response; in the example above, the "strongly agree" pole would be scored as 5, and the "strongly disagree" pole scored as 1 (note, however, that if the item had been worded "this bank is *un*reliable," then the scoring would be reversed, with "strongly agree" scored as 1). An overall attitude score can then be computed for each test respondent; if 100 items are in the initial pool, overall attitude scores could range from 100 (the most negative attitude possible) to 500 (the most positive attitude).

An item analysis is then undertaken, in which responses to each item are correlated with the overall attitude score. The 20 or 25 items with the highest correlations are then selected for the final attitude scale. The selected items are presumably the best indicators of attitude because they are the items most strongly associated with (most predictive of) the overall attitude score.

On the final attitude scale, the selected items are presented as in the test research, with 5-point scales assessing the respondent's agreement with the item. Overall attitude is estimated by the total across the items.

Features of Quasi-Direct Techniques. There is a good deal of variation in quasi-direct attitude assessment techniques, but as a rule, these procedures provide more information than do direct attitude measurement techniques. For example, when a Thurstone or Likert scale has been employed, a researcher can see what specific items were especially likely to be endorsed by respondents with particular attitudes; an investigator who finds, for instance, that those with unfavorable attitudes toward the bank very often agreed with the statement that "this bank has unfriendly personnel" may well have learned about a possible cause of those negative attitudes. Similarly, ranking techniques can give information about a large number of attitudes and so provide insight about comparative evaluations; techniques in which the respondent indicates separately the degree of positive and negative feeling toward the object (e.g., Kaplan, 1972) offer the possibility of distinguishing respondents with neutral attitudes from those who are indifferent; and so on. Precisely because quasi-direct procedures involve acquiring attitude-relevant information (rather than direct attitude assessments), these procedures offer information not available with direct measurement techniques.

But this additional information is obtained at a cost. Thurstone and Likert attitude scales have to be constructed anew for each attitude object; obviously, one cannot use the First Federal Bank attitude scale to assess attitudes toward Greg's Golf Shop or Carol's Chemical Company, or even toward City Savings and Loan. (Indeed, the substantial effort needed to obtain a sound Thurstone or Likert scale is often a deterrent to the use of such techniques.) Procedures such as paired-comparison ratings or ranking tasks may take more time to administer than would direct attitude measures.

Indirect Techniques

Indirect attitude measurement techniques assess attitude not by directly eliciting an evaluation of the attitude object, or even by eliciting information obviously relevant to such an overall evaluation, but instead by some more roundabout (indirect) means. Quite a few indirect techniques have appeared in the literature; useful reviews include Dawes and Smith (1985) and Kidder and Campbell (1970). Three examples of indirect attitude assessment procedures are discussed here: physiological indices, information tests, and the lost-letter technique.

Physiological Indices. One group of indirect attitude measurement techniques relies on physiological indices as potential indicators of attitude. These have included measures of pupil dilation and contraction, electrodermal indices (concerning aspects of skin electricity such as resistance), heart rate, respiration rate, and perspiration rate. Each physiological index has spawned a body of research bearing on the use of that index as a possible indicator of attitude, and different substantive issues arise in those various directions of research. Nevertheless, a general conclusion seems appropriately drawn about the physiological indices mentioned above: These indices may assess general arousal but do not measure attitude (Cacioppo & Sandman, 1981; Mueller, 1970; Petty & Cacioppo, 1983; Woodmansee, 1970). Specifically, the evidence suggests that at best these indices can indicate something about a respondent's degree of arousal but cannot distinguish the direction of the associated affect (cannot distinguish positive arousal from negative arousal); of course, this inability to distinguish the direction of evaluation makes these indices unsuitable as measures of attitude. Some work suggests that an index of facial electromyographic (EMG) activity—the contractions of muscles in the face—holds some promise as a physiological attitude measure (e.g., Cacioppo, Petty, Losch, & Kim, 1986; for a general discussion, see Cacioppo, Petty, & Geen, 1989; cf. Cacioppo, Bush, & Tassinary, 1992). An even more likely physiological basis for attitude assessment appears to lie in brain wave activity (see, e.g., Cacioppo, Crites, & Gardner, 1996; Cacioppo, Crites, Gardner, & Berntson, 1994).

Information Tests. Another class of indirect attitude assessment procedures consists of "information tests." These tests are based on the idea that persons' attitudes can influence their factual judgments, and hence that by examining a respondent's judgments about factual matters, one can learn something about the respondent's attitude.

K. R. Hammond's (1948) error-choice attitude measurement technique is a classic example of an information-test attitude measure. In this procedure, respondents are presented with multiple-choice questions concerning matters of fact, with two answers available for each question—but both answers are incorrect. The respondent is forced into choosing a wrong answer (hence the label "error-choice"), with the respondent's attitude inferred from the nature of the wrong answer chosen. For example, Hammond's assessment of labor-management attitudes included an item such as this: "Financial reports show that out of every business dollar, (a) 16 cents is profit, (b) 3 cents is profit," with the true figure midway between those given. The assumption (which Hammond showed to be sound) was that persons with promanagement attitudes would likely underestimate profits, whereas those with prolabor attitudes would probably give an overestimate.

Other information-test ways of assessing attitude can be seen as variations on this basic procedure (see Kidder & Campbell, 1970, pp. 351-358). One can provide more than two erroneous choices (to assess the respondent's degree of error), one can include items for which the truth is indeterminate but force respondents to choose between two extreme answers, one can ask open-ended questions ("What percentage of business dollar volume is profit?"), and so forth. Whatever form an information-test attitude measure takes, however, the critical question is whether the items on the instrument are diagnostic of attitude, that is, whether persons' attitudes are being reflected in their answers to the items. One cannot justifiably assume that answers to a given question will be influenced by attitude;

instead, validating evidence needs to be acquired in the course of constructing the attitude measure.

Lost-Letter Technique. The lost-letter technique (Milgram, Mann, & Harter, 1965) is an indirect means of assessing attitudes in a community. Briefly, the technique involves addressing a large number of envelopes to two (fictitious) organizations that appear to have opposing views on the attitude topic. If the topic is abortion rights, for instance, the researcher addresses half the envelopes to an organization whose name clearly indicates that the organization is pro-life; the other half of the envelopes are addressed to an organization that is clearly pro-choice. These envelopes are stamped and then randomly scattered in the community. A person who comes upon an envelope will presumably treat it as a lost letter that was supposed to be mailed. The question is whether the finder will mail the letter, and the presumption is that finders will not be willing to mail letters to organizations opposing their views but will mail letters to organizations whose attitudes are compatible with their own. All the mailed envelopes, of course, come to the researcher, who tallies the number of pro-life and pro-choice letters received. If, for instance, many more pro-choice letters than pro-life letters are received, the conclusion will be that in the community studied, pro-choice attitudes predominate. (For examples and discussion of this technique, see Bolton, 1974; Hines, 1980; Shotland, Berger, & Forsythe, 1970; Stern & Faber, 1997.)

A common problem with this technique, as noted by Dawes and Smith (1985, p. 544), is that the return rate tends to be closer to a 50-50 split than more direct attitude measures (such as public opinion surveys in the community) suggest; it may be that some people mail the letters no matter what their own opinions are, and others do not mail the letters no matter what their opinions are, thus tending to minimize the impact of those persons whose letter mailing is influenced by their attitudes.

Features of Indirect Techniques. Indirect attitude assessment techniques are a varied lot: Some involve paper-and-pencil questionnaires (as in the error-choice technique), but others do not; some can be used to assess the attitude of particular individuals, but others (such as the lost-letter technique) cannot; some can be effectively employed only in a laboratory setting (the physiological techniques, for instance, require the appropriate equipment), but others are equally at home in laboratory or field settings.

These techniques have in common, of course, that they are indirect. Their indirectness naturally suggests the most appropriate circumstances for use: Indirect attitude assessment techniques are likely to be most attractive in circumstances in which one fears respondents may, for whatever reason, distort their true attitudes. In most research on persuasion, however, these circumstances are rather uncommon (respondents are ensured anonymity, message topics are generally not unusually sensitive ones, etc.); consequently, indirect attitude measures are rarely employed.

Summary

As this survey suggests, a variety of attitude measurement techniques are available. The overwhelmingly most frequently used attitude measurement procedures are direct or quasi-direct techniques; reliability and validity are more readily established for attitude measures based on these techniques than for measures derived from indirect procedures. Direct procedures are often preferred over quasi-direct techniques because of the effort required for constructing Thurstone or Likert scales. But which specific attitude assessment procedure an investigator employs in a given instance will depend on the particulars of the situation. Depending on what the researcher wants to find out, the time available to prepare the attitude questionnaire, the time available to question respondents, the sensitivity of the attitude topic, and so forth, different techniques will recommend themselves.

ATTITUDES AND BEHAVIORS

The General Relationship

Attitude has been taken to be a key mental state relevant to persuasion because of a presumed relationship between attitudes and actions. The assumption has been that attitudes are important determinants of behavior and, correspondingly, that one avenue to changing a person's behavior will be to change that person's attitudes. For a period, however, it appeared as if the assumption of a close relationship between attitudes and behaviors was mistaken. Some classic studies (e.g., LaPiere, 1934) and some extensive reviews (e.g., Wicker, 1969) suggested that people's actions were commonly inconsistent with their attitudes.

It has turned out that these pessimistic conclusions about the attitude-behavior relationship were overdrawn. Subsequent research has confirmed that attitudes and behaviors are generally consistent (for some reviews, see Eckes & Six, 1994; M.-S. Kim & Hunter, 1993a; Kraus, 1995).[2] The degree of attitude-behavior consistency, however, has been found to vary depending on other factors. A large number of possible moderating variables have been explored, including the degree to which the behavior is effortful (Bagozzi, Yi, & Baumgartner, 1990); having a vested interest in a position (Crano & Prislin, 1995); attitude accessibility (Fazio, Powell, & Williams, 1989; Kokkinaki & Lunt, 1997); affective-cognitive consistency (R. Norman, 1975); self-monitoring (Ajzen, Timko, & White, 1982; Shepherd, 1985; Snyder & Kendzierski, 1982); and analyzing reasons for one's attitude (T. D. Wilson, Dunn, Bybee, Hyman, & Rotondo, 1984). The next section discusses three well-studied illustrative factors: the correspondence between the attitudinal and behavioral measures, the basis on which the attitude was formed, and the perceived relevance of the attitude to the action.

Moderating Factors

Correspondence of Measures. One factor that influences the observed consistency between an attitudinal measure and a behavioral measure is the nature of the measures involved. Good evidence indicates that substantial attitude-behavior correlations will be obtained only when the attitudinal measure and the behavioral measure correspond in specificity (Ajzen & Fishbein, 1977). For example, a general attitude will probably not be especially strongly correlated with any one particular specific behavior. A general attitude measure corresponds to a general behavioral measure, not to a specific one, and hence general attitude measures should be correlated more strongly with general behavioral measures than with specific ones.

For example, general attitudes toward religion might or might not be strongly correlated with performance of the particular act of (say) reading books about religious philosophy. But attitudes toward religion may well be strongly correlated with a general religious behavior index—an index based on multiple behaviors (whether the person reads books about religious philosophy, attends religious services, listens to religious programs on radio or television, owns records of religious music, donates money to religious institutions, consults clergy about personal problems, and so on). No one of these behaviors may be very strongly predicted by religious attitude, but the overall pattern of these behaviors might well be associated with religious attitude. That is, although the correlation of the general attitude with any one of these behaviors might be relatively small, the correlation of the general attitude with a multiple-act behavioral measure may be much greater.[3]

Several investigations have yielded information about the relative strength of the attitude-behavior association when single-act and multiple-act behavioral measures are predicted on the basis of general attitudes. In these studies, the average correlation between general attitude and any single-act index of behavior was roughly .30; by contrast, the average correlation between general attitude and a multiple-act behavioral measure was approximately .65 (Babrow & O'Keefe, 1984; Fishbein & Ajzen, 1974; O'Keefe & Shepherd, 1982; Sjoberg, 1982; Weigel & Newman, 1976; see also Oskamp et al., 1991). These findings plainly indicate that attitudinal measures and behavioral measures are likely to be rather more strongly associated when there is substantial correspondence between the two measures and underscore the folly of supposing that a single specific behavior will necessarily or typically be strongly associated with a person's general attitude (for some relevant reviews, see Eckes & Six, 1994; M.-S. Kim & Hunter, 1993a; Kraus, 1995).

Correspondingly, these findings underscore the importance of carefully considering the focus of persuasive efforts. For instance, to encourage participation in a community recycling program, it might seem natural to construct persuasive messages aimed at inducing favorable attitudes toward protecting the environment. But this is not likely to be a particularly efficient persuasive strategy. Even if the messages succeed in producing positive environmental protection attitudes, those general attitudes may not be especially strongly associated with the specific behavior that is wanted (recycling program participation). A more effective focus for persuasive efforts might well be specific attitudes toward participation in the recycling program, rather than general environmental attitudes.[4]

Formative Basis of Attitude. A second factor influencing attitude-behavior consistency is the manner in which the attitude was formed or shaped. Attitudes based on direct behavioral experience with the attitude object have been found to be more predictive of later behavior toward the object than are attitudes based on indirect experience. (For some examples and discussion, see Doll & Ajzen, 1992; Doll & Mallu, 1990; Eagly & Chaiken, 1993, pp. 194-200; Fazio & Zanna, 1978, 1981; Steffen & Gruber, 1991. For some complexities, see Millar & Millar, 1996a, 1998.)

For example, during a housing shortage at Cornell University—well publicized on campus—some new students had to be placed in temporary quarters (thus giving them firsthand experience with the problem); other new students were given permanent dormitory rooms (and so knew of the problem less directly). The two groups had equally negative attitudes regarding the housing crisis, but the strength of the attitude-behavior relationship differed. Those whose attitudes were formed on the basis of direct experience exhibited greater consistency between their attitudes and behaviors aimed at alleviating the crisis than did students whose attitudes were based on indirect experience (Regan & Fazio, 1977).

A similar effect was observed by R. E. Smith and Swinyard (1983), who compared attitude-behavior consistency for product attitudes that were based either on a trial experience with a sample of the product (direct experience) or on exposure to advertising messages about the product (indirect experience). Much greater attitude-behavior consistency was observed for those persons who had had the opportunity to try the product than for those who had merely read about it. For example, purchase of the product was more highly correlated with attitudes based on product trial (.57) than with attitudes based on product advertising (.18).

This finding does not mean that product trial influence strategies (e.g., providing free samples through the mail, offering grocery store shoppers a taste of a new food product, etc.) will be more effective (in producing sales) than advertising strategies. Attitudes based on direct experience are more predictive of behavior than are attitudes based on indirect experience—which means (for example) that persons with negative product attitudes based on direct experience are less likely to purchase the product than are persons with similarly negative attitudes based on indirect experience. The shopper who has a negative attitude toward a food product because of having read about it might still come to purchase the product; the shopper whose negative attitude is based on tasting the product, however, is much less likely to do so.

In short, attitudes induced by direct experience will be more strongly correlated with behavior than attitudes induced by indirect experience. Two persons may have equally positive attitudes but may differ in whether they act consistently with those attitudes because of underlying differences in the ways in which the attitudes were formed.

Perceived Relevance of Attitude to Action. Whether individuals will act consistently with their attitudes surely depends in part on whether they perceive their attitudes as relevant to their behavioral choices. For example, investors who see their environmental protection attitudes as relevant to their investment decisions will, obviously, make different investments than if they thought those attitudes were not relevant to those actions. In general, "it may be only when individuals explicitly define their attitudes as relevant and appropriate guides to action that they can be expected to turn to their general attitudinal orientations for guidance in making their behavioral choices" (Snyder, 1982, p. 114). That is, one factor influencing attitude-behavior consistency is the perceived relevance of the attitude to the action.

For example, in a study by Snyder and Kendzierski (1982), participants read arguments in an affirmative action court case and rendered individual verdicts in the case. Participants' affirmative action attitudes had been obtained earlier, permitting assessment of attitude-behavior consistency (consistency between their general attitudes toward affirmative action and their judicial decisions in the particular case). The critical experimental manipulation consisted of giving some participants instructions from the judge that emphasized that the case dealt with a contemporary issue (affirmative action) and thus that decisions in this case could have implications not only for the involved parties but also for affirmative action programs generally (because of the precedent-setting nature of judicial decisions). The judge did not explicitly tell these participants to make their decisions on the basis of their attitudes, but the instructions did offer the opportunity for participants to see the relevance of their attitudes for their decision. The participants who did not receive the instructions exhibited little consistency between their affirmative action attitudes and their decisions (the correlation was .08). But those who received the instructions suggesting the relevance of those attitudes to their decision displayed substantially greater consistency (the correlation was .51).

Summary. Research has examined a great many possible moderators of attitude-behavior consistency (for some general discussions, see Ajzen & Sexton, 1999; Eagly & Chaiken, 1993, pp. 193-215; Fazio & Towles-Schwen, 1999; Kraus, 1995). The three mentioned here, although relatively prominent, are only illustrative.

Encouraging Attitude-Consistent Behavior

Even with the acknowledgment that attitudes and actions will often be consistent, it still remains the case that sometimes a persuader's challenge will be to encourage people to act consistently with their attitudes. That is, sometimes the task facing the persuader is not that of inducing or changing an attitude—the desired attitude is already present; instead, the job is that of getting the audience to act consistently with the existing attitude. For example, it is not enough to convince people to have favorable attitudes toward good health (indeed, they probably already have such attitudes); needed is to convince people to make attitude-consistent behavioral choices about exercise, diet, medical care, and the like. Similarly, persons who express positive attitudes toward energy conservation and environmental protection may nevertheless need to be induced to act consistently with those views—to engage in recycling, consider packaging considerations when buying products, choose appropriate thermostat settings, and so on. Thus the question arises of how persuaders might approach such tasks. At least three related strategies can be identified.

Enhance Perceived Relevance. One strategy for enhancing attitude-behavior consistency is to encourage people to see their attitudes as relevant to their behavioral choices. As just discussed, persons are likely to act more consistently with their attitudes when they see the attitudes as relevant to the behavior in question. It is possible to create conditions under which the perceived relevance of an attitude to an action is heightened (as Snyder & Kendzierski, 1982, did in the affirmative-action case study described earlier). A second study by Snyder and Kendzierski (1982) offers another illustration. Participants in this investigation were undergraduates known to have attitudes favorable to psychological research; they were asked to volunteer to participate in extra sessions of a psychology experiment. This was an especially demanding request (involving returning on different days, at inconvenient times, and so on). Indeed, in the control condition—despite the favorable attitudes—only 25% of the participants volunteered. Before responding to the request, each participant overheard a conversation between two other students (confederates of the experimenters) who were discussing the request. The first student said, "I don't know if I should volunteer or if I shouldn't volunteer. What do you think?" In the control condition, the second student responded, "Beats me—it's up to you." In the experimental condition, the response was, "Well, I guess that whether you do or whether you don't is really a question of how worthwhile you think experiments are"—a response designed to underscore the relevance of attitudes toward psychological research as guides for decision making in this situation. Although only 25% of the control condition participants agreed to volunteer (i.e., acted consistently with their favorable attitudes), 60% of the experimental condition participants agreed.

Obviously, then, when the relevance of an attitude for an action is heightened, behavior is more likely to be consistent with that attitude—and hence one means of influencing behavior is the strategy of emphasizing the relevance of an existing attitude to a current behavioral choice. Little systematic research evidence concerns this strategy (see Borgida & Campbell, 1982; Prislin, 1987; Shepherd, 1985; Snyder, 1982; Snyder & Kendzierski, 1982), but as a testimony to the strategy's potential effectiveness, consider the millions of home computers (and computer programs, encyclopedias, tutoring sessions, and so on) purchased by parents who were prodded by sellers asking, "You want your children to have a good education, don't you? To have an edge in school? To get ahead in life?" Fundamentally, these questions attempt to get the parent to see the relevance of existing attitudes to the behavioral decision at hand and reflect the seller's understanding that enhancing the perceived relevance of an attitude to an action can be a means of increasing attitude-behavior consistency.

Induce Feelings of Hypocrisy. A second strategy for encouraging attitude-behavior consistency can be appropriate in situations in which people have previously acted inconsistently with their attitudes: the strategy of hypocrisy induction. As discussed more thoroughly in Chapter 4 (concerning cognitive dissonance theory), a number of studies suggest that when persons have been hypocritical (in the sense of believing one thing but doing something different), one way of encouraging attitude-consistent behavior can be to draw persons' attention to the hypocrisy. Specifically, the research evidence suggests that when both the existing attitude and the previous inconsistency are made salient, persons are likely subsequently to act more consistently with their attitudes. For example, Stone, Aronson, Crain, Winslow, and Fried (1994) varied the salience of participants' positive attitudes about safe sex practices (by having some participants write and deliver a speech about the importance of safe sex) and varied the salience of previous behavior that was inconsistent with such attitudes (by having some participants be reminded of their past failures to engage in safe sex practices, through having to list circumstances surrounding their past failures to use condoms). The combination of salient attitudes and salient inconsistency induced greater subsequent attitude-behavior consistency (reflected in greater likelihood of buying condoms, and buying more condoms, at the end of the experiment) than either one alone. Thus one means of inducing attitude-behavior consistency may be to lead people to recognize their hypocrisy.[5]

Encourage Anticipation of Feelings. A third strategy for enhancing attitude-behavior consistency is to invite people to consider how they will feel if they fail to act consistently with their attitudes. As discussed more extensively in Chapter 5 (concerning theories of behavioral intention), feelings of anticipated emotions such as regret and guilt shape people's behavioral choices—and hence one way of influencing such choices is precisely by activating such anticipated feelings. A number of studies have influenced the salience of anticipated emotions simply by asking about such feelings, with consequent effects on intention or behavior. For example, Richard, van der Pligt, and de Vries (1996b) asked people either to indicate how they would expect to feel *after* having unprotected sex (by rating the likelihood of experiencing various positive and negative emotions) or to indicate how they felt *about* having unprotected sex (using similar ratings). Those participants whose attention was drawn to their anticipated feelings were more likely to intend to use condoms (and subsequently were more consistent condom users) than the other participants. Such results plainly suggest that making salient the emotion-related consequences of contemplated attitude-inconsistent behavior may have the effect of enhancing attitude-behavior consistency.

Summary. These three strategies all seek to tap some general desire for consistency as a way of influencing behavior in a circumstance in which persons will have an opportunity to act consistently with some existing attitude. But the strategies vary in the means of engaging that motivation. The perceived relevance strategy amounts to saying, "You might not have realized it, but this really is an opportunity to act consistently with your attitude." The hypocrisy induction strategy says, in effect, "You haven't been acting consistently with your attitude, but here is an opportunity to do so." The anticipated feelings strategy implicitly says, "Here is an opportunity to act consistently with your attitude—and think how bad you'll feel if you don't."[6] It remains to be seen what factors moderate the success of these strategies (e.g., what circumstances make one or another more likely to be effective).

▨ ASSESSING PERSUASIVE EFFECTS

Attitude Change

Attitude measurement procedures obviously provide means of assessing persuasive effects. To see whether a given message changes attitudes, an investigator can assess attitudes before and after exposure to the message (perhaps also collecting parallel attitude assessments from persons not exposed to the message, as a way of reducing ambiguity about the potential causes of any observed changes). Indeed, such attitude assessment procedures are the most common ones used in studies of persuasive effects. The concrete realizations of attitude assessment may vary depending on the particulars of the research design (for example, in an experiment in which participants are randomly assigned to conditions, one might dispense with the premessage attitude assessment and examine only postmessage differences, on the assumption that random assignment makes substantial initial differences unlikely), but effects on attitude are the effects most frequently considered in persuasion research.

Beyond Attitude

Although attitude has historically been considered the key mental state relevant to persuasive effects—and hence attitude change the key relevant outcome—attitudes are not the only possible focus for persuasive efforts.

Obviously, when other psychological states are of interest, other assessments will be useful or necessary.

Sometimes the focus of a persuasive effort will be some determinant of attitude, such as a particular belief about the attitude object. For example, an advertising campaign might try to persuade people that a product is environmentally friendly (as a means of influencing persons' attitudes toward the product and, eventually, product purchase). The appropriate assessment of the campaign's persuasive effectiveness would involve changes in that specific belief about the product, not changes in the overall attitude toward the product. The belief that the product is environmentally friendly might well influence the overall attitude, but to see whether the target belief is changed by the persuasive effort, assessments of that belief will be needed.

Sometimes persuaders want to influence some property of an attitude other than its valence (positive or negative) and extremity. That is, rather than influencing whether (or the degree to which) an attitude is positive or negative, a persuader might want to influence some other attribute of the attitude, such as its salience (prominence, accessibility), the confidence with which it is held, the degree to which it is linked to other attitudes, and so forth (for discussions of some such attitudinal properties, see Bromer, 1998; Eagly & Chaiken, 1998; Petty & Krosnick, 1995; Roskos-Ewoldsen, 1997). For example, when consumers already have positive attitudes toward one's product, the persuasive task may be to ensure that those attitudes are salient (activated) at the right time, perhaps by somehow reminding people of their attitudes.

Such attitudinal properties have been grouped together under the general heading of "attitude strength" (for some discussions, see Bassili, 1996; Petty & Krosnick, 1995; Raden, 1985). Conceptualizations of attitude strength vary, but a useful illustration is provided by Krosnick and Petty's (1995) proposal that attitude strength is best understood as an amalgam of persistence (stronger attitudes are more persistent than are weaker ones), resistance (stronger attitudes are more resistant to change than are weaker ones), impact on information processing and judgments (stronger attitudes are more likely to affect such processes than are weaker attitudes), and impact on behavior (stronger attitudes will have more effect on behavior than will weaker ones). It should be apparent that persuaders might have an interest in influencing not merely attitude (valence and extremity) but attitude strength as well.[7]

Finally, persuasive efforts sometimes will be concerned not with any aspect of attitudes but rather with other mental states. For example, the key to changing some behaviors might involve not influencing persons' attitudes but rather changing their normative beliefs (their conceptions of what others think they should do) or their perceived self-efficacy (their perceived ability to perform the desired behavior). (For discussion of such persuasion targets, see Chapter 5 concerning the theory of reasoned action and the theory of planned behavior.) Consider, for instance, a smoker who has a positive attitude toward quitting but has not yet really tried to do so; one can imagine such a person finally making a serious attempt to quit because of becoming convinced that family members really want the smoker to quit (normative considerations) or that quitting is indeed possible (self-efficacy).

In short, it should be apparent that persuasive efforts might seek changes in mental states other than attitude, and hence researchers will want correspondingly different outcome assessments (for illustrations of such diversity in the context of advertising, see W. D. Wells, 1997). Attitude change will often, but not always, be a persuader's goal.

Perceived and Expected Persuasive Effects

Studies of persuasive effects have sometimes employed outcome measures involving self-reports of perceived persuasiveness (e.g., "How much did that message influence you?" or "How persuasive was that message?") or expected persuasiveness (e.g., "How persuasive do you think that message would be?"). For example, Struckman-Johnson, Gilliland, Struckman-Johnson, and North (1990) assessed the effectiveness of various condom advertisements by asking respondents to rate "the overall effectiveness of the ad in terms of getting you personally to buy the product" (p. 1402). Garramone (1984) asked persons whether they were influenced by particular negative political advertisements. Kettlewell and Evans (1991) examined the effects of a museum's donation solicitation letters by asking respondents "to mark on the scale for each letter how likely it would be that they would contribute to the museum if they received the letter in the mail" (p. 580). (For other examples, see Eayrs & Ellis, 1990; Edgar, Freimuth, Hammond, McDonald, & Fink, 1992; Ho, 1994; Snyder & DeBono, 1985, Study 1.)

But discrepancies have been found between actual persuasive effects and expected or perceived persuasive effects. For example, Thornton, Kirchner, and Jacobs (1991) found that although participants expected that using a photograph would increase the effectiveness of a door-to-door campaign soliciting charitable contributions (Experiment 1), there was no significant effect of including the photograph (Experiments 2 and 3). Collins, Taylor, Wood, and Thompson (1988) found that respondents judged vivid messages to be more persuasive than nonvivid messages, but vivid and nonvivid messages did not differ on measures of actual attitude change. In Dillman, Singer, Clark, and Treat's (1996) research, focus group participants strongly believed that appeals based on benefits to one's group or region would be more successful in encouraging census responses than would appeals emphasizing that responding is required by law, but direct comparison of the persuasiveness of these appeals failed to confirm those expectations. (For other illustrations of such discrepancies, see Gibbon & Durkin, 1995, Study 1; Gilham, Lucas, & Sivewright, 1997; Hoeken, 1999; N. Miller, Lee, & Carlson, 1991; Rook, 1986.)[8]

The clear implication of such discrepancies is that in assessing persuasive effects (whether attitude change or some other outcome), assessments of actual persuasive effects are preferable to assessments of perceived or expected effects. Whether people expect or perceive a message to be persuasive is not necessarily a good guide to whether the message will actually be persuasive (for additional discussion, see Gilham et al., 1997; O'Keefe, 1993b). The perceived persuasiveness of a message might, however, be a matter of independently motivated investigation. For example, persons varying in the personality characteristic of self-monitoring appear to differ in their perceptions of the persuasiveness of different types of advertisements (at least for some products): High self-monitors are inclined to think that image-oriented ads will be more persuasive than ads focused on product quality, whereas the reverse is more likely to be the case for low self-monitors (see Shavitt & Lowrey, 1992; Snyder & DeBono, 1985, Study 1). These differing perceptions are consonant with theoretical expectations concerning how self-monitoring might influence such perceptions. But the point here is that such judgments of perceived persuasiveness should not be taken as proxies for assessments of actual persuasiveness. More generally, lay beliefs about persuasion (about how persuasion works, about how to resist persuasive messages, about what makes messages persuasive, and so forth) can be a focus for interesting research (see Friestad & Wright, 1994), in part because such beliefs can influence receivers' reactions to persuasive messages (e.g., T. D. Wilson, Houston, & Meyers, 1998), but lay beliefs about a message's persuasiveness are not a completely dependable substitute for assessments of actual persuasive effects.

▨ CONCLUSION

This introductory chapter has elucidated the concepts of persuasion and attitude, described some common attitude assessment procedures, sketched the relationship of attitudes and behavior, and discussed the assessment of persuasive effects. In the following chapters, extant social-scientific theory and research about persuasion are reviewed. Several theoretical perspectives that have been prominent in the explanation of persuasive effects are discussed in Chapters 2 through 6. Research on various factors influencing persuasive effects is explored in Chapters 7 through 10.

▧ NOTES

1. For those familiar with the distinctions among locutionary, illocutionary, and perlocutionary speech acts (Searle, 1969): This point can also be expressed by saying that to persuade is a perlocutionary act, whereas (for example) to urge is an illocutionary act.

2. These reviews have used different procedures and analyzed different numbers of studies, but their estimates of the mean attitude-behavior correlation range from .38 to .47 (Eckes & Six, 1994; M.-S. Kim & Hunter, 1993a; Kraus, 1995). Larger mean correlations are reported when various methodological artifacts are corrected (Eckes & Six, 1994; M.-S. Kim & Hunter, 1993a) or with optimal levels of moderator variables.

3. Ajzen and Fishbein's (1977) analysis specifies four ways in which attitudes and behaviors might correspond (action, target, context, and time). So, for example, the behavior of attending church services on campus this Sunday corresponds most directly to the attitude toward attending church services on campus this Sunday; this attitude and behavior correspond in the action specified (attending), the target toward which the action is directed (church services), the context of the action (on campus), and the time of the action (this Sunday). A more general behavior (for example, one without a specified context or time, such as attending church services) corresponds most directly to a more general attitude (obviously, the attitude toward attending church services). Thus for an attitude toward an object (e.g., a consumer product), the corresponding behavioral measure would include assessments involving various actions, contexts, and times—which is the point of the multiple-act behavioral measure.

4. Notably, the theory of reasoned action and theory of planned behavior (discussed in Chapter 5) include attitudes toward specific behaviors as a key determinant of behavioral intentions.

5. As discussed in Chapter 4 (on cognitive dissonance theory), however, hypocrisy induction efforts can also backfire as a behavioral influence mechanism; instead of changing their future behaviors to be more consistent with their attitudes, people might change their attitudes to be consistent with their previous behavior (Fried, 1998).

6. Actually, (some sense of) hypocrisy may be a deeper connecting thread among these strategies. The perceived relevance strategy and the anticipated feelings strategy might be described as alerting people to hypocrisy (or to potential hypocrisy or hypocrisy-related feelings). So, for example, the reason that heightening the perceived relevance of an attitude to an action enhances attitude-behavior consistency may be precisely that such enhanced perceived relevance leads to an increased recognition of past inconsistency (and thus to feelings of hypocrisy, guilt, and so on—which then motivate attitude-consistent future behavior) and/or to an

increased expectation that negative feelings (guilt, regret, and so forth) will arise if attitude-inconsistent behavior is undertaken (with attitude-consistent behavior then motivated by a desire to avoid such negative feelings).

7. Research on attitudinal properties other than evaluation (that is, other than valence and extremity) is somewhat unsettled conceptually. For example, Krosnick and Petty's (1995, p. 4) approach treats strength's effects (persistence, resistance, and impact on information processing, judgments, and behavior) as the "defining features" of strength. But if strength is defined as (say) resistance, then it is necessarily true that "strong" attitudes are resistant. That is, this leaves unanswered the question of what makes attitudes resistant (saying "these attitudes are resistant because they are strong" would be akin to saying "these men are single because they are unmarried"). An alternative approach might define attitude strength not by its effects but by the conjunction of various effect-independent properties of attitude (e.g., an attitude's interconnectedness with other attitudes, its importance, and the certainty with which it is held) or even dispense with any overarching concept of attitude strength in favor of studying the particular individual effect-independent features (see Eagly & Chaiken, 1998, pp. 290-292). It will obviously be a substantial undertaking to distinguish these various features conceptually and to investigate their empirical interrelationships and effects.

8. A caveat here: These apparent discrepancies—which take the form of a statistically significant difference between conditions for perceived effectiveness measures but a nonsignificant difference for actual effectiveness measures—might simply reflect poor statistical power for detecting the latter effect (as noted by Dillard & Peck, 2000, pp. 491-492) or (given equal power) a difference in the size of the effect on the two measures. The key question is that of the magnitude of the relationship between indices of perceived effectiveness and indices of actual effectiveness. It would be surprising if there were not typically a positive relationship between these measures, but it is not plain that the relationship is so robust as to enable one to confidently employ one measure as a proxy for the other. For example, in research by Collins et al. (1988, p. 13, Table 3), the mean correlation between perceived effectiveness and actual attitude change was .12; Piccolino (1966) reported a correlation of -.02 between perceived and actual effectiveness. Not entirely unrelated is the finding by Janis and Field (1956) that various self-reports of perceived general susceptibility to social influence were correlated between .06 and .26 with observed general persuasibility.

Functional Approaches to Attitude   2

One general approach to the analysis of attitudes focuses on the functions that attitudes can serve. The basic idea is that attitudes may serve various functions for persons, that is, may do different jobs, meet different needs or purposes. The relevance of this idea for understanding persuasion is that the most effective technique for changing an attitude may vary depending on the attitude's function. Functional analyses of attitude have a long history; the treatment here first discusses one classic example of such an analysis and then turns to more recent developments. (For useful collections and discussions concerning functional approaches to attitude, see Eagly & Chaiken, 1993, pp. 479-490; Eagly & Chaiken, 1998, pp. 303-309; Maio & Olson, 2000b; Pratkanis, Breckler, & Greenwald, 1989.)

A CLASSIC FUNCTIONAL ANALYSIS

In a well-known analysis, Katz (1960) proposed four attitude functions: utilitarian, ego-defensive, value-expressive, and knowledge (see also Katz, McClintock, & Sarnoff, 1957; Sarnoff & Katz, 1954). The utilitarian function is represented by attitudes that help people maximize rewards and minimize punishments. For example, students who experience success with essay exams are likely to develop favorable attitudes toward such exams. Attitudes serving a utilitarian function, Katz suggested, will be susceptible to change when the attitude (and related activities) no longer effectively maximizes rewards and minimizes punishments. Thus utilitarian attitudes are probably most effectively changed by either creating new rewards and punishments (as when, for instance, a company creates a new incentive program to encourage suggestions by employees) or by changing what is associated with existing rewards and punishments (as when a company changes the basis on which salespeople's bonuses are based).

Attitudes serving an ego-defensive function do the job of defending one's self-image. Ego-defensive attitudes are exemplified most clearly by prejudicial attitudes toward minorities; such attitudes presumably bolster the holder's self-image (ego) by denigrating others (see, e.g., Fein & Spencer, 1997). The most promising avenues to changing attitudes serving such a function, Katz suggested, might involve removing the threat to the ego (thus removing the need for self-defense) or giving persons insight into their motivational dynamics (getting people to see that their attitudes are not substantively well-grounded but simply stem from ego-defensive needs).

With attitudes serving a value-expressive function, persons get satisfaction from holding and expressing attitudes that reflect their central values and self-images. For example, a person whose self-image is that of a conservative Republican might get satisfaction from supporting a balanced budget amendment because such a viewpoint reflects the person's self-image. Attitudes serving a value-expressive function are thought to be likely to change either when the underlying beliefs and self-images change (because then there would be no need to express the old values) or when an alternative, superior means of expressing the values is presented (as when a political candidate says, "If you're looking for a *real* conservative [or liberal or whatever], then vote for me, because I represent those values better than the other candidates do").

The knowledge function of attitudes reflects the role of attitudes in organizing and understanding information and events. For example, one way of making sense of complex sociopolitical situations (such as in the Middle East or the Balkans) can be to, in effect, identify the "good guys" and the "bad guys." That is, attitudes (evaluations) can serve as at least a superficial mechanism for organizing one's understandings of such situations. Attitudes serving a knowledge function, Katz suggested, are especially susceptible to change through the introduction of ambiguity (as when the good guys do something bad or the bad guys do something good); such ambiguity indicates that the attitudes are not functioning well to organize information, thus making the attitudes more likely to change.

Katz's description of these four attitude functions provides a useful concrete example of a functional analysis of attitudes. It is appropriately nuanced; for example, it acknowledges that a given attitude might serve more than one function. It makes plain the connection between functional attitude analysis and the understanding of alternative persuasion mechanisms by suggesting means of influence especially well tailored to each functional attitude type. (The analysis claims not that the recommended means of changing each type of attitude will be guaranteed to be successful but only that a given attitude type is more likely to be changed when approached with the appropriate means of influence.)

Katz's analysis did not initially attract much research attention, in good part because of perceived difficulties in assessing attitude function (for some discussion, see C. A. Kiesler, Collins, & Miller, 1969, pp. 302-330; Lutz, 1981; Shavitt, 1989). But functional analyses of attitude have subsequently flowered.

SUBSEQUENT DEVELOPMENTS

Identifying General Functions of Attitude

Katz's list of attitude functions is only one of many proposed function typologies. In other analyses, different functions have been proposed, the relationships among various functions reconsidered, and alternative organizational schemes considered.

For example, M. B. Smith, Bruner, and White (1956) suggested a social-adjustive function, in which attitudes help people adjust to social situations and groups. As described by Snyder and DeBono (1989), persons hold attitudes serving a social-adjustive function because such attitudes "allow them to fit into important social situations and allow them to interact smoothly with their peers" (p. 341); expression of the attitude may elicit social approval, make it easier to adapt to social situations, and the like.[1] Shavitt's (1990) taxonomy distinguished a utilitarian function, a social identity function (understood as including both social-adjustive and value-expressive functions), and a self-esteem maintenance function (including ego-defensive purposes). Gastil (1992) proposed six attitude functions: personal utility, social utility, value expressive, social adjustment (easing social interaction), social identity (forging one's identity), and self-esteem maintenance.

But there is not yet a consensus on any one functional typology. This surely reflects the lack of any simple, easily assessed source of evidence for or against a given function list. An attitude function taxonomy presumably shows its worth by being broadly useful, across a number of applications, in illuminating the underlying motivational bases of attitude. Expressed generally, this illumination consists of showing that the scheme in question permits one to detect or predict relevant events or relationships, but this evidence can be quite diverse. A given typology's value might be displayed by showing that knowledge of an attitude's function (as captured by the typology in question) permits one to predict or detect (for example) the product features that persons will find most appealing, the relative effectiveness of various persuasive messages, the connection between personality traits and attitude functions, and so on. But because for any given typology there commonly is relatively little research evidence distinctively bearing on that scheme, there is at present little basis for supposing that any given specific typology is unquestionably superior to all others. (There is even less evidence comparing the usefulness of alternative taxonomies; for an example, see Gastil, 1992.)

This lack of consensus makes for a rather chaotic and unsettled situation, one in which a genuine accumulation of results (and corresponding confident generalization) is difficult. If there was one widely agreed-on set of specific functions, then research could straightforwardly be accumulated; more could be learned about (say) what personality traits or situational features incline persons to favor this or that function, what sorts of messages are best adapted for changing attitudes serving the various functions, and so forth. Instead, most of the research evidence concerning functional attitude analyses is of a piecemeal sort: One study compares personality correlates of social-adjustive and value-expressive functions, another examines different means of influencing attitudes serving ego-defensive functions, and so on.

In such a circumstance, one promising approach might be to paint in broader strokes, deferring matters of detailed functional typologies in favor of identifying some general functional differences. One broad functional distinction has been found widely useful and seems contained (implicitly or explicitly) in a great many attitude function analyses: a distinction between symbolic and instrumental attitude functions (see Abelson & Prentice, 1989; Ennis & Zanna, 2000, pp. 396-397). Briefly expressed, symbolic functions focus on the symbolic associations of the object; attitudes serving a symbolic function do the jobs of expressing fundamental moral beliefs, symbolizing significant values, projecting self-images, and the like. Instrumental functions focus on the intrinsic properties of the object; attitudes serving instrumental functions do the jobs of summarizing the desirable and undesirable aspects of the object, appraising the object through specific intrinsic consequences or attributes, and so forth. (For related ideas, see Kinder & Sears's [1981] distinction between self-interest politics and symbolic politics as two bases of public opinion, Herek's [1986] distinction between evaluative and expressive functions, and Pratkanis & Greenwald's [1989] distinction between sense-making functions and self functions.)

For example, concerning stricter gun control laws in the United States, a supporter's positive attitudes might have a predominantly symbolic basis (beliefs such as "It represents progress toward a more civilized world") or an instrumental basis ("It will reduce crime because criminals won't be able to get guns so easily"); similarly, an opponent's negative attitudes might be motivated by largely symbolic considerations ("It represents impingement on constitutional rights") or by largely instrumental considerations ("It will increase crime because criminals will still have guns, but law-abiding citizens won't"). Of course, it is possible for a person's attitude on a given topic to have a mixture of symbolic and instrumental underpinnings. And an attitude's function might change through time. For instance, an attitude might initially serve a symbolic function but subsequently come to predominantly serve instrumental ends (see Mangleburg et al., 1998). But the general distinction between symbolic and instrumental attitude functions appears to be a broadly useful one (see, e.g., Crandall, Glor, & Britt, 1997; Herek & Capitanio, 1998; Le Poire, 1994; Prentice & Carlsmith, 2000; J. B. Pryor, Reeder, Vinacco, & Kott, 1989).

Assessing the Function of a Given Attitude

Given a typology of attitude functions, the question that naturally arises is how one can tell what function an individual's attitude is serving. Indeed, one recurring challenge facing functional attitude theories has been the assessment of attitude functions (see Shavitt, 1989).

One straightforward procedure for assessing the function of a given attitude involves coding (classifying) relevant free-response data (data derived from open-ended questions). For example, Shavitt (1990) asked participants to write down "what your feelings are about the attitude object, and why you feel the way you do. . . . Write down all of your thoughts and feelings that are relevant to your attitude, and try to describe the reasons for your feelings" (p. 130). Responses were then classified on the basis of the apparent attitude function. For example, responses concerning what the attitude communicates to others were coded as indicating a social identity function, whereas responses focused on attributes of the attitude object were classified as reflecting a utilitarian function.

Such free-response data can be elicited in various ways (participants might write essays or simply list their beliefs), and the classification system will vary depending on the functional typology being used (for example, one might simply contrast symbolic and instrumental bases of attitudes; see

Ennis & Zanna, 1993). But the general principle behind these procedural variants is that different attitude functions will have different characteristic clusters of affiliated beliefs, spawned by the different motivations behind (different functions of) the attitude, and hence examination of such freely elicited beliefs will illuminate attitude functions. (For other examples of such procedures, see Herek, 1987; Maio & Olson, 1994.)

A second avenue to the assessment of attitude functions is the use of a questionnaire with standardized scale response items. The leading example is Herek's (1987) Attitude Functions Inventory, which presents respondents with statements about different possible bases for their views (statements of the form "My views about X mainly are based on . . ."); respondents are asked to indicate the degree to which each statement is true of them (giving answers on a scale anchored by the phrases "very true of me" and "not at all true of me"). So, for instance, in an item assessing the value-expressive function, persons are asked about the degree to which it is true that their views are based on their "moral beliefs about how things should be"; for the ego-defensive function, one item asks whether the respondent's views are based on "personal feelings of disgust or revulsion." (Each attitude function is assessed using several items.) As another example of such procedures, Clary, Snyder, Ridge, Miene, and Haugen (1994) had participants rate the importance of 30 possible reasons for volunteering (six reasons for each of five attitude functions). For example, "I can gain prestige at school or work" was one utilitarian reason, whereas "members of a social group to which I belong expect people to volunteer" was a social-adjustive reason. (For other examples of the use of these or similar instruments, see D. S. Anderson & Kristiansen, 1990; Clary et al., 1998; Ennis & Zanna, 1993; Gastil, 1992; Herek, 2000; Shavitt, 1990; Wyman & Snyder, 1997.)

In much attitude function research, however, a third approach has been adopted, that of using proxy indices such as personality characteristics to stand in for more direct assessments of function (on the basis of associations between such characteristics and attitude functions). Among these, the most frequently employed has been the individual-difference variable of self-monitoring (Snyder, 1974). Self-monitoring refers to the control or regulation (monitoring) of one's self-presentation, and specifically to the tendency to tailor one's behavior to fit situational considerations. Broadly speaking, high self-monitors are concerned about the image they project to others and tailor their conduct to fit the particular circumstances they are in. Low self-monitors are less concerned about their projected image and mold their behavior to fit inner states (their attitudes and values) rather than external circumstances (social norms of appropriateness). In a well-established questionnaire used to assess self-monitoring, high self-monitoring is reflected by agreement with statements such as "I guess I put on a show to impress or entertain others" and "I would probably make a good actor"; low self-monitoring is reflected by agreement with statements such as "I have trouble changing my behavior to suit different people and different situations" and "I can only argue for ideas which I already believe" (see Gangestad & Snyder, 2000; Snyder & Gangestad, 1986).

Self-monitoring is taken to be broadly reflective of differences in likely attitude function. For example, as described by DeBono (1987), the expectation is that high self-monitors will emphasize social-adjustive functions (letting the high self-monitor behave in ways appropriate to the social situation), whereas low self-monitors will favor value-expressive functions (in the sense that the low self-monitor's attitudes will be chosen on the basis of the degree to which the attitude is consistent with the person's underlying values). So, for example, high self-monitors are likely to especially stress the image-related aspects of products (because of the social-adjustive function), whereas low self-monitors are more likely to focus on whether the product's intrinsic characteristics and qualities match the person's criteria for such products.

For any such proxy measure, of course, the key question will be the degree to which the proxy is actually related to differences in attitude function, a question probably best addressed by examining the relationship between proxy measures and more direct assessments. In the specific case of personality characteristics such as self-monitoring, presumably such characteristics merely incline persons (in appropriate circumstances) to be more likely to favor one or another function. For instance, it is surely not the case that all the attitudes of high self-monitors (whether toward aspirin or automobiles or affirmative action) serve social-adjustive functions. (See Herek, 2000, pp. 332-335, for commentary on the use of such proxy measures.)

Influences on Attitude Function

A variety of factors might influence the function that a given attitude serves. Three such classes of factors merit mention: individual differences (from person to person), the nature of the attitude object, and features of the situation.

Individual Differences. Different persons can favor different attitude functions, as straightforwardly illustrated by self-monitoring. As just discussed, high self-monitors appear to favor social-adjustive functions, whereas low self-monitors seem more likely to adopt value-expressive functions. Other personality correlates of attitude function differences have not received so much recent research attention, although plainly it is possible that other individual-difference variables might be related to differences in attitude function (see, e.g., Katz et al., 1957; Zuckerman, Gioioso, & Tellini, 1988). But apart from any underlying personality differences, people's motivations can vary. For example, different people can have different reasons for volunteering, although those differences might not be systematically related to any general personality disposition.

Attitude Object. The function of an attitude toward an object may also be shaped by the nature of the object because objects can differentially lend themselves to attitude functions. For example, Shavitt (1990) found that air conditioners commonly evoked predominantly utilitarian thoughts ("keeps the air cool," "expensive to run"), whereas wedding rings were more likely to elicit social identity thoughts ("represents a sacred vow"). Similarly, Mittal, Ratchford, and Prabhakar (1990) found that attitudes toward shampoo were determined more by instrumental attributes (such as conditioning hair) than by symbolic ones (such as being a high-fashion brand), whereas for perfume, symbolic attributes were more influential than instrumental ones.

Each of these objects (air conditioners, shampoo, wedding rings, and perfume) appears to predominantly encourage one particular attitude function (and so might be described as unifunctional). But other objects are multifunctional, in the sense of easily being able to accommodate different attitude functions. For instance, automobiles can readily permit both symbolic and instrumental functions; a person's attitude toward an automobile might have a largely instrumental basis ("provides reliable transportation"), a largely symbolic one ("looks sexy"), or some mixture of these.

It should be noticed that the attitude functions served by a given object can be influenced by larger social forces (see Herek, 2000, pp. 328-329). For example, in the United States, coffee has become a symbolically significant object (whereas previously it was largely seen in instrumental terms) and hence can now accommodate symbolic function attitudes more easily than it once might have.

Situational Variations. Different situations can elicit different attitude functions (for a general discussion, see Shavitt, 1989, pp. 326-332). For example, if the situation makes salient the intrinsic attributes and outcomes associated with an object, presumably instrumental (utilitarian) functions will be more likely to be activated; by contrast, social identity functions might be engaged by "situations that involve using or affiliating with an attitude object, or expressing one's attitude toward the object, in public or in the presence of reference group members" (p. 328). Thus attitude functions may vary depending on features of the immediate situation.

Multifunctional Attitude Objects Revisited. As noted above, attitude objects differ in the degree to which they accommodate multiple attitude functions, and this influences the role that individual-difference variations and situational variations can play in determining attitude function. For unifunctional attitude objects (those eliciting predominantly one function), individual-difference variations and situational variations may not have much impact. For example, aspirin is likely to be generally (that is, across individuals and across situations) perceived largely in instrumental terms. But (as emphasized by Shavitt, 1989) multifunctional attitude objects (such as automobiles) represent objects for which individual-difference variations and situational variations are likely to have greater impact on attitude function. It is possible for the attitudes of high and low self-monitors toward automobiles to serve different functions because the attitude object can accommodate different functions. Similarly, situational factors can influence the salience of various functions only if the attitude object permits different attitude functions. The larger point is that the attitude object, individual differences, and situational factors all intertwine to influence attitude function.

Persuasion: Function Matching

The functional approach suggests that the key to effective persuasion is the matching of the persuasive appeal to the functional basis of the attitude. For example (see Herek, 1986), if a negative attitude toward a neighborhood facility for persons with AIDS is based on a symbolic association of AIDS and homosexuality, then perhaps that attitude might be changed by information emphasizing that AIDS also attacks heterosexuals. But if that negative attitude is based on instrumental concerns about the contagiousness of AIDS, then different arguments (about the lack of contagiousness) will be needed; indeed, in this latter case, the first sort of message (emphasizing heterosexuals' potential susceptibility to AIDS) would presumably backfire—illustrating the potential importance of using persuasive appeals that match the functional basis of receivers' attitudes.

The Persuasive Effects of Matched and Mismatched Appeals. Consistent with this analysis, a variety of investigations have found that messages with appeals matching the receiver's attitude function are indeed more persuasive than messages containing mismatched appeals. A good number of these studies have used self-monitoring as an indirect index of variation in attitude function and have focused on how self-monitoring differences are related to differential susceptibility to various types of appeals in consumer product advertising. As discussed above, high self-monitors are expected to favor social-adjustive functions and low self-monitors to favor value-expressive functions; the appeal variation consists of using arguments emphasizing correspondingly different aspects of the attitude object and in the specific domain of consumer products can be characterized as a difference between appeals emphasizing the *image* of the product or its users (a social-adjustive appeal) and appeals emphasizing the intrinsic *quality* of the product (a value-expressive appeal; see, e.g., Snyder & DeBono, 1987). This contrast is exemplified by a pair of experimental magazine advertisements for Canadian Club whiskey (Snyder & DeBono, 1985, Study 1). Both ads showed a bottle of the whiskey resting on a set of blueprints for a house; for the image-oriented advertisement, the slogan read, "You're not just moving in, you're moving up," whereas the product quality-oriented advertisement claimed, "When it comes to great taste, everyone draws the same conclusion."

Across a number of studies, high self-monitors have been found to react more favorably to image-oriented advertisements than to product quality-oriented ads, whereas the opposite effect is found for low self-monitors (e.g., DeBono & Packer, 1991; Lennon, Davis, & Fairhurst, 1988; Snyder & DeBono, 1985; Zuckerman et al., 1988; cf. Bearden, Shuptrine, & Teel, 1989; Browne & Kaldenberg, 1997; for related work, see DeBono & Snyder, 1989; DeBono & Telesca, 1990).[2] Outside the realm of consumer product advertising, parallel differences (between high and low self-monitors) have been found with related appeal variations. For example, concerning the topic of institutionalization of the mentally ill, DeBono (1987) found that low self-monitors were more persuaded by value-expressive messages (indicating what values were associated with positive attitudes toward institutionalization) and high self-monitors by social-adjustive messages (indicating that a substantial majority of the receiver's peers favored institutionalization); similar effects concerning dating attitudes and voting have been reported by, respectively, Bazzini and Shaffer (1995) and Lavine and Snyder (1996).

Similar findings have been reported in investigations that assessed individual attitude function differences in ways other than self-monitoring differences. For example, Clary et al. (1994) initially assessed attitude function through participants' ratings of the importance of various possible reasons for volunteering. Participants were then presented with pro-volunteering messages that were matched or mismatched to their attitude functions; matched messages were more persuasive than mismatched messages in inducing intentions to volunteer (see also Clary et al., 1998). In

Celuch and Slama's (1995) research, variations in the degree to which persons' self-presentation motives emphasized "getting ahead" or "getting along" were related to the persuasiveness of messages emphasizing either the self-advancement aspects of a product or the conformity-relevant aspects of a product.[3]

Parallel results obtain when considering the effectiveness of different appeals for different types of products. Shavitt (1990, Study 2) compared the effects of a utilitarian or social identity appeal for either a utilitarian product (such as air conditioners) or a social identity product (such as greeting cards). Participants read pairs of ads for different fictitious brands of a product, one ad with a utilitarian appeal and one with a social identity appeal; brands advertised with function-relevant appeals were preferred over brands advertised with function-irrelevant appeals (so that, for example, ads using utilitarian appeals were preferred over ads using social identity appeals when air conditioners were advertised, but this preference was reversed when greeting cards were advertised).

In short, substantial evidence suggests that persuasive appeals that are matched to the receiver's attitude function will be more persuasive than mismatched appeals. Although a systematic review remains to be done, it is worth noticing that studies in this area often report relatively large effects, suggesting the substantive importance of functionally matched messages.[4]

Explaining the Effects of Function Matching. Exactly why are function-matched appeals typically more persuasive than unmatched appeals? The answer to this question is not yet entirely clear, but there are two broad possibilities. One is that functionally matched appeals simply speak to a receiver's psychological needs in ways that unmatched appeals do not. This explanation is unsurprising, really—after all, such correspondence is what makes the appeals matched. A receiver who values a vehicle's gas mileage more than the image projected by the vehicle will naturally be more persuaded by appeals based on the former than by those based on the latter. Correspondingly, people are likely to perceive functionally matched messages as containing better arguments than mismatched messages (Lavine & Snyder, 1996, 2000; see, relatedly, Shavitt & Lowrey, 1992).

A second possibility is that function-matched messages are processed more carefully than mismatched messages. For example, in Petty and Wegener's (1998b) study, high and low self-monitors read consumer product messages that varied in the functional match of the appeals (image-based versus product quality-based appeals) and in the quality of the supporting arguments (strong versus weak arguments). Attitudes were more strongly influenced by argument quality when the message contained matched appeals than when it contained mismatched appeals. For instance, high self-monitors were more influenced by the strength of the arguments when the appeals were image-based than when the appeals were product quality-based. This effect suggests that receivers more carefully scrutinized messages with appeals matching their functional attitude bases than they did messages with mismatched appeals (see also DeBono, 1987; Lavine & Snyder, 1996, 2000; Petty, Wheeler, & Bizer, 2000). Relatedly, several studies have reported findings suggesting that high self-monitors more carefully process messages from attractive than unattractive (or expert) communicators (DeBono & Harnish, 1988; DeBono & Telesca, 1990), findings that might reflect the propensity for high self-monitors to favor social-adjustive attitude functions. And this explanation is at least not inconsistent with evidence suggesting that function-matched messages may be better remembered than mismatched messages (DeBono & Packer, 1991, Study 3).

If this second explanation is sound, then at least sometimes function-matched messages should be *less* persuasive than mismatched messages, namely, when the messages contain poor-quality arguments (as indeed was observed by Petty & Wegener, 1998b). The weaknesses of such poor-quality messages will be recognized by receivers who scrutinize the message closely but can go unnoticed by receivers who do not process so carefully. So this explanation supposes that the widely observed greater persuasiveness of function-matched messages is actually a consequence of the generally high argumentative quality of the appeals; with poorer-quality arguments, function-matched messages might not have displayed such a persuasive advantage.

Both explanations might turn out to have some merit. For example, it may be that when message scrutiny is already likely to be high, the different intrinsic appeal of matched and mismatched arguments will play a key role, whereas in other circumstances, the functional match or mismatch of arguments will influence the degree of scrutiny given (see Petty et al., 2000).[5] Further research on these questions will be welcomed.

▧ COMMENTARY

Generality and Specificity in Attitude Function Typologies

The general enterprise of functional attitude analysis is driven by the search for a small set of universal, exhaustive, and mutually exclusive attitude functions that can be used to dependably and perceptively distinguish any and all attitudes. But as discussed in the previous section, there is not yet a consensus on any such set of functions, and perhaps there never will be such consensus. This lack of agreement might appear to provide a decisive objection to functional analyses.

The general idea of functional analysis, however, can still be of use in illuminating attitudes and persuasion processes, even without some universal scheme of attitude functions. It has proved possible, for at least some attitude objects or issues, to distinguish different attitudinal functions in a way that is dependable (reliable) and that provides insight into attitudes on that subject. For example, functional analyses have provided insight concerning attitudes on such matters as volunteering (Clary & Snyder, 1991; Clary et al., 1998; Snyder, Clary, & Stukas, 2000); persons with HIV/ AIDS (J. B. Pryor et al., 1989); and democracy (Gastil, 1992). In particular, a number of studies have illuminated attitudes on various AIDS-related issues by considering the relative contributions of symbolic and instrumental attitudinal underpinnings (e.g., Crandall et al., 1997; Herek & Capitanio, 1998; Le Poire, 1994; J. B. Pryor et al., 1989; Schneider, Snyder-Joy, & Hopper, 1993). That is, the functions served by attitudes on a given subject can be analyzed even in the absence of a general typology of attitude functions; insights into the motivational dynamics of particular attitudes are possible even without having some universal set of functions.

Of course, there is variation in the specific functional typologies used to analyze these different particular attitudes. On one subject, it may be helpful to distinguish various subtypes of a function, but distinguishing those subtypes may not be necessary when considering attitudes on a different topic. For instance, a generalized utilitarian function might suffice when analyzing the functions of attitudes toward amusement parks, whereas when analyzing attitudes toward democracy, it is useful to distinguish personal utility functions (my beliefs about how democracy benefits me personally) and social utility functions (my beliefs about how democracy benefits society as a whole; see Gastil, 1992). The larger point is that although one may hope that continuing research will eventuate in a well-evidenced small set of general and well-articulated attitude functions, one need not wait for such an outcome to appreciate the value of functional attitude analyses. Indeed, even if there comes to be some consensus on a general attitude function typology, analyses of specific attitudes will still almost certainly require the typology to be modified (elaborated, refined, adapted) to provide maximum illumination of the particular attitude under study.

Functional Confusions

Some Functional Distinctions. There is some underlying murkiness in the conceptualization of attitude functions. This can be displayed by considering that there are distinctions—often unappreciated—among the functions of an *attitude,* the functions of *expressing* an attitude, and the functions of the *attitude object.*

Consider first that there is a distinction to be drawn between the functions of an attitude (that is, the functions of having that attitude) and the functions of expressing an attitude. For example, imagine that John has unfavorable views about (a negative attitude toward) minorities. His *having* that attitude might serve an ego-defensive function, a self-esteem maintenance function, that is, having that attitude makes him feel better about himself—even if he never reveals his views to anyone else. On the other hand, his *expressing* that attitude around his bigoted friends might serve a social-adjustive function, one of letting him fit in with people who are expressing similar attitudes. Thus the job done by the attitude (the having of the attitude) and the job done by the expression of the attitude can be different.[6]

Similarly, there is a plain distinction between the functions of an attitude and the functions of an attitude object. After all, no one would give the same answer to the question, "What are attitudes toward amusement parks good for?" and the question, "What are amusement parks good for?" The functions of an attitude (the jobs that the evaluation does) and the functions of an object (the jobs that the object does) are plainly different.

Finally, there is a distinction between the functions of an attitude object and the functions of expressing an attitude. The purposes served by abolition of capital punishment (the attitude object) are different from the purposes served by a person's saying, "I support the abolition of capital punishment" (the expression of the attitude). Consider, for example, that a person might believe that abolishing capital punishment would serve an instrumental function ("Doing away with capital punishment would prevent execution of the innocent"), but this does not mean that the person's *expressing* opposition to capital punishment serves an instrumental function; depending on the circumstances, expression of that attitude might serve some thoroughly symbolic end (symbolizing one's values, for instance). Thus there is a difference between the jobs done by the attitude object (the product, the policy) and the jobs done by expressing attitudes concerning that object.[7]

Conflating the Functions. These three elements—the functions of an attitude, the functions of expressions of an attitude, and the functions of an attitude object—are commonly conflated in theory and research on attitude functions. For example, the functions of having an attitude and the functions of expressing an attitude are often not carefully distinguished. Such conflation can be detected in (among other places) Katz's (1960,

p. 187) discussion of voting behavior as reflecting a value-expressive function, in Snyder and DeBono's (1989, p. 341) description of social-adjustive attitudes as allowing people to fit into social situations smoothly, and in Shavitt and Nelson's (2000, p. 55) treatment of the meanings communicated by a person's consumer product choices as an aspect of a social identity function of attitudes. All these would seem to be more accurately characterized as describing functions of expressing attitudes, rather than functions of having attitudes.

Similarly, the functions of attitudes and the functions of attitude objects are often treated as if these were indistinguishable. For instance, Clary et al. (1994) quietly shift from discussing the idea that "attitudes could serve a variety of distinct social and psychological functions" (and that "the same attitude could serve very different motivational functions for different people") to discussing "the relevant motivations underlying volunteerism" (note: motivations underlying volunteerism, not motivations underlying attitudes toward volunteerism) and "the specific functions served by volunteerism" (pp. 1130-1131; again, not the specific functions served by positive or negative attitudes toward volunteerism but the functions served by volunteerism itself). Similarly, Ennis and Zanna's (1993) opening paragraphs slide from discussion of "the psychological functions of attitudes" to discussion of "the psychological functions of a product" (p. 662; see also Ennis & Zanna, 2000). In discussions of attitude function, such elision of the functions of attitudes, the functions of attitude objects, and the functions of attitude expressions is common (see, e.g., Lavine & Snyder, 2000; Pratkanis & Greenwald, 1989; Shavitt, 1990). This state of affairs suggests that it may be useful to reconsider the assessment and conceptualization of attitude function with the relevant distinctions in mind.

Reconsidering the Assessment and Conceptualization of Attitude Function

Assessment of Attitude Function Reconsidered. The common conflation of attitude function and attitude object function naturally raises some questions about procedures for assessing attitude function. The procedures that assess attitude function through coding free-response data or through standardized scale item data rest on the idea that the function an attitude serves is reflected in the beliefs held about the attitude object, the reasons given for the attitude, the importance of alternative reasons for the attitude, and so forth. But all these may most directly reflect not the function served by the respondent's attitude but rather the respondent's perceptions of what is valuable—the attitude object's useful properties, the value of the purposes served by the attitude object, and so forth.

To concretize this, imagine asking people questions of the form, "What's important about X?" or "What's right or wrong (or good or bad) about X?"—that is, questions of the sort one might use in an open-ended questionnaire designed to assess attitude function. Depending on the topic, a variety of answers might be received. For example, when asked, "What's right or wrong about gun control?" Al says, "It encourages crime by disarming citizens," but Bob says, "It infringes rights." When asked, "What's good or bad about this automobile?" Christine says, "It gets good gas mileage," whereas Donna says, "It makes me look cool." Asked, "What's important about volunteering?" Ed says, "It helps me develop job skills," but Frank says, "It contributes to the community."

One straightforward way of understanding the variation in these answers is to see it simply as reflecting differences in people's wants (where "wants" is understood broadly, as encompassing people's desires, values, goals, what ends they want to serve, what attributes they value in particular types of objects, and so on). That is, these sorts of differences—which commonly have been taken to indicate differences in attitude functions—might more lucidly be characterized as simply differences in what people want from (what they value in) attitude objects.

Consider, for example, the procedure in which attitude function assessment is based on respondents' perceived importance of various reasons for volunteering (Clary et al., 1998; Clary et al., 1994). On the face of things, it seems that this procedure classifies persons on the basis of their perceived importance of various functions of the *action of volunteering* (jobs that volunteering performs, outcomes of volunteering), not on the basis of any functions of their *attitudes*. So, for instance, someone who says that improving one's résumé is an important reason for volunteering appears to be identifying a perceived important function of (job done by, purpose served by) the action—which is not the same as identifying a function of one's positive or negative attitude toward that action.

Proxy measures of attitude function such as self-monitoring are, if anything, even more susceptible to being understood in this way. For example, it is plain that high and low self-monitors can (in appropriate circumstances) have systematically different beliefs about attitude objects. But these different beliefs appear to correspond to differences in how self-monitors value certain functions of the object. (For example, high self-monitors value identity projection functions of automobiles more than do low self-monitors.) Just because high self-monitors value certain functions of objects more than do low self-monitors does not show that the attitudes of high self-monitors serve different functions than do the attitudes of low self-monitors.

To put it another way: High and low self-monitors want different things from their consumer products. But this does not mean that high and low self-monitors want different things from their *attitudes*. One might plausibly say that high and low self-monitors want their attitudes to do the same job—the job of identifying good and bad products for them.[8] Thus instead of the supposition that high and low self-monitors have attitudes that serve different functions, what seems invited is the conclusion that although high and low self-monitors may sometimes differ in the criteria they use to appraise objects, the underlying function of the evaluation (the function of the attitude) is identical.

In sum, the procedures commonly used for assessing attitude functions can instead be understood as assessing variations in the perceived value or importance of functions of (or attributes of) the attitude object.[9]

Utilitarian and Value-Expressive Functions Reconsidered. Against this backdrop, it may be useful to reconsider how utilitarian and value-expressive attitude functions have been conceptually differentiated. In Katz's (1960) treatment of these two functions, utilitarian attitudes are exemplified by attitudes based on economic gain or other concrete rewards (p. 171), whereas value-expressive attitudes are concerned with abstract "central values" and self-images (p. 173). Indeed, Katz specifically described value-expressive attitudes as different from attitudes aimed at "gaining social recognition or monetary rewards" (p. 173).

A similar way of distinguishing utilitarian and value-expressive functions appears in Maio and Olson's (1994, 1995) research examining the hypothesis that persons with value-expressive attitudes will exhibit closer connections between attitudes and values than will persons with utilitarian attitudes. In this work, the values implicated in value-expressive attitudes are conceived of as abstract ends such as equality, honesty, and freedom (Maio & Olson, 1994, p. 302), as opposed to the narrower self-interested ends represented by utilitarian attitudes; values are "evaluations of abstract ideas (e.g., equality, honesty) in terms of their importance as guiding principles in one's life" (Maio & Olson, 1995, p. 268). From this point of view, a person considering whether to make a charitable donation who thinks about "the importance of helping others" has a value-expressive attitude, whereas people who think about "whether they can afford to donate" have utilitarian attitudes (Maio & Olson, 2000a, p. 251).

That is, value-expressive attitudes have commonly been distinguished from utilitarian attitudes on the basis of the nature of the outcomes sought: Abstract, prosocial ends indicate value-expressive attitudes, whereas concrete, self-enhancing ends indicate utilitarian attitudes. But plainly, this way of distinguishing attitudes seems less a matter of attitude function than a matter of the abstractness or nobility of the ends served by the object. On the conventional view, "protecting the environment" might be a value, but "protecting my savings account" would not be. Yet obviously, each represents a potential outcome that can be valued, and hence each represents a basis of assessment of objects (assessment of objects for the degree to which the objects realize the outcome). Thus value-expressive attitudes and utilitarian attitudes arguably do not actually serve different attitude functions; the underlying attitude function is identical in the two cases (evaluative object appraisal in the service of obtaining satisfactory outcomes), although the criteria for assessing objects (that is, the outcomes of interest) may vary.

Indeed this sort of reasoning has led Maio and Olson (2000a, pp. 258-260) to introduce the idea of "goal-expressive" attitudes, precisely meant to "encompass what Katz referred to as value-expressive and utilitarian functions" (p. 259). By collapsing value-expressive and utilitarian attitudes into one functional category, this approach abandons the idea that value-expressive and utilitarian attitudes serve different purposes; it recognizes their similarity in abstract attitude function (appraisal) while not losing sight of the variation possible in substantive motivational content (for a related view, see Eagly & Chaiken, 1998, p. 304).

Summary. Taken together, these considerations invite a simpler, more straightforward account of much research on attitude function variation. Specifically, this work might more perspicaciously be described as work identifying variation in people's wants (broadly understood—their values, goals, evaluations of various properties of objects, and so on). As indicated above, both the procedures commonly used to differentiate attitude functions and the conceptual treatment of value-expressive and utilitarian functions can be seen to distinguish cases on the basis of persons' wants, not on the basis of attitude function.

Persuasion and Function Matching Revisited

Existing research on persuasion and function matching is entirely congenial with the idea that apparent attitude function variation reflects variation in people's wants. Indeed, approached from such a perspective, it is hardly surprising that function-matched messages are so often more persuasive than unmatched messages—because the matched messages speak to what people value.

For example, high and low self-monitors characteristically differ in their evaluation of various outcomes and object attributes. For instance, high self-monitors characteristically place a higher value on aspects of self-image presentation. Given this difference in wants, it is perhaps unsurprising that high self-monitors find image-oriented appeals and certain normatively oriented appeals (concerning what their peers think) to be especially congenial (e.g., DeBono, 1987; Snyder & DeBono, 1985); such appeals fit their wants (not their attitude functions).

As another example, consider the previously mentioned finding that variations in the degree to which persons' self-presentation motives emphasize "getting ahead" or "getting along" are related to the persuasiveness of messages emphasizing either the self-advancement aspects of a product or the conformity-relevant aspects of a product (Celuch & Slama, 1995). These results can obviously be straightforwardly described as a matter of matching appeals to the motivations (wants, desires, values, goals) of message receivers (specifically, motivations for self-presentation).

The same holds true for appeals matched not to individual-difference variations but to variations in the nature of the object. Different objects are valued for different types of reasons. People generally want certain sorts of things from air conditioners and different sorts of things from greeting cards—and hence appeals matched to what people want from these objects (not to what they want from their attitudes toward those objects but to what they want from those objects) will naturally be likely to enjoy some persuasive advantage (as observed by Shavitt, 1990). Similarly, for situational variations: When certain wants (values, outcomes, etc.) are made more salient, persuasive appeals engaging those wants are likely to be more successful than appeals engaging nonsalient desires (see Maio & Olson, 2000a, Study 4).

Finally, this redescription is congenial with the proposed account of function-matching persuasion effects that suggests that functionally matched messages engender greater message scrutiny. It would not be surprising that a receiver's attention be especially engaged by messages that appear to be talking about something important to the receiver (some important outcome, attribute, goal, value, etc.).

In short, existing research concerning attitude functions and persuasive appeals appears to be well captured by two core ideas: (a) What is wanted varies. Different persons can have different wants (with systematic relationships here, such as connected with self-monitoring differences); different types of objects are characteristically wanted (valued) for different reasons; and as situations vary so can the salience of different wants. (b) Persuasive messages are more effective when they engage what people want than when they do not.

These two ideas are currently clothed in talk about variation in attitude function, but such talk is at least misleading and arguably dispensable in favor of talk about variation in wants.[10] In the long run, however, clear treatment of variation in wants will require some typology of wants, that is, some systematic analysis of the ways in which wants (values, goals, desired properties of objects, etc.) can vary. The empirical success of research using attitude function categories suggests that these categories might provide some leads in this regard (although now the consequences of the lack of agreement about a functional taxonomy may be more acutely felt). For example, a carefully formulated version of the symbolic-instrumental contrast might serve as one way of distinguishing variation in wants (see Eagly & Chaiken, 1998, p. 304). It may be profitable, however, to consider other sources as well and, in particular, to consider work on typologies of values as a potential source of further insight (as recommended by Maio & Olson, 2000a).

Reviving the Idea of Attitude Functions

The analysis offered in the preceding section might appear to recommend jettisoning the idea of attitude functions and replacing it with an analysis of systematic differences in what people value. Such an approach seems to capture much of the work conducted under the aegis of functional approaches to attitude. That reframing, however, arguably fails to appreciate the contribution afforded by considering differences in genuine attitude function.

The wants-based reframing of attitude functions implicitly focuses on only one attitude function, that of (broadly) object appraisal (evaluative appraisal in the service of satisfaction of wants). But this overlooks another apparent general function of attitudes, a self-maintenance function, as exemplified by Katz's (1960) ego-defensive function.[11] The ego-defensive function is genuinely a function of an attitude, not a function of an attitude object. For example, the ego-defensive function of prejudicial attitudes toward a minority group is different from the function of the minority group itself: The minority group does not serve the function of bolstering the person's self, but the negative attitude toward the minority group can.[12]

This suggests that there are at least two distinguishable broad functions of attitude.[13] But most of the work on persuasion and attitude functions has implicitly addressed attitudes serving object appraisal functions and so has focused on adapting messages to different bases of object appraisal. Scant work is concerned with (for example) how persuasion might be effected when attitudes serve ego-defensive ends or with how to influence attitudes adopted because of the reference group identification purposes served by holding the attitude.[14]

Thus there is good reason to want to retain some version of the idea of different attitude functions, as illustrated by the apparent usefulness of a contrast between object-appraisal functions and self-maintenance functions.[15] But if the idea of attitude function is to be revived, a consistent and clear focus on the functions of attitudes (as opposed to the functions of objects or the functions of attitude expression) will be needed, accompanied by attention to the continuing challenge of attitude function assessment.

▨ CONCLUSION

Despite some conceptual unclarities, work on the functional approach to attitudes has pointed to some fundamentally important aspects of attitude and persuasion. In cases in which attitudes are primarily driven by an interest in object appraisal, persuaders will want to attend closely to the receiver's basis for assessing the attitude object. What people value can vary, and hence the persuasiveness of a message can depend in good measure on whether the message's appeals match the receiver's wants.

▨ NOTES

1. Snyder and DeBono's (1989) description of the social-adjustive function implicitly focuses not on the function of the attitude but on the function of the attitude expression. By contrast, M. B. Smith et al.'s (1956) discussion of this function emphasized that "one must take care to distinguish the functions served by holding an opinion and by expressing it" (p. 41). The potential social-adjustive function of attitude expression is straightforward enough (e.g., one can fit into social situations by expressing this or that opinion). The social-adjustive function of simply holding an attitude, on the other hand, is "at once more subtle and more complex" (p. 42). At base, it involves the creation of feelings of identification or similarity through attitudes (in ways similar to the identification processes discussed by Kelman, 1961); the mere holding of certain attitudes can be "an act of affiliation with reference groups" (M. B. Smith et al., 1956, p. 42), independent of any overt expression of the attitude. Unhappily, as discussed below, the distinction between attitude functions and attitude expression functions has not commonly been closely observed.

2. With respect to consumer product advertising, the differences between high and low self-monitors extend beyond the differential appeal of image-based and product quality-based ads. There are also related differences in the ability to remember whether an ad has been seen before (e.g., high self-monitors more accurately remember exposure to image ads than to quality ads; DeBono & Packer, 1991, Study 3); in how self-relevant ads are perceived to be (e.g., high self-monitors see image ads as more self-relevant than quality ads; DeBono & Packer, 1991, Study 2); in the types of advertisements they create for multiple-function attitude objects such as watches (e.g., low self-monitors prefer to use utilitarian appeals, whereas high self-monitors prefer social identity arguments; Shavitt & Lowrey, 1992); and in the impact of the appearance of the product (the better-looking the

car, the higher the quality ratings given by high self-monitors; DeBono & Snyder, 1989).

3. Actually, there are a number of studies that (a) are not commonly treated as representing research on attitude function matching and (b) may not even cite attitude function-matching research but that nevertheless (c) examine the relative effectiveness of persuasive appeals that have been designed to match variations in receivers' psychological needs as extrapolated from some individual-difference variable (thus paralleling the research format of much function-matching research). Studies by Faber, Karlen, and Christenson (1993), Kowert and Homer (1993), and Settle and Mizerski (1974)—examining, respectively, compulsive versus normal buyers, firstborns versus laterborns, and inner- versus other-directed persons—provide just three examples.

4. For example, effect sizes corresponding to correlations of about .20 or greater are at least not rare (e.g., Clary et al., 1994; DeBono, 1987; Shavitt, 1990; Snyder & DeBono, 1985). These effects, however, may in part reflect the use—more common in this research area than in others—of an experimental design in which participants see two versions of a message (representing contrasting appeal variations) in sequence (e.g., Shavitt, 1990; Snyder & DeBono, 1985). As Shavitt (1990, pp. 141-142) has noted, the juxtaposition of the versions may create larger effect sizes than would be found with other designs (in which participants see both versions but temporally separated, or in which each participant sees only one version of a message).

5. Some readers will recognize fragments of elaboration likelihood model reasoning here (see Chapter 6), and specifically the idea that the variable of functional matching versus mismatching might (like many variables) play multiple roles in persuasion, depending on the circumstance; for some amplification, see Petty et al. (2000, p. 145).

6. To further cement that distinction, notice that persons might express attitudes they do not hold—because the (deceptive) expression of the attitude serves some purpose, some function. A lifelong committed Democrat, newly introduced to a group of Republicans, is asked by them about a preference among presidential candidates. The Democrat strongly prefers the Democratic candidate but—not wanting to initiate a potentially unpleasant discussion—says, "I prefer the Republican." The function served by the negative attitude toward the Republican candidate is obviously different from the function served by expressing a positive attitude toward that candidate. The larger point is that the functions of attitudes should not be confused with the functions of expressing attitudes. (A complexity: One job done by—one purpose served by—the possessing of an attitude can be the job of having the attitude available for ready expression. But this does not underwrite confusing the functions of attitudes with the functions of expressing attitudes.)

7. There is a complexity here, however. The functions of an object and the functions of expressing an attitude toward that object can sometimes overlap (or coincide), at least in the realm of attitude objects that can be possessed or used, such as consumer products. For such objects, possession or use of the attitude object presumably counts as expression of the corresponding favorable attitude

(one's ownership of the object presumably expresses one's liking for the object), and hence similar jobs can be potentially done by the attitude object (that is, one's having or using the attitude object) and by other means of expressing the attitude (e.g., saying one likes the object).

8. In a sense, of course, the consumer product attitudes of high and low self-monitors do different jobs, because the attitudes of high self-monitors focus on one type of product attribute and the attitudes of low self-monitors focus on another type: High self-monitors want their attitudes to do the job of identifying objects that satisfy high self-monitor values, and low self-monitors want their attitudes to do the job of identifying objects that satisfy low self-monitor values. Such a way of differentiating attitude functions could be taken to absurd lengths, in that whenever two persons differentially valued some attribute of an object, their attitudes would be said to serve different functions; if Alice values, but Betty does not, an automobile's having power seats, then their attitudes toward automobiles serve different functions (in that only Alice's attitude would do the job of identifying cars that satisfy Alice's valuing of power seats). The real question is one of how to group different possible attitude jobs (when to lump them together, when to distinguish them), and the suggestion here is that it will be useful to recognize that although high and low self-monitors may vary in what they value, there is a sense in which the fundamental job done by their attitudes—evaluative appraisal in the service of value satisfaction—is the same. (In particular, as will be suggested shortly, attitudes driven by this sort of interest look rather different from attitudes driven by an interest in ego protection.)

9. As Eagly and Chaiken (1993, p. 490; 1998, p. 308) have stressed, early functional approaches emphasized latent motivational aspects of attitudes, aspects not necessarily apparent in manifest belief content or conscious thought—and hence not necessarily well captured by coding the manifest content of answers to open-ended questions or by examining responses to standardized self-report instruments.

10. For a related attempt at reinterpreting function-matching appeal research in ways that do not involve reference to attitude functions, see Brannon and Brock (1994), who propose that "schema-relevance," not attitude function relevance, actually underlies the findings of attitude function research.

11. A self-maintenance function might include not only ego-defensive functions but also those social-adjustive functions of holding (as opposed to expressing) attitudes, as described by M. B. Smith et al. (1956, p. 42) and mentioned above in note 1; having a given attitude can create feelings of identification or similarity, thus serving the function of creating and maintaining one's view of oneself.

12. The ego-defensive function of the attitude may also be shared, however, by the attitude expression. That is, expressing prejudicial attitudes may serve an ego-defensive function. But the focus here is on functions of attitudes (not functions of attitude expression), and the point is that ego defense is indeed one job that can be done by the holding of an attitude.

13. In fact, Pratkanis and Greenwald's (1989) analysis proposed just these two functions: "First, an attitude is used to make sense of the world and to help the organism operate on its environment. . . . Second, an attitude is . . . used to define

and maintain self-worth" (p. 249). This latter function unfortunately elides attitude function and attitude expression function: "We attach different labels to this self-related function of attitude, depending on the audience (public, private, or collective) that is observing the attitude and its expression" (p. 249).

14. Some work exists concerning attitudes about *objects* that serve self-related purposes (such as attitudes about class rings), but this is different from work concerning *attitudes* serving self-related purposes.

15. To be sure, even this contrast is contestable, in the following sort of way: "Self-maintenance is itself a value, something wanted. Thus even ego-defensive attitudes actually reflect an object appraisal function (evaluative appraisal in the service of value satisfaction); it's just that 'self-maintenance' is the value that's being served instead of some other value." And it is certainly true that understood in a sufficiently abstract way, all attitudes presumably (indeed, perhaps by definition) serve some broad appraisal function. Still, there looks to be a difference between appraisal that is in some sense object driven (I know what I'm looking for in aspirin or automobiles or whatever, and I engage in object appraisal to see how this candidate stacks up) and appraisal that seems somehow self-driven (I want to ensure a certain sort of self-evaluation, and I engage in object appraisal to produce that outcome). Expressed differently: The attitude functions of high self-monitors ("I like the car because it's sexy") and low self-monitors ("I like the car because it's reliable") look rather similar when contrasted with those of the bigot's ego-defensive prejudices. And that contrast is particularly sharp from a persuader's point of view: The same general sort of approach might be taken to persuade high and low self-monitors (emphasizing different object attributes, to be sure, but otherwise a similar approach), whereas persuading bigots likely requires something rather different.

Belief-Based Models of Attitude

This chapter discusses belief-based approaches to the analysis of attitude and attitude change. The central theme of these approaches is that one's attitude toward an object is a function of the beliefs that one has about the object. There are a number of variants of this general approach, with the variations deriving from differences in what features of beliefs are seen to contribute to attitude and from differences in how beliefs are seen to combine to yield an attitude. One particular belief-based approach, Martin Fishbein's summative model of attitude, has enjoyed special prominence among students of persuasion and social influence and hence is the focus of the chapter's attention. (The summative model also figures in the theory of reasoned action and the theory of planned behavior; see Chapter 5.)

SUMMATIVE MODEL OF ATTITUDE

The Model

The summative model of attitude (Fishbein, 1967b, 1967c) is based on the claim that one's attitude toward an object is a function of one's salient beliefs about the object. For any given attitude object, a person may have a large number of beliefs about the object. But at any given time, only some of these are likely to be salient (prominent)—and it is those that are claimed to determine one's attitude. In, say, a public opinion or marketing questionnaire, one might elicit the respondent's salient beliefs (e.g., about a product or a political candidate) by asking the respondent to list the characteristics, qualities, and attributes of the object. Across a number of respondents, the most frequently mentioned attributes represent the modally salient beliefs, which can be used as the basis for a standardized questionnaire. (For discussion of procedures for identifying salient beliefs, see Ajzen & Fishbein, 1980, pp. 68-71; Ajzen, Nichols, & Driver, 1995; Fishbein & Ajzen, 1975, pp. 218-219; Fishbein & Middlestadt, 1995; van der Pligt & de Vries, 1998b; for some complexities, see Roskos-Ewoldsen & Fazio, 1997.)

In particular, the model holds that one's attitude toward an object is a function of belief strength (that is, the strength with which one holds one's salient beliefs about the object) and belief evaluation (the evaluation one has of these beliefs).[1] Specifically, the relation of belief strength and belief evaluation to attitude is said to be described by the following formula.

$$A_o = \Sigma b_i e_i$$

where A_o is the attitude toward the object, b_i is the strength of a given belief, and e_i is the evaluation of a given belief. The sigma (Σ) indicates that one sums across the products of the belief strength and belief evaluation ratings for each belief. That is, one multiplies each belief evaluation by the strength with which that belief is held and then sums those products to arrive at an estimate of the overall attitude toward the object. If there are five salient beliefs about the object, then the attitude estimate is given by $b_1e_1 + b_2e_2 + b_3e_3 + b_4e_4 + b_5e_5$.

The procedures for assessing the elements of this model are well established (see, e.g., Fishbein & Raven, 1962). One's attitude toward the object (A_o) can be obtained by familiar attitude measurement techniques. The evaluation of a belief (e_i) is assessed through semantic-differential evaluative scales such as good-bad, desirable-undesirable, favorable-unfavorable, and the like. The strength with which a belief is held (b_i) can be assessed through scales such as likely-unlikely, probable-improbable, and true-false.

As an example: Suppose that a preliminary survey had indicated that the most salient beliefs held about Senator Smith by the senator's constituents were that the senator supports defense cuts, is helpful to constituents, is respected in the Senate, and is unethical. One might assess the strength with which the first of these beliefs was held by respondents through items such as the following:

Senator Smith supports defense cuts.

likely	___ ___ ___ ___ ___ ___ ___	unlikely
true	___ ___ ___ ___ ___ ___ ___	false
probable	___ ___ ___ ___ ___ ___ ___	improbable

The evaluation of that belief can be assessed with items such as the following:

Supporting defense cuts is

good	___ ___ ___ ___ ___ ___ ___	bad
desirable	___ ___ ___ ___ ___ ___ ___	undesirable
harmful	___ ___ ___ ___ ___ ___ ___	beneficial

Suppose (to simplify matters) that for each belief, belief strength and belief evaluation were assessed by a single scale (perhaps "likely-unlikely" for belief strength, "good-bad" for belief evaluation) scored from +3 (likely or good) to −3 (unlikely or bad). A particular respondent might have the following belief strength and belief evaluation ratings for the four salient beliefs about Senator Smith.

	b_i	e_i	$b_i e_i$
supports defense cuts	+3	−2	−6
helpful to constituents	−3	+3	−9
respected in the Senate	+2	+1	+2
unethical	−2	−3	+6
			−7 $= \Sigma b_i e_i$

This particular respondent believes that it is quite likely that the senator supports defense cuts (belief strength of +3), and supporting defense cuts is seen as a moderately negative characteristic (evaluation of −2); the respondent thinks it very unlikely that the senator is helpful to constituents (helpfulness to constituents being thought to be a very good quality); the respondent thinks it moderately likely that Smith is respected in the Senate, and that is a slightly positive characteristic; and the respondent thinks it rather unlikely that Smith possesses the highly negative characteristic of being unethical.

Because (in this example) each belief strength score (b_i) can range from -3 to $+3$ and each belief evaluation score (e_i) can range from -3 to $+3$, each product ($b_i e_i$) can range from -9 to $+9$, and hence the total (across the four beliefs in this example) can range from -36 to $+36$. A person who thought that the qualities of supporting defense cuts, being helpful to constituents, and being respected in the Senate were all very positive characteristics (belief evaluations of $+3$ in each case) and who thought it very likely that the senator possessed each of these qualities (belief strength of $+3$ for each), and who also thought it quite unlikely (-3 belief strength) that the senator possessed the strongly negative (-3 belief evaluation) characteristic of being unethical would have a total ($\Sigma b_i e_i$) of $+36$, indicating an extremely positive attitude toward the senator—as befits such a set of beliefs. By comparison, the hypothetical respondent with a total of -7 might be said to have a slightly negative attitude toward Senator Smith.

Perhaps it is apparent how this general approach could be used for other attitude objects (with different salient beliefs, of course). In consumer marketing, for example, the attitude object of interest is a product or brand, and the salient beliefs typically concern the attributes of the product or brand. Thus, for instance, the underlying bases of consumers' attitudes toward a given brand of toothpaste might be investigated by examining the belief strength and belief evaluation associated with consumers' salient beliefs about that brand's attributes: whitening power, taste, ability to prevent cavities, cost, ability to freshen breath, and so forth.

As another example of application, persons' attitudes toward public policy proposals can be studied; here the salient beliefs might well include beliefs about the consequences of adoption of the policy. Consider, for instance, some possible cognitive bases of attitudes toward capital punishment. Does capital punishment deter crime (belief strength), and how good an outcome is that (belief evaluation)? Is capital punishment inhumane, and how negatively valued is that? Is capital punishment applied inequitably, and how disadvantageous is that? And so forth. Two persons with opposed attitudes on this issue might equally value crime deterrence—that is, have the same evaluation of that attribute—but disagree about whether capital punishment has that attribute (has the consequence of deterring crime). Or two people with opposed attitudes might agree that capital punishment has the characteristic of satisfying the desire for vengeance but differ in the evaluation of that characteristic.

Persuasive Strategy Implications

The summative model points to a number of alternative ways in which attitude might be influenced and suggests means for identifying plausible foci for messages.

Alternative Persuasive Strategies. Because, on this view, one's attitude is taken to be a function of the strength and evaluation of one's salient beliefs about the object, attitude change will involve changing these putative bases of attitude. The model thus suggests ways in which attitude might be changed. For example, in attempting to induce a favorable attitude toward a given attitude object (e.g., Senator Smith), one might attempt to lead the receiver to add a new salient positive belief about the object ("You might not have realized it, but Senator Smith has been working to fix the problems with Social Security"). A second possibility is to attempt to increase the favorability of an existing positive belief ("Senator Smith is, as you know, respected in the Senate, but you may not realize just how desirable that is: It means Senator Smith can be more effective in passing legislation to help our state"). Third, a persuader might attempt to increase the belief strength (likelihood) of an existing positive belief ("You already know it's true that Senator Smith has worked hard for the people of this state—but you don't know just how true that is . . ."). Fourth, one might try to decrease the unfavorability of an existing negative belief ("Sure, Senator Smith was only an average student—but then again, being an average student isn't so bad"). Fifth, one might attempt to decrease the belief strength (likelihood) associated with an existing negative belief ("It's simply not true that Senator Smith accepted kickbacks"). Finally, attitude could be changed without adding any new beliefs and without changing the strength or evaluation of any existing beliefs—simply by shuffling the current beliefs around in such a way that a different set of beliefs is salient. That is, changing the relative saliency of currently held beliefs can presumably influence attitudes ("Have you forgotten that five years ago Senator Smith helped keep XYZ Industries from moving out of state?"). Obviously, these are not mutually exclusive possibilities; a persuader might well offer arguments designed to implement all these strategies.

Identifying Foci for Appeals. The summative attitude model can also be useful in identifying likely foci for persuasive appeals. This facet of the model is particularly apparent when considering mass persuasion contexts. Suppose, for example, that one was planning a persuasive campaign concerning the construction of nuclear power plants and had undertaken a survey assessing the beliefs of those favoring and those opposing such plants, with survey results that included the following findings (with these means having a possible range of +3 to –3).

Nuclear Power Attributes	b_i		e_i	
	Pro-Nuclear Power	Anti-Nuclear Power	Pro-Nuclear Power	Anti-Nuclear Power
Prevents a future energy crisis	+2.8	–2.5	+2.7	+2.7
Increases risk of nuclear accident	–2.4	+2.9	–2.8	–2.6
Creates waste disposal problems	+2.2	+2.3	–1.3	–2.8
Leads to higher energy costs	+1.9	+2.0	–2.5	–2.4

These results suggest that (among these hypothetical respondents) those who favor and oppose nuclear power equally value the attribute of preventing an energy crisis (mean belief evaluations of 2.7 in each group) but that those favoring nuclear power think this outcome much more likely (mean belief strength rating of 2.8) than do those opposing nuclear power (mean belief strength rating of –2.5). Both groups of respondents negatively evaluate any increased risk of a nuclear accident, but only those opposed to nuclear power think this outcome very likely. Both groups think nuclear power will create waste disposal problems, but those opposed to nuclear power think this a much more undesirable outcome than do those favoring nuclear power. And everybody thinks nuclear power is reasonably likely to lead to the negatively evaluated consequence of higher energy costs.

It is probably apparent how one can quickly identify the most likely avenues for persuasive efforts in this circumstance—and how one can also identify probable blind alleys. For instance, suppose one's campaign is aimed at inducing favorable attitudes toward nuclear power (and so aimed at persuading those who are anti-nuclear power). There would not be much point in constructing messages aimed at showing just how desirable it would be to prevent a future energy crisis—because even those respondents opposed to nuclear power already believe that such an outcome is quite desirable. With respect to the attribute of "preventing a future energy crisis," these opponents of nuclear power need to be persuaded not whether such an outcome is desirable but rather whether nuclear power will produce such a result. By contrast, the campaign's messages concerning potential waste disposal problems might well profitably focus on receivers' evaluations of such problems (rather than trying to instill the belief that such problems will occur). (For examples of such analyses, see Gerber, Newman, & Martin, 1988; Woo & Castore, 1980; relatedly, see van der Pligt & de Vries, 1998a.)

🔲 RESEARCH EVIDENCE AND COMMENTARY

The commentary that follows initially takes up some questions addressed specifically to the summative model (the general evidence concerning the model; the roles of attribute importance, belief content, and belief strength in the model; and the procedures for scoring the model's scales), then turns to another belief-based model (offering an alternative image of how beliefs are related to attitudes) and to the general question of the sufficiency of belief-based analyses of attitude; a concluding section reconsiders the persuasive strategies suggested by the summative model.

General Correlational Evidence

A number of investigations have examined the correlation between a direct measure of the respondent's attitude toward the object (A_o) and the predicted attitude based on the summative formula ($\Sigma b_i e_i$) using modally salient beliefs. Reasonably strong positive correlations have commonly been found, ranging roughly from .55 to .80 with a variety of attitude objects including public policy proposals (e.g., Infante, 1971, 1973; Peay, 1980; Petkova, Ajzen, & Driver, 1995); political candidates (e.g., M. H. Davis & Runge, 1981; Holbrook & Hulbert, 1975); and consumer products (e.g., Holbrook, 1977; Nakanishi & Bettman, 1974).[2] That is, attitude appears to often be reasonably well predicted by this model.

This correlational evidence, however, does not offer compelling support for the claim that attitude is determined by salient beliefs. Several studies have found that attitude can be equally well predicted (using $\Sigma b_i e_i$) from salient and from nonsalient beliefs (e.g., Ajzen et al., 1995; A. J. Smith & Clark, 1973). Such findings might reflect respondents' use of their current attitudes as guides to responding to items concerning nonsalient beliefs (for example, if I have a negative attitude toward the object, and the standardized belief list asks for my reactions to statements associating the object with some attribute that I had not considered, I might well give relatively unfavorable responses precisely because I already have a negative attitude toward the object). Moreover, when standardized belief lists (that is, lists containing modally salient beliefs) and individualized belief lists (in which each respondent gets an individually constructed questionnaire, listing only his or her particular salient beliefs) have been compared as the basis for attitude prediction, often there is no dependable difference (e.g., Agnew, 1998; Bodur, Brinberg, & Coupey, 2000; Kaplan & Fishbein, 1969; Rutter & Bunce, 1989). So the correlational evidence in hand certainly shows that belief assessments can indicate a person's attitude (if only because persons give attitude-consistent responses to questionnaire items about beliefs) but falls short of showing that attitudes are determined by salient beliefs. (For a careful discussion of these matters, see Eagly & Chaiken, 1993, pp. 232-234.)

Attribute Importance

Several investigations have explored the potential role of attribute importance or relevance in predicting attitude. The summative model, it will be noticed, uses only belief strength and belief evaluation to predict attitude; some researchers have thought that the predictability of attitude might be improved by adding the importance or relevance of the attribute as a third variable. That is, in addition to assessing belief strength and belief evaluation, one also obtains measures of the relevance or importance of each belief to the respondent; then some three-component formula, such as $\Sigma b_i e_i I_i$ (where I_i refers to the importance of the attribute), is used to predict attitude.[3]

But the evidence in hand suggests that adding relevance or importance to the summative formula does not improve the predictability of attitude (e.g., L. R. Anderson, 1970; Hackman & Anderson, 1968; Holbrook & Hulbert, 1975). In understanding this result, it may be helpful to consider the possibility that the attributes judged more important or relevant may also have more extreme evaluations; the assessment of belief evaluation (e_i) may already involve indirect assessment of relevance and importance (e.g., Holbrook & Hulbert, 1975; cf. van der Pligt & de Vries, 1998a). Moreover, if an investigator is careful to select only salient attributes as the basis for attitude prediction, then presumably all the attributes assessed are comparatively relevant and important ones—and hence adding importance or relevance ratings would not be expected to improve the prediction of attitude. In any event, there appears to be little reason to suppose that the predictability of attitude from the original summative formula ($\Sigma b_i e_i$) can be improved by adding a belief importance or belief relevance component.[4]

Enhancing the predictability of attitude, however, is arguably not the main relevant research goal. The larger purpose is that of illuminating how beliefs contribute to attitude; given that attitude can be predicted even from nonsalient beliefs (as discussed above), the use of predictability as the relevant criterion is a bit misleading. Indeed, with that larger goal in mind, belief importance ratings can be seen to be valuable in another way (that is, beyond whether they add to the predictability of attitude from $\Sigma b_i e_i$). Suppose, for example, that an investigator has not been careful to ensure (by pretesting) that the listed beliefs are modally salient for respondents. Although many of the listed beliefs are not actually ones that determine the respondents' attitudes, it is still possible that the belief list will produce a reasonably strong correlation between $\Sigma b_i e_i$ and attitude (because, as discussed earlier, respondents can use their current attitudes as guides to responding to these nonsalient belief items). In such a circumstance, importance ratings might indicate which of the listed beliefs are actually salient for the respondents. Indeed, even if the belief list has been pretested to ensure that it contains *modally* salient beliefs, belief importance ratings may still give some insight into what underlies attitudes, especially if there is some reason to think that different respondents (or subgroups of respondents) may have importantly different sets of salient beliefs. In short, although belief importance might not add to the predictability of attitude from $\Sigma b_i e_i$, belief importance ratings may be crucial in permitting the identification of those beliefs (on a standardized list) that actually determine the respondent's attitude—and hence the beliefs that warrant a persuader's attention. (For illustrations of such a role for importance ratings, see, e.g., Elliott, Jobber, & Sharp, 1995; van der Pligt & de Vries, 1998a, 1998b; van der Pligt & Eiser, 1984. For a general discussion, see van der Pligt, de Vries, Manstead, & van Harreveld, 2000.)

Belief Content

The summative model offers what might be called a content-free analysis of the underpinnings of attitude. That is, for the summative model's analysis, the content of a belief is irrelevant; what matters is simply how the belief is evaluated and how strongly it is held. Ignoring content may indeed be appropriate given an interest simply in attitude prediction. But for other purposes, systematic attention to belief content may be important.

Functional approaches to attitude (discussed in Chapter 2) provide a useful contrast here. Functional approaches identify different syndromes (coherent sets) of beliefs based on belief content; different attitude functions correspond to substantively different (sets of) salient beliefs. So, for example, two automobile owners may have equivalent attitudes, but one has beliefs about gas mileage and frequency-of-repair records, whereas the other has beliefs about what identity is conveyed by the automobile.

Such differences in belief content can figure importantly in persuasion. Consider, for example, the persuasive strategy of creating a more positive attitude by inducing belief in some new positive attribute. If content is ignored, one positive attribute might seem as good as another for this purpose. But a functional perspective recommends considering the substantive content of the belief to be instilled; after all, if the receiver has predominantly image-oriented beliefs about the object, then trying to add some product quality-oriented belief ("gets good gas mileage") may not be successful.

The point here is not that such considerations cannot be represented within a summative model framework. For example, one might say that the "good gas mileage" attribute is more likely to be salient for (or valued by) one person than another or that that attribute is more likely to be perceived as associated with the attitude object by one person than by another.[5] Rather, the point is that the summative model provides no systematic ways of thinking about belief content, although such content is manifestly important. In a sense, then, one might think of these approaches as complementary: Functional approaches emphasize the (manifest or latent) content of beliefs, whereas belief-based attitude models (such as the summative model) are aimed at illuminating how underlying beliefs contribute to an overall attitude.

Role of Belief Strength

There is good reason to think that the apparent contribution of belief strength scores to the prediction of attitude does not reflect a genuine role for belief strength in determining attitude but instead is a methodological artifact. The relevant evidence comes from research comparing Σe_i (that is, the simple sum of the belief evaluations) with $\Sigma b_i e_i$ (the summative formula) as predictors of attitude. The relative success of these two formulas varies, depending on the way in which the list of salient beliefs is prepared.

The most common way of preparing the list of salient beliefs (in research on this attitude model) is by eliciting beliefs from a test sample, identifying the most frequently mentioned beliefs, and using these on the questionnaire. In this procedure, a standardized belief list is composed (i.e., every respondent receives the same set of modally salient beliefs). An alternative procedure is to elicit salient beliefs from each respondent individually and so have each respondent provide belief strength and belief evaluation ratings for his or her unique set of salient beliefs. That is, an individualized belief list can be constructed for each respondent.

The research evidence indicates that when individualized belief lists are used, Σe_i and $\Sigma b_i e_i$ are equally good predictors of attitude; adding belief strength scores to the formula does not improve the predictability of attitude. With standardized belief lists, however, $\Sigma b_i e_i$ is a better predictor than is Σe_i. That is, belief strength scores significantly improve the predictability of attitude only when standardized (as opposed to individualized) belief lists are used (Cronen & Conville, 1975; Delia, Crockett, Press, & O'Keefe, 1975; Eagly, Mladinic, & Otto, 1994).[6] On reflection, of course, this result makes good sense. With individualized belief lists, the respondent has just indicated that he or she thinks the object possesses the attribute; only beliefs that the respondent already holds are rated for belief strength. By contrast, with standardized belief lists, belief strength scores distinguish those beliefs the respondent holds from those the respondent does not hold. The use of standardized lists thus creates a predictive role for belief strength scores (namely, the role of differentiating those beliefs the respondent holds from those the respondent does not hold), but the predictive contribution of belief strength scores is a methodological artifact, not an indication of any genuine place for belief strength in the cognitive states underlying attitude.

To put the point somewhat differently: These results suggest that—insofar as the underlying bases of attitude are concerned—we may more usefully think of persons' beliefs about an object as rather more categorical ("I think the object has the attribute," "I don't think the object has the attribute," or "I'm not sure") than continuous ("I think that the probability that the object possesses the attribute is thus-and-so"). The belief strength scales give the appearance of some continuous gradation of belief probability, but these scales make a contribution to attitude prediction only because standardized belief lists are used. When individualized belief lists are used, belief strength scores are unhelpful in predicting attitude because in each case the individual thinks that the object has the attribute—and it is that simple categorical judgment (not variations in the reported degree of probabilistic association) that is important in determining the individual's attitude.[7]

Scoring Procedures

There has been a fair amount of discussion in the literature concerning how the belief strength and belief evaluation scales should be scored (e.g., Ajzen & Fishbein, 1980, p. 71; Bagozzi, 1984; Bettman, Capon, & Lutz,

1975; Fishbein & Ajzen, 1975, pp. 82-86; Lauver & Knapp, 1993; J. L. Smith, 1996; Steinfatt, 1977). By way of illustration, two common ways of scoring a 7-point scale are from −3 to +3 (bipolar scoring) and from 1 to 7 (unipolar scoring). (There are possibilities in addition to −3 to +3 or 1 to 7, but these provide a useful basis for discussion.) With belief strength and belief evaluation scales, one might score both scales −3 to +3, score both scales 1 to 7, or score one scale −3 to +3 and the other 1 to 7. But (because the scales are multiplied) these different scoring procedures can yield different correlations of $\Sigma b_i e_i$ with attitude, and hence a question has arisen concerning which scoring procedures are preferable.

Sometimes conceptual considerations have been adduced as a basis for choosing a scoring method. These arguments commonly take one of two forms. One is an appeal to the nature of the relevant psychological states; for example, it is sometimes suggested that evaluation is naturally better understood as bipolar rather than as unipolar, or that belief strength scales should not be scored in a bipolar way because it is not psychologically meaningful for attitude objects to be negatively associated with attributes. (For examples of such arguments, see Bagozzi, 1984; Ryan & Bonfield, 1975.) The other considers the plausibility of the consequences of employing various combinations of scoring procedures; for example, to take the simplifying case of a person with just one salient belief, a respondent who strongly believes that the object possesses a very undesirable characteristic should presumably have the least favorable attitude possible—but if both scales are scored from 1 to 7, that respondent will not have the lowest possible strength-times-evaluation product (which thus suggests the implausibility of such scoring). In particular, the combination of bipolar scoring for belief evaluation and unipolar scoring for belief strength has often been argued to be the theoretically most appropriate scoring combination (e.g., Steinfatt, 1977).

But the main criterion for assessing scoring procedures has been the predictability of attitude thereby afforded. That is, the criterion has been the observed correlation between $\Sigma b_i e_i$ and attitude.[8] Several studies have compared the predictability of attitude using different scoring methods. Although results vary, the most common finding seems to have been that scoring both scales in a bipolar fashion yields larger correlations (of $\Sigma b_i e_i$ with attitude) than do alternative combinations and, in particular, is superior to the intuitively appealing bipolar evaluation and unipolar strength combination (Ajzen, 1991; Bettman et al., 1975; Lutz, 1976; P. Sparks, Hedderley, & Shepherd, 1991; cf. Hewstone & Young, 1988).

This conclusion is also recommended by several studies using optimal scaling procedures, which assign scale values in such a fashion as to maximize the resulting correlation. With these procedures, a constant is added to each belief strength score and another is added to each belief evaluation score; the constants are computed precisely to produce the largest possible correlation between $\Sigma b_i e_i$ and attitude (see Bagozzi, 1984; Holbrook, 1977).[9] Several studies have reported that the computed scaling constants suggest that both scales should be bipolar (Ajzen, 1991; Holbrook, 1977; cf. Doll, Ajzen, & Madden, 1991).

But now the task becomes explaining why bipolar scoring for both scales appears to maximize the correlation between $\Sigma b_i e_i$ and attitude. Bipolar scoring seems to make intuitive psychological sense in the case of belief evaluation scales, but the general empirical success of bipolar scoring for belief strength scales may appear puzzling. One possibility is simply this: When standardized lists of modal salient beliefs are used, bipolar scoring of belief strength scales may permit participants to remove all effects of beliefs that they do not have (or beliefs that are not salient for them). When such beliefs appear on the standardized belief list, a mark at the midpoint of belief strength scales is a sensible response (the respondent does not know, or is not sure, whether the object has the attribute, so marks the midpoint rather than favoring either "likely" or "unlikely"). With bipolar scoring, such a response is scored as zero—which, when multiplied by the corresponding belief evaluation, will yield a product of zero (no matter what the evaluation is); this has the entirely appropriate effect of removing that belief from having any impact on the respondent's predicted attitude.[10] In short, the common superiority of bipolar (over unipolar) scoring of belief strength scales might be a consequence of the use of standardized lists of beliefs and so may be a methodological artifact rather than a source of substantive information about how belief strength perceptions operate.

Alternative Integration Schemes

The summative model depicts beliefs as combining in a particular way to yield an overall evaluation, namely, in an additive way (summing across the $b_i e_i$ products). Hence, for instance, everything else being equal, adding a new positive belief will make an attitude more favorable. But different integration schemes—that is, different images of how beliefs combine to yield attitudes—have been proposed. The most prominent of these is an averaging model, as embedded in Anderson's information integration theory (N. H. Anderson, 1971, 1981b, 1991).[11] Crudely expressed, an averaging model suggests that attitude is determined by the average, not the sum, of the relevant belief properties.

An averaging image (of how beliefs combine to yield attitudes) can produce some counterintuitive predictions. For example, it suggests that adding a new positive belief about an object will not necessarily make the attitude more positive. Suppose that a person's current attitude toward the object is based on four beliefs evaluated +3, +3, +3, and +2. Imagine that the person acquires a new belief that is evaluated +2 (and, to simplify matters, assume equal belief strength weights for each belief). A summative picture of belief combination expects the additional belief to make the attitude more positive (because the sum of the evaluations would be 13 rather than 11), but an averaging model predicts that the overall attitude would be less positive: The average of the initial four beliefs is 2.75, but the average of the set of five beliefs is 2.60 (that is, adding the new attribute lowers the average evaluation).

For a time, a fair amount of research attention was devoted to comparing summative and averaging (and other) models of belief integration. But for various reasons, no general conclusion issues from this research. For one thing, in many circumstances, the models make equivalent predictions (and so cannot be empirically distinguished); moreover, in circumstances in which the models do make divergent predictions, each can point to some evidence suggesting its superiority over the other (e.g., N. H. Anderson, 1965; Fishbein & Hunter, 1964). Thus neither seems to provide an entirely satisfactory general account of how beliefs are related to attitudes; indeed, there may be no single simple rule by which persons combine beliefs into an attitude. (For some reviews and discussion, see Eagly & Chaiken, 1993, pp. 241-255; Wyer, 1974, pp. 263-306.)

An inability to display any decisive general superiority of one model over the other is in some ways unfortunate, as summative and averaging models can yield different recommendations to persuaders. Suppose, for example, that voters have a generally favorable attitude toward some policy issue (e.g., gun control) that appears as a referendum ballot item. The organizers of the campaign favoring that policy discover some new advantage to the proposed policy. Naturally enough, they undertake an advertising campaign to publicize this new positive attribute of the policy, hoping to make voters' attitudes even more favorable toward their position.

The initiation of this new campaign rests implicitly on a summative image of how this new information will be integrated: Adding a new positive belief about an object should make attitudes toward that object more favorable. But (as just suggested) an averaging model will predict that at least under some circumstances, the addition of this new positive attribute could make attitudes toward the policy *less* favorable than they had been—

and hence might conclude that this new advertising campaign is ill-advised. In the absence of good evidence about just what sort of belief combination principle might best describe what will occur in a circumstance such as this, one can hardly give persuaders firm recommendations.

The Sufficiency of Belief-Based Analyses

Belief-based attitude models depict beliefs about the object as the sole determinants of attitudes. But the question has arisen whether such beliefs are a sufficient basis for understanding attitudes; the issue is whether some non-belief-based (noncognitive) elements might independently contribute to attitude (independent, that is, of representations of belief structure such as $\Sigma b_i e_i$).

The central research evidence here takes the form of studies investigating whether a given noncognitive element makes a contribution to the prediction of attitude beyond that afforded by measures of belief structure ($\Sigma b_i e_i$). A convenient illustration is provided by research concerning the effects of consumer advertising. Advertising presumably attempts to influence the consumer's beliefs about the product's attributes or characteristics, thereby influencing the consumer's attitude toward the product. But evidence suggests that at least under some circumstances, the influence of advertising on receivers' attitudes toward a given brand or product may come about not only through receivers' beliefs about the product's characteristics but also through the receivers' evaluation of the advertisement itself (the receivers' "attitude toward the ad"). As receivers have more favorable evaluations of the advertising, they come to have more favorable attitudes toward the product being advertised. And several studies have reported that this effect occurs over and above the advertising's effects on product beliefs—that is, attitude toward the ad and $\Sigma b_i e_i$ jointly have been found to be more successful in predicting attitude than is $\Sigma b_i e_i$ alone (e.g., Gardner, 1985; Mitchell, 1986; Mitchell & Olson, 1981; for related findings, see Lutz, MacKenzie, & Belch, 1983; MacKenzie, Lutz, & Belch, 1986; for a review, see S. P. Brown & Stayman, 1992). Such evidence appears to point to some influence on attitudes beyond beliefs about the object and hence suggests the insufficiency of a purely belief-based analysis of the determinants of attitude.

The research evidence bearing on these matters is not uncontroversial. Fishbein and Middlestadt (1995) argued that most of the research purporting to show an independent effect for noncognitive elements (including attitude toward the ad) is methodologically flawed (for discussion, see, e.g., Fishbein & Middlestadt, 1997; Herr, 1995; Miniard & Barone, 1997;

Priester & Fleming, 1997; Schwarz, 1997). One illustration of such flaws is that if an investigator is not careful to ensure that salient beliefs are being assessed, then the apparent ability of some noncognitive factor to add to the predictability of attitude beyond $\Sigma b_i e_i$ might reflect not some genuine influence of the noncognitive factor but rather a shortcoming in the assessment of beliefs; the suggestion is that with better belief assessment, the apparent noncognitive contribution might disappear (see, e.g., Mittal, 1990).[12]

There does, however, seem to be good evidence pointing to an independent role for some noncognitive elements, however, namely, feelings (emotions, affect). The suggestion is that attitude might be influenced either by cognitive (belief-related) considerations or by affective (feeling-related) considerations. So, for example, a person's evaluation of a politician might reflect cognitions concerning the politician's personal attributes or issue positions or might be based on the feelings that the politician evokes in the person (hope, anger, disgust, pride, etc.). Consistent with this suggestion, several studies have reported that attitudes are often better predicted from a combination of affective and cognitive assessments than from either one alone (e.g., Abelson, Kinder, Peters, & Fiske, 1982; Bodur et al., 2000; Crites, Fabrigar, & Petty, 1994; Eagly et al., 1994; Haddock & Zanna, 1998). Such evidence invites a picture of attitudes as potentially having both affective and cognitive determinants (as offered by, e.g., Eagly & Chaiken, 1993, pp. 14-16; Zanna & Rempel, 1988) and suggests the incompleteness of a purely belief-based analysis of attitude.[13]

Of course, if belief is understood sufficiently broadly, none of this is necessarily inconsistent with a belief-based model of attitude. The distinction between affect and cognition might sensibly be said to be one of emphasis: No cognition is free from affect (every belief has some evaluative aspect, even if neutral), and even self-reported feelings amount to reports about what people believe (what people believe their feelings are). Indeed, these (and other) considerations have led some commentators to suggest that perhaps the more useful contrast is not between (pure) affect and (pure) cognition but between what might be called affective beliefs and cognitive beliefs (see, e.g., Trafimow & Sheeran, 1998).

Even approached in such a fashion, however, the evidence in hand suggests the importance of being alert to the different types of beliefs (affective and cognitive) that might underlie attitudes.[14] Some attitudes might be primarily based on affective considerations, others predominantly on cognitive considerations, and still others on a mixture of affective and cognitive elements.[15] And, of course, understanding the current basis of a person's attitude is commonly a first step toward understanding how the attitude might be changed.

Persuasive Strategies Reconsidered

The various research findings discussed above invite some reconsideration of the persuasive strategies suggested by the summative model. Expressed compactly, those strategies involve changing the strength of a current belief, changing the evaluation of a current belief, or changing the set of salient beliefs (by adding new beliefs or by altering the relative salience of current ones). Scant evidence directly compares the relative effectiveness of these different strategies (see, e.g., Infante, 1975; Stutman & Newell, 1984), but other research provides some insight into the likely utility of the various alternatives.[16]

Belief Strength as a Persuasion Target. The apparently artifactual role of belief strength scores suggests the implausibility of certain persuasive strategies that the summative model might recommend. Consider a persuader who is trying to induce a favorable attitude toward Boffo Beer. Suppose that a particular respondent has the salient belief that Boffo Beer tastes good and on 7-point scales (scored −3 to +3) indicates that this attribute is highly desirable (+3 for belief evaluation) and that it is moderately likely (+2 for belief strength) that Boffo Beer tastes good. The summative attitude model suggests that this respondent's attitude could be made more positive by influencing the belief strength rating for this attribute—specifically, by getting the respondent to believe that it is very likely that Boffo Beer tastes good (+3 for belief strength).

But if belief strength does not actually influence attitude, then such a strategy is misguided; if a person already has the relevant categorical judgment in place, trying to influence the *degree* of association between the object and the attribute will not influence attitude. Thus if our hypothetical respondent already believes that Boffo Beer tastes good, there appears to be little point in seeking changes in the exact degree of the respondent's subjective probability judgment that Boffo Beer tastes good.

Of course, if our respondent thinks Boffo Beer *does not* taste good (or has no opinion about Boffo's taste), then in seeking to induce a positive attitude toward the beer, a persuader may well want to influence that belief by attempting to induce the belief that Boffo does taste good. But this will be a matter of changing the relevant categorical judgment (e.g., from "Boffo Beer doesn't taste good" to "Boffo Beer does taste good") and need not be approached as though there is some psychologically real probabilistic degree of perceived association between object and attribute. That is, the key distinction will be between whether the person does or does not have the belief, not between finer gradations of belief strength.[17]

Belief Evaluation as a Persuasion Target. Little research directly addresses the persuasive strategy of changing the evaluation of a currently
held belief. Lutz (1975a) found that messages designed specifically to
change laundry detergent attribute evaluations had little effect on those
evaluations (and, correspondingly, little effect on attitudes; cf. Kohn,
1969). It may be that as Eagly and Chaiken (1993, p. 237) suggest, some
attribute evaluations are relatively stable by virtue of their basis in prior experience. For example, the evaluation of the laundry detergent attribute
"gets your clothes clean" might well be expected to be relatively stable for
most people.

Still, sometimes attribute evaluations appear to be a useful focus for persuaders. For example, a consumer may know that a faster Internet connection can be purchased but may not realize just how desirable that would be.
Death penalty opponents might seek to convince the public that vengeance
is a base and unworthy motive—and hence that capital punishment's attribute of providing vengeance is less desirable than one might previously
have thought. Although it may not be easy to influence the evaluations
associated with existing beliefs, changing such evaluations may nevertheless sometimes be a key aspect of a persuader's campaign.

Changing the Set of Salient Beliefs as a Persuasion Mechanism. Changing
the set of salient beliefs might be accomplished in two (not mutually exclusive) ways, by adding new salient beliefs or by altering the relative salience
of existing beliefs.

Adding a new appropriately valenced belief (e.g., adding a belief that
associates some new positive attribute with the object, to make the attitude
more favorable) would appear to be relatively attractive as an avenue to attitude change.[18] But the previously discussed research evidence suggests that
two considerations should be kept in mind here. First, the content (not just
the evaluation) of the advocated new belief may need to be considered
closely, as some candidate new beliefs may be more compatible than others
with the current set of beliefs. For instance, a receiver with predominantly
concrete, instrumental beliefs about a given automobile ("It gets bad gas
mileage" or "It gets good gas mileage") may not be receptive to advertising invoking image-oriented appeals ("You'll feel so sexy driving it"); for
such a person, adding new instrumentally oriented beliefs ("It's a very safe
vehicle") might be a more plausible approach.[19]

Second, the possibility that belief integration occurs in some nonsummative way indicates that persuaders should not automatically assume
that adding a new belief will necessarily move the attitude in the evaluative
direction of that belief. If beliefs combine in a way that involves averaging
the evaluations of the individual beliefs (rather than summing them), then

it is possible that (for example) adding a new positive belief may not make the attitude more positive.[20]

The other broad way of changing the set of salient beliefs (besides adding new salient beliefs) is to alter the relative salience of currently held beliefs. For example, a persuader might seek to make the audience's beliefs about positive attributes more salient, thereby enhancing the attitude. There is little direct evidence about implementing this as a persuasive strategy, and it is not plain whether substantial changes in attitude can be expected from such a strategy (see Delia et al., 1975; Shavitt & Fazio, 1990). Nevertheless, it is easy to see that (for example) one purpose of point-of-purchase displays (e.g., in grocery stores) can be to influence which of the product's attributes are salient.

In employing such a strategy, it is important to identify just which beliefs are already actually salient, and (as intimated earlier) belief importance ratings can be especially valuable for this purpose when standardized lists (of modally salient beliefs) are used. For example, as van der Pligt et al. (2000) have pointed out, smokers do not necessarily evaluate the undesirable health consequences of smoking any less negatively than do nonsmokers (nor do they necessarily give different belief strength ratings), but the health consequences are less important (less salient)—and other consequences more important—for smokers than for nonsmokers. Thus attempting to shift the relative salience of these beliefs—to make the negative consequences more prominent and the positive consequences less salient—may be a more productive avenue for persuasion than attempting to influence belief evaluation (or strength).

▧ CONCLUSION

The general idea that the beliefs one has about an object influences one's attitude toward that object is enormously plausible, and, correspondingly, it seems obvious that one natural avenue to attitude change involves influencing beliefs. Hence it is not surprising that belief-based models of attitude have received such attention from students of persuasion. Indeed, the summative model of attitude obviously offers some straightforward recommendations to persuaders.[21] Still, many particulars of the relationship of beliefs and attitudes remain elusive, with corresponding uncertainties for the understanding of persuasion.

▧ NOTES

1. The summative model of attitude is sometimes referred to as an expectancy-value (EV) model of attitude. An EV model of attitude represents attitude as a

function of the products of the value of a given attribute (e.g., the attribute's desirability) and the expectation that the object has the attribute (e.g., belief strength). The summative model is only one version of an EV model, however; this basic EV idea has been formulated in various ways (e.g., Peak, 1955; Rosenberg, 1956; Sheth & Talarzyk, 1972). But the summative model is the best studied, appears to have been the most successful empirically, and indeed is the standard against which alternative EV models have commonly been tested (e.g., Bettman et al., 1975; Holbrook & Hulbert, 1975). (For some general discussions of EV models of attitude, see Bagozzi, 1984, 1985; J. B. Cohen, Fishbein, & Ahtola, 1972; Eagly & Chaiken, 1993.)

2. This attitude model is embedded in the theory of reasoned action and the theory of planned behavior (see Chapter 5). Research addressed to those theories has produced evidence concerning the use of the summative formula to predict specifically attitudes toward behaviors (A_B), with similar results (for some review discussions, see Conner & Sparks, 1996; Eagly & Chaiken, 1993, p. 176).

3. Although they are not discussed here, the potential complexities in assessing belief importance should not be underestimated; see Jaccard, Brinberg, and Ackerman (1986); Jaccard, Radecki, Wilson, and Dittus (1995); Jaccard and Sheng (1984); and van der Pligt et al. (2000, pp. 145-155).

4. Relatedly, equally good correlations of $\Sigma b_i e_i$ with attitude have been observed using a list of modally salient beliefs and using a smaller set of beliefs identified by the respondent as most important (see Budd, 1986; van der Pligt & de Vries, 1998a; van Harreveld, van der Pligt, & de Vries, 1999; cf. Elliott et al., 1995). As with the previously mentioned findings concerning the predictability of attitude from nonsalient beliefs, these results might reflect the use of one's current attitude as a guide to responding to whatever belief items are presented.

5. For efforts at representing functional ideas in expectancy-value terms, see Belch and Belch (1987) and Lutz (1981).

6. Esses, Haddock, and Zanna (1993) report a related but slightly different finding. With individualized belief lists, attitudes toward various social groups were equally well predicted by the average of the attribute evaluations (that is, $\Sigma e_i /n$, where n is the number of beliefs) and by the average of a multiplicative composite in which each attribute evaluation was multiplied by the individual's judgment of the percentage of the group to which each attribute applies (that is, $\Sigma b_i P_i /n$, where P is the relevant percentage).

7. Notably, the failure of belief strength scores to contribute to attitude prediction with individualized belief lists is apparently not due to a lack of variability in belief strength scores; see Delia et al. (1975, p. 16). For some evidence suggesting a more categorical than purely continuous image of belief strength, see Weinstein (2000, esp. pp. 72-73).

8. This is a curious criterion, because the goal of maximizing the predictability of attitude from $\Sigma b_i e_i$ (that is, maximizing the correlation between attitude and $\Sigma b_i e_i$) is at best an interim research goal. The goal is understandable, because predictive accuracy provides evidence bearing on the adequacy of the summative model. But (as intimated earlier) such predictability does not necessarily show that

the model's implicit depiction of the underlying psychological processes is correct (recall, for example, that attitude can be predicted even from lists of nonsalient beliefs). Some measure of predictability is surely a necessary condition for the model's adequacy, but the more important question concerns the substantive adequacy of the model, that is, whether the model provides an accurate account of the relationship of beliefs and attitudes.

9. The $\Sigma b_i e_i$-attitude correlations that result from optimal scaling are not themselves good evidence for the summative model (after all, the data have been manipulated to maximize the correlations) and are not meant that way. Instead, the result of interest is the particular scaling constants recommended—not necessarily the specific numerical values (as these might bounce around from study to study) but rather what general sort of scale the constants recommend. For example, a researcher might start with a belief strength scale scored in a unipolar fashion, but the optimal scaling constants might be such as to transform it into a bipolar scale. That is, optimal scaling results can give evidence about whether unipolar or bipolar scoring will maximize the correlation.

10. Notice the contrast: With bipolar belief strength scoring, it does not matter what the respondent's evaluation is of an attribute for which the respondent has marked the midpoint of the belief strength scales (because the strength-times-evaluation product for that attribute will be zero). But with unipolar belief strength scoring, the strength-times-evaluation product will vary depending on the respondent's evaluation of that attribute. Hence even if a respondent is completely uncertain about whether the object has the attribute (and so marks the midpoint of the belief strength scales), the respondent would nevertheless be predicted to have a relatively more favorable attitude if the attribute were evaluated positively than if the attribute were evaluated negatively. Scott Moore helped me see this point clearly.

11. Anderson's information integration theory is much broader than a simple averaging model (see, e.g., N. H. Anderson, 1981a, 1991). The general notion is that there are many information integration principles that persons employ, one of which is a weighted-averaging principle (for useful general discussions, see Eagly & Chaiken, 1984, pp. 321-331; 1993, pp. 241-253). My purpose here is simply to introduce the idea that nonsummative images of belief combination are possible; an uncomplicated averaging model provides a convenient example.

12. There are actually some rather difficult methodological challenges here. For instance, the very assessment of beliefs may create apparent consistency between attitudes and belief-based elements (as when existing attitudes guide one's responses to nonsalient belief items). Such consistency may suggest the operation of a belief-based attitude process even where none exists. For example, an attitude might be formed in a wholly non-belief-based way, then used to guide responses to belief items in such a way that the attitude appears to be largely determined by those belief elements (for discussion of such problems, see Fishbein & Middlestadt, 1997, pp. 112-113; Herr, 1995).

13. The idea that attitudes might have multiple underlying components—including both affective and cognitive bases—has a long history in the study of

attitudes (e.g., Rosenberg & Hovland, 1960), but (as pointed out by Eagly et al., 1994) only recently has research explicitly taken up the question of whether the predictability of attitude can be enhanced by including non-belief-based considerations. And although multicomponent views of attitude commonly treat affect and cognition as representing just two of three attitudinal bases (the third being conation or behavioral elements, as when one's past behavior influences one's attitudes through self-perception processes; see, e.g., Bem, 1972), recent research has come to focus on only the affective and cognitive elements (see, e.g., Haddock & Zanna, 1998, p. 328, n. 4; Verplanken, Hofstee, & Janssen, 1998, p. 24, n. 1).

14. There is good reason to think that the wording of belief elicitation questionnaires (that is, questionnaires asking persons to report their beliefs about the attitude object) may influence the types of beliefs that people report. For example, some common procedures may generally elicit predominantly instrumental-utilitarian beliefs rather than symbolic beliefs (see Ennis & Zanna, 1993, 2000). This suggests the importance of carefully designing belief elicitation procedures to minimize the possibility that some important class of underlying beliefs will be missed. For example, it is possible to ask different questions to elicit affective considerations and cognitive ones (e.g., Haddock & Zanna, 1998).

15. A contrast between affective beliefs and cognitive beliefs can be thought of as another way of analyzing belief content. That is, this distinction points to a substantive variation in the beliefs underlying attitudes, namely, whether the beliefs are predominantly affective or cognitive, and in that sense can be seen to be similar to elements of functional analyses of attitude (discussed in Chapter 2). However, functional analyses offer the idea that beliefs characteristically coalesce in substantively different motivationally coherent packages or syndromes, whereas a general distinction between affective and cognitive beliefs need not imply that an individual's beliefs commonly cluster together on the basis of being affective or cognitive (but see Trafimow & Sheeran, 1998).

16. Some general evidence indicates covariation between attitude change and change in the underlying bases of attitude. That is, changes in belief strength and evaluation (or $\Sigma b_i e_i$) have been found to be accompanied by corresponding changes in attitude (e.g., Carlson, 1956; DiVesta & Merwin, 1960; Infante, 1972; Lutz 1975a, 1975b; Peay, 1980). Such evidence is consistent with the model's suggestions that attitude change can be influenced by changes in belief strength and belief evaluation, but other uncertainties (e.g., the apparent artifactual contribution of belief strength scores) make such evidence less helpful than it might be.

17. J. W. Hass, Bagley, and Rogers (1975) examined the effects of messages aimed at influencing the perceived likelihood of an energy crisis and messages aimed at influencing the perceived undesirability of an energy crisis. Both messages were effective in influencing their respective targets (participants who read a message depicting a crisis as very likely perceived an energy crisis to be more likely than did those receiving a low-likelihood message, and those who read a message emphasizing very undesirable consequences of an energy crisis perceived an energy crisis to be more undesirable than those receiving a message suggesting minor negative consequences). Only the evaluation-focused message, however,

was dependably related to intentions to reduce energy consumption: The high-undesirability message produced stronger intentions than did the low-undesirability message. Notably, across message conditions, an energy crisis was perceived to be moderately likely; the perceived likelihood of an energy crisis (on a 10-point scale) was 5.9 in the low-likelihood message condition and 6.9 in the high-likelihood message condition. These findings thus are consistent with the idea that so long as the relevant categorical judgment is in place, smaller variations in belief strength may not be consequential (and thus are not a useful target for persuasive efforts). (See K. D. Levin, Nichols, & Johnson, 2000, pp. 182-183, for other evidence raising doubts about belief strength as a persuasive target.)

18. Adding a new belief might be thought of as influencing belief strength but only in the sense that it involves changing some categorical judgment (e.g., from "I don't know whether the object has attribute X" to "I think the object has attribute X"). That is, it need not be understood as necessarily involving some gradation of subjective probability.

19. Given the previously discussed distinction between affectively oriented and cognitively oriented beliefs, one might naturally hypothesize that attitudes would most effectively be changed by appeals that invoke the same sorts of considerations as underlie the attitude—that affectively oriented appeals would be more persuasive than cognitively oriented appeals for affectively based attitudes, for instance (with the reverse holding for cognitively based attitudes). The evidence on this matter is not clear-cut (see, e.g., Edwards, 1990; Fabrigar & Petty, 1999; Millar & Millar, 1990).

20. As a complexity: Adding a new salient belief may cause some existing belief to become less salient. The number of beliefs that can be salient is surely limited (given that human information-processing capacity is not unbounded). If the current set of beliefs has exhausted that capacity, then the addition of some new salient belief will necessarily mean that some old belief has to drop from the set of salient beliefs. Presumably in such a circumstance, a comparison of the evaluations of the two beliefs in question (the new salient one and the previously salient one) will, ceteris paribus, indicate the consequences for attitude change.

21. The model, however, implicitly emphasizes message content as central to persuasive effects and does not directly speak to the roles played by such factors as communicator credibility, message organization, receiver personality traits, and so forth. From the model's point of view, all such factors only indirectly influence message-induced attitude change—indirectly in the sense that their influence is felt only through whatever effects they might have on belief strength, evaluation, and salience.

Cognitive Dissonance Theory

4

A number of attitude theories have been based on the idea of cognitive consistency—the idea that persons seek to maximize the internal psychological consistency of their cognitions (beliefs, attitudes, etc.). Cognitive inconsistency is taken to be an uncomfortable state, and hence persons are seen as striving to avoid it (or, failing that, seeking to get rid of it). Heider's (1946, 1958) balance theory was perhaps the earliest effort at developing such a consistency theory (for discussion and reviews, see Crockett, 1982; Eagly & Chaiken, 1993, pp. 133-144). Osgood and Tannenbaum's (1955) congruity theory represented another variety of consistency theory (for discussion and reviews, see Eagly & Chaiken, 1993, pp. 460-462; Wyer, 1974, pp. 151-185).

But of all the efforts at articulating the general notion of cognitive consistency, the most influential and productive has been Leon Festinger's (1957) cognitive dissonance theory. This chapter offers first a sketch of the general outlines of dissonance theory and then a discussion of several areas of research application.

▨ GENERAL THEORETICAL SKETCH

Elements and Relations

Cognitive dissonance theory is concerned with the relations among cognitive elements (also called cognitions). An element is any belief, opinion, attitude, or piece of knowledge about anything—about other persons, objects, issues, oneself, and so on.

Three possible relations might hold between any two cognitive elements. They might be *irrelevant* to each other, have nothing to do with each other. My belief that university tuition will increase next year and my favorable opinion of Swiss chocolate are presumably irrelevant to each other. Two cognitive elements might be *consonant* (consistent) with each other; they might hang together, form a package. My belief that golf is a noble game and my liking to play golf are presumably consonant cognitions.

Finally, two cognitive elements might be *dissonant* (inconsistent) with each other. The careful specification of a dissonant relation is this: Two elements are said to be in a dissonant relation if the opposite of one element follows from the other. Thus (to use Festinger's classic example) my cognition that I smoke and my cognition that smoking causes cancer are dissonant with each other; from my knowing that smoking causes cancer, it follows that I should not smoke—but I do.[1]

Dissonance

When two cognitions are in a dissonant relation, the person with those two cognitions is said to have dissonance, to experience dissonance, or to be in a state of dissonance. Dissonance is taken to be an aversive motivational state; persons will want to avoid experiencing dissonance, and if they do encounter dissonance, they will attempt to reduce it.

Dissonance may vary in magnitude: one might have a lot of dissonance, a little, or a moderate amount. As the magnitude of dissonance varies, so will the pressure to reduce it; with increasing dissonance, there will be increasing pressure to reduce it. With small amounts of dissonance, there may be little or no motivational pressure.

Factors Influencing the Magnitude of Dissonance

Expressed most broadly, the magnitude of dissonance experienced will be a function of two factors. One is the relative proportions of consonant and dissonant elements. Thus far, dissonance has been discussed as a simple two-element affair, but usually two *clusters* of elements are involved. A smoker may believe, on the one hand, that smoking reduces anxiety, makes one appear sophisticated, and tastes good and, on the other hand, also believe that smoking causes cancer and is expensive. There are here two clusters of cognitions, one of elements consonant with smoking and one of dissonant elements. Just how much dissonance this smoker experiences will depend on the relative size of these two clusters. As the proportion of consonant elements (to the total number of elements) increases, less and less dissonance will be experienced, but as the cluster of dissonant elements grows (compared with the size of the consonant cluster), the amount of dissonance will increase.

The second factor that influences the degree of dissonance is the importance of the elements or issue. The greater importance this smoker assigns to the expense and cancer-causing aspects of smoking, the greater the dissonance experienced; correspondingly, the greater importance assigned to anxiety reduction and the maintenance of a sophisticated appearance, the less dissonance felt. If the entire question of smoking is devalued in importance, less dissonance will be felt.

Means of Reducing Dissonance

There are two broad means of reducing dissonance, corresponding to the two factors influencing the magnitude of dissonance. The first way to reduce dissonance is by changing the relative proportions of consonant and dissonant elements. This can be accomplished in several ways. One can add new consonant cognitions; the smoker, for instance, might come to believe that smoking prevents colds—a new consonant cognition added to the consonant cluster. One can change or delete existing dissonant cognitions; the smoker might persuade him- or herself that, say, smoking does not really cause cancer.

The other way to reduce dissonance is by altering the importance of the issue or the elements involved. The smoker could reduce dissonance by deciding that the expense of smoking is not that important (devaluing the importance of that dissonant cognition), might come to think that reducing anxiety is an important outcome (increasing the importance of a consonant cognition), or might decide that the whole question of smoking just is not that important. (For illustrations of this means of dissonance reduction, see Simon, Greenberg, & Brehm, 1995.)

▨ SOME RESEARCH APPLICATIONS

Cognitive dissonance theory has produced a great deal of empirical work (for general reviews, see Eagly & Chaiken, 1993, pp. 469-478; Harmon-

Jones, in press). In the study of persuasive communication, four research areas are of interest: decision making, selective exposure to information, induced compliance, and hypocrisy induction.

Decision Making

One application of dissonance theory comes in the area of decision making (or choice making). Dissonance is said to be a postdecisional phenomenon; dissonance arises after a decision or choice has been made. When facing a decision (in the simplest case, a choice between two alternatives), one is said to experience conflict. But after making the choice, one will almost inevitably experience at least some dissonance, and thus one will be faced with the task of dissonance reduction. So the general sequence is (a) conflict, (b) decision, (c) dissonance, and (d) dissonance reduction.

Conflict. Virtually every decision a person makes is likely to involve at least some conflict. Rarely does one face a choice between one perfectly positive option and one absolutely negative alternative. Usually, one chooses between two (or more) alternatives that are neither perfectly good nor perfectly bad—and hence there is at least some conflict, because the choice is not without some trade-offs. Just how much conflict is experienced by a person facing a decision will depend (at least in part) on the initial evaluation of the alternatives. When (to take the simplest two-option case) the two alternatives are initially evaluated similarly, the decision maker will experience considerable conflict; two nearly equally attractive options make for a difficult choice.

This conflict stage is the juncture at which persuasive efforts are most obviously relevant. Ordinarily, persuasive efforts are aimed at regulating (either increasing or decreasing) the amount of conflict experienced by decision makers. If one's friend is inclined toward seeing the new action-adventure film, rather than the new romantic comedy, one can attempt to undermine that preference and so increase the friend's conflict (by saying things aimed at getting the friend to have a less positive evaluation of the action film and by saying things aimed at producing a more positive evaluation of the comedy), or one can attempt to persuade the friend to follow that inclination and so reduce the friend's conflict (by saying things aimed at enhancing the evaluation of the already preferred action film and by saying things aimed at reducing further the evaluation of the comedy).

Of course, a persuader might attempt to regulate a decision maker's conflict by trying to alter the evaluation of only *one* (not both) of the alternatives; I might try to get you to have a more positive attitude toward my preferred position on the persuasive issue, although I do not attack the opposing point of view. But—perhaps not surprisingly—a review of the research evidence (O'Keefe, 1999a) suggests that persuasive communications that only make arguments only supporting the persuader's position (one-sided messages) are generally not as effective as are messages that undertake in addition to refute arguments favoring the opposing side (refutational two-sided messages). This research (also discussed in Chapter 9) suggests that as a rule persuaders are most likely to successfully regulate the conflict experienced by the persuadee if they attempt to influence the evaluation not only of their preferred alternative but of other options as well.

In any case, by regulating the degree of conflict experienced, the persuader can presumably make it more likely that the persuadee will choose the option desired by the persuader. But after the persuadee has made a choice (whether or not the one wanted by the persuader), the persuadee will almost inevitably face at least some dissonance—and, as will be seen, the processes attendant to the occurrence of dissonance have important implications for persuasion.

Decision and Dissonance. At least some dissonance is probably inevitable after a decision because in virtually every decision, at least some aspects of the situation are dissonant with one's choice. Somewhat more specifically, there are likely to be some undesirable aspects to the chosen alternative and some desirable aspects to the unchosen alternatives; each of these is dissonant with the choice made, and hence at least some dissonance is likely to be created.

Consider, for example, a person's choosing where to eat lunch. Al's Fresco Restaurant offers good food and a pleasant atmosphere but is some distance away and usually has slow service. The Bistro Cafe has so-so food, and the atmosphere isn't much, but it's nearby and has quick service. No matter which restaurant is chosen, there will be some things dissonant with the person's choice. In choosing the Bistro, for instance, the diner will face certain undesirable aspects of the chosen alternative (e.g., the poor atmosphere) and certain desirable aspects of the unchosen alternative (e.g., the good food the diner could have had at Al's).

Factors Influencing the Degree of Dissonance. The amount of dissonance that one faces following a choice is taken to depend most centrally on two factors. One is the similarity of the initial evaluations: The closer the initial evaluations of the alternatives, the greater the dissonance. Thus a choice between two nearly equally attractive sweaters is likely to evoke more dissonance than a choice between one fairly attractive and one fairly unattractive sweater. The other factor is the relative importance of the decision, with more important decisions predicted to yield more dissonance. A choice about what to eat for dinner this evening is likely to provoke less dissonance than a choice of what career to pursue.

These two factors represent particularized versions of the general factors influencing the degree of dissonance experienced: the relative proportions of consonant and dissonant elements (because when the two alternatives are evaluated similarly, the proportions of consonant and dissonant elements will presumably approach 50-50) and the importance of the issue or elements (here represented as the importance of the decision).

Dissonance Reduction. One convenient way in which a decision maker can reduce the dissonance felt following a choice is by reevaluating the alternatives. By evaluating the chosen alternative *more* positively than one did before and by evaluating the unchosen alternative *less* positively than before, the amount of dissonance felt can be reduced. Because this process of re-rating the alternatives will result in the alternatives being less similarly evaluated than they were prior to the decision, this effect is sometimes described as the "postdecisional spreading" of alternatives (in the sense that the alternatives are spread further apart along the evaluative dimension than they had been). If (as dissonance theory predicts) people experience dissonance following decisions, then one should find dissonance reduction in the form of this postdecisional spreading of the alternatives, and one should find greater spreading (i.e., greater dissonance reduction) in circumstances in which dissonance is presumably greater.

In simplified form, the typical experimental arrangement in dissonance-based studies of choice making is one in which respondents initially give evaluations of several objects or alternatives and are then faced with making a choice between two of these. After making the choice, respondents are then asked to reevaluate the alternatives, with these rankings inspected for evidence of dissonance reduction through postdecisional spreading of alternatives.

In general, the research evidence appears to indicate that one does often find the predicted changes in evaluations following decisions (e.g., Brehm, 1956; G. L. White & Gerard, 1981); the evidence is not so strong that the magnitude of dissonance reduction is greater when the conditions for heightened dissonance are present (as when the two alternatives are initially rated closely, or the decision is important), because conflicting findings have been reported, especially for the effects of decisional importance (for discussion, see Converse & Cooper, 1979).

The general finding of postdecisional spreading in the evaluations of the alternatives suggests that decision maker satisfaction will (in the words of Wicklund & Brehm, 1976) "take care of itself" (p. 289). Because persons are likely to more positively value that which they have freely chosen, then if one can induce persons to choose a given alternative, they will be likely to more positively value that alternative just because they have chosen it. For example, if persons are induced to buy a product, they will likely have a more positive attitude toward the product just as a consequence of having chosen to buy it. Of course, this does not mean that every purchaser is guaranteed to end up being a satisfied customer; it still may happen that (say) a new-car buyer decides that the car purchased is a lemon and returns it to the dealer. Nevertheless, there are forces at work that incline persons to be happier with whatever they have chosen, just because they have chosen it.

Persuaders might infer from this that once a persuadee has been induced to decide the way the persuader wants, then the persuader's job is done; after all, having made the choice, the persuadee is likely to become more satisfied with it through the ordinary processes of dissonance reduction. This inference is unsound, however; persuaders who reason in this fashion may find their persuasive efforts failing in the end, in part because of the occurrence of regret.

Regret. Although not anticipated in Festinger's original (1957) treatment of decision making, the phenomenon of regret has emerged as an important aspect of postdecisional cognitive processes (see Festinger, 1964). What appears to happen is that after the decision has been made but before the dissonance has been reduced (through postdecisional spreading of alternatives), the alternatives are temporarily evaluated *more similarly* (that is, rated closer together) than they were initially. (Some readers will recognize "buyer's remorse" in these changes.) Then, following this regret phase (during which dissonance presumably increases), the person moves on to the matter of dissonance reduction, with the evaluations of the alternatives spreading farther apart (see Festinger & Walster, 1964; Walster, 1964).

One plausible account of this regret phenomenon is that having made the choice, the decision maker now faces the task of dissonance reduction. Naturally, the decision maker's attention focuses on those cognitions that are dissonant with his or her choice—on undesirable aspects of the chosen option and on desirable aspects of the unchosen option, perhaps in the hope of eventually being able to minimize each. As the decision maker focuses on undesirable aspects of the chosen alternative, that alternative may seem (at least temporarily) less attractive than it had before; focusing on desirable aspects of the unchosen option may make that option seem (at least temporarily) more attractive than it had before. With the chosen alternative becoming rated less favorably, and the unchosen alternative becoming rated more favorably, the two alternatives naturally become evaluated more similarly than they had been.

During this regret phase, it is even possible that the initial evaluations become reversed, so that the initially unchosen alternative becomes rated more favorably than the chosen option. In such a circumstance, the decision maker may back out of the original choice. This outcome becomes more likely when the two alternatives are initially evaluated rather similarly because in such a circumstance, comparatively small swings in absolute evaluations can make for reversals in the relative evaluations of the alternatives.

There is a moral here for persuaders concerning the importance of follow-up persuasive efforts. It can be too easy for a persuader to assume that the job is done when the persuadee has been induced to choose in the way the persuader wants, but the possibility of regret, and particularly the possibility that the decision maker's mind may change, should make the persuader realize that simply inducing the initial decision may not be enough.

A fitting example is provided by an investigation of automobile buying. In purchases of automobiles from a dealer, ordinarily some time elapses between the buyer's agreeing to buy the car and the actual delivery of the car to the buyer. It sometimes happens that during this interval, the would-be purchaser changes his or her mind and backs out of the decision to buy the car. (There are likely any number of reasons why this happens, but it should be easy enough to imagine that at least some of the time something such as regret is at work.) In Donnelly and Ivancevich's (1970) investigation, during the interval between decision and delivery, some automobile purchasers received two follow-up telephone calls from the seller; the calls emphasized the desirable aspects of the automobile that had been chosen, reassured the purchaser of the wisdom of the decision, and (one might say) encouraged the purchaser to move past the regret phase and on to the stage of dissonance reduction. Other purchasers received no such call. Significantly fewer of the purchasers receiving the follow-up calls backed out of their decisions than did those not receiving the call (the back-out rate was cut in half), underlining the potential importance of follow-up persuasive efforts.

Selective Exposure to Information

A second area of dissonance theory research that is relevant to persuasion concerns persons' propensities to expose themselves selectively to information. Below, the dissonance-theoretic analysis of information exposure is presented, followed by a review and discussion of the relevant research.

The Dissonance Theory Analysis. If dissonance is an aversive motivational state, then naturally persons will want to do what they can to avoid dissonance-arousing situations and will prefer instead to be in circumstances that do not arouse dissonance (or that even increase the consonance of their cognitions). This general idea finds specific expression in the form of dissonance theory's selective exposure hypothesis. Broadly put, this hypothesis has it that persons will prefer to be exposed to information that is supportive of (consonant with) their current beliefs rather than to nonsupportive information (which presumably could arouse dissonance).

At one point in the study of the effects of mass communication, this selective exposure hypothesis was especially attractive to researchers. Early in the study of mass communication's effects, it was commonly presumed that the mass media had significant and far-reaching impacts on the audience's attitudes and beliefs. But it proved rather difficult to find convincing evidence of the supposedly powerful effects of mass communication. As a result, the focal question for researchers became not, "Why and how does mass communication have these powerful effects?" but instead, "Why *doesn't* mass communication have the tremendously powerful and obvious effects we expected it to have?" (for discussion of these developments, see Blumler & Gurevitch, 1982; DeFleur & Ball-Rokeach, 1982).[2]

Against this backdrop, the attractiveness of the selective exposure hypothesis should be plain. If persons generally seek out only media sources that confirm or reinforce their prior beliefs (and, correlatively, avoid exposure to nonsupportive or inconsistent information), then the powerful effects of the mass media would naturally be blunted: Media messages would only be preaching to the converted (at least on topics on which persons already had well-established attitudes).

More generally, of course, the selective exposure hypothesis suggests that persuaders (through the mass media or otherwise) may need to be concerned about getting receivers to attend to their messages. If, as dissonance theory suggests, there is a predisposition to avoid nonsupportive information, then persuaders may face the task of somehow overcoming that obstacle so that their communications can have a chance to persuade.

The Research Evidence. In the typical experimental research paradigm for the investigation of selective exposure, respondents' attitudes on a given issue are assessed. Then respondents are given the choice of seeing (reading, hearing) one of several communications on the issue. These communications are described in a way that makes clear what position on the issue is advocated by each, and both supportive and nonsupportive messages are included. The respondent is then asked to select one of the messages. Support for the selective exposure hypothesis consists of respondents' preferring to see supportive rather than nonsupportive communications.

For some time, it proved difficult to detect any consistent selective exposure principle at work in persons' informational preferences. Indeed, several early reviews concluded that little or no evidence supported the selective exposure hypothesis (Freedman & Sears, 1965a; Sears & Freedman, 1967); there did not seem to be any general preference for supportive information such as had been expected from dissonance theory. Other observers, however, argued that much of the experimental work failed to control for possible confounding factors and so never offered a realistic chance for the detection of a preference for supportive information (for discussions of some problems with early research on selective exposure, see Rhine, 1967; Wicklund & Brehm, 1976).

Subsequent research that attempted to avoid the weaknesses of earlier studies was able to detect a preference for supportive information (e.g., Cotton & Hieser, 1980; Olson & Zanna, 1979). Thus the accumulated research on selective exposure seems to suggest that there is some preference for supportive information—but this research has also pointed up other (often competing) influences on information exposure (for useful reviews, see Cotton, 1985; Frey, 1986).[3]

Other Influences on Exposure. One such additional influence on information exposure appears to be the perceived utility of the information, with persons preferring information with greater perceived utility. Consider, for example, an investigation in which undergraduates initially chose to take either a multiple-choice exam or an essay exam. The students were then asked for their preferences among reading several articles, some supporting the decision and some obviously nonsupportive. For instance, for a student who chose the multiple-choice exam, the nonsupportive articles were described as arguing that students who prefer multiple-choice tests would actually be likely to do better on essay exams. Contrary to the selective exposure hypothesis—but not surprisingly—most of the students preferred articles advocating a change from the type of exam they had chosen (Rosen, 1961). Obviously, in this study, the nonsupportive communication offered information that might be of substantial usefulness to the students, and the perceived utility of the information could well have outweighed any preference for supportive information.

Surely another influence on information exposure is sheer curiosity, as illustrated in a study in which participants listened to a tape recording of an interview in which the interviewee came off as either exceptionally well suited or exceptionally poorly suited to the position being sought (Freedman, 1965). Participants were asked to indicate their own judgment of the applicant's suitability for the position; as one might expect, these judgments were heavily influenced by which of the two versions of the interview was heard. Participants were then given the opportunity of reading either a supportive or a nonsupportive communication. For instance, a participant who heard the poorly suited applicant's interview and who realized the applicant was poorly suited for the position could read either a communication confirming that judgment or a communication asserting that the applicant was well qualified. Participants did not exhibit a general preference for supportive information and overwhelmingly preferred to see the contradictory evaluation. One plausible explanation for this result is that often the participants were simply curious about the basis for the opposing judgment ("How could *anybody* think that guy was qualified? I want to see that evaluation!").

Fairness norms may also play a role in information exposure. In certain social settings, there is an emphasis on obtaining the greatest amount of information possible, on being fair to all sides, on being open-minded until all the evidence is in. One such setting is the trial. In Sears's (1965) study, participants received brief synopses of a murder case and then rendered a judgment about the guilt of the defendant. They were subsequently offered a chance of seeing either confirming or disconfirming information (e.g., for a mock juror who thought the defendant was guilty, disconfirming information consisted of information indicating that the defendant was innocent). Participants showed a general preference for nonsupportive information, perhaps because the trial setting was one that made salient the norms of fairness and openness to evidence.

Summary. All told, there may be some (slight) preference for supportive information, as expected by dissonance theory. This preference is only one of many (often competing) influences on information exposure, however, and hence this preference may be overridden by other considerations. This general conclusion—based largely on experimental laboratory investigations—is consistent with the results of field research concerning information exposure. As a rule, investigations of selectivity in exposure to mass communications have turned up little evidence of strong selective exposure effects (e.g., Bertrand, 1979; Chaffee & Miyo, 1983; Swanson, 1976). Hence even if there is some general preference for supportive over nonsupportive information, the existence of other competing preferences may mean that in practice the effects of a preference for supportive material will often be washed out. Even so, persuaders who hope to encourage attention to their messages will want to be attentive to the factors influencing information exposure, as these may suggest avenues by which such attention can be sought (see, e.g., Flay, McFall, Burton, Cook, & Warnecke, 1993).

Induced Compliance

Perhaps the greatest amount of dissonance-theory-inspired research concerns what is commonly called "induced compliance." Induced compliance is said to occur when an individual is induced to act in a way discrepant from his or her beliefs and attitudes.

One special case of induced compliance is counterattitudinal advocacy, which is said to occur when persons are led to advocate some viewpoint opposed to their position. Most of the research on induced compliance concerns counterattitudinal advocacy because that circumstance has proved a convenient focus for study. (For a detailed discussion of induced-compliance research, see Eagly & Chaiken, 1993, pp. 505-521.)

Incentive and Dissonance in Induced-Compliance Situations. Obviously, induced-compliance situations have the potential to arouse dissonance; after all, a person is acting in a way discrepant from his or her beliefs. Dissonance theory suggests that the amount of dissonance experienced in an induced-compliance situation will depend centrally on the amount of incentive offered to the person to engage in the discrepant action. Any incentive offered for performing the counterattitudinal action (for example, some promised reward or threatened punishment) is consistent with engaging in the action—that is, is consonant with engaging in the action. Thus someone who performs a counterattitudinal action with large incentives for doing so will experience relatively little dissonance.

To use Festinger's (1957) example: Suppose you are offered a million dollars to publicly state that you like reading comic books (assume, for the purpose of the example, that you find this offer believable and that you do not like reading comic books). Presumably, you would accept the money and engage in the counterattitudinal advocacy. You might experience some small amount of dissonance (from saying one thing and believing another)—but the million dollars is an important element that is consonant with your having performed the action, and hence overall there is little dissonance experienced.

But if the incentive had been smaller (less money offered), then the amount of dissonance experienced would have been greater. The greatest possible dissonance would occur if the incentive were only just enough to induce compliance (if the incentive were the minimum needed to get you to comply). Suppose (to continue the example) that you would not have agreed to engage in the counterattitudinal advocacy for anything less than $100. In that case, an offer of exactly $100—the minimum needed to induce compliance—would have produced the maximum possible dissonance. Any incentive larger than that minimum would only have reduced the amount of dissonance experienced.

When substantial dissonance is created through induced compliance, pressure is created to reduce that dissonance. One easy route to dissonance reduction is to bring one's private beliefs into line with one's behavior. For example, if you declared that you liked reading comic books when offered only $100 (your minimum price) for doing so, you would experience considerable dissonance and could easily reduce it by deciding that you think reading comic books isn't quite as bad as you might have thought.

What happens if the incentive offered is insufficient to induce compliance? That is, what are the consequences if a person is offered some incentive for engaging in a counterattitudinal action, and the person does not comply? To continue the example, suppose that you had been offered only $10 to say that you like to read comic books. You would decline the offer, thereby losing the possibility of getting the $10—and hence you would experience some dissonance over that ("I could have had that $10"). But you would not experience much dissonance, and certainly not as much as if you had turned down an offer of $90. That is, you would experience more dissonance if you declined a $90 offer than if you declined a $10 offer. Faced with the dissonance of having turned down $90, one natural avenue to dissonance reduction is to strengthen one's initial negative attitude ("I was right to turn down that $90, because reading comic books really is pretty bad").

So the relationship between the amount of incentive offered and the amount of dissonance experienced is depicted (by dissonance theory) as something like an inverted V. With increasing incentive, there is increasing dissonance—up to the point at which compliance occurs (up to the point at which the incentive is sufficiently large to induce compliance). But beyond that point, increasing incentive produces decreasing dissonance, such that with very large incentives, there is little or no dissonance experienced from engaging in the counterattitudinal action. Thus so long as the amount of incentive is sufficient to induce compliance, additional incentive will make it less likely that the person will come to have more favorable attitudes toward the position being advocated.

In a classic experiment, Festinger and Carlsmith (1959) obtained striking evidence for this analysis. In this study, participants performed an exceedingly dull and tedious task. At the conclusion of the task, they were asked to tell a student who was waiting to participate in the experiment (the student was a confederate of the experimenter) that the task was enjoyable and interesting. As incentive for performing this counterattitudinal behavior, participants were offered money; half were offered $1 (low incentive), and half were offered $20 (high incentive). After engaging in the counterattitudinal advocacy, participants' attitudes toward the task were assessed.

Festinger and Carlsmith found, consistent with dissonance theory's predictions, that those receiving $1 came to think that the task was significantly more enjoyable than did those who complied for $20. Those who complied under the influence of a large incentive ($20) presumably experienced less dissonance from engaging in the counterattitudinal act (because they had the $20 that was consonant with performing the act)—and so had little need for attitude change. By contrast, participants receiving the small incentive ($1) presumably experienced more dissonance and hence had more motivation to change their attitudes to reduce dissonance; they reduced their dissonance by coming to have a more favorable attitude toward the dull task.

Subsequent investigations provided additional confirming evidence (for a collection of studies on induced compliance, see Elms, 1969). For example, E. Aronson and Carlsmith (1963) found that children prohibited from playing with an attractive toy by a mild threat (of punishment for disobedience) subsequently found the toy less attractive than did children prohibited by a severe threat. That is, those who engaged in the counterattitudinal action of avoiding the toy when given only mild incentive to do so apparently experienced greater dissonance (than did those who avoided the toy when given strong incentives to do so) and hence displayed greater underlying attitude change. There have been relatively fewer studies of circumstances in which the incentives offered are insufficient to induce compliance, but this evidence is also generally consistent with dissonance theory predictions. For instance, Darley and Cooper (1972) found that persons who were offered insufficient incentives (to engage in counterattitudinal advocacy) were inclined to strengthen their initial attitudes, and—as expected from dissonance theory—greater strengthening occurred with larger incentives.

The "Low, Low Price Offer." An example of induced-compliance processes is provided by the familiar marketing ploy of the "low, low price offer." This offer is sometimes cast as a straightforward lower price ("fifty cents off"), sometimes as "two for the price of one" (or "three for the price of two," etc.), but in any case, the central idea is that a lower price is offered to the consumer. Presumably, the lower price will make purchase more likely.

Now imagine a situation in which a particular consumer is faced with competing brands of (say) soap. This consumer does not have an especially positive impression of Brand A—it's not the consumer's usual brand—but Brand A is running a really good low-price special ("three bars for the price of one"). From a dissonance theory view, this lower price represents an increased incentive for the consumer to purchase Brand A (increased incentive to engage in the counterattitudinal behavior of buying Brand A). As the deal gets better and better—that is, as the price gets lower and lower— there is more and more incentive to comply (incentive to purchase). For example, there is more incentive to comply when the deal is "three for the price of one" than when the deal is "two for the price of one."

The key insight offered by dissonance theory here is this: The greater the incentive to comply, the less dissonance created by the purchase—and hence less chance for favorable attitude change toward the brand. This consumer might buy Brand A this time (because the price is so low), but the consumer's underlying unfavorable attitude toward Brand A is not likely to change—precisely because the incentive to comply was so great. That is, the "low, low price offer" might boost sales for a while, but it can also undermine the development of more positive attitudes toward the brand.

An illustration of these processes was offered in a set of five field experiments concerning the effects of low introductory selling prices. House brands of common household products (e.g., aluminum foil, toothpaste, and light bulbs) were introduced in various stores in a chain of discount houses. In some of the stores, the brands were introduced at the regular price, whereas at other stores, the brands were introduced with a low introductory price offer for a short period (before the price increased to the regular price). As one might expect, when the low-price offer was in effect, sales were higher at the stores offering the lower prices. But when prices returned to normal, the subsequent sales were greater at the stores that had the initial higher prices (Doob, Carlsmith, Freedman, Landauer, & Tom, 1969). That is, introducing these products at low introductory prices proved to be harmful to long-run sales, presumably because there was relatively little brand loyalty established by the low introductory selling price. Thus the greater incentive created by the lower price apparently prevented the development of sufficiently positive attitudes toward the brand.

One should not conclude from this that the low-price offer is a foolish marketing stratagem that should never be used. The point is that this marketing technique can set in motion forces opposed to the development of positive attitudes toward the brand and that these forces are greater as the incentive becomes greater (as the deal gets better). But some low-price offers are better than others (from the view of creating favorable attitude change): A low-price offer that is only just barely good enough to induce purchase—an offer that provides just enough incentive to induce compliance—will create the maximum possible dissonance (and so, a marketer might hope, maximum favorable attitude change toward the product). Low-price offers may also be useful as strategies for introducing new brands; the marketer's plan is that the low price would induce initial purchase and that this exposure to the brand's intrinsic positive characteristics will create a positive attitude toward the brand (thereby enhancing long-term sales). Of course, if the brand does not have sufficiently great intrinsic appeal (as was likely with the house brands studied by Doob et al., 1969), then using low introductory prices to induce trial will not successfully create underlying positive attitudes toward the brand. (For indications of the complexity of the effects of price promotion on attitudes, see S. Davis, Inman, & McAlister, 1992; Raghubir & Corfman, 1999.)

Limiting Conditions. Researchers have not always obtained the induced-compliance effects predicted by dissonance theory. Indeed, with the accumulation of more and more such instances (instances of failure to reproduce the dissonance effects), investigators began to search for the factors that determine whether one would obtain the expected results. A number of hypotheses were proposed and discarded (for examples and discussion, see Carlsmith, Collins, & Helmreich, 1966; Elms, 1969; C. A. Kiesler et al., 1969, pp. 213-214; Rosenberg, 1965).

But two important limiting conditions have been successfully identified. First, in general, one finds the predicted dissonance effects only when the participants feel that they had a choice about whether to comply (e.g., about whether to perform the advocacy). That is, freedom of choice seems to be a necessary condition for the appearance of dissonance effects in induced-compliance situations (the classic work on this subject is Linder, Cooper, & Jones, 1967). Thus one can expect that inducing counterattitudinal action with minimal incentive will produce substantial dissonance (and corresponding favorable attitude change) only when the person freely chooses to engage in the counterattitudinal behavior.[4]

Second, the predicted dissonance effects are obtained only when there is no obvious alternative cause to which the feelings of dissonance can be attributed. The general idea is that feelings of dissonance, like other feelings, are subject to attributional processes. That is, because feelings do not come already labeled as to their natures or causes, persons are faced with the task of (nonconsciously) arriving at an explanation of their feelings. Hence if persons can attribute their dissonance feelings to some cause other than their counterattitudinal behavior, the usual dissonance effects will not be observed.

A classic illustration of such attributional processes is provided by Zanna and Cooper's (1974) investigation in which participants took a pill (actually a placebo) before engaging in (freely chosen) counterattitudinal advocacy. Participants who were told that the pill would have no effect on them displayed the expected dissonance effects. By contrast, those told that the pill might make them feel tense took the opportunity to blame their uncomfortable feelings on the pill rather than on the counterattitudinal advocacy and hence did not display the usual attitude change. (For related work, see J. Cooper, 1998, Study 1; Fazio, Zanna, & Cooper, 1977; Fried & Aronson, 1995; Zanna & Cooper, 1976.)[5]

Summary. Dissonance theory's expectations about the effects of incentive for counterattitudinal action on attitude change can, in the end, be said to have been confirmed in broad outline—although not without the discovery of unanticipated limiting conditions. When a person freely chooses to engage in counterattitudinal action (without an apparent alternative account of the resulting feelings), increasing incentive for such action leads to lessened pressure for making one's beliefs and attitudes consistent with the counterattitudinal act. Hence a persuader seeking long-term behavioral change (by means of underlying attitude change) ought not to create intense pressure to engage in the counterattitudinal behavior; rather, the persuader should seek to offer only just barely enough incentive to induce compliance and let dissonance reduction processes encourage subsequent attitude change.

So consider, for example, those marketing contests in which consumers are invited to submit a slogan for the product or to write an essay explaining why they like the product, with prizes (cash or goods) to be received by those whose entries are randomly selected. When the slogan or essay writing is counterattitudinal ("I don't really like the product, I just want to try to win the prize"), one might expect that larger prizes would minimize the development of more favorable attitudes toward the advocated product (compared with smaller prizes, that is, compared with a smaller incentive).

Or consider some social influence tasks commonly faced by parents. In hoping to encourage the young child not to play with the expensive electronic equipment, parents ought to provide only just enough punishment to induce compliance; excessive punishment might produce short-term obedience but not underlying change (e.g., when the parents are present, the child will not play with the equipment—but the child will still *want* to, and when the back is turned . . .). Or in trying to encourage children to do their homework, parents ought to think carefully about offering extremely large rewards for compliance; such rewards can undermine the development of positive attitudes toward homework (whereas a minimal reward can induce immediate compliance while also promoting the development of positive attitudes). All these examples illustrate the potential application of the general principle that smaller incentives for freely chosen counterattitudinal behavior are more likely (than larger incentives) to produce underlying favorable attitudes toward that behavior.

Hypocrisy Induction

Hypocrisy as a Means of Influencing Behavior. Sometimes a persuader's task is not so much to encourage people to have the desired attitudes as it is to encourage people to act on existing attitudes. For example, people commonly express positive attitudes toward recycling, natural resource conservation, condom use, and so forth—yet often fail to act accordingly.

Such inconsistencies might be exploited by persuaders, however, as suggested by dissonance research on hypocrisy induction. The basic idea is that calling attention to the inconsistency of a person's attitudes and actions—that is, the person's hypocrisy—can arouse dissonance, which then is reduced through behavioral change (altering the behavior to make it consistent with the existing attitude).[6]

For example, Stone et al. (1994) varied whether participants engaged in public proattitudinal advocacy concerning the importance of safe sex and whether participants were (by listing circumstances surrounding their past failures to use condoms) made mindful of their past failures to engage in safe sex practices. The combination of advocacy and mindfulness (the hypocrisy condition) was expected to induce greater dissonance—and so greater subsequent behavioral consistency—than either treatment alone (or than a no-advocacy-and-no-reminder condition). Consistent with this expectation, hypocrisy-condition participants (compared with those in other conditions) were more likely to buy condoms (and bought more condoms on average) at the end of the experiment. That is, faced with the reality of their inconsistent actions, these persons reduced their dissonance by bringing their behaviors in line with their safe sex attitudes. (For other examples and relevant research, see E. Aronson, Fried, & Stone, 1991; Dickerson, Thibodeau, Aronson, & Miller, 1992; Fried & Aronson, 1995; Linz, Fuson, & Donnerstein, 1990; Stone, Wiegand, Cooper, & Aronson, 1997.)

Hypocrisy Induction Mechanisms. It is not yet clear how hypocrisy is induced. That is, the specific interventions or treatments that might be used have not yet been carefully distinguished or explored. Most hypocrisy induction studies to date have employed structured proattitudinal advocacy exercises of the sort used by Stone et al. (1994), but presumably the underlying mechanism involves the salience of attitude-behavior inconsistency.

The general idea is that existing inconsistencies between beliefs and behavior can, if made sufficiently salient, prompt consistency seeking (e.g., in the form of changing actions to accord with attitudes). Having persons engage in proattitudinal advocacy is one possible way, but surely not the only possible means, of enhancing the salience of an existing inconsistency. For instance, in the right circumstances, a simple reminder of one's attitudinal commitments might be sufficient.

Consider, for example, Aitken, McMahon, Wearing, and Finlayson's (1994) research concerning water conservation. Households given feedback about their water consumption, combined with a reminder of their previously expressed belief in their responsibility to conserve water, significantly reduced their consumption. Feedback alone was useful in reducing consumption but not as effective as the combination of feedback and the (presumably hypocrisy-inducing) reminder. (For a similar intervention, with similar results, concerning electricity conservation, see Kantola, Syme, & Campbell, 1984.)

To date, it appears that successful hypocrisy induction treatments involve a combination of two key elements: (a) ensuring the salience of the relevant attitude (e.g., through proattitudinal advocacy or through being explicitly reminded of one's commitment to the attitude) and (b) ensuring the salience of past failures to act in ways consistent with that attitude (e.g., by having the person recall such failures or by giving feedback indicating such failures). When only one of these elements is present, hypocrisy effects are weaker or nonexistent (Aitken et al., 1994; E. Aronson et al., 1991; Dickerson et al., 1992; Kantola et al., 1984; Stone et al., 1994; Stone et al., 1997, Experiment 1; see also S. J. Sherman & Gorkin, 1980). It will plainly be useful to have some clarification of alternative means of implementing these two elements, identification of circumstances in which one or another form of implementation is more powerful, and so forth.

Backfire Effects. It might appear straightforward enough to use hypocrisy as a means of inducing behavioral change, but it is important to consider that faced with evidence of inconsistency between attitudes and actions, persons can achieve consistency in two (not mutually exclusive) ways. They might change their behavior to align it with their attitudes, or they might change their attitudes to align them with their behavior. In the hypocrisy induction studies discussed thus far, the inconsistency was generally resolved by changing behaviors to be consistent with the attitude. But the other effect has also been observed.

Fried (1998) had participants engage in public advocacy about the importance of recycling, under one of three conditions varying the salience of past inconsistent behavior. Some participants listed their past recycling failures anonymously (as in previous hypocrisy induction manipulations), some listed their past failures in ways that permitted them to be personally identified, and some did not list past failures (the no-salience condition). Persons in the anonymous-salience condition exhibited the usual behavioral effects of hypocrisy (e.g., they pledged larger amounts of money to a recycling fund than did persons in the no-salience condition), but persons in the identifiable-salience condition did not. These persons, instead of changing behaviors to become consistent with their prorecycling attitudes, changed their attitudes to become consistent with their recycling failures— specifically, they displayed a reduced belief in the importance of recycling.

It is not yet clear exactly how to explain such reversal of effects, how general such outcomes are, the conditions under which they are likely to occur (perhaps, say, with relatively unimportant attitudes), and so forth. But persuaders will certainly want to take note of the potential dangers of hypocrisy induction as an influence mechanism. As a means of changing a person's behavior, pointing out that the person's conduct is inconsistent with the person's professed beliefs might lead to the desired behavioral change—or might lead to belief revision (and so backfire on the persuader).

▧ REVISIONS OF, AND ALTERNATIVES TO, DISSONANCE THEORY

A number of revisions to dissonance theory have been suggested, and several competing explanations have also been proposed. These various alternative possibilities (whether competitors to, or reframings of, dissonance theory) are numerous and individually complex (for example, some are focused specifically on explaining induced-compliance effects, whereas others offer broader reinterpretations of dissonance work), and the relevant research evidence is both extensive and contested, to the point that the details of the alternatives and the arguments cannot be reproduced here (for references and careful discussion, see Eagly & Chaiken, 1993, pp. 505-552). But by way of illustration, it may be useful to discuss one facet that is common to a number of the alternatives, namely, an emphasis on the centrality of the concept of self to dissonance phenomena.

For example, E. Aronson (1968, 1992, 1999) has suggested that dissonance arises most plainly from inconsistencies that specifically involve the self. That is, "dissonance is greatest and clearest when it involves not just any two cognitions but, rather, a cognition about the self and a piece of our behavior that violates that self-concept" (E. Aronson, 1992, p. 305). For example, induced-compliance situations involve actions inconsistent with one's self-concept and hence set in motion processes designed to restore consistency. In general, "any action that violates an important self-view has the potential to cause feelings of dissonance" (Stone et al., 1994, p. 126). This self-concept model of dissonance is better seen as a revision (or respecification) of Festinger's original formulation than as an alternative to dissonance theory.

Another view that also emphasizes the centrality of self but that is offered more as a competitor to dissonance theory is Steele's self-affirmation theory (Steele, 1988; Steele & Liu, 1983; for a review, see J. Aronson, Cohen, & Nail, 1999). On this view, the key motivating force behind dissonance phenomena is actually a desire for self-integrity. That is, the various attitudinal and behavioral changes attendant to dissonance are argued to reflect the desire to maintain an image of the self as "adaptively and morally adequate, that is, as competent, good, coherent, unitary, stable, capable of free choice, capable of controlling important outcomes, and so on." Processes of self-affirmation are "activated by information that threatens the perceived adequacy or integrity of the self," with the aim of such processes being the restoration of the perception of self-integrity (Steele, 1988, p. 262).

The key suggestion is that dissonance phenomena can be explained without assuming that there is any "motivation for consistency" of the sort so central to dissonance theory. So, for example, self-affirmation theory points to cases in which persons appeared unmoved by induced-compliance inconsistencies so long as they were able to affirm their self-integrity in other ways (Steele, 1988). Thus whereas E. Aronson's (1968) self-concept elaboration of dissonance theory can be seen to abandon any general consistency motive (for cognitions generally) in favor of emphasizing consistency among specifically self-relevant cognitions, self-affirmation theory "simply goes the next revisionary step" (Steele & Spencer, 1992, p. 345) by abandoning consistency motivation entirely in favor of exclusively self-integrity motives.

It remains to be seen how successful these and other alternatives will prove to be.[7] (For examples and discussion of various approaches, see Beauvois & Joule, 1996, 1999; J. Cooper, 1999; J. Cooper & Fazio, 1984; Leippe & Eisenstadt, 1999; Stone, 1999.) The general question is the degree to which a given framework can successfully encompass the variety of findings currently housed within dissonance theory, while also pointing to new phenomena recommending distinctive explanation. For example, one contested question has been whether the findings generated by self-affirmation theory are actually inconsistent with dissonance theory (see E. Aronson, 1992; J. Cooper, 1999; Steele & Spencer, 1992). But no matter the particulars of the resolution of such issues, it is plain that dissonance-related phenomena continue to provide rich sources of theoretical and empirical development. For students of persuasion, these various alternatives bear watching because of the possibility that these new frameworks will shed additional light on processes of social influence.

▨ CONCLUSION

Dissonance theory does not offer a systematic theory of persuasion (and was not intended to). But dissonance theory has served as a fruitful source of ideas bearing on social influence processes and has stimulated substantial relevant research. To be sure, the theory's expectations have sometimes received only weak confirmation (as in studies of selective exposure), and unanticipated findings have emerged (as in the discovery of limiting conditions on induced-compliance effects). Nevertheless, cognitive dissonance theory has yielded a number of useful and interesting findings bearing on processes of persuasion.

▨ NOTES

1. This "follows from" is, obviously, a matter of psychological implication, not logical implication. What matters is whether I *think* that one belief follows from another—not whether it logically does so follow.

2. This paragraph reproduces the conventional wisdom concerning the history of mass communication effects research. For discussion and correctives, see Bineham (1988), Chaffee and Hochheimer (1985), Delia (1987), Wartella (1996), and Wartella and Reeves (1985).

3. As Eagly and Chaiken (1993, pp. 591-592) have pointed out, assessments of information preference have involved both measures of selective exposure per se (choosing to be exposed to one or another message) and measures of selective attention (e.g., time spent engaged in exposure to one or another message), suggesting that it might prove useful to distinguish such assessments. Research designs in this area have also often not distinguished selective avoidance (avoidance of nonsupportive information) and selective approach (seeking out supportive information); both can contribute to the appearance of selective exposure effects. Although there is not yet much evidence on the matter, it appears that selective avoidance effects are weaker than selective approach effects (Cotton, 1985, p. 26; Frey, 1986, pp. 69-70).

4. This description adopts the conventional language that characterizes choice as a necessary condition for the induced-compliance effects predicted by dissonance theory. But any claims about necessary conditions for dissonance-predicted effects have to be offered rather tentatively, if only because the research evidence (concerning not only choice but other putatively necessary conditions as well) has commonly not been analyzed in ways entirely conducive to supporting such claims. There is a difference between saying (for example), "Choice is necessary for

the appearance of dissonance-predicted effects" and "Dissonance-predicted effects are larger under conditions of choice than under conditions without choice." The former depicts choice as a necessary condition, the latter as a moderating factor; the former thus predicts null (zero) effects in no-choice conditions, the latter only that the size of the effect will be smaller in no-choice conditions. Any hypothesis of zero effect, however, is almost certainly literally false; a more appropriate hypothesis would presumably be that the effects would be trivially small (note: small in size, not "statistically nonsignificant"). There has not been discussion of what "trivially small" might be in this context, however. The evidence that is usually advanced to support necessary-condition claims about choice commonly takes the form of (a) a finding that a dissonance-predicted effect is statistically significantly different from zero under choice conditions but not under no-choice conditions or (b) a finding that a dissonance-predicted effect is significantly larger under choice than under no-choice conditions. But neither of these is good evidence for the necessary-condition claim (and only the latter is good evidence for a moderating-factor claim). The evidentiary situation is more complicated, but no more satisfactory, in the case of the claim that a particular *combination* of conditions is necessary. In short, although it has become customary to characterize research in this area as having identified various necessary conditions for the appearance of dissonance-predicted effects, these characterizations should be seen as deserving further attention (especially focused on matters of effect size and statistical power).

5. Those familiar with the standard social-psychological treatment of induced-compliance research will have noticed that this characterization of the limiting conditions diverges somewhat from the usual rendition. The evidence is rather good that the appearance of dissonance-predicted effects in counterattitudinal advocacy situations requires—or at least is maximized by—a combination of free choice (about performing the advocacy), commitment to the advocacy (e.g., by performing it publicly), and the expectation of some foreseeable, irrevocable aversive event resulting from the advocacy (for a review, see Eagly & Chaiken, 1993, pp. 511-521). But counterattitudinal advocacy is only a special case of induced compliance (albeit the case that has received the most research attention), and it is not clear that this more extensive list of limiting conditions applies to induced compliance generally (as opposed to counterattitudinal advocacy specifically). Indeed, it is arguable that there are cases of induced compliance that (a) are not cases of counterattitudinal advocacy, (b) do yield results interpretable using dissonance-theoretic analyses of induced compliance, (c) do seem to require at least free choice for the appearance of dissonance effects, and yet (d) appear not to involve aversive consequences of the sort usually contemplated. For example, the research (discussed in Chapter 8) concerning the differential effectiveness of liked and disliked communicators seems to satisfy these requirements (e.g., R. A. Jones & Brehm, 1967).

6. Notice the contrast with induced-compliance situations, in which counterattitudinal behavior is induced by some incentive and (under appropriate conditions) leads to dissonance and subsequent attitudinal realignment. In hypocrisy induction circumstances, counterattitudinal behavior need not be induced because

it already has occurred. But in the colloquial sense of hypocrisy, both counter-attitudinal advocacy situations and hypocrisy induction situations represent cases of hypocrisy (in which a person says one thing but thinks or does another).

7. It is surprising that in considering possible reframings of dissonance research, little explicit consideration seems to have been given to guilt (and correspondingly little attention to potentially relevant research findings concerning guilt). As note 6 indicates, in both counterattitudinal advocacy situations and hypocrisy induction situations, persons are (made) aware of being hypocritical (in the colloquial sense of saying one thing but thinking or doing another)—and such hypocrisy is a paradigmatic guilt-arousing circumstance. Although it is implausible to think that dissonance is nothing but guilt (some phenomena, such as selective exposure, appear to be easily accommodated within a dissonance framework but not so easily explained as guilt based), it might be useful to seek closer connections between these two research literatures (O'Keefe, 2000). As one possible illustration, consider that (a) one common source of guilt feelings is having told a lie (e.g., Keltner & Buswell, 1996, Study 1); (b) another common source of guilt is having inflicted harm on others (e.g., Baumeister, Reis, & Delespaul, 1995, Study 2; Tangney, 1992); and (c) presumably doing both these things would (ceteris paribus) arouse greater guilt than doing either alone. From this perspective, it should not be surprising that (a) counterattitudinal advocacy, even without aversive consequences, has the capacity to arouse dissonance (e.g., Harmon-Jones, Brehm, Greenberg, Simon, & Nelson, 1996; for a review, see Harmon-Jones, 1999); (b) aversive consequences, even from proattitudinal advocacy, have the capacity to arouse dissonance (e.g., Scher & Cooper, 1989); and (c) the combination of counterattitudinal advocacy and aversive consequences arouses greater dissonance than does either element alone (e.g., R. W. Johnson, Kelly, & LeBlanc, 1995).

Theories of Behavioral Intention

5

T he behaviors of central interest to persuaders are voluntary actions, ones under the actor's volitional control. The most immediate determinant of such an action is presumably the actor's behavioral intention—what the person intends to do. Influencing behavior, then, is to be accomplished through influencing persons' intentions. For example, getting voters to vote for a given political candidate will involve (at a minimum) getting the voters to *intend* to vote for the candidate. The question that naturally arises is, "What determines intentions?" This chapter discusses two theoretical approaches—the theory of reasoned action (TRA) and the theory of planned behavior (TPB)—that provide alternative accounts of the determinants of intention (and hence alternative models of voluntary action); a concluding section discusses the relationship of intentions and actions.

THEORY OF REASONED ACTION

The TRA is a general account of the determinants of volitional behavior developed by Martin Fishbein and Icek Ajzen (Ajzen & Fishbein, 1980; Fishbein & Ajzen, 1975). In what follows, the TRA model is described, the current state of research on the theory is reviewed, and the theory's implications for persuasive messages are considered.

The Determinants of Intention

The TRA proposes that one's intention to perform or not perform a given behavior is a function of two factors: one's attitude toward the behavior in question and one's subjective norm, which represents one's general perception of whether important others desire the performance or nonperformance of the behavior. That is, intentions are influenced both by personal attitudinal judgments (my personal evaluation of the action) and by social-normative considerations (what I think other people think I should do).

These two factors will not always contribute equally to the formation of intentions. In some circumstances, one's intentions may be determined largely by one's attitude toward the behavior, and normative considerations may play little or no role, but for other circumstances, the normative factor may carry a great deal of weight while one's personal attitudes are put aside. That is, the attitudinal and normative factors may carry varying weights in influencing intention.

The TRA expresses this algebraically, as follows:

$$BI = A_B(w_1) + SN(w_2)$$

Here, BI refers to one's behavioral intention; A_B represents one's attitude toward the behavior; SN represents one's subjective norm; and w_1 and w_2 represent the weights for each factor.[1] One's behavioral intentions are thus a joint function of an attitudinal component and a normative component, each appropriately weighted.

The procedures for assessing the various elements of this model are reasonably well established (for details, see Ajzen & Fishbein, 1980). In assessing behavioral intention, a questionnaire item such as the following is commonly employed:

I intend to smoke cigarettes.

likely   ____   ____   ____   ____   ____   ____   ____   unlikely

To measure the attitude toward the behavior (A_B), several evaluative semantic differential scales can be used.

My smoking cigarettes is

good	___	___	___	___	___	___	___	bad
harmful	___	___	___	___	___	___	___	beneficial
pleasant	___	___	___	___	___	___	___	unpleasant

To obtain an index of the SN, an item such as the following is commonly employed.

Most people who are important to me think

| I should | ___ | ___ | ___ | ___ | ___ | ___ | ___ | I should not |

smoke cigarettes.

The relative weights of the attitudinal and normative components are determined empirically. These weights are not readily determinable for any single person. That is, there is not any satisfactory way to assess the relative weights of the components for Pat Smith's intention to smoke cigarettes. One can, however, assess the relative weights of the components (for a given behavior) across a group of respondents. For example, for a group of nonsmoking male adolescents, one can estimate the relative influence of attitudinal and normative considerations on smoking intentions.[2]

The Determinants of Each Component

The attitudinal (A_B) and normative (SN) components of the model are themselves seen to have distinct sets of determinants.

The Determinants of the Attitudinal Component. An individual's attitude toward the behavior is taken to be a function of his or her salient beliefs about the act (which commonly are beliefs concerning outcomes of the behavior). More specifically, the proposal is that the evaluation of each belief (e_i) and the strength with which each belief is held (b_i) jointly influence one's attitude toward the behavior, as represented in the following equation:

$$A_B = \Sigma b_i e_i$$

This is the same summative conception of attitude discussed in Chapter 3 (concerning belief-based attitude models). The assessment procedures are identical; the same sorts of belief strength scales (e.g., probable-improbable, true-false) and belief evaluation scales (e.g., good-bad, desirable-undesirable) are employed. For instance, the following items assess the respondent's belief strength (b_i) concerning a particular outcome of cigarette smoking:

My smoking cigarettes will increase my risk of cancer.

likely	___ ___ ___ ___ ___ ___ ___	unlikely
true	___ ___ ___ ___ ___ ___ ___	false
probable	___ ___ ___ ___ ___ ___ ___	improbable

The evaluation of that outcome (e_i) can be assessed with items such as the following:

Increasing my risk of cancer is

good	___ ___ ___ ___ ___ ___ ___	bad
desirable	___ ___ ___ ___ ___ ___ ___	undesirable
harmful	___ ___ ___ ___ ___ ___ ___	beneficial

The Determinants of the Normative Component. An individual's subjective norm is taken to be based on his or her judgment of the normative expectations of specific salient others (what I think my parents want me to do, what I think my best friend wants me to do, and so on). The subjective norm is also based on the individual's motivation to comply with each of those referents (how much I want to do what my parents think I should, etc.). Specifically, then, a person's subjective norm is suggested to be a joint function of the normative beliefs that one ascribes to particular salient others (NB_i) and one's motivation to comply with those others (MC_i). This is expressed algebraically as follows:

$$SN = \Sigma NB_i MC_i$$

An individual's normative beliefs (NB_i) are commonly obtained through a set of items in which the normative expectation of each referent is assessed. For example,

My parents think

I should ____ ____ ____ ____ ____ ____ ____ I should not

smoke cigarettes.

The motivation to comply with each referent (MC_i) is typically assessed through a question such as this:

Generally speaking, how much do you want to do
what your parents think you should do?

Not at all ____ ____ ____ ____ ____ ____ ____ Very much

If I believe that my parents, my best friend, my physician, and others who are important to me all think that I should not smoke cigarettes, and I am motivated to comply with each referent's expectations, then I will surely have a negative subjective norm regarding cigarette smoking (I am likely to think that in general, most people who are important to me think I should not smoke cigarettes).

▨ RESEARCH CONCERNING THE TRA MODEL

The theory of reasoned action has spawned a great deal of empirical research.[3] The following sections review research evidence concerning the determinants of intention and the determinants of each of the model's components.

Research on the Determinants of Intention

General Evidence. Behavioral intentions have proved to be rather predictable from A_B and SN, across a variety of behaviors, including voting (Bowman & Fishbein, 1978; Fishbein & Ajzen, 1981a; Fishbein, Ajzen, & Hinkle, 1980); consumer purchases (Fishbein & Ajzen, 1980; Warshaw, 1980); family planning (Fishbein, Jaccard, Davidson, Ajzen, & Loken, 1980); seat belt use (Budd, North, & Spencer, 1984); eating in fast-food restaurants (Brinberg & Durand, 1983); conserving home energy (Seligman, Hall, & Finegan, 1983); paper recycling (R. E. Jones, 1990); anti-pollution behavior (Hamid & Cheng, 1995); dental care (Hoogstraten, de Haan, & ter Horst, 1985; Tedesco, Keffer, & Fleck-Kandath, 1991); using credit union services (Gur-Arie, Durand, & Bearden, 1979); exercise (for a review, see Hausenblas, Carron, & Mack, 1997); physician prescribing of antibiotics (Lambert et al., 1997); breast and testicle self-examination (Brubaker & Wickersham, 1990; S. M. Moore, Barling, & Hood, 1998); and consumer complaining (Bearden & Crockett, 1981). The multiple correlations (obtained using A_B and SN to predict BI) in these applications are roughly in the range of .50 to .90. Although the predictability of intention from TRA components varies, for the most part the research findings have been generally supportive, with an average multiple correlation of between .65 and .70 (for some review discussions, see Conner & Sparks, 1996; Eagly & Chaiken, 1993, pp. 168-186; Sheppard, Hartwick, & Warshaw, 1988; Sutton, 1998).

The Relative Influence of the Two Components. It may be of some interest that the attitudinal component is commonly more strongly correlated with intention than is the normative component. Even when both components are significantly weighted (that is, even when SN makes a statistically significant contribution to the prediction of intention), A_B is still commonly the better predictor (see Farley, Lehmann, & Ryan, 1981; Trafimow & Finlay, 1996). Generally speaking, then, it seems that the attitudinal component typically exerts more influence on intention than does the normative component. To be sure, this generalization may be of limited utility: It is always an open question whether a specific intention will be predicted by attitude, norm, or both; for any given intention, it might turn out that normative considerations are more influential than attitudinal ones. But in the absence of information to the contrary, one should probably assume that A_B will be a more powerful influence on intention than will SN.

The question naturally arises of whether any systematic factors are at work that permit one to predict the likely relative influence of the components. A variety of individual and situational factors have been examined, including self-monitoring (DeBono & Omoto, 1993); mood (Armitage, Conner, & Norman, 1999); degree of group identification (Terry & Hogg, 1996); state versus action orientation (Bagozzi, Baumgartner, & Yi, 1992); private versus collective self-concepts (Trafimow & Finlay, 1996; Ybarra & Trafimow, 1998); and others (Crawley & Coe, 1990; Thuen & Rise, 1994). Much of this work is preliminary, so confident conclusions are premature at present, but useful generalizations may be on the horizon (see Trafimow, 2000).

The Relation of the Two Components. When researchers report the correlation between the TRA's attitudinal and normative components, the correlation is commonly a significant positive one (e.g., Bearden & Crockett, 1981; Elliott et al., 1995; Hamid & Cheng, 1995; Miniard & Cohen, 1981; Myeong & Crawley, 1993; Ryan, 1982; Shepherd & D. J. O'Keefe, 1984; P. Sparks & Guthrie, 1998; Warshaw, 1980): Persons with negative subjective norms are likely to also have relatively unfavorable attitudes toward the behavior (and vice versa); as the attitude toward the behavior becomes more positive, so does the subjective norm (and vice versa), and so on. Even when the intercorrelation is not reported, it can often be deduced from other information reported; typically, the components turn out to be positively correlated—often substantially so. For example, for the studies compiled by Ajzen and Fishbein (1980), the smallest intercorrelation is over .40 (Fishbein, Jaccard, et al., 1980); the largest is over .70 (Fishbein, Ajzen, & Hinkle, 1980, p. 181); and the remainder are between .50 and .70 (Fishbein & Ajzen, 1980, p. 170; Fishbein, Ajzen, & McArdle, 1980, p. 233; Fishbein, Bowman, Thomas, Jaccard, & Ajzen, 1980, p. 210; Sperber, Fishbein, & Ajzen, 1980, p. 123), with most of these between .60 and .70.

These interrelationships (and allied conceptual considerations) have led some to suggest that the attitudinal and normative components are not actually distinct (e.g., Miniard & Cohen, 1979, 1981), but this conclusion seems overdrawn. Considerable evidence indicates that the two components are different. For example, as mentioned above, the relationships of A_B to intention and of SN to intention vary for different persons. Moreover, experimental manipulations have been observed to have distinct effects on the two components or their relationships to intention (Fishbein & Ajzen, 1981b; Trafimow & Fishbein, 1994a, 1994b). In short, although the two components are often related empirically, they are nevertheless distinct (for a general discussion of this matter, see Trafimow, 1998).

Thus the relevant question now seems to be this: Just when will the attitudinal and normative components be substantially positively correlated, and when will they be largely unrelated (or perhaps even negatively related)? There is not much good evidence bearing on this question, and hence it is not yet possible to specify the factors that influence the magnitude of the intercorrelation (for some discussion, see Oliver & Bearden, 1985; Shepherd, 1987; Shimp & Kavas, 1984). As a general rule, it seems, one should expect at least moderately positive correlations between the components; this appears to be the overwhelmingly most common finding in the research literature. Indeed, reported intercorrelations below .30 are rare (Cochran, Mays, Ciarletta, Caruso, & Mallon, 1992; Zuckerman & Reis, 1978).[4]

Research on the Determinants of Each Component

The Determinants of the Attitudinal Component. The TRA's claims about the determinants of one's attitude toward the act have commonly received rather good empirical support, with correlations between $\Sigma b_i e_i$ and A_B averaging more than .50 (for review discussions, see Conner & Sparks, 1996; Eagly & Chaiken, 1993, p. 176). Correlations more than .60 have been observed in a number of investigations (e.g., Bagozzi, 1982; Fishbein, Ajzen, & Hinkle, 1980; Jaccard & Davidson, 1972; G. W. King, 1975; McCarty, Morrison, & Mills, 1983; Myeong & Crawley, 1993; Riddle, 1980; Tedesco, Keffer, Davis, & Christersson, 1993).[5]

The Determinants of the Normative Component. The TRA's claims about the determinants of the SN have also appeared to receive good empirical support, with correlations between $\Sigma NB_i MC_i$ and SN commonly in the range of .50 to .70. (For review discussions, see Conner & Sparks, 1996; Eagly & Chaiken, 1993, p. 176. For some examples, see Elliott et al., 1995; Gallois, Terry, Timmins, Kashima, & McCamish, 1994; Myeong & Crawley, 1993; Tedesco et al., 1993; Terry, Galligan, & Conway, 1993.) Despite this evidence, considerable worries have been raised about the TRA's treatment of the SN and its determinants. These worries are of two sorts, one concerning specifically the TRA's analysis of the determinants of the SN, the other concerning the adequacy of the TRA's general representation of normative influences.

Concerning the TRA's analysis of the determinants of SN, several troubling empirical results have been reported. For example, ΣNB_i has sometimes been found to be a better predictor of SN than $\Sigma NB_i MC_i$ (that is, deleting the motivation-to-comply element improves the prediction of SN; Budd et al., 1984; Doll & Orth, 1993; Kantola, Syme, & Campbell, 1982; Miniard & Page, 1984). Correspondingly, studies have found that intentions are more predictable from ΣNB_i than from $\Sigma NB_i MC_i$ (Budd & Spencer, 1984b; Chassin et al., 1981; DeVries & Ajzen, 1971; McCarty, 1981; Saltzer, 1981; Schlegel, Crawford, & Sanborn, 1977; Sutton, McVey, & Glanz, 1999). Moreover, there are uncertainties about the most appropriate way to phrase motivation-to-comply questionnaire items; these items can be worded in a way that focuses on the specific behavior of interest ("When it comes to voting for Senator Smith, how much do you want to do what your best friend thinks you should do?"), in a general way ("In general, how much do you want to do what your best friend thinks you should do?"), or at some intermediate level of specificity ("When it comes to politics, how much . . .")—and it is not clear how one might most appropriately choose among these.[6]

These specific difficulties concerning the subjective norm and its determinants have been acknowledged for some time (see Ajzen & Fishbein, 1980, pp. 246-247), but there is also a second, broader, worry that perhaps the TRA's subjective norm construct does not adequately capture the diverse forms in which normative influences on intention and behavior can arise. The TRA's subjective norm represents the actor's perceptions concerning specifically other people who are important to the actor (the normative beliefs the actor ascribes to them, the actor's motivation to comply with them). But arguably, other normative elements are not well captured by this construct.

For example, perceptions concerning what most people do—sometimes called a descriptive norm (Cialdini, Kallgren, & Reno, 1991)—plainly can play a role in influencing one's intentions. For example, I think that most people who are important to me think that I should not drive over the speed limit (negative subjective norm), but I think most people do drive faster than the speed limit—and that descriptive norm underwrites my intention to speed. As another illustration of possible normative factors not captured by the subjective norm, consider that persons might have beliefs—sometimes termed moral norms—about what is intrinsically right or wrong conduct (see Manstead, 2000). One's beliefs about what is morally proper can obviously diverge from one's subjective norm and thus might independently influence one's intentions and actions. (Moral norms receive further attention below, in the context of the theory of planned behavior.)

In any case, it seems that the TRA's subjective norm represents at best only one specific aspect of normative influences on intention and action; other facets of normative influence seem not well captured by the TRA. (For a broader general treatment of the roles that norms can play in conduct, see Cialdini et al., 1991.)

▨ IMPLICATIONS FOR PERSUASION

The TRA rather straightforwardly identifies three conditions under which a person's intention to perform a given behavior may change: if the attitudinal component changes (and is significantly weighted), if the normative component changes (and is significantly weighted), or if the relative weighting of the two components changes.

It is presumably apparent why inducing change by altering the attitudinal or normative component requires that the component be significantly weighted. The TRA underscores the futility of attempts to change, say, the normative component in circumstances in which only the attitudinal component is significantly related to intention. Perhaps not surprisingly, empirical evidence indicates that changing a component will lead to a change in intentions only when the component is significantly associated with intention (Ajzen, 1971; Ajzen & Fishbein, 1972; McCarty, 1981).

Changing the Attitudinal Component

One goal for a persuader might be the induction of change in the attitudinal component—influencing the receiver's attitude toward the behavior. According to the TRA, A_B is a function of the belief strength (b_i) and evaluation (e_i) of salient beliefs about the action. There are thus a number of possible avenues to changing A_B. For example, in attempting to induce an unfavorable attitude toward a given behavior (e.g., smoking), one might attempt to lead the receiver to add a new salient negative belief about the act ("Maybe you didn't realize that smoking leaves a bad odor on your clothes"). A second possibility is to attempt to increase the unfavorability of an existing negative belief ("You probably already know that smoking can lead to blood circulation problems—but you may not realize just how *serious* such problems are. Impaired circulation is *very* undesirable, even dangerous, . . ."). Third, a persuader might attempt to increase the belief strength (likelihood) of an existing negative belief ("You probably already realize that smoking *can* lead to health problems. But maybe you don't realize just how *likely* it is to do so. You really are at risk . . ."). Fourth, one might try to decrease the favorability of an existing positive belief ("Maybe smoking does give you something to do with your hands, but that's a pretty trivial thing"). Fifth, one might attempt to decrease the belief strength (likelihood) associated with an existing positive belief ("Actually, smoking *won't* help you keep your weight down"). Finally, the attitude toward the action could be changed without adding any new beliefs and without changing the belief strength or evaluation of any existing beliefs, simply by shuffling the current beliefs around in such a way that a different set of beliefs is salient; because the attitude toward the act is based on the salient beliefs about the act, changing the relative saliency of currently held beliefs can presumably influence attitudes ("Have you forgotten just how expensive cigarettes are nowadays?"). Obviously, these are not mutually exclusive possibilities; a persuader might well offer arguments designed to implement all these strategies.

Changing the Normative Component

The normative component is a second possible focus for influence attempts. According to the TRA, one would influence SN by influencing NB_i

and MC_i, in ways precisely parallel to the ways in which A_B is influenced through b_i and e_i. For example, one might attempt to reconfigure the set of salient referents by adding a new referent or by increasing the relative salience of an existing potential referent: "Have you considered what your *mother* would think about your doing this?" Or one might attempt to change the normative belief attributed to a current referent: "Oh, no, you're wrong—I talked to George, and he thinks you *should* go ahead and do this." Or one might try to change the motivation to comply with a current referent: "You really shouldn't worry about what *he* thinks—he has no sense when it comes to things like this."

But the previously mentioned uncertainties concerning the nature and determinants of the subjective norm make for some corresponding difficulties here. For example, if one attempts to influence a receiver's motivation to comply with a particular referent, it is not clear whether one should attempt to change the receiver's motivation to comply (with that referent) generally, or concerning the relevant broad behavioral domain, or regarding the specific behavior at hand. Moreover, altering motivation to comply with a given referent may not affect the receiver's SN; recall the research evidence that SN has been better predicted by ΣNB_i than by $\Sigma NB_i MC_i$, evidence suggesting that changing the motivation to comply component may not affect the SN in the ways predicted by the TRA. Given all this, perhaps it is not surprising that some investigators have found it difficult to manipulate the normative component through persuasive messages (McCarty, 1981).

Yet it is plainly possible to devise successful interventions based on something like alterations of the subjective norm. For example, Kelly et al. (1992; St. Lawrence et al., 1994) identified "trendsetters" who subsequently communicated HIV risk reduction information to gay men in their communities, producing substantial and sustained risk reduction behavior; one way of understanding such effects is to see them as reflecting changes in the receivers' subjective norms (and specifically in normative beliefs).

However, to the extent that the TRA's subjective norm construct does not adequately represent the variety of potential roles of normative factors in intention and action, to that same extent persuaders will want to broaden their sights insofar as normative influences are concerned. For instance, in some circumstances it may be useful to attempt to change the receiver's descriptive norm (the receiver's perception of what most people do). As one example, college students appear to commonly overestimate the frequency of drug and alcohol use on their campuses (e.g., Perkins, Meilman, Leichliter, Cashin, & Presley, 1999; cf. Wechsler & Kuo, 2000). Interventions aimed at correcting such descriptive norm misperceptions might be helpful in reducing drug and alcohol abuse (e.g., Haines & Spear,

1996; D. T. Miller, Monin, & Prentice, 2000, pp. 106-107; Steffian, 1999; cf. Werch et al., 2000).[7]

Changing the Relative Weights of the Components

The final possible avenue of influence suggested by the TRA is changing the relative weights of the attitudinal and normative components. For instance, suppose a person has a positive attitude toward the act of attending law school but has a negative subjective norm (thinks that important others think that she should not go to law school)—and because at present the person places greater emphasis on normative than on attitudinal considerations in making this behavioral decision, she intends not to go to law school. A persuader who wanted to encourage the person's attending law school might try to emphasize that insofar as a decision such as this is concerned, one's personal feelings ought to be more important than what others think ("It's *your* career choice, *your* life, not theirs; in situations like this, you need to do what's right for you—you're the one who has to live with the consequences, not them—and that means basing your choice on what you want, not what somebody else wants" and so on). That is, the persuader might attempt to have the receiver place more emphasis on attitudinal than normative considerations in forming the relevant intention.

But this strategy can succeed in changing intention only when the attitudinal and normative components incline the receiver in opposite directions. If a persuader wishes to encourage a receiver to attend law school, and the receiver has both a negative attitude toward the act *and* a negative subjective norm, then changing the relative weights of the two components will not create a positive intention. In this connection, it is important to recall the generally positive correlations that have been observed between the two components. As a rule, it is unlikely that the attitudinal and normative components will pull a person in opposite directions.[8] Consequently, the strategy of influencing intention by influencing the relative weights of the two components is not likely to find wide application.

Identifying Foci for Persuasive Efforts

In two ways, the TRA provides a general scheme for identifying plausible targets for persuasive efforts. First, it can indicate whether a persuader might usefully focus on changing the attitudinal component, the normative component, or the relative weights of the two components. For example, if both components incline the receiver against the persuader's advocated action but only the attitudinal component is significantly weighted, then obviously it would be futile to seek to influence either the normative component or the relative weights of the components.[9]

Second, if changing the attitudinal or normative component is the persuasive focus, the TRA may provide some guidance in identifying more specific foci for persuasive messages. For example, TRA-based questionnaires can be used to identify differences between those who already intend to perform the persuader's advocated action ("intenders") and those who do not ("nonintenders")—differences in what outcomes are associated with the action, differences in the normative beliefs ascribed to various referents, and so forth (for examples of such research, see Gottleib, Gingiss, & Weinstein, 1992; B. V. Marin, Marin, Perez-Stable, Otero-Sabogal, & Sabogal, 1990; Seligman et al., 1983; Thuen & Rise, 1994). These differences can then be used as the basis for constructing persuasive messages— messages focused on changing those specific elements known to distinguish intenders and nonintenders (see, e.g., Brubaker & Fowler, 1990; Strader & Katz, 1990).[10]

▨ TRA SUMMARY

The TRA has obviously enjoyed considerable empirical support, with many successful specific applications. Given such success, one question that naturally arises is whether the predictability of intentions might be enhanced by adding further predictors (beyond the TRA's attitudinal and normative components). Various possible additional components have been explored, but one addition has been especially widely studied and hence merits special attention: perceived behavioral control, as suggested by the theory of planned behavior.

▨ THEORY OF PLANNED BEHAVIOR

The Determinants of Intention

The TPB was developed by Ajzen (1985, 1991) in an attempt to extend the TRA beyond easily performed voluntary behaviors. The TPB suggests that in addition to the attitudinal and normative influences identified by the TRA, a third element—perceived behavioral control (PBC)—also influences behavioral intention, and thus the TPB adds PBC as a third predictor of intention. PBC refers to the person's perception of the ease or difficulty of performing the behavior. PBC is similar to the concept of self-efficacy, which refers to a person's perceived ability to perform or control a behavior (see Bandura, 1977). The TPB model is expressed algebraically as follows:

$$BI = A_B(w_1) + SN(w_2) + PBC(w_3)$$

Thus the suggestion is that PBC influences persons' intentions, above and beyond any effect of SN and A_B.[11]

The general plausibility of the TPB can perhaps be seen by considering that sometimes the obstacle to behavioral performance appears to reside not in negative attitudes or subjective norms but rather in a perceived lack of ability to perform the action. For example, a person might have a positive attitude toward exercising regularly ("I think exercising regularly would be a good thing") and a positive subjective norm ("Most people who are important to me think I should exercise regularly") but believe himself incapable of engaging in the action ("I can't do it, I don't have the time"—negative perceived behavioral control), and so he does not even form the intention to exercise regularly. As another illustration, in a comparison of householders who recycled and those who did not, De Young (1989) found that recyclers and nonrecyclers had similar positive attitudes about recycling, but nonrecyclers perceived recycling as much more difficult to do than did recyclers and indicated uncertainty about exactly how to perform the behavior. That is, the barrier to recycling appeared to be a matter of perceived inability to perform the action, not a negative attitude toward the behavior.

Perceived behavioral control can be assessed in various ways, but questionnaire items commonly take forms such as these:

For me to exercise regularly would be

very easy   ____   ____   ____   ____   ____   ____   ____   very difficult

If I wanted to, I could easily exercise regularly.

strongly   ____   ____   ____   ____   ____   ____   ____   strongly
agree   disagree

How much control do you have over whether you exercise regularly?

complete   ____   ____   ____   ____   ____   ____   ____   absolutely
control   no control

The Determinants of PBC

PBC is taken to be a function of the person's beliefs about the resources and obstacles relevant to performance of the behavior. More specifically, the determinants of PBC are taken to reflect jointly the person's perception of (a) the likelihood or frequency that a given control factor will occur and (b) the power of the control factor to inhibit or facilitate the behavior. PBC is expressed algebraically as follows:

$$PBC = \Sigma c_i p_i$$

where c_i refers to the individual control belief (the perceived likelihood or frequency that the control factor will occur) and p_i refers to the perceived facilitating or inhibiting power of the individual control factor. Procedures for assessing these variables are not well established, but an individual's control beliefs (c_i) might be assessed using items such as this:

Where I live, bad weather occurs

very frequently   ____ ____ ____ ____ ____ ____ ____   very rarely

The perceived power of each control factor (p_i) can be assessed through a question such as this:

Bad weather makes it

very easy   ____ ____ ____ ____ ____ ____ ____   very difficult

to exercise regularly.

If, for example, I think that bad weather occurs frequently where I live, that I don't have ready access to exercise facilities, and that I don't have much spare time, and I think that each of these conditions makes it very difficult to exercise regularly, then I will likely perceive that I have relatively little control over whether I exercise regularly.[12]

▨ RESEARCH CONCERNING THE TPB MODEL

Research on the Determinants of Intention

The empirical evidence indicates that as the TPB suggests, adding PBC to the original TRA does often improve the predictability of intention. Such effects have been obtained across a variety of behaviors, including exercising (e.g., Gatch & Kendzierski, 1990; for reviews, see Blue, 1995;

Hausenblas et al., 1997); voting (Netemeyer & Burton, 1990); donating blood (Giles & Cairns, 1995); the use of protective gloves by health care workers (P. F. Levin, 1999); flossing (Rise, Astrom, & Sutton, 1998; relatedly, see Tedesco et al., 1991); driving violations (Parker, Manstead, Stradling, Reason, & Baxter, 1992); condom use (e.g., Basen-Engquist & Parcel, 1992; for reviews, see Albarracin, Johnson, Fishbein, & Mueller-leile, 2001; Sheeran & Taylor, 1999); and a number of other behaviors (e.g., Madden, Ellen, & Ajzen, 1992). (For some relevant reviews and discussions, see Conner & Armitage, 1998; Conner & Sparks, 1996; Eagly & Chaiken, 1993, pp. 186-193; Godin & Kok, 1996; Notani, 1998; Sutton, 1998.) Although the TPB does not always outperform the TRA (see, e.g., Fishbein & Stasson, 1990), the number and diversity of supportive findings suggest that the TPB will often provide a superior model.

The question thus becomes one of specifying the circumstances under which PBC can be expected to contribute to the prediction of intention (over and above the predictability afforded by the TRA components, A_B and SN). At present, relatively little firm empirical guidance is available.[13] There has been some suggestion, for example, that when a behavior is generally perceived to be controllable, PBC may not add to the predictability of intention (Sheeran & Orbell, 1999a), but such an effect might reflect simply a lack of variability in PBC (which would minimize the opportunity for the detection of covariation; see, relatedly, Brenes, Strube, & Storandt, 1998; Sutton, 1998, pp. 1330-1331).

Research on the Determinants of PBC

Relatively little research attention has been given to the TPB's claims about the determinants of PBC. Many TPB studies have not collected data about c_i, p_i, and PBC (and of those that have, some do not report the relevant correlation between $\Sigma c_i p_i$ and direct measures of PBC; e.g., Armitage & Conner, 1999a, 1999c; Brenes et al., 1998; Crawley & Koballa, 1992; P. Norman, Bennett, & Lewis, 1998). The few reported results are not especially encouraging, as the correlations commonly range from roughly .10 to .35 (see, e.g., Cheung, Chan, & Wong, 1999; Kasprzyk, Montano, & Fishbein, 1998; Parker, Manstead, & Stradling, 1995; Povey, Conner, Sparks, James, & Shepherd, 2000a; Valois, Desharnais, Godin, Perron, & LeComte, 1993). However, stronger relationships have been reported between direct assessments of PBC and other belief-based measures, including measures based on questions about only likelihood of occurrence (i.e., Σc_i), questions about only powerfulness (Σp_i), questions that appear to involve some amalgam of likelihood of occurrence and powerfulness considerations (e.g., "Which of the following reasons would be likely to stop you from exercising regularly?"), and questions about the perceived importance of various barriers; using measures such as these, correlations with PBC measures of between roughly .25 and .60 have been obtained (Ajzen & Madden, 1986; Courneya, 1995; Estabrooks & Carron, 1998; Godin, Valois, & Lepage, 1993; P. Norman & Smith, 1995; Sutton et al., 1999; Theodorakis, 1994; Trafimow & Duran, 1998).[14]

Interpretation of these findings is complicated by variation in the direct assessments of PBC, in the means of establishing the set of control beliefs, and in the assessments of likelihood (c_i) and powerfulness (p_i). Taken together, however, these findings do suggest that in some fashion perceptions of behavioral control are belief based, in the sense of being related to persons' beliefs about resources and obstacles relevant to behavioral performance. The TPB may not yet have an adequate account of exactly how beliefs combine to yield perceptions of behavioral control, but it seems plain that assessments of the resources for, and obstacles to, behavior play some role in shaping persons' perceptions of control.

▨ PBC AS A PERSUASION TARGET

Obviously, the TPB identifies another general persuasion target (beyond the TRA's attitudinal and normative components), namely, perceived behavioral control (self-efficacy). In some general sense, PBC reflects a person's judgment of the obstacles and resources relevant to a given behavior, and hence altering PBC will mean somehow changing those perceptions. The lack of a well-articulated and well-evidenced account of the determinants of PBC, however, means that there is less guidance than one might like concerning specific means of influencing PBC. One can nevertheless point to four broad alternative means by which a persuader might influence PBC. The appropriateness of each mechanism will vary depending on the particular target behavior, and combinations of these approaches may prove more effective than any one individually, but each offers an avenue to influencing perceptions of behavioral control.

One means of influencing PBC may be for the persuader to directly remove an obstacle to behavioral performance. Some such obstacles are the result of a lack of relevant information, and in such cases persuaders might find success simply by providing the information. For example, parents' self-efficacy for lowering the temperature setting of a water heater (to prevent tap water scalding of infants) can be enhanced by a simple informational brochure describing how to perform the action (Cardenas & Simons-Morton, 1993). Adolescents may not know how to use condoms properly, voters may not know the location of their polling places, and potential first-time home buyers may not understand the process of buying a house; in all these cases, simply providing the relevant information may remove a barrier to behavioral performance.

Even when the obstacle is substantive (rather than informational), persuaders may be able to address it. For example, among low-income patients whose initial medical test results indicate a need for a return hospital visit, transportation problems might represent a significant barrier to returning; Marcus et al. (1992) found that providing such patients with free bus passes or parking permits significantly increased the likelihood of a return visit.[15]

Second, a persuader might create the opportunity for successful performance of the behavior in question. The core idea is that rehearsal of a behavior—practice at performing the behavior successfully—will enhance perception of control over the action (the underlying reasoning being something such as "I've done it before, so I can do it again"). For instance, several studies have found that self-efficacy for condom use can be enhanced by interventions that include role-playing (or mental rehearsal) of discussions with sexual partners, practice at using condoms correctly, and the like (Maibach & Flora, 1993; Weeks et al., 1995; Weisse, Turbiasz, & Whitney, 1995; Yzer, Fisher, Bakker, Siero, & Misovich, 1998). For other suggestions of the effect of successful performance on self-efficacy, see Duncan, Duncan, Beauchamp, Wells, and Ary (2000); Luzzo, Hasper, Albert, Bibby, and Martinelli (1999); Mishra et al. (1998); and Steffen, Sternberg, Teegarden, and Shepherd (1994).

Third, a persuader can provide examples of others (models) performing the action successfully; such modeling can enhance self-efficacy (by receivers reasoning that "if they can do it, I can do it"). For example, compared with a no-treatment control group, preservice teachers who viewed a videotape that described and demonstrated various effective behavior management techniques subsequently reported enhanced self-efficacy for using such techniques (Hagen, Gutkin, Wilson, & Oats, 1998). For other examples of the potential effects of modeling on self-efficacy, see R. B. Anderson (1995, 2000); Mahler, Kulik, and Hill (1993); and Ng, Tam, Yew, and Lam (1999); for some discussion of factors relevant to the choice of models, see Corby, Enguidanos, and Kay (1996) and R. B. Anderson and McMillion (1995).

Finally, simple encouragement may make a difference. That is, hearing a communicator say (in effect) "you can do it" may help enhance a person's perceived ability to perform an action. For instance, assuring receivers that they can successfully prevent a friend from driving while drunk can enhance receivers' self-efficacy for that action (compared with a no-treatment control condition; R. B. Anderson, 1995).[16]

Research is only beginning to accumulate concerning the effects of any of these individual mechanisms on perceived behavioral control (self-efficacy), and there is even less evidence concerning their relative effectiveness. Several studies have examined multicomponent self-efficacy interventions (that is, interventions that combine different potential means of influencing self-efficacy, such as modeling and information; see, e.g., Eden & Kinnar, 1991; Gist, Schwoerer, & Rosen, 1989), and self-efficacy treatments have sometimes been included as part of a larger intervention package (as when, for instance, participants receive information designed to persuade participants of the importance of the behavior in combination with a self-efficacy treatment; for examples, see Bryan, Aiken, & West, 1996; Fisher, Fisher, Misovich, Kimble, & Malloy, 1996). Such designs can provide evidence for the influenceability of self-efficacy but obviously cannot provide information about the relative impact of different specific mechanisms of influence. It will be valuable to have research that identifies the conditions under which one or another mechanism (or combination of mechanisms) is most effective.[17]

▧ COMMENTARY ON THE TPB

Two general aspects of the TPB merit some comment. One is the unusual character of PBC as an influence on intention; the other is the question of possible additions to the TPB.

Curious Status of PBC

There is some reason to think that PBC is not the same sort of influence on intention that A_B and SN are. It makes sense that everything else being equal, a more positive A_B should be associated with more positive intentions; similarly, it makes sense that everything else being equal, a more positive SN should be associated with more positive intentions. But it does not make sense that everything else being equal, greater perceived control should be associated with more positive intentions. There are many actions that I perceive to be entirely under my control—for instance, setting fire to my office—that I have no intention of performing. Just because I think I have the capability to perform an action surely does not mean that I am more likely to intend to do so.

One possibility is that rather than being a straightforward influence on intention (in the ways that A_B and SN are), PBC might instead be a necessary (but not sufficient) condition for the formation of intention. That is, if I do not think I have the ability to perform the behavior, then of course I will not intend to perform the action, but if I do think I have the ability to perform the behavior, then I might or might not intend to perform it (depending on my attitude and subjective norm).

This reasoning suggests an image in which A_B and SN influence intention when PBC is relatively high, but when PBC is relatively low, then A_B and SN will be less strongly related to intention. For example, if I think I am capable of performing the behavior of mountain climbing, then my attitude and subjective norm influence my intentions (if I like mountain climbing, then I'll intend to do it; if I don't like it, then I won't intend to do it), but if I think the behavior is not under my control (there are no mountains where I live, it's hard to travel to the mountains, and so forth), then my attitude and norm are irrelevant (I don't think I *can* go mountain climbing, so—no matter what my attitude and subjective norm are—I don't intend to). That is, PBC might be thought of not as a variable that straightforwardly influences intention in the way that A_B and SN do but rather as a variable that moderates the influence of A_B and SN on intention (PBC might be said to enable A_B and SN, in the sense that those variables will influence intention only when PBC is sufficiently high).

If this image is correct, persuaders would want to be alert to a possible pitfall in focusing on PBC as a persuasion target. Specifically, increasing PBC seems likely to increase behavioral intentions only when A_B or SN is already positive. So, for example, persuading a person that exercising regularly is under her control would presumably lead her to intend to exercise only if she thought exercising regularly was a good idea (positive A_B) or thought that people important to her thought she should exercise (positive SN). Thus if PBC is not exactly on a plane with A_B and SN with respect to influencing intention, then persuaders ought not expect that changing PBC will necessarily have much influence on intention.

If PBC operates in this sort of moderating fashion, then the usual statistical tests of TPB should reveal an interaction effect such that the relationships of intention to A_B and SN would vary depending on the level of PBC (and, specifically, that the relationships would vary in the way sketched above, that is, as PBC increases, there should be stronger relations of A_B and SN to intention). But such interaction effects are commonly not observed (see, e.g., Crawley, 1990; Giles & Cairns, 1995; Netemeyer & Burton, 1990; Terry & Hogg, 1996). There might be various reasons for this (poor statistical power for detecting such interactions or inadequate procedures for assessing PBC), but one plain possibility is simply that this otherwise appealing image of PBC's operation is incorrect.

Still, that PBC is not quite on all fours with A_B and SN is perhaps indicated by the finding that PBC can be significantly *negatively* related to intentions. Wall, Hinson, and McKee (1998) observed such a relationship in a study of excessive drinking; the less control that people thought they had over excessive drinking, the more likely they were to report intending to drink to excess. (Relatedly, PBC has been found to be negatively related to binge drinking, that is, frequent binge drinkers were less likely than others to think that the behavior was under their control; P. Norman et al., 1998.) In a similar vein, Conner and McMillan (1999) found PBC to be significantly negatively related to intentions to use marijuana. Such results certainly indicate that PBC is something rather different from A_B and SN and are consistent with Eagly and Chaiken's (1993, p. 189) supposition that increasing PBC might enhance intention only to the degree that the behavior is positively evaluated.

Indeed, such findings invite the conclusion that PBC can be a repository for rationalization. "Why do I keep doing these bad things that I know I shouldn't (drinking to excess, smoking, and so forth)? Because I can't help myself; it's not really under my control. And why do I fail to do these good things I know I should do (exercising, recycling, and so on)? Gee, I'd like to do them, I really would—but I just can't, it's out of my hands, not under my control." That is, if one negatively evaluates the behavior but intends to do it anyway, one may come to believe that the behavior cannot be prevented; if one positively evaluates the behavior but nevertheless does not intend to perform it, one may come to think that it is impossible to perform the action. Persuaders will want to notice that removing such rationalizations may lay the groundwork for subsequent behavioral change.

Additions to the TPB?

Given the enhanced predictability of intention commonly obtained by the TPB's addition of PBC to the original TRA, the question naturally arises of whether still better prediction might be obtained by adding other determinants of intention. Of the possibilities that have been explored, three suggestions—anticipated affect, self-identity, and moral norms— have received notable research attention.[18]

Anticipated Affect. Behaviors sometimes have affective (feeling-related) consequences—they can arouse regret, happiness, guilt, and so forth—and actors can often foresee these consequences (as when one scans the shelves at the video rental store, looking for a mood-brightening comedy). Such anticipated emotional consequences can be assessed by asking participants to indicate how they would expect to feel in a given circumstance. For example, Richard, van der Pligt, and de Vries (1995) had respondents imagine having had unsafe sex and then indicate their anticipated reactions on scales with anchors such as worried-not worried, regret-no regret, and tense-relaxed.

A good deal of research now indicates that various anticipated emotions are dependably related to intentions and behavior. Several studies have reported such effects specifically for anticipated regret (e.g., McConnell et al., 2000; Simonson, 1992); for instance, Lechner, De Vries, and Offermans (1997) found that among women who had not previously undergone mammography, the best predictor of participation intentions was anticipated regret (that is, the greater the regret anticipated from not undergoing mammography, the greater the intention to do so). Related effects have been reported for anticipated guilt; for instance, people avoid health risk actions that they expect would make them feel guilty (Birkimer, Johnston, & Berry, 1993), and people who anticipate feeling guilty for future tax evasion are less likely (than persons without such anticipated guilt) to expect to cheat on their taxes (Grasmick & Scott, 1982; Thurman, St. John, & Riggs, 1984). More generally, broad composite measures of anticipated emotions have been found to have such effects. For example, composite indices of anticipated positive and negative emotions have been found to be related to intentions concerning dieting and exercise (Bagozzi, Baumgartner, & Pieters, 1998), to salespersons' intentions to be planful and effortful in sales behaviors (S. P. Brown, Cron, & Slocum, 1997), and to safe sex behaviors (e.g., Richard et al., 1995).

Moreover—specifically relevant to the TPB—anticipated emotions have been found to influence intentions above and beyond A_B, SN, and PBC. Studies of safe sex behaviors (Conner, Graham, & Moore, 1999; Richard, de Vries, & van der Pligt, 1998; Richard et al., 1995), lottery playing (Sheeran & Orbell, 1999a), safe driving (Parker et al., 1995), and using drugs, using alcohol, and eating fast food (Richard, van der Pligt, & de Vries, 1996a) have reported that various measures of anticipated emotional states (some general, others more specific) have improved the predictability of behavioral intentions beyond that afforded by the TPB (for some discussion, see Conner & Armitage, 1998, pp. 1446-1448). Although it is premature to identify possible moderating factors, one should probably expect that the strength of this contribution will vary from case to case.

Notice that the observed independent effect of anticipated affect implies that anticipated affective reactions are distinct from A_B and from SN. One might have imagined that the expected affective consequences of an action would already be included in A_B (because those consequences would contribute to the overall evaluation of the action) or in SN (through recognition of the views of significant others; e.g., "My mother would want me to do this, and I'll feel bad if I disappoint her") and hence would not make a separate contribution to the prediction of intention. But these studies suggest otherwise.

Correspondingly, such studies suggest that anticipated affective reactions provide a distinctive persuasive target. There is good evidence that the anticipation of emotion can indeed be influenced, primarily by heightening the salience of such anticipations. Several studies have apparently influenced the salience of anticipated emotions simply by asking about such feelings, with consequent effects on intention or behavior. For example, Richard et al. (1996b) found that persons who were asked to indicate how they would expect to feel *after* having unprotected sex (by rating the likelihood of experiencing various positive and negative feelings) were more likely to intend to use condoms (and subsequently were more consistent condom users) than were persons who rated their feelings *about* having unprotected sex. Similarly, Sheeran and Orbell (1999a, Study 4) found that persons who answered a questionnaire item about regretting not playing the lottery (and so who presumably were induced to anticipate regret) intended to buy more lottery tickets than persons who did not answer such a question. (For related manipulations, see Hetts, Boninger, Armor, Gleicher, & Nathanson, 2000; Simonson, 1992.) Thus it seems that one straightforward mechanism for engaging anticipated emotions is simply to invite receivers to consider how they will feel if they follow (or do not follow) a particular course of action.

A more focused mechanism might involve suggesting that receivers would experience a given emotion if they followed a particular course of action—say, that they would feel guilty if they cheated on their taxes. The potential of such an approach is illustrated by Parker, Stradling, and Manstead's (1996) research, in which participants saw one of four videos aimed at influencing intentions to speed in residential areas; the videos were meant to influence either normative beliefs, behavioral beliefs, perceived behavioral control, or anticipated regret. The anticipated regret video appeared to evoke greater anticipated regret than other videos, and only the anticipated regret video proved more successful than a control video in inducing negative attitudes toward speeding. A similar illustration is offered by an antilittering campaign in Oklahoma (employing appeals meant to make people feel guilty if they littered), which seems to have produced substantial increases in the proportion of residents who said that they would feel guilty if they littered (Grasmick, Bursik, & Kinsey, 1991).

The potential influenceability of anticipated emotions is perhaps also suggested by the occurrence of certain forms of advertising. For example, guilt-based consumer advertising often seeks to engage anticipated guilt feelings; Huhmann and Brotherton (1997) examined guilt-based advertisements in popular magazines for a 2-year period and found that most of the guilt appeals were "anticipatory" appeals (offering consumers the opportunity to avoid a guilt-inducing transgression) as opposed to appeals meant to arouse guilt. Sweepstakes promoters and lottery advertising often seem to seek to induce thoughts about anticipated emotions—including not just the potential positive emotional consequences of winning but also the regret of not playing ("Suppose you've been assigned the winning mega-prize number, but because you didn't enter we had to give the 10 million dollars to someone else"; see Hetts et al., 2000, p. 346; Landman & Petty, 2000).

All the examples thus far are ones in which a persuader seeks to encourage the anticipation of particular emotions. But sometimes a persuader might want to prevent the anticipation of certain emotions. In consumer purchases, one type of possible anticipated regret involves the prospect of finding a lower price elsewhere ("If I find a lower price at another store, I'll regret buying the product now—hence I'll postpone my purchase"). An appropriate price guarantee (in which the seller promises that if the buyer finds the product offered at a lower price elsewhere, the seller will match that price) can undermine the creation of that anticipated regret (as observed by McConnell et al., 2000).

In short, it seems clear that persuaders can indeed effectively engage anticipated emotions, perhaps even through relatively simple mechanisms that make anticipated emotions more salient. To the extent that anticipated affect influences intentions beyond the factors identified by the TPB, anticipated affect will correspondingly be an important potential target for persuaders.

Self-Identity. A second possible addition to the TPB is self-identity, which refers to a salient facet of an actor's self-perception, some relatively enduring significant aspect of one's self-concept. For example, a person might think of herself as "someone concerned about environmental issues." Researchers have assessed self-identities with various types of questionnaire items, including items that assess the perceived applicability of identity labels (e.g., in a study of intentions to eat a low-fat diet, "I think of myself as a health-conscious person"; P. Sparks & Guthrie, 1998) and items concerning the importance of the behavior to the person's conception of self (e.g., "To engage in household recycling is an important part of who I am"; Terry, Hogg, & White, 1999).

A number of studies have indicated that self-identity can influence intention independent of A_B, SN, and PBC. For example, Armitage et al. (1999) found that self-identity (e.g., "I think of myself as someone who is concerned about the health consequences of what I eat") contributed to the prediction of intentions to eat healthily above and beyond the predictability provided by the three TPB components. Similar effects have been reported in studies of recycling (Terry et al., 1999), drug and alcohol use (Conner & McMillan, 1999; Conner, Warren, Close, & Sparks, 1999), dietary choices (Armitage & Conner 1999a, 1999b, 1999c; P. Sparks & Guthrie, 1998; P. Sparks & Shepherd, 1992), and exercise (Theodorakis, 1994); for a review, see Conner and Armitage (1998, pp. 1444-1446). These studies exhibit some variation in the size of the relationship between self-identity and intention (see Conner & Armitage, 1998, p. 1446), but it is not yet clear what factors might influence such variation.

As with anticipated affect, the apparent independent contribution of self-identity to the prediction of intention suggests that self-identity may be a distinctive target for social influence. But there is not yet much systematic research concerning how persuaders might engage receivers' self-identities or concerning the relative efficacy of various means of doing so (for a useful discussion, see Pratkanis, 2000). There appear to be two broad possible avenues to influence here. One is to create some new self-identity for the receiver, one deemed relevant to the intention of interest. This might seem daunting at first look, but sometimes this is simply a matter of inviting receivers to think of themselves in some new attractive way (for example, to see their past behavior as reflecting some value or concern that they had not realized was operating, with such behavioral reconstrual thus providing the basis for a new aspect of self-identity). The other is to engage some existing self-identity—and for that, surely one general mechanism of influence is to make the relevant identities more salient for the receiver, perhaps just by mentioning them ("Chris, I know you're someone who is . . .").

The potential effectiveness of identity-based influence strategies is suggested by research concerning the effects of simply offering the receiver some relevant self-characterization. For example, in R. L. Miller, Brickman, and Bolen's (1975) study, fifth graders who were told they were neat and tidy subsequently littered less (compared with those in a no-treatment control condition—and compared with those told they should be neat and tidy). Other studies of this labeling strategy have not always produced such effects (see, e.g., DeJong & Oopnik, 1992; E. M. Moore, Bearden, & Teel, 1985), but obviously at least sometimes this simple mechanism can be successful.[19]

Moral Norms. A third possible addition to the TPB is what can be called moral norms (also sometimes termed personal norms or moral obligation), that is, a person's conception of morally correct or required behavior. Questionnaires for assessing moral norms have included items concerning perceived obligation (e.g., "I feel a strong personal obligation to use energy-saving light bulbs"; Harland, Staats, & Wilke, 1999) or perceived moral propriety (e.g., "It would be morally wrong for me to use marijuana"; Conner & McMillan, 1999; "Not using condoms would go against my principles"; Conner, Graham, & Moore, 1999).[20]

Several studies have found that moral norms can enhance the prediction of intention above and beyond the predictors already contained in the TPB. Such increased predictability has been found, for example, in studies of marijuana use (Conner & McMillan, 1999), condom use (Conner, Graham, & Moore, 1999; Godin et al., 1996), environmental protection behaviors (Harland et al., 1999; cf. Lam, 1999), volunteering (Warburton & Terry, 2000), and information disclosure by insurance agents (Kurland, 1995). (For review discussions concerning moral norms, see Conner & Armitage, 1998, pp. 1441-1444; Manstead, 2000.) One supposes that the inclusion of moral norms will not always contribute to the prediction of intention, but there is little firm evidence yet concerning relevant moderating factors (see Gorsuch & Ortberg, 1983; Manstead, 2000, pp. 27-28).

As with the other potential additions to TPB, the apparent influence of moral norms on intention suggests that such norms may be a distinctive focus of influence efforts. Paralleling social identity influence mechanisms, two general influence paths are possible: One involves the creation of some new perceived moral norm, the other (surely more generally useful and plausible) involves making some existing moral norm more salient. But there is little explicit research guidance on such questions.

The Relations Among Anticipated Affect, Self-Identity, and Moral Norms. At least in some circumstances, one's anticipated affect, self-identity, and moral norms are likely to be closely intertwined. If I think of myself as a particular sort of person, I might feel corresponding moral obligations, and I might well expect to feel guilty or regretful if I fail to live up to my personal standards. For example, the beliefs "I'm the kind of person who donates to charity" (self-identity), "I feel I have a moral obligation to donate to charity" (moral norm), and "I'll feel bad (guilty, regretful) if I fail to donate to charity" (anticipated affect) naturally hang together.[21] The unifying theme seems to involve self-conceptions (including conceptions of the norms or standards to which one holds oneself) and the anticipated affective consequences of violating those self-images.

But these various elements may sometimes also be usefully distinguished with respect to their influences on intention. For example, a committed environmentalist's expectations of guilt feelings from failing to recycle is probably different from a person's anticipated regret about not playing the lottery (found by Sheeran & Orbell, 1999a, Study 4, to influence intention beyond TPB components); the former is more closely bound up with significant personal identity questions, the latter probably more with potentially forgone monetary gains. The larger point is that although there are plainly connections to be explored among anticipated affect, self-identity, and moral norms, one probably should not fuse these into a single element.

The Assessment of Potential Additions. The impulse to add predictors to the TPB is a natural one. After all, the TPB added PBC to the TRA (commonly to good effect), and hence pursuit of still further additions is to be expected. But in assessing possible new predictors, two criteria might be kept in mind. One is the size of the improvement in predictability afforded by a given candidate addition. It will not be enough that a given variable make a dependable (statistically significant) additional contribution to the prediction of intention; a large additional contribution is what is sought (for some relevant discussion, see Sutton, 1998).

The second is the breadth of behaviors across which the proposed addition is useful. In articulating a general model of behavioral intentions, one wants evidence suggesting that a proposed addition is broadly useful. It might be the case that improved prediction results from including variable X when predicting behavioral intention Y, but this result (even if frequently replicated in studies of Y) does not show that X adds to the prediction of intention sufficiently broadly (that is, across enough different behaviors) to merit the creation of a new general model that includes X.

But it is important also to bear in mind that there is a natural tension between a generally useful model and accurate prediction (of intention) in a given application. In studying a particular behavior, an investigator might add variables that improve the prediction of that intention, never mind whether those added variables would be helpful in improving prediction in other applications. Thus when one's interest concerns some particular behavior of substantive interest (as opposed to concerning the elaboration of general models), TRA or TPB might be thought of as providing useful general starting points. In some particular application, there might be additional predictors (beyond A_B, SN, and PBC) that prove to be useful in illuminating the behavior of interest—even if those additional factors are not generally useful (that is, even if not useful in studying other behaviors). And, of course, any potential addition to the TPB (whether general or case-specific) is another distinguishable potential target for persuaders.

▨ THE INTENTION-BEHAVIOR RELATIONSHIP

The TRA and the TPB focus on factors influencing the formation of behavioral intentions, but such a focus promises to illuminate persuasion only to the extent that intentions are related to action. As it happens, there is good evidence that voluntary actions can often be successfully predicted from intentions. Several broad reviews have reported mean intention-behavior correlations ranging from .41 to .53 (Eckes & Six, 1994; M.-S. Kim & Hunter, 1993b; Sheppard et al., 1988), and reviews of selected subsets of relevant work have reported similar magnitudes (e.g., .46 by Godin & Kok, 1996; .52 by Hausenblas et al., 1997; .54 by Ouellette & Wood, 1998; .45 by Randall & Wolff, 1994; .44 by Sheeran & Orbell, 1998). Given that measures of intention are thus often reasonably strongly related to behavioral assessments, the question that naturally arises is what variables influence the strength of this relationship. A variety of factors have been examined as possible influences on the intention-behavior relationship (for some examples, see Brubaker & Wickersham, 1990; Pieters & Verplanken, 1995; Sheeran, Norman, & Orbell, 1999). Three factors are discussed here as illustrative.

First, the degree of correspondence between the measure of intention and the measure of behavior influences the strength of the observed intention-behavior relationship (see Ajzen, 1991; Ajzen & Fishbein, 1980, pp. 42-47; Courneya, 1994). For instance, a questionnaire item asking about my intention to buy diet cola at the grocery tonight may well be strongly related to whether I buy diet cola at the grocery tonight—but it will be less strongly related to whether I buy Diet Coke (specifically) at the grocery tonight or to whether I buy diet cola at the cafeteria tomorrow. That is, as the degree of correspondence between the two measures weakens, the intention becomes a poorer predictor of (less strongly related to) the behavior. This methodological consideration emphasizes how different means of assessing intention and behavior can affect the size of the observed association.

A second apparent influence on the intention-behavior relationship is the temporal stability of intentions. If a person's intentions fluctuate a good deal through time, then a measure of intention (taken at one particular time) may not necessarily be predictive of subsequent behavior (Ajzen & Fishbein, 1980, pp. 47-51; Sheeran, Orbell, & Trafimow, 1999).[22] In part, this is a methodological point, in the sense that if the value of a predictor variable is volatile over time, then of course any single assessment of it is likely to be relatively weakly related to a subsequent assessment of an outcome variable (even if the two properties are actually closely related). That is, even if behavior is entirely determined by whatever the actor's intention is at the moment of behavioral performance, an earlier assessment of intention will be predictive of that behavioral performance only if the (earlier) assessed intention matches the (later) at-the-moment-of-action intention. Thus if people's intentions are stable over time, then there is a good chance that their earlier intentions will match their later ones, thus yielding a strong observed relationship between the measure of intention and the measure of behavior. But if people's intentions are variable over time, then the observed relationship will be weaker—not because intentions do not actually influence actions but because the temporal instability of intention inevitably introduces error into the intention measure.

But there is also a substantive point here, because of the possibility that some intentions (for some people or for some types of behaviors) are generally more stable than others. There is not yet much accumulated research on this matter, but (for example) some evidence suggests that for behaviors deemed relatively important (e.g., ones taken to be closely related to one's self-image), intentions may be more stable (compared with corresponding intentions for less important behaviors) and hence more closely related to action (see Granberg & Holmberg, 1990; Kendzierski & Whitaker, 1997; Radecki & Jaccard, 1999; Sheeran & Orbell, 2000a). In any case, the general point to notice is that to the degree that persons' intentions are unstable, to that same degree intentions may not provide a good basis for predicting subsequent action.

Third, explicit planning about behavioral performance can strengthen the relationship between intentions and actions. In several studies, participants who specified when and where they would perform the action were more likely (than control group participants) to subsequently engage in the behavior (Gollwitzer & Brandstatter, 1997; Orbell, Hodgkins, & Sheeran, 1997; Orbell & Sheeran, 2000; Sheeran & Orbell, 1999b; relatedly, see Kendzierski, 1990). For example, Sheeran and Orbell (2000b) found that participants who specified when, where, and how they would make an appointment for a medical screening test were much more likely to subsequently attend the screening than those in a control condition. In a similar vein, persons who intended to use a condom in an initial sexual encounter and who reported having planned about doing so were more likely (than nonplanners with equivalent intentions) to have used a condom (Abraham et al., 1999).

Notably, these effects of planning do not necessarily involve enhancing intentions (see, e.g., Sheeran & Orbell, 1999b). Explicit planning appears to be able to influence the likelihood of subsequent behavior not by strengthening intention but by strengthening the link between intention and action—that is, by increasing the likelihood that the intention will be realized in behavior. One common persuasive challenge is precisely that of encouraging people to translate their existing good intentions into action. For example, people may form an initial intention to exercise (or recycle or eat a healthier diet) but then fail to follow through. Obviously, encouraging receivers to engage in explicit behavioral planning is a possible mechanism for addressing such challenges.

One other general aspect of the intention-behavior relationship worth considering is the question of whether intention is a sufficient basis for the prediction of voluntary action. The TRA and the TPB propose that intention is the only significant influence on (volitional) behavior; any additional factors that might be related to behavior are claimed to have their effect indirectly, via intention (or via the determinants of intention).[23] The question at issue is this: Are there factors that have effects on behavior that are not mediated through intention? Alternatively put: Are there additional variables that might improve the prediction of behavior (over and above the predictability afforded by intention)?

Among various possibilities, the most prominent and well-studied suggestion focuses on past behavior (that is, prior performance of the behavior in question). Some studies have found the prediction of behavior to be improved by taking prior behavior into account (e.g., Bentler & Speckart, 1979; De Wit, Stroebe, De Vroome, Sandfort, & van Griensven, 2000; Wittenbraker, Gibbs, & Kahle, 1983); specifically, persons who had performed the action in the past were more likely to perform it in the future—over and above the effects of intention on future performance. But other studies have failed to find such an effect (e.g., Brinberg & Durand, 1983). A systematic review of this research has indicated that a key differentiating factor is whether the behavior is routinized (Ouellette & Wood, 1998). Specifically, prior behavior makes an independent contribution (to the prediction of behavior) only when the behavior has become habitual and routine (and so, in a sense, automatic rather than fully intentional); where conscious decision making is required, this effect disappears, as the influence of prior behavior seems to largely be mediated through intention or its determinants.

For persuaders, these findings serve as a reminder of the persuasive difficulties created by entrenched behavioral patterns; past behavior may exert an influence on conduct that is not mediated by intention, and hence securing changes in intention may not be sufficient to yield changes in well-established behavioral routines. On the other hand, these findings also suggest the durability of persuasive effects that involve establishing such habits (for some discussion of the establishment of habitual or routinized behavior, see Aarts, Paulussen, & Schaalma, 1997; McCaul, Glasgow, & O'Neill, 1992).

▨ CONCLUSION

The TRA and the TPB have undergone extensive empirical examination, with repeated and widespread supporting evidence. From time to time, various alternative models of the determinants of behavior have been suggested (e.g., Bagozzi, 1992; Bagozzi & Warshaw, 1990; Bentler & Speckart, 1979; Triandis, 1980), although none has enjoyed the same degree of empirical scrutiny (or success) as the TRA and the TPB. In illuminating the underpinnings of behavioral intention, the TRA and the TPB provide manifestly useful applications to problems of persuasion, primarily by identifying potential points of focus for suasory efforts.

▨ NOTES

1. The attitude of interest here is specifically the attitude toward the behavior in question. The suggestion is that, for example, the intention to buy a Ford automobile is influenced most directly by one's attitude toward the behavior of buying a Ford automobile rather than by one's attitude toward Ford automobiles. Attitudes toward objects may have some relationship to attitudes toward actions, but the TRA suggests that attitudes toward actions are the more immediate determinant of intentions.

2. The customary procedure obtains the weights through examination of the beta weights from a multiple regression analysis. Briefly put: In such an analysis, the attitudinal and normative components are used simultaneously to predict intention; the relative size of the correlation of each component with intention (in conjunction with other information, specifically, the correlation between the two components) will yield an indication of the relative weight of each component. (For instance, if the attitudinal component is strongly correlated with intention, and the normative component is not, the attitudinal component will receive a larger weight—reflecting its greater influence on intention.) This procedure— rather than simply asking people directly how important the attitudinal and normative considerations are to them—is used because there is reason to think such self-reports are not sufficiently accurate (Fishbein & Ajzen, 1975, pp. 159-160). The inadequacy of these self-reports has prevented satisfactory estimation of the weights for a given individual's intention to perform a given behavior (for exploration of some possibilities other than such self-reports, see Budd & Spencer, 1984a; Hedeker, Flay, & Petraitis, 1996).

3. At least some of the research generated by the theory is not entirely satisfactory for assessing the theory. For example, sometimes researchers have sought to predict intentions using assessments of the determinants of each component (rather than direct assessments of the two components). And although Fishbein and Ajzen have emphasized the importance of assessing respondents' *salient* beliefs and referents and have described procedures for identifying the modal salient beliefs about the act and the modal salient referents for a given population of respondents (Ajzen & Fishbein, 1980, pp. 68-76), these careful procedures are not always followed by other investigators.

4. The two correlations of A_B and SN with intention constrain the possible values for the correlation between A_B and SN. For example, if the correlations of A_B and SN with intention are .60 and .40, then it is mathematically impossible that the

correlation between A_B and SN be (for instance) $-.50$; if the correlations are .80 and .60, it is impossible for A_B and SN to be negatively correlated at all; if the correlations are .80 and .80, the correlation between A_B and SN must be at least .28; and so on. The general point is that lower limits on the correlation between A_B and SN are established by the individual correlations of the components with intention, with the lower limit rising as the individual correlations increase. So it may be that whenever the model is successful in predicting intention from both A_B and SN individually, A_B and SN will likely be at least moderately positively correlated.

5. Many of the issues that have arisen in the context of belief-based models of attitude (see Chapter 3)—such as the potentially artifactual contribution of belief strength scores to the prediction of attitude—can naturally arise here as well, because the same summative model of attitude is involved (e.g., Valiquette, Valois, Desharnais, & Godin, 1988).

6. In addition, the issues discussed in Chapter 3 (on belief-based models of attitude) concerning alternative scale scoring procedures also arise in the context of scoring normative belief and motivation to comply items. For some discussion of the phrasings and scorings of such items, see Fishbein and Ajzen (1981b), Gagne and Godin (2000), Kantola et al. (1982), and Miniard and Cohen (1981, esp. p. 332, n. 9).

7. Some persons might be relatively more susceptible than others to certain sorts of normative appeals. In particular, high self-monitors seem swayed more by persuasive messages emphasizing that the advocated view is endorsed by their peers than by messages suggesting that the advocated view provides an opportunity to express their own values (see Bazzini & Shaffer, 1995; DeBono, 1987).

8. To be careful here: A positive correlation between the two components does not necessarily mean that if one component is positive, the other will be as well; it means only that the two components vary directly (so that as one becomes more positive, so does the other). Imagine, for example, that in a group of respondents, each respondent has a positive attitude toward the behavior and a negative subjective norm; those with very strongly positive attitudes, however, have only slightly negative subjective norms, whereas those with only slightly positive attitudes have very strongly negative norms. There is a positive correlation between the two components (as the attitude becomes more positive, the norm also becomes more positive—that is, less negative), although for each individual, one component is positive and the other is negative. But insofar as the persuasive strategy of altering the weights is concerned, the implication is (generally speaking) the same: Altering the weights of the components is not likely to be a broadly successful way of changing intention (because of the unusual requirements for the strategy's working— e.g., a dramatic change in the weights may be necessary).

9. A word of caution: It may be tempting to examine the beta weights for the two components as a means of identifying the most promising target for persuasion, reasoning that if one component has a substantially larger beta weight than the other, then that more heavily weighted component is correspondingly the more important persuasion target. But when the predictors are substantially correlated (as the two TRA components commonly are), beta weights can be misleading

about differences in relative influence, because small differences in zero-order correlations can produce large differences in beta weights. For a concrete illustration, imagine two circumstances. In one, intention is correlated .70 with A_B and .65 with SN, and A_B and SN are correlated .80; this yields a multiple correlation of .72, with A_B having a beta weight of .50 and SN having a beta weight of .25. In the other circumstance, A_B and SN are again correlated .80, but the zero-order correlations are switched (intention is correlated .65 with A_B and .70 with SN); the multiple correlation remains .72, but now A_B has a beta weight of .25 and SN has a beta weight of .50. That is, a rather small difference between the correlations (.65 and .70) can yield a large difference between the beta weights (.25 and .50). In drawing conclusions about which component is the more important persuasion target, persuaders would be well advised to examine the zero-order correlations as well as the beta weights. (Some readers will recognize this as simply an example of the general point that the presence of multicollinearity conditions the interpretation of partial coefficients.)

10.   Nonintenders might be further subdivided on the basis of other characteristics, and those subgroups compared for potential differences (in salient referents, behavioral beliefs, and so forth) relevant to constructing persuasive messages. For instance, in designing antismoking appeals, it may be important to recognize differences between less-educated smokers and better-educated smokers (Sengupta, 1996); in designing messages aimed at encouraging condom use, differences between persons relatively more or less knowledgeable about AIDS risk behaviors may be relevant (Jemmott & Jemmott, 1991).

11.   The TPB also expects that sometimes PBC will appear to have a direct relationship to behavior. In circumstances in which actual (not perceived) behavioral control influences performance of the behavior (that is, circumstances in which the behavior is actually not under purely volitional control), then to the extent that persons' perceptions of behavioral control are accurate (and so covary with actual behavioral control), then to that same extent PBC will be related to behavior.

12.   Different types of resources and obstacles will want different phrasings of questionnaire items, especially with respect to control beliefs (likelihood or frequency of occurrence). For instance, although the control belief associated with bad weather could be assessed by asking respondents how frequently bad weather occurs where they live (with scales end anchored by phrases such as "very frequently" and "very rarely"), the control belief concerning a lack of facilities might better be assessed by asking a question such as "I have easy access to exercise facilities" (with end anchors such as "true" and "false"). In addition, because $\Sigma c_i p_i$ is a multiplicative composite (as are $\Sigma b_i e_i$ and $\Sigma NB_i MC_i$), the same scale-scoring issues (e.g., unipolar vs. bipolar) can arise (see Gagne & Godin, 2000).

13.   Notani (1998) has sought to identify conditions that affect the strength of the relationship between PBC and intention or behavior, but this is not the same as identifying conditions under which TPB outperforms TRA.

14.   The lack of any standardized item format for assessing control beliefs and powerfulness—necessitated by variation in the types of factors under study (see note 12 above)—has produced considerable diversity in the details of these belief-

based assessments, and it is not always clear how best to characterize the measures employed. For example, P. Norman and Smith (1995) presented respondents with a list of seven barriers to physical activity (such as a lack of time or the distance from facilities), and asked respondents to indicate, "Which of the following reasons would be likely to stop you from taking regular exercise?" (with responses given on a 7-point scale anchored by "extremely likely" and "extremely unlikely"). Although based on likelihood ratings, the resulting index appears not to assess control beliefs (the perceived frequency or likelihood of occurrence of a control factor); it might better be seen as amalgamating assessment of powerfulness and likelihood of occurrence (notice that the question asks for the likelihood that the factor will prevent the behavior—not the likelihood that the factor will occur) or perhaps even as assessing simply the factor's powerfulness (the question might be taken to mean, "Which of the following reasons would, if hypothetically it occurred, be likely to stop you from taking regular exercise?").

15. The effect of including the parking permit or bus pass was only partly attributable to its removal of transportation obstacles. Apparently, the inclusion of the permit/pass also helped convince recipients of the value of making a return visit ("This must be important, otherwise they would not send me a bus pass"), which in turn helped boost return rates (Marcus et al., 1992, p. 227). Sometimes persuasion happens in unexpected ways.

16. This list of alternative mechanisms reflects some parallels with Bandura's (1986, pp. 399-401; 1997, pp. 79-115) analysis of sources of self-efficacy, which include "enactive attainment" (experiences of genuine mastery of the behavior), "vicarious experience" (seeing or imagining others perform successfully), and "verbal persuasion" (having others provide assurances about one's possession of the relevant capabilities).

17. Several commentators have suggested that it may be useful to distinguish different facets of PBC/self-efficacy (e.g., Cheung et al., 1999; Estabrooks & Carron, 1998; McCaul, Sandgren, O'Neill, & Hinsz, 1993). In particular, there is something to recommend a distinction between internal and external aspects of PBC/self-efficacy, that is, between internal resources and obstacles to action (motivation, personal capabilities, and the like) and external resources and obstacles (facilities, equipment, cooperation of others, and so forth). Something like this distinction has surfaced in a number of places (e.g., Norwich & Duncan, 1990; Povey et al., 2000a; P. Sparks, Guthrie, & Shepherd, 1997; Terry & O'Leary, 1995; K. M. White, Terry, & Hogg, 1994), although with varying labels (e.g., "self-efficacy" is used to refer to internal factors, and "perceived control over behavior" to external factors, by Armitage and Conner, 1999a, 1999c). Although it remains to be seen whether this will turn out to be the best (or a satisfactory) way to unpack PBC/self-efficacy, it is worth noticing that internal and external control elements represent distinct possible targets of persuasion and might well be differentially responsive to different influence mechanisms.

18. As an example of another possibility: Because the TPB retains the TRA's subjective norm as its representation of normative influences, concerns about the adequacy of this representation have spurred studies suggesting that the TPB's

prediction of intention might be enhanced by including consideration of descriptive norms (Conner & McMillan, 1999; Sheeran & Orbell, 1999a; cf. Povey, Conner, Sparks, James, & Shepherd, 2000b).

19. The labeling strategy has the potential to be effective both with those who already have the relevant self-concept (because it makes the existing self-characterization more salient) and with those who had not previously thought of themselves in the suggested way (because it invites the new self-characterization).

20. An early form of the TRA included personal normative beliefs as an influence on intention (Fishbein, 1967a), but this component was subsequently omitted because it was taken to represent simply an alternative measure of intention (e.g., Ajzen & Fishbein, 1980, p. 247; Fishbein & Ajzen, 1975, pp. 305-306); see Manstead (2000, pp. 11-15).

21. In fact, some measures of moral norms (or personal norms or moral obligation) have included items concerning anticipated affective states (such as "I would feel guilty if I . . ."); see Conner and McMillan (1999), Godin et al. (1996), Harland et al. (1999), and Warburton and Terry (2000).

22. It has sometimes been suggested that the strength of the intention-behavior relationship will be affected by the time interval between the assessment of intention and the assessment of behavior (the idea being that as the time interval increases, the predictability of behavior from intention will decrease; see, e.g., Ajzen, 1985; Ajzen & Fishbein, 1980, p. 47). One rationale for this suggestion is precisely the possibility of change in intentions through time (that is, temporal instability in intentions), because the supposition is that with an increased time interval (between intention assessment and behavioral assessment), there would be increased opportunity for a change in intention. As it happens, it is not clear that variations in the size of the time interval have general effects on the intention-behavior relationship (for a review, see Randall & Wolff, 1994, but also see Sheeran & Orbell, 1998, pp. 234-235). But of course if (for a particular behavior) persons' intentions are relatively stable across time, then variations in the interval between assessments would not show much effect on the intention-behavior relationship. The relevant points to notice here are that (a) time interval variation is a poor proxy measure of temporal instability in intentions, and (b) an apparent absence of broad time interval effects on the strength of the intention-behavior relationship is not necessarily inconsistent with the hypothesis that temporal instability of intentions influences the strength of the intention-behavior relationship.

23. There is a slight complexity here, as the TPB acknowledges that in addition to intention, PBC may also have a direct relationship with behavior, by virtue of a possible correspondence between PBC and actual barriers to action.

Elaboration
Likelihood Model

6

The elaboration likelihood model (ELM) of persuasion is an approach developed by Richard Petty, John Cacioppo, and their associates (the most comprehensive single treatment of the ELM is provided by Petty & Cacioppo, 1986a; for a briefer recent presentation, see Petty & Wegener, 1999). The ELM suggests that important variations in the nature of persuasion are a function of the likelihood that receivers will engage in elaboration of (that is, thinking about) information relevant to the persuasive issue. Depending on the degree of elaboration, two types of persuasion process can be engaged (one involving systematic thinking and the other involving cognitive shortcuts)—with different factors influencing persuasive outcomes depending on which process is activated. In the sections that follow, the nature of variations in the degree of elaboration are described, factors influencing the degree of elaboration are discussed, the two persuasion processes (and the correspondingly different influences on persuasive effects) are treated, and the complexities and consequences of persuasion processes are considered.

The ELM is an example of a dual process approach to social information-processing phenomena (see Chaiken & Trope, 1999)—an example focused specifically on persuasion phenomena. An alternative dual process image of persuasion has been provided by the heuristic-systematic model

(HSM; see Chaiken, 1987; S. Chen & Chaiken, 1999). Although the two models differ in some important ways, the ELM and HSM share the broad idea that persuasion can be achieved through two general avenues (varying in the amount of careful thinking involved).

▨ VARIATIONS IN THE DEGREE OF ELABORATION: CENTRAL VERSUS PERIPHERAL ROUTES TO PERSUASION

The Nature of Elaboration

The ELM is based on the idea that under different conditions, receivers will vary in the degree to which they are likely to engage in elaboration of information relevant to the persuasive issue. By "elaboration" is meant (roughly) engaging in issue-relevant thinking. Thus sometimes receivers will engage in extensive issue-relevant thinking: They will attend closely to a presented message, carefully scrutinize the arguments it contains, reflect on other issue-relevant considerations (e.g., other arguments recalled from memory or arguments they devise), and so on. But sometimes receivers will not undertake so much issue-relevant thinking; no one can engage in such effort for every persuasive topic or message, and hence sometimes receivers will display relatively little elaboration.[1]

A number of means have been developed for assessing variations in the degree of elaboration that occurs in a given circumstance (for discussion, see Petty & Cacioppo, 1986a, pp. 35-47). Perhaps the most straightforward of these is the thought-listing technique: Immediately following the receipt of a persuasive message, receivers are simply asked to list the thoughts that occurred to them during the communication (for a more detailed description, see Cacioppo, Harkins, & Petty, 1981, pp. 38-47; for a broad review of such techniques, see Cacioppo, von Hippel, & Ernst, 1997). The number of issue-relevant thoughts reported is presumably at least a rough index of the amount of issue-relevant thinking.[2] Of course, the reported thoughts can also be classified in any number of ways (e.g., according to their substantive content or according to what appeared to provoke them); one classification obviously relevant to the illumination of persuasive effects is one that categorizes thoughts according to their favorability to the position being advocated by the message. That is, it is possible to see whether a given message appears to evoke predominantly favorable or predominantly unfavorable thoughts about the advocated position.

As is probably already apparent, the degree to which receivers engage in issue-relevant thinking forms a continuum, from cases of extremely high elaboration to cases of little or no elaboration. One might be tempted to think that in circumstances in which little or no elaboration occurs, little or no persuasion will occur (after all, the receiver has not really engaged the message and has not undertaken much issue-relevant thinking). But the ELM suggests that persuasion can take place at any point along the elaboration continuum—although the nature of the persuasion processes will be different as the degree of elaboration varies. To bring out the differences in these persuasion processes, the ELM offers a broad distinction between two routes to persuasion: a central and a peripheral route.

Central and Peripheral Routes to Persuasion

The central route to persuasion represents the persuasion processes involved when elaboration is relatively high. When persuasion is achieved through the central route, it commonly comes about through extensive issue-relevant thinking: careful examination of the information contained in the message, close scrutiny of the message's arguments, consideration of other issue-relevant material (e.g., arguments recalled from memory, arguments devised by the receiver), and so on. In short, persuasion through the central route is achieved through the receiver's thoughtful examination of issue-relevant considerations.

The peripheral route represents the persuasion processes involved when elaboration is relatively low. When persuasion is achieved through peripheral routes, it commonly comes about because the receiver employs some simple decision rule (some heuristic principle) to evaluate the advocated position. For example, receivers might be guided by whether they like the communicator or by whether they find the communicator credible. That is, receivers may rely on various peripheral cues (such as communicator credibility) as guides to attitude and belief, rather than engaging in extensive issue-relevant thinking.

Thus as elaboration decreases, peripheral cues presumably become progressively more important determinants of persuasive effects, but as elaboration increases, peripheral cues should have relatively smaller effects on persuasive outcomes. Indeed, one indirect marker of the amount of elaboration (in a given circumstance) is precisely the extent to which observed persuasive effects are a function of available peripheral cues as opposed to (for example) the quality of the message's arguments. If, in a given experimental condition, variations in peripheral cues have more influence on persuasive outcomes than do variations in the strength of the message's arguments, then presumably relatively little elaboration occurred. That is, the persuasive outcomes were presumably achieved through a peripheral, not a central, route (but see Bless & Schwarz, 1999).

This distinction between the two routes to persuasion should not be permitted to obscure the underlying elaboration continuum. The central and peripheral routes to persuasion are not two exhaustive and mutually exclusive categories or kinds of persuasion (cf. Stiff, 1986); they simply represent prototypical extremes on the high-to-low elaboration continuum (for an illuminating discussion, see Petty, Cacioppo, Kasmer, & Haugtvedt, 1987; Petty, Kasmer, Haugtvedt, & Cacioppo, 1987; Stiff & Boster, 1987). The ELM recognizes, for example, that at moderate levels of elaboration, persuasion involves a mixture of central route and peripheral route processes, with correspondingly complex patterns of effects (see, e.g., Petty & Cacioppo, 1986a, pp. 206-207; Petty & Wegener, 1999, pp. 44-48). Thus in considering the differing character of persuasion achieved through central and peripheral routes, it is important to bear in mind that these routes are offered as convenient idealized cases representing different points on the elaboration continuum.

A useful illustration of the distinction between central and peripheral routes to persuasion is provided by Petty, Cacioppo, and Goldman's (1981) study of the effects of argument strength and communicator expertise on persuasive effectiveness. In this investigation, the personal relevance of the message topic for receivers was varied, such that for some receivers the topic was quite relevant (and so presumably disposed receivers to engage in high elaboration), whereas for other receivers the topic was much less relevant (and hence these receivers would presumably be less likely to engage in elaboration). The design also varied the quality of the message's arguments (strong vs. weak arguments) and the expertise of the communicator (high vs. low).

High-topic-relevance receivers were significantly affected by the quality of the arguments contained in the message (being more persuaded by strong arguments than by weak arguments) but were not significantly influenced by the communicator's degree of expertise. By contrast, low-topic-relevance receivers were more affected by expertise variations (being more persuaded by the high-expertise source than by the low) than by variations in argument quality. That is, when receivers were inclined (by virtue of topic relevance) to engage in extensive elaboration, the results of their examination of the message's arguments were much more influential than was the peripheral cue of the communicator's expertise. But when receivers were not inclined to invest the cognitive effort in argument scrutiny, the peripheral cue of expertise had more influence.

As this investigation indicates, persuasion can be obtained either through a central route (involving relatively high elaboration) or through a peripheral route (in which little elaboration occurs). But the factors influencing persuasive success are different in the two cases, as illustrated by this study; moreover, as will be seen, the consequences of persuasion are not identical for the two routes. It thus becomes important to consider what factors influence the degree of elaboration that receivers are likely to undertake, because with variations in elaboration, different sorts of persuasion processes are engaged.

▨ FACTORS AFFECTING THE DEGREE OF ELABORATION

Two broad classes of factors influence the degree of elaboration that a receiver will likely undertake in any given circumstance. One concerns the receiver's motivation for engaging in elaboration, the other the receiver's ability to engage in such elaboration. For extensive elaboration to occur, both ability and motivation must be present. High elaboration will not occur if the receiver is motivated to undertake issue-relevant thinking but is unable to do so, nor will it occur if the receiver is able to engage in elaboration but is unmotivated to do so.

Factors Affecting Elaboration Motivation

A variety of factors have received research attention as influences on receivers' motivation to engage in issue-relevant thinking, including the receiver's mood (e.g., Bless, Bohner, Schwarz, & Strack, 1990; Bless, Mackie, & Schwarz, 1992; Bohner, Crow, Erb, & Schwarz, 1992; Worth & Mackie, 1987; but also see Bless & Schwarz, 1999); the receiver's attitudinal ambivalence (that is, the degree to which the attitude is based on a mixture of positive and negative elements; e.g., Maio, Bell, & Esses, 1996; Maio, Esses, & Bell, 2000); and the presence of multiple sources with multiple arguments (e.g., Harkins & Petty, 1987; D. J. Moore & Reardon, 1987). Two influences are discussed here as illustrative: the personal relevance of the topic to the receiver and the receiver's degree of need for cognition.

Personal Relevance. The most studied influence on the receiver's motivation for engaging in issue-relevant thinking is the personal relevance of the topic to the receiver. As a given issue becomes increasingly personally relevant to a receiver, the receiver's motivation for engaging in thoughtful consideration of that issue presumably increases—and indeed investigations have reported findings confirming this expectation (e.g., Petty & Cacioppo, 1979b, 1981, 1984; Petty, Cacioppo, & Goldman, 1981; Petty, Cacioppo, & Schumann, 1983).[3]

The ELM's research evidence on this matter has employed a clever methodological innovation (introduced by Apsler & Sears, 1968). In many earlier studies of the effect of topic relevance variations on persuasive processes, researchers commonly employed two message topics, one presumably quite relevant for the population from which receivers were drawn and one not so relevant. This obviously creates difficulties in interpreting experimental results because any observed differences between high- and low-relevance conditions might be due not to the relevance differences but to some factor connected to the topic differences (e.g., the necessarily different arguments used in the messages on the two topics).

The procedure followed by ELM researchers is exemplified in a study by Petty and Cacioppo (1979b). Receivers in this investigation were college undergraduates; the persuasive messages advocated the adoption of senior comprehensive examinations as a graduation requirement—either at the receivers' college (the high-relevance condition) or at a different, distant college (the low-relevance condition). With this form of manipulation, receivers in parallel high- and low-relevance conditions could hear messages identical in every respect (e.g., with the same arguments and evidence) save for the name of the college involved, thus simplifying interpretation of experimental findings.

A note about terminology: In ELM research reports, these variations in personal relevance have often been labeled as variations in the receiver's level of "involvement" with the message topic (and so, for instance, in the high-relevance condition, receivers would be said to be "highly involved" with the topic). But in persuasion research, the term "involvement" has also been used to cover other variations in the sort of relationship that message recipients have to the topic of advocacy, including the person's judgment of the importance of the issue, the degree to which the person is strongly committed to a stand on the issue, the extent to which the person's sense of self is connected to the stand taken, and as an omnibus concept meant to encompass a number of such elements. But these different properties are distinguishable. For instance, an issue might be personally relevant to me (e.g., faculty parking privileges), but I might not think it an especially important issue; I might be committed to my stand on an issue (such as whether the earth is round) without my sense of self being bound up with that issue; and so on. Thus it is important to bear in mind that the involvement manipulations in ELM research are specifically ones that induce variation in the personal relevance of the topic.[4]

Need for Cognition. A second factor influencing elaboration motivation is the receiver's level of need for cognition, which refers to "the tendency for an individual to engage in and enjoy thinking" (Cacioppo & Petty, 1982, p. 116). This tendency varies among people; some persons are generally disposed to enjoy and engage in effortful cognitive undertakings, whereas others are not. Need-for-cognition scales have been developed to assess this individual difference (e.g., Cacioppo & Petty, 1982). Persons high in need for cognition tend to agree with statements such as "I really enjoy a task that involves coming up with new solutions to problems" and "I like to have the responsibility of handling a situation that requires a lot of thinking," whereas individuals low in need for cognition are more likely to agree with statements such as "I like tasks that require little thought once I've learned them" and "I think only as hard as I have to." (For a general review of research on need for cognition, see Cacioppo, Petty, Feinstein, & Jarvis, 1996.)

As one might suppose, a good deal of research suggests that need for cognition influences elaboration likelihood. Persons high in need for cognition are likely to report a larger number of issue-relevant thoughts (following message exposure) than are persons low in need for cognition (e.g., S. M. Smith, Haugtvedt, & Petty, 1994; for a review, see Cacioppo, Petty, et al., 1996, pp. 230-231). Relatedly, those high in need for cognition are more influenced by the quality of the message's arguments than are those low in need for cognition (e.g., Axsom, Yates, & Chaiken, 1987; Cacioppo, Petty, Kao, & Rodriguez, 1986; Cacioppo, Petty, & Morris, 1983; Haugtvedt, Petty, Cacioppo, & Steidley, 1988; for a review, see Cacioppo, Petty, et al., 1996, pp. 229-230).[5] Such findings, of course, are consistent with the supposition that persons high in need for cognition have generally greater motivation for engaging in issue-relevant thinking than do persons low in need for cognition.[6]

Factors Affecting Elaboration Ability

Several possible influences on receivers' ability to engage in issue-relevant thinking have been investigated, including such variables as message repetition (Cacioppo & Petty, 1985) and the receiver's body posture (Petty, Wells, Heesacker, Brock, & Cacioppo, 1983). Two factors with relatively more extensive research support are discussed here: the presence of distraction in the persuasive setting and the receiver's prior knowledge about the persuasive topic.

Distraction. In this context, distraction refers to the presence of some distracting stimulus or task accompanying a persuasive message. Research concerning the effects of such distractions has used a variety of forms of distraction, including having an audio message be accompanied by static or beep sounds and having receivers monitor a bank of flashing lights, copy a list of two-digit numbers, or record the location of an *X* flashing from time to time on a screen in front of them (for a general discussion of such manip-ulations, see Petty & Brock, 1981).

The theoretical importance of distraction effects to the ELM should be plain. Under conditions that would otherwise produce relatively high elab-oration, distraction should interfere with such issue-relevant thinking. Such interference should enhance persuasion in some circumstances and reduce it in others. Specifically, if a receiver would ordinarily be inclined to engage in favorable elaboration (that is, to predominantly have thoughts favoring the advocated position), then distraction, by interfering with such elaboration, would presumably reduce persuasive effectiveness. But if a receiver would ordinarily be inclined to predominantly have thoughts un-favorable to the position advocated, then distraction should presumably enhance the success of the message (by interfering with the having of those unfavorable thoughts).[7]

Quite a bit of research concerns distraction's effects on persuasion, although regrettably little of it is completely suitable for assessing the pre-dictions of the ELM (for some general discussions of this literature, see Baron, Baron, & Miller, 1973; Buller, 1986; Buller & Hall, 1998; Petty & Brock, 1981). But what relevant evidence exists does seem largely compat-ible with the ELM. For example, studies reporting that distraction en-hances persuasive effects have commonly relied on circumstances in which elaboration likelihood was high and predominantly unfavorable thoughts would be expected (see Petty & Brock, 1981, p. 65). More direct tests of the ELM's predictions have also been generally supportive (for a review, see Petty & Cacioppo, 1986a, pp. 61-68). For instance, Petty, Wells, and Brock (1976, Experiment 1) found that increasing distraction increased the effectiveness of a counterattitudinal message containing weak argu-ments but decreased the effectiveness of a counterattitudinal message con-taining strong arguments. The weak-argument message ordinarily evoked predominantly unfavorable thoughts, and hence distraction—by inter-fering with such thoughts—enhanced persuasion for that message, but the strong-argument message ordinarily evoked predominantly favorable thoughts, and thus distraction inhibited persuasion for that message.

Prior Knowledge. A second factor influencing elaboration ability is the receiver's prior knowledge about the persuasive topic: The more extensive such prior knowledge, the better able the receiver is to engage in issue-relevant thinking. Several studies have indicated that as the extent of re-ceivers' prior knowledge increases, more issue-relevant thoughts occur, the influence of argument strength on persuasive effects increases, and the influence of peripheral cues (such as source likability and message length) decreases (Laczniak, Muehling, & Carlson, 1991; Wood, 1982; Wood &

Kallgren, 1988; Wood, Kallgren, & Preisler, 1985; for related work, see Cacioppo, Petty, & Sidera, 1982).[8] As one might expect, this suggests that when receivers with extensive prior knowledge encounter a counter-attitudinal message, such receivers are better able to generate counterargu-ments (i.e., arguments opposing the message's advocated position) and hence in general are less likely to be persuaded (in comparison with re-ceivers with less extensive topic knowledge). But receivers with extensive prior knowledge are also more affected by variations in message argument strength; hence increasing the strength of a counterattitudinal mes-sage's arguments will presumably enhance persuasion for receivers with extensive knowledge but will have little effect on receivers with less exten-sive knowledge.[9]

Summary

As should be apparent, a variety of factors can influence the likelihood of elaboration in a given circumstance by affecting the motivation or the abil-ity to engage in issue-relevant thinking. With variations in elaboration like-lihood, of course, different sorts of persuasion processes are engaged: As elaboration increases, peripheral cues have diminished effects on persua-sive outcomes, and central route processes play correspondingly greater roles. But the factors influencing persuasive effects are different, depend-ing on whether central or peripheral routes to persuasion are followed. Thus the next two sections consider what factors influence persuasive out-comes when elaboration likelihood is relatively high and when it is rela-tively low.

▨ INFLUENCES ON PERSUASIVE EFFECTS UNDER CONDITIONS OF HIGH ELABORATION: CENTRAL ROUTES TO PERSUASION

The Critical Role of Elaboration Valence

Under conditions of relatively high elaboration, the outcomes of per-suasive efforts will largely depend on the outcomes of the receiver's thoughtful consideration of issue-relevant arguments (as opposed to largely depending on the operation of simple decision principles activated by peripheral cues). Broadly put, when elaboration is high, persuasive effects will depend on the predominant valence (positive or negative) of the receiver's issue-relevant thoughts: To the extent that the receiver is led to have predominantly favorable thoughts about the advocated position, the message will presumably be relatively successful in eliciting attitude change in the desired direction, but if the receiver has predominantly unfavorable thoughts, then the message will presumably be relatively unsuccessful. Thus the question becomes this: Given relatively high elaboration, what influences the predominant valence (the overall evaluative direction) of elaboration?

Influences on Elaboration Valence

Of the many influences on the evaluative direction of receivers' issue-relevant thinking, two factors merit attention here: whether the message's advocated position is proattitudinal or counterattitudinal and the strength (quality) of the message's arguments.

Proattitudinal Versus Counterattitudinal Messages. The receiver's initial attitude and the message's advocated position, considered jointly, will surely influence the valence of elaboration. When the advocated position is one toward which the receiver is already favorably inclined—that is, when the message advocates a proattitudinal position—the receiver will presumably ordinarily be inclined to have favorable thoughts about the position advocated. By contrast, when the message advocates a counterattitudinal position, receivers will ordinarily be inclined to have unfavorable thoughts about the view being advocated. That is, everything else being equal, one expects proattitudinal messages to evoke predominantly favorable thoughts and counterattitudinal messages to evoke predominantly unfavorable thoughts.

But of course, this cannot be the whole story—otherwise nobody would ever be persuaded by a counterattitudinal message. At least sometimes people are persuaded by the arguments contained in counterattitudinal communications, and hence the ELM suggests that a second influence on elaboration valence is the strength of the message's arguments.

Argument Strength. Recall that under conditions of high elaboration, receivers are motivated (and able) to engage in extensive issue-relevant thinking, including careful examination of the message's arguments. Presumably, then, the valence of receivers' elaboration will depend (at least in part) on the results of such scrutiny: The more favorable the reactions evoked by that scrutiny of message material, the more effective the message should be. If a receiver's examination of the message's arguments reveals shoddy arguments and bad evidence, one presumably expects little persuasion, but a different outcome would be expected if the message contains powerful arguments, sound reasoning, good evidence, and the like.

That is, under conditions of high elaboration, the strength (the quality) of the message's arguments should influence the evaluative direction of elaboration (and hence should influence persuasive success). Many investigations have reported results indicating just such effects (e.g., Heesacker, Petty, & Cacioppo, 1983; Petty & Cacioppo, 1979b, 1984; Petty, Cacioppo, & Goldman, 1981; Petty, Cacioppo, & Schumann, 1983).

Unhappily, this research evidence is not as illuminating as one might suppose because of the way in which argument strength is operationally defined. To obtain experimental messages containing strong or weak arguments, ELM researchers commonly pretest various messages: A strong-argument message is defined as "one containing arguments such that when subjects are *instructed* to think about the message, the thoughts that they generate are predominantly favorable," and a weak-argument message is defined as one in which the arguments "are such that when subjects are instructed to think about them, the thoughts that they generate are predominantly unfavorable." That is, ELM research has "postponed the question of what specific qualities make arguments persuasive by defining argument quality in an empirical manner" (Petty & Cacioppo, 1986a, p. 32).

The consequence of this research practice is that it is not possible to say just what made these strong-argument messages effective under conditions of high elaboration. (It's not that the messages contained strong arguments—if the messages had not been effective under conditions of close scrutiny, they would not have been labeled strong-argument messages in the first place.) Hence it is not yet possible to provide much direction to persuaders about just how to compose effective messages under conditions of high elaboration likelihood. One can say, "Use strong arguments," but that amounts to saying, "Use arguments that will be effective." It remains to be seen just what sorts of particular characteristics will make messages effective when elaboration likelihood is high.

Other Influences on Elaboration Valence. Some research has examined other possible influences on elaboration valence. For example, some evidence indicates that when elaboration likelihood is high, warning receivers of an impending counterattitudinal message encourages receivers to have more unfavorable thoughts about the advocated position than they otherwise would have had (Petty & Cacioppo, 1977, 1979a). As another example, when elaboration is high, the receiver's mood may incline the receiver to have mood-congruent thoughts (that is, the better the receiver's mood, the more favorable the thoughts; Petty, Schumann, Richman, & Strathman, 1993; cf. Bohner, Chaiken, & Hunyadi, 1994). But the greatest amount of research evidence relevant to influences on elaboration valence has concerned variations in argument strength.

Summary: Central Routes to Persuasion

Under conditions of high elaboration (e.g., high personal relevance of the topic to the receiver), the outcome of persuasive efforts depends on the valence of receivers' elaboration: When a persuasive message leads receivers to have predominantly favorable thoughts about the position being advocated, persuasive success is correspondingly more likely. And the valence of receivers' elaboration will depend (at least in part) on the character of the message's arguments.[10]

▨ INFLUENCES ON PERSUASIVE EFFECTS UNDER CONDITIONS OF LOW ELABORATION: PERIPHERAL ROUTES TO PERSUASION

The Critical Role of Heuristic Principles

The ELM suggests that under conditions of relatively low elaboration, the outcomes of persuasive efforts will not generally turn on the results of the receiver's thoughtful consideration of the message's arguments or other issue-relevant information. Instead, persuasive effects will be much more influenced by the receiver's use of simple decision rules or heuristic principles.[11] These heuristic principles (or heuristics, for short) represent simple decision procedures requiring little information processing. The principles are activated by peripheral cues, that is, by extrinsic features of the communication situation such as the characteristics of the communicator (e.g., credibility). For example, in a circumstance in which elaboration likelihood is low, receivers may display agreement with a liked communicator because a simplifying decision rule ("If I like the source, I'll agree") has been invoked.

Heuristic principles have ordinarily not been studied in a completely direct fashion—and for good reason. One would not expect (for instance) that self-report indices of heuristic use would be valuable; presumably, these heuristics are commonly used in a tacit, nonconscious way, and thus receivers may well not be in a good position to report on their use of such principles (Chaiken, 1987, p. 24; S. Chen & Chaiken, 1999, pp. 86-87; Petty & Cacioppo, 1986a, p. 35). Instead, the operation of heuristic principles has been inferred from the observable influence of peripheral cues on persuasive outcomes. The ELM expects particular patterns of cue effects on persuasion: The influence of peripheral cues should be greater under conditions of relatively low elaboration likelihood (e.g., lower topic relevance) or under conditions in which the cue is relatively more salient.

The primary evidence for the operation of heuristic principles consists of research results conforming to just such patterns of effect (for some discussion, see Bless & Schwarz, 1999).

Varieties of Heuristic Principles

Although a number of heuristic principles have been suggested, three heuristics have received relatively more extensive research attention: the credibility, liking, and consensus heuristics.[12]

Credibility Heuristic. One heuristic principle is based on the apparent credibility of the communicator and amounts to a belief that "statements by credible sources can be trusted" (for alternative expressions of related ideas, see Chaiken, 1987, p. 4; Cialdini, 1987, p. 175). As discussed in Chapter 8, studies have indicated that as the personal relevance of the topic to the receiver increases, the effects of communicator credibility diminish (e.g., H. H. Johnson & Scileppi, 1969; Petty, Cacioppo, & Goldman, 1981; Rhine & Severance, 1970). Similar results have been obtained when elaboration likelihood has been varied in other ways (e.g., S. B. Kiesler & Mathog, 1968; Ratneshwar & Chaiken, 1986). Thus consistent with ELM expectations, the peripheral cue of credibility has been found to have greater impact on persuasive outcomes when elaboration likelihood is relatively low. Moreover, some research suggests that variations in the salience of credibility cues lead to corresponding variations in credibility's effects (Andreoli & Worchel, 1978; Worchel, Andreoli, & Eason, 1975). All told, there looks to be good evidence for the existence of a credibility heuristic in persuasion.

Liking Heuristic. A second heuristic principle is based on how well the receiver likes the communicator and might be expressed by beliefs such as these: "People should agree with people they like" and "People I like usually have correct opinions" (for alternative formulations of this heuristic, see Chaiken, 1987, p. 4; Cialdini, 1987, p. 178). When this heuristic is invoked, liked sources should prove more persuasive than disliked sources. As discussed in more detail in Chapter 8, the research evidence does suggest that the ordinary advantage of liked communicators over disliked communicators diminishes as the personal relevance of the topic to the receiver increases (e.g., Chaiken, 1980, Experiment 1; Petty, Cacioppo, & Schumann, 1983). Confirming findings have been obtained in studies in which elaboration likelihood varied in other ways (e.g., Wood & Kallgren, 1988) and in studies varying the salience of liking cues (e.g., Chaiken &

Eagly, 1983): As elaboration likelihood declines or cue saliency increases, the impact of liking cues on persuasion increases. Taken together, then, these studies point to the operation of a liking heuristic that can influence persuasive effects.

Consensus Heuristic. A third heuristic principle is based on the reactions of other people to the message and could be expressed as a belief that "if other people believe it, then it's probably true" (for variant phrasings of such a heuristic, see Chaiken, 1987, p. 4; Cialdini, 1987, p. 174). When this heuristic is employed, the approving reactions of others should enhance message effectiveness (and disapproving reactions should impair effectiveness). A number of studies now indicate the operation of such a consensus heuristic in persuasion (for a more careful review, see Axsom et al., 1987). For example, several investigations have found that receivers are less persuaded when they overhear an audience expressing disapproval (versus approval) of the communicator's message (e.g., Hylton, 1971; Landy, 1972; Silverthorne & Mazmanian, 1975). (For some related work, see Darke et al., 1998; Hocking, Margreiter, & Hylton, 1977; Reingen, 1982. For complexities, see Beatty & Kruger, 1978.)

Other Heuristics. Various other principles have been suggested as heuristics that receivers may employ in reacting to persuasive messages. For example, it may be that the number of arguments in the message (Chaiken, 1980, Experiment 2; Petty & Cacioppo, 1984) or the sheer length of the message (Wood et al., 1985) can serve as cues that engage corresponding heuristic principles ("the more arguments, the better" or "the longer the message, the better its position must be"). But for the most part, relatively little research evidence concerns such heuristics, and hence confident conclusions are perhaps premature.

Summary: Peripheral Routes to Persuasion

Under conditions of low elaboration likelihood, the outcome of persuasive efforts depends less on the valence of receivers' issue-relevant thinking than on the operation of heuristic principles, simple decision rules activated by peripheral cues in the persuasion setting. When receivers are unable or unmotivated to engage in extensive issue-relevant thinking, their reactions to persuasive communications will be guided by simpler principles such as the credibility, liking, and consensus heuristics.

 COMPLEXITIES AND CONSEQUENCES IN PERSUASION PROCESSES

Complexities in Persuasion

In at least three ways, the ELM identifies important complexities in persuasion processes. First, and most obviously, it points to the existence of fundamentally different possible routes to persuasion. Persuasion is complicated in the sense that it does not come about in just one way but might be accomplished through either central or peripheral routes.

Second, the ELM acknowledges persuasion's complexity by its recognition of the broad trade-off between elaboration valence and peripheral cues as influences on persuasion (a trade-off that creates the possibility that a mixture of central and peripheral processes might operate simultaneously). Recall that there is a continuum of elaboration; the distinction between central route and peripheral route persuasion is simply a convenient way of expressing the variation represented at the extremes of this continuum. What is crucial is not the (useful but too-simple) distinction between the two persuasion routes but rather the underlying elaboration continuum, which creates something of a trade-off between peripheral cues and elaboration valence as influences on persuasive outcomes: As elaboration increases, the impact of peripheral cues declines, and the impact of the valence of the receiver's issue-relevant thinking increases.[13] For example, as variations in argument strength make more difference in outcomes, variations in communicator expertise play smaller roles as peripheral cues (e.g., Petty, Cacioppo, & Goldman, 1981). The ELM does not claim that (for instance) variations in argument strength will make no difference when elaboration is low or that variations in peripheral cues will make no difference when elaboration is high. Rather, the suggestion is that broadly speaking, the relative impact of elaboration valence and peripheral cues will vary as the amount of elaboration varies. With greater elaboration, persuasive effects come to depend more and more on the valence of elaboration (and less and less on peripheral cues); as elaboration decreases, the impact of peripheral cues increases (and that of elaboration valence declines). Thus at intermediate levels of elaboration, one should expect correspondingly complex possible combinations of central route and peripheral route processes.[14]

As a third complexity, the ELM acknowledges that a given variable might play multiple roles in persuasion. Viewed through the lens of the ELM, a variable might influence persuasion in three broad ways. First, it might influence the degree of elaboration (and thus influence the degree to which central route or peripheral route processes are engaged). Second, it might serve as a peripheral cue (and so influence persuasive outcomes when peripheral route persuasion is occurring). Third, it might influence the valence of elaboration (and so influence persuasive outcomes when central route persuasion is occurring), by being an argument or by otherwise biasing (that is, encouraging one or another valence of) elaboration.[15]

The ELM emphasizes that a given variable need not play one and only one of these roles (e.g., Petty & Cacioppo, 1986a, pp. 204-215; Petty & Wegener, 1998a, 1999). In different circumstances, a variable might affect persuasion through different mechanisms. For example, consider the variable of message length (the simple length of a written message). This might serve as a peripheral cue that activates a length-based heuristic (such as "longer messages probably have lots of good reasons for the advocated view"; see Wood et al., 1985). When message length operates this way, longer messages will be more persuasive than shorter ones.

But message length might also (or instead) influence elaboration motivation. For example, on a highly technical subject, the length of the message might serve as a sign of whether the message was likely to be worth close examination. Shorter messages might get little attention (because receivers would think that the message could not possibly contain the necessary amount of technical information), whereas longer messages would be examined more carefully. (For some evidence of such a phenomenon, see Soley, 1986.) In such a circumstance, obviously, a longer message would not necessarily be more persuasive than a shorter one; the persuasiveness of the longer message would turn on the outcome of the closer scrutiny engendered by the message's length.

Similarly, communicator attractiveness might operate as a peripheral cue (engaging some version of the liking heuristic), might influence the amount of elaboration (a communicator's attractiveness might draw attention toward or away from the message), or might serve as an argument (e.g., in advertisements for beauty products) and hence influence elaboration valence (see, e.g., Puckett, Petty, Cacioppo, & Fischer, 1983). Another example: The articulation of justification (supporting argumentation and evidence) in a message might influence the amount of elaboration (as when the presence of such support leads receivers to think that paying close attention to the message's arguments will be worthwhile), might serve as a peripheral cue (by suggesting the credibility of the communicator or by activating a heuristic such as "if the message cites information sources, the position must be worthy of belief"), or might influence elaboration valence by encouraging more positive thoughts about the advocated view (see O'Keefe, 1998).

The possibility of different persuasion roles for a single variable directly implies considerable complexity in persuasion. Consider, for instance: What will be the effect (on persuasive outcomes) of varying the communicator's attractiveness? The ELM's analysis implies that no simple prediction can be made; instead, the effects will be expected to vary depending on (among other things) whether attractiveness operates as an influence on the extent of elaboration, as an influence on the valence of elaboration, or as a peripheral cue. So, for instance, increasing the communicator's attractiveness might enhance persuasion (e.g., if attractiveness operates as a peripheral cue that activates a liking-implies-correctness heuristic, if attractiveness enhances message scrutiny and the message contains strong arguments, if attractiveness reduces message scrutiny and the message contains weak arguments, or if greater attractiveness encourages positive elaboration by serving as an argument) or inhibit persuasion (e.g., if attractiveness enhances message scrutiny and the message contains weak arguments or if attractiveness reduces message scrutiny and the message contains strong arguments).

Obviously, the key question that arises concerns specifying exactly when a variable is likely to play one or another role (see, e.g., Petty, Wegener, Fabrigar, Priester, & Cacioppo, 1993, p. 354). Direct research evidence on such matters is sparse, and hence confident generalizations are surely some distance in the future. Even in the absence of some well-articulated account of the circumstances under which a given variable will serve in this or that persuasion role, persuaders will be well-advised to be alert to such complexities (for a general discussion, see Petty & Wegener, 1998a).

Consequences of Different Routes to Persuasion

Although persuasion can be accomplished at any point along the elaboration continuum, this does not mean that the nature of the persuasive effects obtained will be identical. As is already clear, different factors influence persuasive success under different elaboration conditions. But in addition, the ELM suggests that with variations in the amount of elaboration (i.e., variations in the route to persuasion), there are corresponding variations in the character of the persuasive outcomes effected. Specifically, the ELM suggests that attitudes shaped under conditions of high elaboration will (compared with attitudes shaped under conditions of low elaboration) display greater temporal persistence, be more predictive of intentions and subsequent behavior, and be more resistant to counterpersuasion.

Each of these claims enjoys both some supportive direct research evidence and some previous research that can be interpreted as indicating such effects. For example, Petty, Cacioppo, and Schumann (1983) reported that attitudes were more strongly correlated with intentions when the attitudes were formed under conditions of high (as opposed to low) personal relevance of the topic; Cacioppo, Petty, Kao, and Rodriguez (1986) found that persons high in need for cognition (and so presumably higher in elaboration motivation) displayed greater attitude-intention and attitude-behavior consistency than did persons lower in need for cognition; Verplanken (1991) reported greater persistence of attitudes and greater attitude-intention consistency under conditions of high (rather than low) elaboration likelihood (as indicated by topic relevance and need for cognition); MacKenzie and Spreng (1992) experimentally varied elaboration motivation and found stronger attitude-intention relationships under conditions of higher (as opposed to lower) elaboration motivation. (For some general reviews and discussions, see Petty & Cacioppo, 1986a, pp. 173-195; Petty, Haugtvedt, & Smith, 1995; Petty & Wegener, 1999, pp. 61-63.)

These effects may seem intuitively plausible (in the sense that the greater issue-relevant thinking affiliated with central route processes might well be expected to yield attitudes that are stronger in these ways), but it is not yet clear exactly what accounts for them. That is, the mechanism by which these outcomes arise is not entirely well understood (for some discussion, see Petty, Haugtvedt, & Smith, 1995, pp. 119-123). Nevertheless, there is good reason for persuaders to presume that persuasion accomplished through high elaboration is likely to be more enduring (less likely to decay through time, less likely to succumb to counterpersuasion) and to be more directive of behavior than is persuasion accomplished through low elaboration.

▧ COMMENTARY

The ELM has stimulated a great deal of research during the last two decades. It is obvious that the ELM provides a framework that offers the prospect of reconciling apparently competing findings about the role played in persuasion by various factors. For example, why might the receiver's liking for the communicator sometimes exert a large influence on persuasive outcomes and sometimes little? One possibility is simply that as elaboration varies, so will the impact of a simple decision rule such as the liking heuristic. Indeed, the ELM's capacity to account for conflicting findings from earlier research makes it an especially important theoretical framework and unquestionably the most influential recent theoretical development in persuasion research. Even so, several facets of ELM theory and research require some commentary.

Argument Strength

It is important to be clear about the nature of ELM research concerning argument strength (argument quality), lest misleading conclusions be drawn. Argument strength, it will be recalled, is operationally defined by argument effects under conditions of high elaboration: A strong-argument message is defined as "one containing arguments such that when subjects are instructed to think about the message, the thoughts that they generate are predominantly favorable," and a weak-argument message is defined as one in which the arguments "are such that when subjects are instructed to think about them, the thoughts that they generate are predominantly unfavorable" (Petty & Cacioppo, 1986a, p. 32).

Hence if in a given investigation, an argument strength manipulation did not influence persuasive effects under conditions of high elaboration (i.e., the message that was thought to contain the stronger arguments did not lead to greater persuasion under such conditions), the conclusion would not be that "this result disconfirms the ELM's prediction" but instead that "the manipulations were somehow defective; either the study did not effectively manipulate argument strength or it did not effectively manipulate the amount of elaboration because by *definition*, stronger arguments lead to greater persuasion under conditions of higher elaboration."

Thus to say, "Under conditions of high elaboration, strong arguments have been found to be more effective than weak arguments" is rather like saying, "Bachelors have been found to be unmarried." Researchers did not need empirical research to find these things out (and indeed, there would be something wrong with any empirical research that seemed to disconfirm these claims). So one ought not be misled by statements such as this:

> A message with strong arguments should tend to produce more agreement when it is scrutinized carefully than when scrutiny is low, but a message with weak arguments should tend to produce less overall agreement when scrutiny is high rather than low. The joint operation of these processes would result in people showing greater attitudinal differentiation of strong from weak arguments when processing is high than when it is low. (Petty & Cacioppo, 1986a, p. 44)

Appearances to the contrary, these are not empirical predictions; these are not expectations that might be disconfirmed by empirical results. If a message does not produce more agreement when scrutinized carefully than when scrutiny is low, then (by definition) it cannot possibly be a message with strong arguments.[16]

It is important to clearly grasp this point because it is important to understand what is and is not known. It is not yet known what it is about the "strong arguments" (used in ELM research) that makes them persuasive under conditions of high elaboration. One can easily be misled into thinking that an explanation is already in hand—"obviously, what makes them persuasive is that they're strong arguments"—but (as should be plain) this provides no explanation at all. Regrettably, inspection of sample ELM messages (e.g., Petty & Cacioppo, 1986a, pp. 54-59) suggests that the strong-versus-weak-argument contrast has often been formed through confounding a number of message features (e.g., the relevance of evidence to proffered conclusions, the desirability of claimed benefits of the advocated position, the apparent self-interest of cited evidence sources, the likelihood that claimed outcomes of the policy would affect the receiver, and so on). It will plainly take some time to sort out just what makes those strong-argument messages more persuasive. One suggestion has been that at least some of the relevant message features can be represented by a belief-based attitude model (as discussed in Chapter 3). That is, the argument strength variations might in part reflect variations in the desirability or likelihood of the attitude-object attributes that are discussed in the message (so that, e.g., strong-argument messages mention attributes that are more desirable than those discussed in weak-argument messages).[17] (For discussion of this and other possibilities, see Areni & Lutz, 1988; Boller, Swasy, & Munch, 1990; Eagly & Chaiken, 1993, pp. 324-325; K. D. Levin et al., 2000, pp. 182-183; Petty & Wegener, 1998a, p. 352.)

There is, however, an alternative way of reading the ELM's interest in argument quality, and that is to treat the manipulation of argument quality as "simply a methodological tool for examining the impact of some other variable on thinking" (Petty & Wegener, 1999, p. 53; similarly, see Petty, Wegener, et al., 1993, pp. 349-350). That is, when argument quality is operationalized as the ELM has defined it, argument quality variations can be thought of as providing nothing more than a means of indirectly assessing the amount of elaboration that has occurred. Thus to see whether a given factor influences elaboration, one can examine the difference in the relative persuasiveness of high- and low-quality arguments as that factor varies: High- and low-quality arguments will be most different in persuasiveness precisely when message scrutiny is high, and hence examining the size of the difference in persuasiveness between high- and low-quality arguments provides a means of assessing the degree of message scrutiny. (For instance, one might detect the effect of distraction on elaboration by noticing that when distraction is present, there is relatively little difference in the persuasiveness of high-quality arguments and low-quality arguments, but that without distraction, there is a relatively large difference in persuasiveness. Such a pattern of effects presumably reflects distraction's effect on elaboration, because—by definition—high- and low-quality arguments differ in persuasiveness when elaboration is high.)

But if this is the case—if the only purpose of varying argument quality is simply "to gauge the extent of message processing by the size of the argument quality effects on attitudes" (Petty & Wegener, 1999, p. 53)—then the ELM will have a curious lacuna. Consider, under this reading, the plight of a persuader who seeks advice about how to construct an effective persuasive message under conditions of high elaboration. Surely, such advice is the sort of thing one is entitled to expect from the ELM, but under this interpretation, the ELM will offer only the extremely unhelpful advice of "say something that will be persuasive." That is, under this reading, the ELM is unconcerned about determining just which message features make arguments persuasive under conditions of high elaboration (i.e., which message features lead arguments to be of high quality), because the ELM's interest in argument quality variations is putatively only as a methodological device, not as something of substantive interest. This would surely be a curious stance for a theory of persuasion.

Hence it seems preferable to treat the ELM as simply having deferred consideration of the elements contributing to the persuasiveness of arguments (as suggested by Petty & Cacioppo, 1986a, p. 32), rather than as disclaiming any interest in such matters.[18] This at least makes the ELM's treatment of argument quality more understandable; no research program can explore and explain everything instantly so some questions necessarily get put off—and it just happens that identification of the active ingredients of argument quality is such a postponed matter.[19]

One Persuasion Process?

The Unimodel of Persuasion. The two persuasion routes sketched by the ELM can be seen to be similar in a key way: In each route, people are trying to reach conclusions about what views to hold, and they do so on the basis of evidence that is available to them. Different sorts of evidence might be relied on in the two cases (peripheral cues in the peripheral route, the carefully scrutinized message arguments in the central route), but—it has been argued—there are not really two fundamentally different underlying processes here. Instead, there is just one process—the process of reasoning to conclusions based on evidence. Hence (this analysis suggests) in place of a dual-process analysis, all that is needed is a unimodel of persuasion. (For some presentations of the unimodel approach, see Kruglanski & Thompson, 1999a, 1999b; Kruglanski, Thompson, & Spiegel, 1999; E. P. Thompson, Kruglanski, & Spiegel, 2000.)

It is important to be clear about exactly how the unimodel approach differs from a framework such as the ELM (see E. P. Thompson et al., 2000, pp. 88-89). The unimodel approach does not deny, for example, the roles played by motivational and ability variables in influencing the degree to which evidence is processed. The key difference is that the unimodel denies, whereas the ELM is said to assert, that a qualitative difference in persuasion processes arises as a consequence of whether persuasion occurs through the processing of message contents as opposed to the processing of extrinsic information (peripheral cues). The unimodel claims that there is an underlying uniformity to the persuasion process, no matter which type of information is processed. That is, the unimodel proposes that there is a "functional equivalence of cues and message arguments" (E. P. Thompson et al., 2000, p. 91), in the sense that cues and message arguments simply serve as evidence bearing on the receiver's conclusion about whether to accept the advocated view.

One way of expressing this equivalence is to see that both peripheral cues and message arguments can be understood as supplying premises that permit the receiver to complete a conditional ("if-then") form of reasoning. In the case of peripheral cues, the reasoning can be exemplified by a receiver who believes that "if a statement comes from an expert, the statement is correct." A message from a source that the receiver recognizes as an expert, then, satisfies the antecedent condition (a statement coming from an expert), and hence the receiver reasons to the appropriate conclusion (that the statement is correct). In the case of message arguments, the reasoning can be exemplified by a receiver who believes (for instance) that "if a public policy has the effect of reducing crime, it is a good policy." Accepting a message argument indicating that current gun control policies have the effect of reducing crime, then, satisfies the antecedent condition (that the policy reduces crime), and hence the receiver reasons to the indicated conclusion (that current gun control policies are good ones). Thus the unimodel proposes that there is really only one type of persuasion process, a process that accommodates different (but functionally equivalent) sources of evidence (viz., cues and message arguments).

Explaining ELM Findings. One question that immediately arises is how the unimodel might explain the substantial accumulated evidence supporting the ELM. For instance, there appears to be considerable evidence showing that receivers vary in their relative reliance on peripheral cues or message arguments depending on such factors as the personal relevance of the topic; such evidence seems to imply that cues and message arguments are not actually functionally equivalent evidence sources.

The unimodel's analysis of such research begins with the point that both peripheral cues and message arguments can vary in their complexity, ease of processing, brevity, and so forth. The unimodel acknowledges that peripheral cues are often the sorts of things that are easily processed (and message arguments are commonly the sorts of things that require more processing), but that need not be so: "Cue and heuristic information need not be briefer, less complex, or easier to process than message information" (Kruglanski & Thompson, 1999b, p. 96).

But (the unimodel suggests) ELM research has commonly confounded the cue-versus-message contrast with other contrasts—in particular, with complexity and temporal location. That is, in ELM research, receivers are offered a simple source of evidence at the beginning of the message in the form of a peripheral cue (e.g., information about source credibility) and then later are given a complex source of evidence (in the form of message arguments). The unimodel analysis suggests that in such a research design, under conditions of low personal relevance (low motivation to process), receivers will naturally be more influenced by the brief, easily processed, initially presented peripheral cue than by the subsequent difficult-to-process argumentative material; when the message arguments appear later in the sequence of information—and require more processing than do the cues—they will likely affect only those receivers who (by virtue of higher topic relevance) have greater motivation to process. Thus the unimodel approach argues that the apparent differences between peripheral cues and message arguments (in their relative impacts on persuasion as personal relevance varies) do not reflect some general difference between cues and arguments (as the ELM is taken to assert) but rather a confounding of evidence type (peripheral cue vs. message argument) and other features of evidence (brevity, ease of processing, and temporal location). If (the unimodel suggests) peripheral cues and message arguments were equalized on these other dimensions, then the putative dual process differences between them would evaporate.

Direct evidence bearing on such claims is only beginning to accumulate. As one example, however, Kruglanski and Thompson (1999b, Study 1) found that when source expertise information was relatively lengthy, source expertise influenced the attitudes of receivers for whom the topic was personally relevant but not the attitudes of receivers for whom the topic was not relevant. In other words, source expertise information and topic relevance interacted in just the way that argument quality and topic relevance have in previous ELM research—thus suggesting the functional equivalence of peripheral cues and message arguments.[20]

Comparing the Two Models. The unimodel analysis raises many complex issues, and it will be some time before these can be sorted out in any clear fashion. One source of complexity is uncertainty about exactly how the unimodel and the ELM differ. The description given here of the unimodel has stressed its putative contrasts with the ELM, but those contrasts may be less substantial than is supposed. For instance, presentations of the unimodel depict the distinction between cues and arguments as crucially important to the ELM, in that the ELM is seen to treat these as functionally different influences on persuasive outcomes (as opposed to the unimodel view, in which cue and argument are simply two content categories and are not functionally different as sources of evidence in the receiver's reasoning processes). It is certainly true that ELM theorists have used the terms "cue" and "argument" in ways that make these into opposed categories (e.g., Petty & Wegener, 1999), which invites some misunderstanding. But at its heart, the ELM wants to emphasize not the contrast between peripheral cues and message arguments but variation along the elaboration continuum that yields a general trade-off between peripheral processes (e.g., as represented by the influence of peripheral cues) and central processes (as represented by elaboration valence, not message arguments specifically) as influences on persuasive outcomes.[21]

Similarly, it is not clear that the ELM is committed to the view (ascribed to it by unimodel advocates) that there are two (sharply different) persuasion processes. Presentations of the ELM have consistently stressed the importance of the underlying elaboration continuum and have offered the two routes as a convenient device for expressing the idea of the continuum by using examples characteristic of its extremes. Unimodel advocates might well reply that if the ELM recognizes only the underlying continuum and does not assert the existence of two different-in-kind processes, then the ELM is not a dual process model at all—which would make the ELM and the unimodel look similar (as noted by, e.g., Kruglanski & Thompson, 1999a, p. 186; Wegener & Claypool, 1999, p. 176).[22]

Given this uncertainty about how the models differ, there is naturally some uncertainty about what research evidence is appropriate to comparing the two models. Empirical evidence will be useful only to the extent that the two models can be seen to issue different predictions, and it is not yet plain that such is the case. Consider, for instance, the findings (mentioned above) indicating that complex information about communicator expertise had more influence on persuasive outcomes when the topic was personally relevant to receivers than when it was not (Kruglanski & Thompson, 1999b, Study 1). From a unimodel perspective, this is inconsistent with the ELM (because the ELM is assumed to expect that source cues will have a smaller influence on persuasion as topic relevance increases). But the ELM can accommodate this finding in a variety of ways, including the possibility that expertise information was processed as an argument or provoked elaboration of self-generated (as opposed to message) arguments (see Petty, Wheeler, & Bizer, 1999, pp. 159-160). The general point is that it is not yet clear whether (or exactly how) the

ELM and the unimodel can be made to offer contrasting empirical predictions.

Even given all these uncertainties about the contrast between the unimodel and the ELM, the unimodel analysis has nevertheless been plainly valuable: It has pointed to the abstract similarity of heuristic-based and elaboration-based persuasion (both involve reasoning from evidence to conclusion), has identified some ambiguities in ELM (or, more broadly, dual process) theorizing (for example, is it true *by definition* that heuristic cues are easy to process?), and has raised some empirical questions (for instance, can extensive processing stimulated by source information produce persuasive effects as persistent and as behavior directive as does extensive processing that is stimulated by other information?). (For some discussion of these and related issues, see, e.g., Chaiken, Duckworth, & Darke, 1999; Eagly, 1999; Manstead & van der Pligt, 1999; N. Miller & Pedersen, 1999; Stroebe, 1999.) One may hope that continuing attention to such matters will lead to theoretical frameworks that are better articulated both conceptually and empirically.

▩ CONCLUSION

The elaboration likelihood model may be seen to contribute two key insights about persuasion. One is the recognition of the variable character of topic-related thinking engaged in by message recipients. Because the extensiveness of topic-relevant thinking varies (from person to person, from situation to situation, etc.), the central factors influencing persuasive success vary: Simple heuristic principles may prevail when little elaboration occurs, but when extensive elaboration is undertaken, then the character of the message's contents takes on greater importance. The second is the recognition that a given variable may play different roles in the persuasion process. The same variable (in different circumstances) might influence the degree of elaboration, might influence the valence of elaboration, and might serve as a peripheral cue—and so might have different effects on persuasive outcomes depending on the situation. Taken together, these two ideas offer the prospect of reconciling apparently conflicting findings in the research literature concerning the role played by various factors in influencing persuasive effects and mark the ELM as an important step forward in the understanding of persuasion.

▩ NOTES

1. There has been some variation in the ELM's definition of elaboration. Elaboration has sometimes been conceived in broad terms (as here), namely, engaging in issue-relevant thinking (e.g., Petty & Wegener, 1999, p. 46). But elaboration

has also been defined more narrowly as issue-relevant thinking undertaken with the motivation of impartially determining the merits of the arguments (e.g., Cacioppo & Petty, 1984, p. 674; Cacioppo, Petty, & Stoltenberg, 1985, p. 229) or as message scrutiny (e.g., Petty & Cacioppo, 1986a, p. 7). But the broadest definition is the most common.

2. Variations in the conceptualization of elaboration (mentioned in note 1) have produced corresponding variations in proposed assessments of elaboration (see, e.g., Cacioppo et al., 1985, p. 229). But most procedures for the assessment of elaboration (as discussed by Petty & Cacioppo, 1986a, pp. 35-47) appear to represent indices of the amount of issue-relevant thinking generally.

3. This research support largely consists of evidence showing that as personal relevance increases, the effects of argument quality increase and the effects of peripheral cues decrease.

4. Other properties captured under the term "involvement" may not have the same effects as does personal relevance. As a simple illustration, the effects on message scrutiny (that is, close attention to the message's contents) may not be the same for increasing personal relevance and for increasing commitment to a position. As personal relevance increases, message scrutiny increases, but as position commitment increases, one can imagine message scrutiny either increasing or decreasing (e.g., increasing when there are cues that message scrutiny will yield position-bolstering material but decreasing when scrutiny looks to yield position-threatening material). For some general discussions of involvement, see B. T. Johnson and Eagly (1989, 1990); K. D. Levin et al. (2000); Park and Mittal (1985); Petty and Cacioppo (1990); Slater (1997); Thomsen, Borgida, and Lavine (1995); and Zaichkowsky (1985).

5. The mean effect (across 11 cases) corresponds to a correlation of roughly .15 (Cacioppo, Petty, et al., 1996, p. 229). There is not a corresponding difference in the influence of peripheral cues. That is, persons low in need for cognition are not dependably more influenced by peripheral persuasion cues than are those high in need for cognition (for a review and discussion, see Cacioppo, Petty, et al., 1996, p. 230).

6. Because need-for-cognition indices are positively correlated with various measures of intellectual ability (mean correlations are roughly in the range of .15 to .30; for a review, see Cacioppo, Petty, et al., 1996, p. 214), one might wonder whether the apparent effects of need for cognition on elaboration likelihood should be ascribed to differences in elaboration motivation or differences in elaboration ability (Chaiken, 1987, pp. 16-17). The evidence in hand appears to favor a motivational difference explanation rather than an ability difference explanation (e.g., Cacioppo, Petty, Kao, & Rodriguez, 1986, Study 1); for instance, the presence of additional motivational incentives (to engage in elaboration) can minimize these effects of need for cognition (e.g., Priester & Petty, 1995), suggesting that a difference in dispositional motivation (not an ability difference) underlies the effects.

7. The ELM's analysis of distraction effects is actually a bit more complex than this. For instance, the ELM acknowledges that when the distraction is so intense as

to become the focus of attention, thus interfering with even minimal message reception, one does not expect to find the otherwise predicted distraction effects. For a more careful discussion, see Petty and Cacioppo (1986a, pp. 61-68).

8. The studies by Wood (1982), Wood and Kallgren (1988), and Wood et al. (1985) all use the same message topic with (it appears) similar messages, which means that this research evidence does not underwrite generalizations as confident as one might prefer.

9. As a further complexity, however, consider that prior knowledge might have still other effects. For instance, although prior knowledge may enhance elaboration ability, it could also diminish elaboration motivation—as might happen if receivers think that they have sufficient information and so expect that there would be little gained from close processing of the message (see B. T. Johnson, 1994; Trumbo, 1999). (For another example of diverse effects of receiver knowledge, see Biek, Wood, & Chaiken, 1996; for a general discussion, see Wood, Rhodes, & Biek, 1995.)

10. The organization of this description of the ELM has separated influences on the amount of elaboration (factors affecting elaboration motivation and/or elaboration ability) and influences on the valence (evaluative direction) of elaboration (following, e.g., Petty & Wegener, 1999, p. 43, Figure 3.1). Alternatively (see Petty & Wegener, 1999, pp. 52-59), one might distinguish (a) variables that affect message processing "in a relatively objective manner" (i.e., that influence elaboration motivation and/or ability in such a way as to affect positive and negative thoughts more or less equally; e.g., distraction interferes with elaboration ability generally) and (b) variables that affect message processing "in a relatively biased manner" (i.e., that influence elaboration motivation and/or ability in selective ways that encourage a particular evaluative direction to thinking; e.g., a message's counterattitudinal stance might enhance motivation to engage in specifically negative elaboration, that is, counterarguing).

11. The ELM suggests that there are other peripheral route processes in addition to heuristic principles—specifically, "simple affective processes" (Petty & Cacioppo, 1986a, p. 8) in which attitudes change "as a result of rather primitive affective and associational processes" (p. 9) such as classical conditioning. Indeed, this additional element is one important difference between the ELM and the HSM. The HSM's systematic processing mode corresponds to the ELM's central route, and the HSM's heuristic mode refers specifically to the use of heuristic principles of the sort discussed here.

Although the ELM's peripheral route is thus broader than is the HSM's heuristic mode, here the peripheral route is treated in a way that makes it look like the heuristic mode. That is, the present treatment focuses on the simple rules/ inferences (the heuristic principles) rather than on the primitive affective processes that are taken to also represent peripheral routes to persuasion. There are several reasons for this. First, the nonheuristic peripheral route processes have not gotten much attention in ELM research. Second, the ELM could abandon a belief in any particular nonheuristic peripheral process (say, classical conditioning) with little consequence for the model, which suggests that the ELM's commitment to any specific such process is inessential to the model. Third, it may be possible to translate some apparently nonheuristic peripheral processes into heuristic principle form (e.g., mood effects might reflect a tacit heuristic such as "if it makes me feel good, it must be right").

12. As Chaiken (1987, p. 5, n. 1) pointed out, a number of heuristic principles appear to be represented in the various compliance principles identified by Cialdini (1984; for a briefer treatment, see Cialdini, 1987; for a recent general discussion, see Cialdini & Trost, 1998).

13. The ELM and HSM diverge in their treatments of the relationship between central (systematic) and peripheral (heuristic) processes. The ELM treats these as broadly antagonistic, in the sense that there is seen to be a general trade-off between central route influences and peripheral route influences. The HSM, on the other hand, suggests that the processes may be additive or interactive. For some discussion and examples of relevant research, see Bohner et al. (1994), Booth-Butterfield et al. (1994), Chaiken and Maheswaran (1994), and S. Chen and Chaiken (1999).

14. As Petty and Wegener (1999, pp. 59-60) stress, that peripheral cues have greater impact as elaboration declines does not necessarily mean that a given specific variable (such as communicator credibility) will have greater impact as elaboration declines. As will be seen shortly, the ELM emphasizes that a given variable can play different roles in persuasion. For example, credibility might operate as a peripheral cue (as discussed in the text) or might serve as an influence on elaboration motivation (e.g., receivers might be more motivated to process messages from a higher-credibility source). Thus it would be wrong to suppose that the ELM predicts that (for instance) as elaboration increases, credibility has less impact on persuasion. Rather, the ELM's view is that as elaboration increases, credibility has less impact on persuasion *as a peripheral cue*. Credibility variations might still affect persuasion under conditions of higher elaboration but would do so in ways other than by serving as a peripheral cue.

15. Presentations of the ELM have expressed this "multiple roles" idea in various ways, but these have not always been as clear as one might like. For instance, one formulation is that "the ELM notes that a variable can influence attitudes in four ways: (1) by serving as an argument, (2) by serving as a cue, (3) by determining the extent of elaboration, and (4) by producing a bias in elaboration" (Petty & Wegener, 1999, p. 51). But the ways in which (what would conventionally be called) arguments can influence attitudes, from the perspective of the ELM, seem to be (a) by serving as a cue (e.g., when the number of arguments activates a heuristic such as "there are many supporting arguments so the position must be correct"), (b) by influencing the extent of elaboration (as when a receiver thinks that "there seem to be a lot of arguments here so maybe it's worth looking at them closely"), and (c) by producing a bias in elaboration (i.e., by influencing the evaluative direction of elaboration). That is, the roles of arguments appear already subsumed in the other three roles (peripheral cue, influence on degree of elaboration, and influence on valence of elaboration); it is not clear how arguments might otherwise function in persuasion within an ELM framework. Hence the presenta-

tion here does not distinguish "serving as an argument" as a distinct role for a persuasion variable.

At least part of the confusion appears to concern the ELM's use of the word "argument," about which three points might be noted. First, "arguments" are sometimes conceived of as "bits of information contained in a communication that are relevant to a person's subjective determination of the true merits of an advocated position" (Petty & Cacioppo, 1986b, p. 133), but taken at face value, such a definition would accommodate at least some peripheral cues as arguments (after all, from the perspective of the heuristic processor, a cue is a bit of information relevant to assessing the true merits of the advocated view—it just happens to provide a shortcut to such assessment), which seems a unimodel-like view (Kruglanski & Thompson, 1999b) surely to be resisted by the ELM. Second, "argument" and "cue" sometimes appear to be used as shorthand to cover anything that affects, respectively, central route and peripheral route persuasion (e.g., Petty & Wegener, 1999, p. 49). But when they are used this way, it is not clear why argument-based persuasion roles are to be distinguished from persuasion roles involving influencing elaboration valence (given that elaboration valence is presumably the engine of persuasion within central route processes). Third, distinguishing "serving as an argument" does at least underscore the broad possible application of "argument" within an ELM perspective. For example, the communicator's physical attractiveness is recognized by the ELM as potentially not simply a peripheral cue but also an argument (as in advertisements for beauty products). Still, when attractiveness serves this argumentative role, it presumably influences persuasive effects by influencing elaboration valence (just as arguments of more conventional form do).

16. Another example: "Subjects led to believe that the message topic (e.g. comprehensive exams) will (vs. won't) impact on their own lives have also been shown to be less persuaded by weak messages but more persuaded by strong ones" (Chaiken & Stangor, 1987, p. 594). Despite the statement's appearance, this is not a discovery; it is not an empirical result or finding, it is not something that research "shows" to be true, it is not something that could have been otherwise (given the effect of topic relevance on elaboration). The described relationship is true by definition (by the definition of argument strength in ELM research).

17. Identification of the active ingredient(s) in argument quality will naturally underwrite new characterizations of existing research findings. To concretize this, consider that one way of formulating existing research results has been to say that "variation in argument quality (that is, in the genuine normative worth of arguments) influences persuasive effects more when receiver involvement is high than when it is low (such that the persuasive advantage of high-quality argumentation increases as receiver involvement increases)." Such a finding is at least interesting, and arguably even a bit surprising. After all, one might well expect that as persons become more involved in an issue, their critical faculties might naturally become a bit clouded by their personal involvement, which in turn would make them less sensitive to variations in the cogency (validity, genuine normative quality) of arguments.

But suppose that the active ingredient in argument quality manipulations turns out to be attribute desirability (e.g., the perceived desirability of policy outcomes), and recall that ELM "involvement" manipulations involve specifically variation in the personal relevance of the topic (e.g., the degree to which the advocated policy will affect the receiver, as in the senior comprehensive exam topic). In such a circumstance, the extant research findings could be described rather differently. One possibility: "Variation in the desirability of a policy's outcomes influences persuasive effects more when the policy affects the receiver than when the policy does not, such that the persuasive advantage of more desirable outcomes (over less desirable ones) increases when the outcomes actually affect the receiver." Empirical confirmation of such a relationship would surely be nice, but this result is perhaps less striking than it might have seemed under other descriptions of the variables.

18. Notice that Petty and Wegener (1998a), although acknowledging that the ELM has thus far "manipulated argument quality primarily as a methodological tool to examine whether some other variable increases or decreases message scrutiny, not to examine the determinants of argument cogency per se," also take up the question of "what makes an argument persuasive" (p. 352).

19. The research literature actually contains three procedures for operationalizing argument quality: pretesting messages for persuasive effectiveness under conditions of high message scrutiny (the ELM procedure; e.g., L. W. Andrews & Gutkin, 1994; Neimeyer, MacNair, Metzler, & Courchaine, 1991; Petty, Cacioppo, & Goldman, 1981; Petty, Cacioppo, & Heesacker, 1981), obtaining participant ratings of argument quality (e.g., J. C. Andrews & Shimp, 1990; Axsom et al., 1987; Burnkrant & Howard, 1984; DeBono, 1992; Helweg-Larsen & Howell, 2000; Munch & Swasy, 1988; Rosselli, Skelly, & Mackie, 1995), and creating unsystematic message variations that might be taken to reflect variations in the normative character of arguments (e.g., Bohner et al., 1994; Hunt, Smith, & Kernan, 1985; Jepson & Chaiken, 1990; Maio et al., 1996). These are not necessarily mutually exclusive procedures (e.g., the pretested effectiveness procedure can be supplemented by eliciting ratings of message quality from main study participants; see, e.g., Burnkrant & Howard, 1984), although they obviously are different (and not necessarily equivalent). But unsystematic message variations actually underlie even the pretested effectiveness and participant rating procedures. These procedures use arguments that have been varied in ways that the investigator hopes will result in appropriate differences (differences in demonstrated effectiveness or in perceived quality), but this manipulating of arguments is undertaken without any well-articulated abstract treatment of the relevant argument properties. That is, none of these approaches to operationalizing argument quality offers an explicit conceptual framework for analyzing and understanding quality-related message features or their roles in persuasion, and hence each leaves the active ingredients of argument quality unidentified (O'Keefe & Jackson, 1995).

20. Kruglanski and Thompson (1999b, pp. 96-97) emphasized that ELM research designs have commonly presented cue information before message arguments, arguing that this temporal ordering has played some part in the observed effects. Although the studies that Kruglanski and Thompson (1999b) reported did

not vary the temporal order of cues and arguments (as noted by N. Miller & Pedersen, 1999), the unimodel account is at least not inconsistent with a number of earlier studies indicating that the impact of credibility variations (on persuasive outcomes) is reduced when information about the communicator is withheld until after the message has been presented (see, e.g., Greenberg & Tannenbaum, 1961; Husek, 1965; for a review, see O'Keefe, 1987).

21. In unimodel presentations and research, the "cue versus argument" distinction sometimes seems to be cast as a "source versus message" distinction (e.g., Kruglanski & Thompson, 1999b, p. 84). But this also does not seem to capture the ELM's assertions. The ELM does not partition source variables and message variables as having intrinsically different roles to play in persuasion but instead emphasizes that each category of variable can serve different persuasion roles in different circumstances (Petty et al., 1999, p. 157; Wegener & Claypool, 1999, pp. 176-177).

22. Unimodel advocates brandish a contrast between "a quantitative difference" ("difference in degree") and a "qualitative difference" ("difference in kind") and insist that the ELM is committed to showing a qualitative difference (see, e.g., Kruglanski & Thompson, 1999a, pp. 185-189); the unimodel, of course, argues that only a quantitative difference exists. But the qualitative-quantitative contrast may itself be seen to be problematic; if nothing else, a large quantitative difference can sometimes look awfully like a qualitative one. That is, the contrast between a difference in degree and a difference in kind may be less sharp than the unimodel needs to press its case against dual process views (see Ajzen, 1999).

The Study of Persuasive Effects

7

The research to be discussed in the next three chapters is, over-whelmingly, experimental research that systematically investigates the influence that various factors (communicator characteristics, message variations, and so on) have on persuasive outcomes. This chapter first provides some general background on the underlying logic of such experimental research and then discusses some problems that arise in the study of persuasive effects.

▧ EXPERIMENTAL DESIGN AND CAUSAL INFERENCE

Various experimental arrangements are used in persuasion effects research, but these can usefully be thought of as variations on a basic design.

The Basic Design

The simplest sort of research design employed in the work to be discussed is an experimental design in which the researcher manipulates a single factor (the independent variable) to see its effects on persuasive outcomes (the dependent variable). For instance, an investigator who wishes to investigate the effects of explicit conclusion drawing on attitude change might design a laboratory investigation of the following sort. The researcher prepares two persuasive messages identical in every respect except that in one message, the persuader's conclusion is drawn explicitly at the end of the message (the explicit-conclusion message), whereas in the other message, the persuader's conclusion is left implicit (the implicit-conclusion message). When participants in this experiment arrive at the laboratory, their attitudes on the persuasive topic are assessed, and then they receive one of the two messages; which message a given participant receives is a matter of chance, perhaps determined by flipping a coin. Thus one set of participants receives the explicit-conclusion message, and a second set receives the implicit-conclusion message. After exposure to the persuasive message, receivers' attitudes are assessed again to ascertain the degree of attitude change produced by the message.

Suppose that (following conventional statistical procedures) the results indicate reliably greater attitude change for those receiving the explicit-conclusion message than for those receiving the implicit-conclusion message. How might such a result be explained? One can rule out systematic bias in assigning participants to hear one or the other of the messages because participants were randomly assigned to hear messages. For instance, one can confidently say that it is unlikely that those hearing the explicit-conclusion message were people who are just generally more easily persuaded than those hearing the implicit-conclusion message (that is, one can rule out this explanation because people who are generally easily persuaded were randomly distributed across the two messages).

The obvious explanation for the obtained results, of course, is precisely the presence or absence of an explicit conclusion. Indeed, because this is the only factor that varies between the two messages, it presumably must be the locus of the observed differences. This is the general logic of experimental designs such as this: These designs are intended to permit unambiguous causal attribution precisely by virtue of experimental control over factors other than the independent variable.

Variations on the Basic Design

There are innumerable ways in which this basic experimental arrangement might be varied. For example, one might dispense with the initial attitude assessment (reasoning that the random assignment of participants to the two experimental conditions would likely ensure that the two groups would have roughly comparable initial attitudes); this is commonly called a posttest-only design (because there would be only a postmessage assessment of attitude). In another example of variation, an investigator might create an independent variable with more than two conditions (more than two levels). For instance, one might compare the persuasive effects of communicators who are high, moderate, or low in credibility.

The most common and important variation, however, is the inclusion of more than one independent variable in a single experiment. Thus (for instance) rather than doing one experiment to study implicit versus explicit conclusions and a second study to examine high versus moderate versus low credibility, a researcher could design a single investigation to study these two variables simultaneously. This would involve creating all six possible combinations of conclusion type and credibility level (3 credibility conditions × 2 conclusion type conditions = 6 combinations).

Experimental designs with more than one independent variable permit the detection of interaction effects involving those variables. An interaction effect is said to occur if the effect of one independent variable depends on the level of another independent variable; conversely, if the effect of one variable does not depend on the level of another variable, then no interaction effect exists. For example, if the effect of having an implicit or explicit conclusion is constant, no matter what the credibility of the source, then no interaction effect exists between credibility and conclusion type. But if the effect of having an implicit or explicit conclusion varies depending on the credibility of the source (say, if high-credibility sources are most effective with explicit conclusions, and low-credibility sources most effective with implicit conclusions), then an interaction effect (involving credibility and conclusion type) exists; the effect of one variable (conclusion type) depends on the level of another (credibility).

▨ TWO GENERAL PROBLEMS IN STUDYING PERSUASIVE EFFECTS

Two noteworthy general problems arise in investigating factors influencing the effectiveness of persuasive messages. One of these concerns the difficulty in making reliable generalizations about the effects of message types; the other concerns the task of defining independent variables in studies of persuasive effects.

Generalizing About Messages

The earlier description of experimental design might make it seem easy to arrive at generalizations about factors influencing persuasive effects. To compare the persuasive effects of (for example) explicit and implicit conclusions, one simply does an experiment of the sort previously described: Create two versions of a given message (one of each conclusion type), and see whether there is any difference in persuasive effect. Indeed, this is overwhelmingly the most common sort of experimental design used in studies of persuasive effects.

But this experimental design has important weaknesses, at least if one is interested in arriving at dependable generalizations about the persuasive effects of variations in message features (such as implicit vs. explicit conclusions). This design uses a single message to represent each general category (level, type) of the message variable. That is, one particular instance of an explicit-conclusion message and one particular instance of an implicit-conclusion message are compared. As Jackson and Jacobs (1983) pointed out, such single-message designs create two important barriers to generalization: One is that the design does not permit unambiguous causal attribution; the other is that the design is blind to the possibility that the effects of a given message factor may not be constant (uniform) across different messages (see also Jackson, 1992).

Ambiguous Causal Attribution. Although the logic of experimental research is designed to permit clear and unambiguous causal attribution, single-message experimental designs inevitably create some ambiguity concerning the cause of any observed differences. This ambiguity arises because manipulating the variable of interest (say, implicit vs. explicit conclusion) inevitably means also concomitantly manipulating other variables that are not of interest.

For example, suppose a researcher created the implicit- and explicit-conclusion messages in the following way. First, the explicit-conclusion message was written. Then, to create the implicit-conclusion message, the researcher simply eliminated the final paragraph (which contained the explicit conclusion). These two messages differ in conclusion type, but that is not the only thing that distinguishes the two messages. For one thing, the explicit-conclusion message is now longer than the implicit-conclusion message.

It is probably apparent what difficulty this poses for arriving at generalizations. If the persuasiveness of the two messages differ, how should that difference be explained? One's initial inclination might well be to interpret the differences as resulting from the type of conclusion used. But one could equally well suppose (given the evidence) that it was message length, not conclusion type, that created the difference. Worse, these are not the only two possibilities. The explicit-conclusion message might be more repetitive than the implicit-conclusion message, it might seem more insulting (because it says the obvious), or it might be more coherent or better organized, and so on. The problem is that one does not know whether conclusion type or some other variable leads to the observed difference in persuasiveness.

There is another way of expressing this same problem (concerning the ambiguities of causal attribution in single-message designs). To put it most generally: In a single-message design, the manipulation of a given message variable can be described in any number of ways, and, consequently, problems of causal attribution and generalization arise.

Consider, for example, the following experimental manipulation. Two persuasive messages are prepared arguing in favor of making the sale of cigarettes illegal. Both messages emphasize the harmful physical consequences of smoking and indeed are generally similar, except for the following sort of variation. Message A reads, "There can be no doubt that cigarette smoking produces harmful physical effects," whereas Message B reads, "Only an ignorant person would doubt that cigarette smoking produces harmful physical effects"; the statement in Message A, "It is therefore readily apparent that the country should pass legislation to make the sale of cigarettes illegal," is replaced in Message B by the statement, "Only the stupid or morally corrupt would oppose passage of legislation to make the sale of cigarettes illegal"; and so forth (with four such alterations in the messages).

What is the independent variable under investigation here? That is, how shall we describe this experimental manipulation? Framing some causal generalization will require that the difference between the two messages be expressed somehow—but exactly how?

As may already be apparent, there are many possible ways to capture the difference between Message A and Message B—and different researchers have described this manipulation in different ways. The original investigators (G. R. Miller & Baseheart, 1969) described this manipulation as a matter of "opinionated language" as opposed to "nonopinionated language," whereby the difference is that opinionated language, in addition to giving the source's views on the topic, also conveys the source's views concerning those who agree or disagree with the source. But Bradac, Bowers, and Courtright (1980) characterized this manipulation as varying "language intensity," which they define as the characteristic of language that indicates the degree to which the speaker's attitude toward a concept deviates from neutrality (pp. 200-201). Abelson (1986) cited this same manipulation as concerning the effects of having a "confident style in debating" (p. 227). McGuire (1985) treated this experimental manipulation under the general headings of "forcefulness of delivery" and "intensity of presentation" and described the experimental manipulation as comparing a "more dynamic style" with a "subdued style" (p. 270). Of course, not even these exhaust the possibilities. For instance, one could describe this as a contrast between extreme and mild (or nonexistent) denigration of those holding opposing views.

These different descriptions of the experimental manipulation could all be correct, but of course they are not identical. The phrases "confident debating style" and "extreme denigration of those holding opposing views" do not mean the same thing. Unfortunately, if one wishes to frame a causal generalization from research using this concrete experimental manipulation, one must choose some particular description. But which one? Given this single-message design, *all* the various interpretations are equally good—which is to say, researchers cannot make the sorts of unambiguous causal attributions we wished to achieve.

Nonuniform Effects of Message Variables. A second barrier to generalization created by single-message designs arises from the possibility (or probability) that the effect of a given message variable will not be uniform (constant) across all messages.

Consider again the example of a single-message study examining the effects of having implicit versus explicit conclusions. Suppose that this study found the explicit-conclusion message to be significantly more persuasive than the implicit-conclusion message (and let's overlook the problem of deciding that it was conclusion type, not some other factor, that was responsible for the difference). Should we conclude that having explicit conclusions will always improve the effectiveness of a message? Not necessarily. After all, there might have been something peculiar about the particular message that was studied (remember that only one message was used). Perhaps something (unnoticed by the researchers) made that particular message especially hospitable to having an explicit conclusion—maybe the topic, maybe the way the rest of the message was organized, or maybe the nature of the arguments that were made. Other messages might not be so hospitable to explicit conclusions.

To put that point more abstractly: The effect of a given message variable may not be uniform across messages. Some messages might be helped a lot by having an explicit conclusion, some helped only a little, and some even hurt by it. But if that is true, then (obviously) looking at the effects of conclusion type on a single message does not really provide a good basis for drawing a general conclusion. So, once again, the typical single-message design used in persuasion effects research creates an obstacle to dependable message generalization because it overlooks the possibility of nonuniform effects across messages.[1]

Designing Future Persuasion Research. It has probably already occurred to the reader that there is a straightforward way of dealing with these two obstacles to dependable message generalization. Because those two obstacles arise from the use of a single message to represent an entire category of messages, the straightforward solution is to use multiple messages to represent each category (Jackson & Jacobs, 1983). For example, a study of implicit versus explicit conclusions would want to have many instances of each message type (multiple instances of explicit-conclusion messages and corresponding multiple instances of implicit-conclusion messages), with as much variation within a category as one could achieve (variation in topic, organization, length, etc.). (For discussion of multiple-message versus single-message designs, see Bradac, 1983; Hewes, 1983; Hunter, Hamilton, & Allen, 1989; Jackson, O'Keefe, & Jacobs, 1988; Jackson, O'Keefe, Jacobs, & Brashers, 1989; Morley, 1988a, 1988b; O'Keefe, Jackson, & Jacobs, 1988; relatedly, see G. L. Wells & Windschitl, 1999.)

With such a multiple-message design, the possibility of nonuniform effects across messages is acknowledged. There is no presumption that the effect of conclusion type will be constant across messages; on the contrary, the design may permit the detection of variation in the effect that conclusion type has across messages. And the chances for unambiguous causal attribution are improved by such a design: Given the variation within the set of messages for a given conclusion type, the researcher can rule out alternative explanations and be more confident in attributing observed differences to the sort of conclusion used.[2]

Beyond the desirability of using multiple-message designs, the generalization problems associated with single-message designs also have implications for how experimental messages are constructed in persuasion research. A number of complex considerations bear on the question of how to construct (or obtain) experimental messages, and the discussion here does not attempt to be a complete one (for more extensive treatments, see Bradac, 1986; Jackson, 1992, pp. 131-149; Jackson, 1993; Jackson & Jacobs, 1983). But a sense of the relevant implications can be obtained by focusing on one particular research practice: the practice of using the same experimental messages more than once.

The problem of generalizing about message types from individual messages would be serious enough if each investigation of persuasive message effects used only one message to represent each message type (category), but with a different concrete message used in each study (so that, for example, every investigation of implicit versus explicit conclusions used only one instance of each type, but every investigation created a new instance of each type). But the problem is worse because occasionally the same messages are used more than once in persuasion research (consider, e.g., Pratkanis, Greenwald, Ronis, Leippe, & Baumgardner, 1986). For example, related messages were used by Holbrook (1978) and Venkatraman,

Marlino, Kardes, and Sklar (1990); by Burnkrant and Howard (1984), Petty, Cacioppo, and Heesacker (1981), and Swasy and Munch (1985); by B. T. Johnson (1994), Petty and Cacioppo (1979b, 1984), Solomon, Greenberg, Psyczynski, and Pryzbylinski (1995), and Sorrentino, Bobocel, Gitta, Olson, and Hewitt (1988); by Kamins and Assael (1987a, 1987b) and Kamins and Marks (1987); and by Wood (1982), Wood and Kallgren (1988), and Wood et al. (1985).

This practice is readily understandable. First, the task of creating satisfactory experimental materials is difficult and time-consuming, and if existing messages already represent the variables of interest, then it can be awfully tempting to employ those materials. Second, in a continuing line of research, a desire for tight experimental control may suggest the reuse of earlier messages. For instance, if a researcher wishes to do a follow-up experiment that investigates the effect of adding some new independent variable to an earlier research design, then the researcher may well want to maximize the comparability of the two investigations. As a means of ensuring such comparability (and thus—in keeping with the general idea behind experimental research—ensuring unambiguous causal inference), the researcher will naturally be led to use the same messages to ruling out one possible source of influence on the results.

But this way of proceeding is, in the end, unsatisfactory, precisely because it complicates, rather than eases, the task of obtaining sound causal generalizations. It complicates this task because single-message instantiations are an unsatisfactory basis for generalizations about message types.[3] Worse, research experience shows that reusing a message may well not provide the hoped-for gain in inferential ability. More than one investigator has reused a set of messages only to find that even under conditions comparable (if not apparently virtually identical) with those in the earlier studies, the messages do not produce the same effects (compare, e.g., Experiments 2 and 3 in M. Burgoon, Jones, & Stewart, 1975; Experiments 1 and 2 in Shepherd & B. J. O'Keefe, 1984). Findings of this sort certainly underscore just how complicated an affair persuasive communication is, but they also suggest that the experimental control gained by reusing messages may be less substantial than one might have thought (cf. Hunter & Hamilton, 1998, pp. 44-45).

Interpreting Past Persuasion Research. Employing multiple-message designs (and avoiding reusing experimental messages) may help future researchers avoid the message generalization problems created by single-message designs, but a great deal of earlier persuasion effects research relied on single-message designs. How should such research be interpreted?

Obviously, any individual single-message study should be interpreted cautiously. The interpretive difficulties created by single-message designs are such that one cannot confidently make broad generalizations from a single study using such a design.

But if several single-message studies address the same research question, then some greater confidence may be warranted. If 10 investigations compare explicit and implicit conclusions, and each one has a different single example of each message category, a review that considers the body of studies taken as a whole can transcend this limitation of the individual investigations and provide a sounder basis for generalization.

The development of statistical techniques for meta-analysis is particularly noteworthy here. Broadly, meta-analysis is a family of quantitative techniques for summarizing the results obtained in a number of separate research studies. Using meta-analytic techniques, a researcher can systematically examine the different effects obtained in separate investigations, combine these separate studies to yield a picture of the overall results obtained, look for variations among the results of different studies, and so on (for a general introduction, see Rosenthal, 1991; for a single comprehensive source, see H. Cooper & Hedges, 1994). Obviously, meta-analysis offers the possibility of overcoming some of the limitations of existing persuasion research using single-message designs. Meta-analysis is not easy to do, and there are disagreements about the desirability, legitimacy, and appropriateness of certain meta-analytic procedures (for examples of discussion, see Erez, Bloom, & Wells, 1996; Hedges & Olkin, 1985; Hedges & Vevea, 1998; B. T. Johnson, Mullen, & Salas, 1995; O'Keefe, 1991, 1999c; Schmidt & Hunter, 1999).[4] Nevertheless, meta-analytic techniques provide an especially attractive way of summarizing existing persuasion effects research (see, e.g., Allen & Preiss, 1998).[5]

Beyond Message Variables. This discussion has focused on the message-generalizing problems associated with single-message designs. These problems are especially salient for persuasion researchers because (despite widespread interest in generalizing across messages) single-message designs have been the norm for studies of persuasive effects (but see Brashers & Jackson, 1999). Of course, the same general considerations apply not just to message factors but to anything; dependable generalizations about a collection of things (messages, people, tables, and so on) commonly require multiple instances of the class. There is, that is, nothing unique about these problems of message generalization (as noted by Bradac, 1983). But some focused attention to matters of message generalization is important, if only because single-message designs have so frequently been employed in the search for generalizations about persuasive effects.

Variable Definition

The other noteworthy problem that occurs in studying persuasive effects might be labeled the variable definition problem because it concerns how independent variables are defined in research practice. Because this problem arises most clearly in the context of defining message variables (that is, message variations or message types), the following discussion focuses on such variables; as will be seen, however, the difficulties that ensue are not limited to message variables.

Message Features Versus Observed Effects. Broadly put, a message variable can be defined in one of two ways: as intrinsic message features or as observed effects on recipients. Most message variables have been defined as message features (as one might expect), but occasionally investigators have defined message types not as message features but rather as engendered recipient responses (that is, the effects observed in message receivers). Because these two ways of defining message variations are consequentially different, the distinction is an important one.

A useful example is provided by the extensive research on fear appeals in persuasive messages. A fear appeal is a particular type of persuasive message, but it has been defined in varying ways. Some investigators define a fear appeal as a message that contains certain sorts of message content (e.g., graphic depictions of consequences of not following the communicator's recommendations, as in gruesome films of traffic accidents in driver education classes). But for other investigators, a fear appeal message is one that arouses fear or anxiety in message recipients (that is, fear appeal is defined by the responses of message receivers).

Obviously, these two definitions will not necessarily correspond. That is, a message that contains gruesome content (a fear appeal by the first definition) might not arouse fear or anxiety in message recipients (i.e., might not be a fear appeal by the second definition); similarly, a message might succeed in arousing fear without containing graphic message content. Neither of these two ways of defining fear appeal is the correct way. There is no "correct" way to define fear appeal (or any other message variation). One can define message types however one likes, so long as one is clear. But it *is* important to be clear about the distinction.

The Importance of the Distinction. It is important to be clear about the different ways of defining message variables (by reference to message features or by reference to effects) because the distinction makes a difference—indeed, it makes several differences.

First, generalizations about message types can only cautiously lump to-gether investigations that employ different ways of defining a given vari-able. Two studies might call themselves studies of fear appeals, but if one defines fear appeal by message content whereas the other defines it by re-cipient response, it may be difficult to draw reliable generalizations that en-compass the two studies.

Second, the different ways of defining message types raise different evi-dentiary issues concerning the soundness of experimental manipulations. Consider that to construct defensible examples of fear appeal messages for use in research, an investigator who defines fear appeal by the presence of certain sorts of message contents need only ensure that the messages do contain the requisite sort of content. By contrast, to have satisfactory in-stances of fear appeal messages, an investigator who defines fear appeal by the engendered audience response must show that the messages engender the required responses.

Third, the different ways of defining message types make for differential immediate utility of research findings for persuaders. Research using mes-sage variation definitions that are based on message features can give obvi-ous direct advice for persuaders concerning the construction of persuasive messages ("Put features X, Y, and Z in your message"), whereas definitions based on effects are likely to be much less helpful ("Do something that en-genders such-and-such effects").

The extended example in this discussion of the problem of variable defi-nition has been that of a particular message variable (fear appeals), al-though other message variables—most notably, the variable of argument strength that figures prominently in elaboration likelihood model research (discussed in Chapter 6)—could have served as well (e.g., Jourdan, 1999). But these issues of variable definition are not limited to message factors. For example, communicator credibility could be defined by observed per-suasive effects (so that, by definition, higher credibility would be associated with greater persuasion) or by other criteria (such as receivers' impressions of the source's believability, expertise, honesty, and the like; see Chapter 8).

Summary. The task of defining independent variables (and especially message variables) in studies of persuasive effects thus raises matters of some delicacy. If an independent variable is defined by the effects it has (at-titude change effects, fear arousal effects, etc.), then it becomes necessarily true that that variable has those effects; a failure of an experimental instantiation of the variable to produce the effects can be interpreted only as a failure to successfully manipulate the variable in question. But if an in-dependent variable is defined in ways that make it conceptually independent of its effects, then a failure to produce expected effects is to be interpreted differently. Neither way of defining independent variables is intrinsically better, but noticing the difference between them (and grasping the implications of the difference) is important.

▨ NOTES

1. Indeed, variability (that is, nonuniformity) in persuasion effects is not just an abstract possibility. Examination of research areas containing multiple studies of the persuasive effects of a given variable (that is, multiple estimates of the size of the variable's effect) suggests that such variability is common and substantial; in such collections of studies, it is rare for the mean size of the effect to be larger than the standard deviation and common for the variability to be twice or three times as large as might be expected given sampling error (O'Keefe, 1999c).

2. It's not enough just to have multiple messages; an appropriate statistical analysis is also required. For a general treatment of these matters, see Jackson (1992); for additional discussion, see M. Burgoon, Hall, and Pfau (1991); Jackson (1991); Jackson and Brashers (1994); Jackson, Brashers, and Massey (1992); Jackson, O'Keefe, and Brashers (1994); and Slater (1991). For discussion of such issues in other research contexts, see H. H. Clark (1973); Fontenelle, Phillips, and Lane (1985); Raaijmakers, Schrijnemakers, and Gremmen (1999); and Richter and Seay (1987).

3. Meta-analytic techniques (discussed shortly) are of little help (as a means of coping with message generalization problems) when the same message is used repeatedly as the instantiation of a message type. Instead of being able to accumulate research results across a large number of versions of the message type in question, a meta-analyst could accumulate research results across only the same concrete messages; the problems of message generalization would remain.

4. Many of the issues concerning the statistical treatment of multiple-message (or, more generally, replicated) designs—as discussed in the references cited in note 2 above—arise in a meta-analytic context as well (see Hedges & Vevea, 1998; Jackson, 1991, 1992).

5. Apart from any other virtues, meta-analysis naturally draws attention to effect sizes, rather than to simple statistical significance. Although null hypothesis significance testing (NHST) has come in for some sharp criticism (see, e.g., Hunter, 1997; Schmidt & Hunter, 1997), at least some of the problems appear to stem from misapprehensions and misapplications of NHST. That is, NHST itself can have a useful role to play (Abelson, 1997; Mulaik, Raju, & Harshman, 1997; Nickerson, 2000), although clearer understandings of statistical significance (and effect size, power, and so forth) are very much to be wished (see J. Cohen, 1990, 1994). In addition, meta-analysis can naturally encourage conceiving of message effects in terms of the effect size distribution (with some mean and variance) associated with a given variable (see Brashers & Jackson, 1999).

Source Factors   8

P ersuasion researchers have quite naturally focused considerable research attention on the question of how various characteristics of the communicator influence the outcomes of the communicator's persuasive efforts. This chapter's review of such research is focused on two particular communicator characteristics—the communicator's credibility and likability—but concludes with a discussion of other source factors, including the communicator's similarity to the audience.

COMMUNICATOR CREDIBILITY

The Dimensions of Credibility

Credibility (or, more carefully expressed, perceived credibility) consists of the judgments made by a perceiver (e.g., a message recipient) concerning the believability of a communicator. Communicator credibility is thus not an intrinsic property of a communicator; a message source may be thought highly credible by one perceiver and not at all credible by another. But this general notion of credibility has been given a somewhat more careful specification in investigations aimed at identifying the basic underlying dimensions of credibility.

Factor-Analytic Research. There have been quite a few factor-analytic studies of the dimensions underlying credibility judgments (e.g., Andersen, 1961; Applbaum & Anatol, 1972, 1973; Baudhuin & Davis, 1972; Berlo, Lemert, & Mertz, 1969; Bowers & Phillips, 1967; Falcione, 1974; Markham, 1968; McCroskey, 1966; Schweitzer & Ginsburg, 1966). In the most common research design in these investigations, re-spondents rate communication sources on a large number of scales. In a few investigations, these scales represent the most frequently mentioned characteristics appearing in previously collected free-response descriptions given of high- and low-credibility communicators (e.g., Berlo et al., 1969; Schweitzer & Ginsburg, 1966), but more commonly, the set of scales used is composed of previously employed items with perhaps some new scales included as well (e.g., Baudhuin & Davis, 1972; Falcione, 1974). The rat-ings given of the sources are then submitted to factor analysis, a statistical procedure that (broadly put) groups the scales on the basis of their intercorrelations: Scales that are comparatively highly intercorrelated will be grouped together as indicating some underlying "factor" or dimension.

Critical discussion of this research has focused especially on the proce-dures for initially selecting scales, the frequent absence of a context within which communicators are to be rated by respondents, the problems of rater-scale and concept-scale interactions, and the criteria for identifying and labeling transsituationally stable factors (see, e.g., Cronkhite & Liska, 1976; Delia, 1976; Hensley, 1974; Infante, 1980; Lewis, 1974; Liska, 1978; McCroskey & Young, 1981; McLaughlin, 1975; Steinfatt, 1974; Tucker, 1971). And at least on the surface, there appears to be substantial variation in the factor structures that have emerged (compare, e.g., Berlo et al., 1969, with Schweitzer & Ginsburg, 1966). At the same time, when there are differences in the sets of initial scales used, the sets of sources rated, the instructions given to raters, and the particular factor-analytic procedures followed—and all these differences do appear in the litera-ture—then perhaps one should not be surprised that differing factor struc-tures have been found.

Expertise and Trustworthiness as Dimensions of Credibility. Without overlooking potential weaknesses in this research or the variations in ob-tained factor structures, one may nevertheless say that with some fre-quency, two broad (and sensible) dimensions have commonly emerged in factor-analytic investigations of communicator credibility. These are vari-ously labeled in the literature, but two useful terms are expertise and trust-worthiness.

The expertise dimension (sometimes called "competence," "expert-ness," "authoritativeness," or "qualification") is commonly represented by scales such as experienced-inexperienced, informed-uninformed, trained-untrained, qualified-unqualified, skilled-unskilled, intelligent-unintelligent, and expert-not expert. These items all seem directed at the assessment of (roughly) whether the communicator is in a position to *know* the truth, to know what is right or correct. Three or more of these scales are reported as loading on a common factor in investigations by Applbaum and Anatol (1972); Baudhuin and Davis (1972); Beatty and Behnke (1980); Beatty and Kruger (1978); Berlo et al. (1969); Bowers and Phillips (1967); Falcione (1974); Hickson, Powell, Hill, Holt, and Flick (1979); McCroskey (1966); Miles and Leathers (1984); Pearce and Brommel (1972); Schweitzer and Ginsburg (1966); and Tuppen (1974). And (as these factor-analytic results would indicate) measures of perceived expertise that are composed of several such items commonly exhibit high internal reliability (for example, reliability coefficients of .85 or greater have been reported by Beatty & Behnke, 1980; Bell, Zahn, & Hopper, 1984; McCroskey, 1966).

The trustworthiness dimension (sometimes called "character," "safety," or "personal integrity") is commonly represented by scales such as honest-dishonest, trustworthy-untrustworthy, open-minded-closed-minded, just-unjust, fair-unfair, and unselfish-selfish. These items all appear to be related to the assessment of (roughly) whether the communicator will likely be inclined to *tell* the truth as he or she sees it. Three or more of these scales are reported as loading on a common factor in investigations by Applbaum and Anatol (1972), Baudhuin and Davis (1972), Berlo et al. (1969), Falcione (1974), Schweitzer and Ginsburg (1966), Tuppen (1974), and Whitehead (1968). Correspondingly, indices of perceived trustworthiness that are composed of several such items have displayed high internal reliability (for example, reliabilities of .80 or better have been reported by Bradley, 1981; Tuppen, 1974).[1]

These two dimensions parallel what have been described as the two types of communicator bias that message recipients might perceive: knowledge bias and reporting bias. "Knowledge bias refers to a recipient's belief that a communicator's knowledge about external reality is nonveridical, and reporting bias refers to the belief that a communicator's willingness to convey an accurate version of external reality is compromised" (Eagly, Wood, & Chaiken, 1978, p. 424; see also Eagly, Wood, & Chaiken, 1981). A communicator perceived as having a knowledge bias will presumably be viewed as relatively less expert; a communicator viewed as having a reporting bias will presumably be seen as comparatively less trustworthy.

Perhaps it is not surprising that both expertise and trustworthiness emerge as basic dimensions of credibility because as a rule, only the conjunction of expertise and trustworthiness makes for reliable communications. A communicator who knows what is correct (has expertise) but who nevertheless misleads the audience (is untrustworthy, has a reporting bias) produces messages that are unreliable guides to belief and action, just as does the sincere (trustworthy) but uninformed (low-expertise, knowledge-biased) communicator.

These two dimensions, however, represent only the most general sorts of credibility-relevant judgments made by recipients about communicators. As a number of researchers (e.g., S. W. King, 1976; Liska, 1978) have indicated, the particular judgments underlying credibility may vary from circumstance to circumstance, as can the emphasis placed on one or another dimension of judgment. Thus it may be useful to develop credibility assessments tailored to particular situations (for some examples, see Frewer, Howard, Hedderley, & Shepherd, 1996; Gaziano & McGrath, 1986; Lagace & Gassenheimer, 1991; Ohanian, 1990; West, 1994).

Factors Influencing Credibility Judgments

Judgments of a communicator's expertise and trustworthiness are surely influenced by a great many factors, and it is fair to say that research to date leaves us rather far from a comprehensive picture of the determinants of these judgments. For the most part, as will be seen, researchers have focused on the effects that message or delivery characteristics have on credibility judgments (as opposed to the effect of, say, information about the communicator's training), perhaps because these characteristics are more nearly under the immediate control of the communicator.[2]

Education, Occupation, and Experience. Although little systematic research investigates exactly how credibility judgments are influenced by information about the communicator's training, experience, and occupation, precisely these characteristics are the ones most frequently manipulated by investigators in experimental studies of the effects of variations in communicator credibility. That is, a researcher who wishes to compare the effects of a high-credibility source with those of a low-credibility source will most commonly manipulate the receiver's perception of the communicator's credibility by varying the information given about the communicator's education, occupation, experience, and the like. For instance, a study of messages about nuclear radiation protection described the high-credibility communicator as "a professor of nuclear research, recognized as a national authority on the biological effects of radioactivity," whereas the low-credibility introduction described the source as "a high school sophomore, whose information was based on a term paper prepared for a social studies class" (Hewgill & Miller, 1965, p. 96).

Similar manipulations are commonplace, and researchers commonly confirm the success of these manipulations by assessing respondents' judgments of the communicators' expertise and trustworthiness. As one might expect, such high-credibility introductions do indeed generally lead receivers to perceive the source as more trustworthy and (particularly) more expert than do low-credibility introductions. What systematic research exists on this matter is (perhaps not surprisingly) consistent with these effects. Receiver judgments of communicator trustworthiness and (especially) expertise have been found to be significantly influenced by information concerning the communicator's occupation, training, amount of experience, and the like (e.g., Hurwitz, Miron, & Johnson, 1992; Ostermeier, 1967; Swenson, Nash, & Roos, 1984).

Nonfluencies in Delivery. There have been a number of investigations of how variations in delivery can influence the credibility judgments made of a speaker. Unfortunately, several of these studies have investigated conceptions of delivery that embrace a number of behavioral features (e.g., Pearce, 1971; Pearce & Brommel, 1972; Pearce & Conklin, 1971). Bowers (1965), for example, compared two speaking styles: One (the "extroverted" delivery style) used rapid, highly fluent speech with negligible pauses, appropriate vocal emphasis, and varied voice quality; the other (the "introverted" delivery style) was less rapid, contained pauses and nonfluencies, emphasized inappropriate words, and had little vocal variety. Obviously, when a construct (such as introverted vs. extroverted delivery style) is defined as a complex of behavioral features, one cannot easily determine just which feature (or set of features) is responsible for any observed effects.[3]

But one delivery characteristic that has been studied in isolation is the occurrence of nonfluencies in the delivery of oral communications. Nonfluencies include vocalized pauses ("uh, uh"), the superfluous repetition of words or sounds, corrections of slips of the tongue, articulation difficulties, and the like. Several investigations have found that with increasing numbers of nonfluencies, speakers are rated significantly lower on expertise, with judgments of trustworthiness typically unaffected (J. K. Burgoon, Birk, & Pfau, 1990; Engstrom, 1994; McCroskey & Mehrley, 1969; G. R. Miller & Hewgill, 1964; Schliesser, 1968; Sereno & Hawkins, 1967).

Speaking Rate. Another delivery characteristic whose effect on credibility perceptions has been investigated is speaking rate. There is a substantial range of possible "normal" speaking rates, and the research question that has arisen is how variations within this range might influence judgments of the communicator's credibility (which is different from asking about the effect of abnormally fast or abnormally slow speaking rates). In two investigations, N. Miller, Maruyama, Beaber, and Valone (1976) found that increasing speaking rates led to significantly greater perceived knowledgeability, intelligence, and objectivity, but this finding is unusual; most other investigators have reported that judgments of expertise and trustworthiness are not dependably affected by speaking rate (Addington, 1971; Gundersen & Hopper, 1976, Study 1; Woodall & Burgoon, 1983). Indeed, not even the direction of effect is consistent across these investigations (for instance, faster speech was found to be nonsignificantly associated with lower perceived expertise and trustworthiness by Addington, 1971). Whatever effects that speaking rate has on credibility, then, those effects are not straightforward.

The speaking rate investigations discussed thus far have all manipulated speaking rate by natural means—having a speaker record a message several times, varying the rate. With natural speech, as speaking rate increases, other vocal characteristics commonly change as well (such as pitch, intonation, and fluency). Using mechanical means called time compression, however, it is possible to alter rate without these other changes. Results of time compression studies are of interest both theoretically (because they offer the prospect of examining the effects of varied rate independent of other factors) and practically (because mechanical alteration of speech, although obviously not useful in face-to-face persuasion settings, could be employed in, for example, radio advertising). As with the work on naturally induced rate variations, however, there is some inconsistency in the research findings concerning the effects of time compression on credibility judgments; the safest conclusion seems to be that time compression does not reliably yield enhanced judgments of expertise or trustworthiness and indeed, under some circumstances, may even significantly reduce perceived expertise and trustworthiness (MacLachlan, 1982; Wheeless, 1971; see also Hausknecht & Moore, 1986; Lautman & Dean, 1983).[4]

Citation of Evidence Sources. Persuaders commonly include evidence in their persuasive messages, that is, relevant facts, opinions, information, and the like, intended to support the persuader's claims. Several investigations have studied how citing the sources of such evidence—as opposed to providing only vague documentation ("Studies show that") or no documentation at all—influences perceived communicator credibility. On the whole, a communicator's citation of the sources of evidence appears to enhance perceptions of the communicator's expertise and trustworthiness, although these effects are sometimes small (e.g., Fleshler, Ilardo, & Demoretcky, 1974; McCroskey, 1967, 1969, 1970; Ostermeier, 1967; Whitehead,

1971; for reviews and discussion, see O'Keefe, 1998; Reinard, 1988, 1998). These investigations employed relevant supporting materials that were attributed (when source citations were provided) to high-credibility sources. One should not expect enhanced communicator credibility to result from citations to low-credibility evidence sources or from citations for poor or irrelevant evidence (Luchok & McCroskey, 1978; Warren, 1969). But the citation of expert and trustworthy sources of evidence in the message appears to influence the communicator's perceived expertise and trustworthiness; in a sense, the high credibility of the cited sources seems to rub off on the communicator.[5]

Position Advocated. The position that the communicator advocates on the persuasive issue can influence perceptions of the communicator's expertise and trustworthiness. Specifically, a communicator is likely to be perceived as more expert and more trustworthy if the advocated position disconfirms the audience's expectations about the communicator's views (when such expectations derive from knowledge of the source's characteristics or circumstances), although certain sorts of trustworthiness judgments (concerning objectivity, open-mindedness, and unbiasedness) appear to be more affected than others (such as sincerity and honesty).

The most straightforward examples of this phenomenon are communicators who argue for positions that are apparently opposed to their own self-interest. Ordinarily, of course, we expect persons to take positions that forward their own interests; sources who support views opposed to their interests thus disconfirm our expectations. If we wonder why a source is taking this (apparently unusual) position, we may well be led to conclude that the communicator must be especially well-informed (expert) and honest (trustworthy): The source must really know the truth and must really be willing to tell the truth, otherwise why would the source be advocating that position? Thus the chemical engineer who testifies that her company's plant was not safely designed, the military officer who argues that defense appropriations should be reduced—these are communicators who, by virtue of the positions they advocate, may be perceived as especially expert and trustworthy.

An empirical demonstration of this phenomenon was provided in several studies in which receivers were presented with messages arguing for either more or less power for courts and prosecutors; these messages were depicted as coming from either a prosecutor or a convicted criminal. Obviously, some of these source-message combinations represent sources arguing for positions that are in their own interest (e.g., the criminal arguing that court power should be restricted), whereas other combinations represent communicators apparently arguing against their own interests (e.g., prosecutors suggesting that prosecutorial powers be reduced). Those communicators arguing for positions opposed to their own interests were perceived as more expert and trustworthy than when they advocated views that favored their self-interests (Walster, Aronson, & Abrahams, 1966).[6]

Of course, receivers' expectations about the position that a communicator will express can derive from sources other than the ordinary presumption that people will favor viewpoints that are in their own interest. A general analysis of the bases of premessage expectancies (and their effects on perceived credibility and persuasive outcomes) has been provided by Eagly et al. (1981). As briefly mentioned earlier, Eagly et al. (1981) distinguished two sorts of communicator bias that receivers can recognize and can use to form premessage expectancies about the communicator's position. One is knowledge bias, which refers to the receiver's belief that the communicator's knowledge of relevant information is somehow biased (perhaps because of the source's background or experience) and thus that the source's message will not accurately reflect reality. The other is reporting bias, which refers to the receiver's belief that a communicator may not be willing to accurately convey relevant information (for instance, because situational pressures might lead the source to withhold or distort information). A receiver's perception of either sort of communicator bias will lead the receiver to have certain expectations about the position that a communicator will express on the issue (and, correspondingly, will provide the receiver with an explanation of why the communicator adopts that position). For example, we naturally expect that a lifelong Democrat will speak in favor of a Democratic political candidate (because of knowledge bias) and that a speaker speaking about gun control legislation to a meeting of the National Rifle Association will likely oppose such legislation (because of reporting bias); when such expectations are confirmed, we have ready explanations for why the communicators acted as they did.

But when a communicator advocates a position that violates an expectancy based on knowledge or reporting bias, the receiver faces the task of explaining why the communicator is defending the advocated position—why the lifelong Democrat is speaking in support of a Republican candidate or why the speaker addressing the National Rifle Association is urging stricter gun control legislation. The most plausible explanation at least sometimes will be that the facts of the matter were so compelling that the communicator was led to override those personal or situational pressures (that had generated the receiver's expectations) and thus defend the advocated position. Correspondingly, the receiver may be led to perceive the communicator as especially expert and trustworthy, precisely because the communicator's expressed position violates the receiver's expectations. Indeed, several investigations have yielded results consistent with this analysis

(Eagly & Chaiken, 1975; Eagly et al., 1978; Wood & Eagly, 1981; see also L. Anderson, 1970; Peters, Covello, & McCallum, 1997).

A related expectancy disconfirmation effect has been observed in studies of advertisements for consumer products. Ordinarily, consumers expect advertisements to tout the advertised product or brand as "the best" on *every* feature or characteristic that is mentioned. Thus (to use an example from R. E. Smith & Hunt, 1978) an advertisement for exterior house paint that claimed that the product was superior to its competitors on only three mentioned product features (durability, number of coats needed, and ease of cleanup) while being equal on two others (number of colors available and nonspill lip on container) would disconfirm receivers' expectations about the message's contents (particularly by contrast to an advertisement claiming that the product was superior on each of these five features). There have been several experimental comparisons of these two types of advertisements—an advertisement suggesting superiority for all the mentioned features of the product (a one-sided advertisement), as opposed to an advertisement that acknowledges (and does not refute or deny) some ways in which the product is not superior (a nonrefutational two-sided advertisement). As one might suppose, when an advertisement acknowledges ways in which competing products are just as good as the advertised product (or acknowledges weaknesses of the advertised product), the ad is commonly perceived as more credible than when the ad claims superiority on every product feature that is mentioned (e.g., Alden & Crowley, 1995a; Kamins & Marks, 1988; Pechmann, 1992; for a review, see O'Keefe, 1999a).[7]

One final point concerning the effects of expectancy disconfirmation on perceived credibility: Although expectancy disconfirmation can enhance perceptions of the communicator's expertise and trustworthiness, the communicator likely to be perceived as the most expert and trustworthy may be a qualified source about whom the audience has *no* expectations so far as message position is concerned. This is suggested by an investigation in which receivers heard either a prolabor or an antilabor message (on the topic of whether labor unions make a significant contribution to inflation) attributed to one of three sources: a labor leader, a management leader, or a university professor of economics. Although premessage expectancies were not assessed in this investigation, one is surely on safe ground thinking that (for example) the labor leader would be expected to offer a prolabor message (arguing that unions do not significantly increase inflation). Thus receivers heard either "biased testimony" (the labor leader with the prolabor message or the management leader with the antilabor message), "reluctant testimony" (the labor leader with the antilabor message or the management leader with the prolabor message), or "unbiased testimony" (the economics professor with either message). As one might suppose, the results indicated that perceptions of expertise and trustworthiness tended to be greater under conditions of reluctant testimony (the expectancy disconfirmation conditions) than under conditions of biased testimony (the expectancy confirmation conditions). But the circumstance that seemed to lead to the greatest perceived expertise and trustworthiness was the unbiased testimony condition, in which presumably the audience had no more than minimal premessage expectancies about the position to be advocated (Arnold & McCroskey, 1967). Thus in a given circumstance, the communicator most likely to be perceived as most expert and trustworthy may be the well-qualified source about whom the audience has few expectations so far as message position is concerned.[8]

Liking for the Communicator. Some indirect evidence indicates that the receiver's liking for the communicator can influence judgments of the communicator's trustworthiness, although not judgments of the communicator's expertise. This evidence, derived from factor-analytic investigations of credibility judgments, is the finding that various general evaluation items often load on the same factor as do trustworthiness scales. For example, items such as friendly-unfriendly, pleasant-unpleasant, nice-not nice, and valuable-worthless have been reported as loading on a common factor with such trustworthiness items as honest-dishonest, trustworthy-untrustworthy, unselfish-selfish, and just-unjust (see, e.g., Applbaum & Anatol, 1972; Bowers & Phillips, 1967; Falcione, 1974; McCroskey, 1966; Pearce & Brommel, 1972). This suggests that liking and trustworthiness judgments are probably more likely to covary than are liking and expertise judgments. Such a pattern of results surely makes good sense: One's general liking for a communicator is much more likely to influence one's judgments about the communicator's dispositional trustworthiness (the communicator's general honesty, fairness, open-mindedness, and the like) than it is to influence one's judgments about the communicator's expertise (experience, training, etc.) on some particular topic or subject matter.[9]

Humor. Including humor in persuasive messages has been found to have rather varied effects on perceptions of the communicator. When positive effects of humor are found, they tend to most directly involve enhancement of the audience's liking for the communicator—and thus occasionally the trustworthiness of the communicator (because liking and trustworthiness are associated)—but rarely judgments of expertise (Chang & Gruner, 1981; Gruner, 1967, 1970; Gruner & Lampton, 1972; Tamborini & Zillmann, 1981). The use of humor, however, can also decrease the audience's liking for the communicator, the perceived trustworthiness of the communicator, and even the perceived expertise of the source (Bryant, Brown, Silberberg, & Elliott, 1981; Munn & Gruner, 1981; P. M. Taylor, 1974); these negative effects seem most likely to obtain when the humor is perceived as excessive or inappropriate for the context. Small amounts of appropriate humor thus may have small enhancing effects on perceived trustworthiness but are unlikely to affect assessments of the communicator's expertise.

Effects of Credibility

What effects do variations in communicator credibility have on persuasive outcomes? It might be thought that the answer to this question is pretty simple: As one's credibility increases, so will one's effectiveness. But the answer turns out to be much more complicated.

Two Initial Clarifications. Two preliminary clarifications need to be made concerning the research on the effects of communicator credibility. The first is that in this research, the two primary dimensions of credibility (expertise and trustworthiness) are usually not separately manipulated. That is, the research commonly compares a source that is relatively high in both expertise and trustworthiness (the high-credibility source) with a source that is relatively low in both (the low-credibility source).

Obviously, because expertise and trustworthiness are conceptually distinct aspects of credibility, it would be possible to manipulate these separately and so examine their separate effects on persuasive outcomes. One could, for instance, compare the effectiveness of a source high in expertise but low in trustworthiness with that of a source low in expertise but high in trustworthiness.

Overwhelmingly, however, expertise and trustworthiness have not been independently manipulated in investigations of credibility's effects. There have been a few efforts at disentangling the effects of expertise and trustworthiness (e.g., McGinnies & Ward, 1980; Mowen, Wiener, & Joag, 1987; O'Hara, Netemeyer, & Burton, 1991; Wiener & Mowen, 1986), but to date no clear generalizations seem possible.[10] The point, thus, of this first clarification is to emphasize the limits of current research on credibility's effects: This research concerns credibility generally, rather than the different dimensions of credibility individually.[11]

The second preliminary clarification concerns the nature of the low-credibility sources in this research: The low-credibility sources are not low in absolute terms but simply relatively low in credibility. In absolute terms, the low-credibility communicators are probably accurately described as no better than moderate in credibility.[12] Several researchers have remarked that it is difficult to create believable experimental manipulations that will consistently yield credibility ratings that are low in absolute terms (Greenberg & Miller, 1966; Sternthal, Dholakia, & Leavitt, 1978).[13] Thus although this discussion (like most in the literature) will be cast as a matter of the differential persuasive effectiveness of high- as opposed to low-credibility communicators, the comparison made in the relevant research is nearly always between a relatively higher-credibility communicator and a relatively lower one, not necessarily between two sources that are in absolute terms high and low in credibility.

With these preliminaries out of the way, we can now turn to a consideration of just how variations in communicator credibility influence persuasive effectiveness. The effects of credibility on persuasive outcomes are not completely straightforward but depend centrally on other factors. These factors can be usefully divided into two general categories: factors that influence the magnitude of credibility's effects and factors that influence the direction of credibility's effects.

Influences on the Magnitude of Effect. The size of the effect that communicator credibility has on persuasive outcomes is not constant but varies from one circumstance to another. Researchers have identified at least two factors that affect just how consequential a role communicator credibility plays in persuasion.

The first is the degree of direct personal relevance that the issue has for the receiver. As the issue becomes more personally relevant for the receiver, variations in the source's credibility make less difference; under conditions of low personal relevance, the communicator's credibility may make a great deal of difference to the outcome, whereas on highly relevant topics, the source's credibility may have little impact (see, e.g., H. H. Johnson & Scileppi, 1969; Petty, Cacioppo, & Goldman, 1981; Rhine & Severance, 1970; for a review, see E. J. Wilson & Sherrell, 1993).[14]

In some ways, it may seem paradoxical that as an issue becomes more personally relevant for a receiver, the source's expertise and trustworthiness become less important. But this relationship may be more understandable when viewed from the perspective of the elaboration likelihood model (ELM; see Chapter 6). For issues of little personal relevance, receivers may be content to let their opinions be shaped by the communicator's apparent credibility; for such an issue, it is not worth the effort to follow the details of the arguments. But for highly relevant topics, receivers will be more likely to attend closely to the details of the message, to scrutinize the communicator's arguments and evidence, and to invest the effort involved in thinking closely about the contents of the message—and that comparatively greater importance of the message contents means that the communicator's credibility will play a smaller role than it otherwise might have.[15]

The second factor influencing the magnitude of credibility's impact is the timing of the identification of the communicator. Often, of course, the communicator's identity is known before the message is received by the audience (e.g., because the source is well-known and can be seen by the audience or because another person introduces the communicator). But in some circumstances, it can be possible to delay identification of the source until after the audience has been exposed to the message (e.g., in television advertisements, in which the source's identity may be withheld until the end of the ad, or even in multipage magazine articles, in which information about the writer may not appear on the first page of the article but instead appears only at the end of the article). The timing of the identification of the source does make a substantial difference in the role that source credibility plays in persuasion.

Specifically, the impact of communicator credibility appears to be minimized when the identity of the source is withheld from the audience until after the message has been presented (e.g., Greenberg & Miller, 1966; Greenberg & Tannenbaum, 1961; Husek, 1965; Mills & Harvey, 1972; Sternthal et al., 1978; Ward & McGinnies, 1974; for a review, see O'Keefe, 1987). When the communicator's identity is delayed until after the audience has received the message, the message is apparently heard more nearly on its own terms, without the influence of the communicator's credibility.

It might be thought that this finding implies that high-credibility communicators should be sure not to delay their identification (but instead should be sure to identify themselves before the message), whereas low-credibility communicators should strive, where circumstances permit, to have their messages received before the audience is given information about their credibility. But that is a mistaken conclusion because it is based on an unsound (although natural) assumption that the direction of credibility's effect is constant, with higher credibility always yielding greater persuasion. As discussed in the next section, sometimes lower-credibility communicators will be more successful persuaders than higher-credibility sources.

Influences on the Direction of Effect. One might plausibly suppose that the direction of credibility's effect would be constant—specifically, that increases in credibility would yield only increases in persuasive effectiveness. Perhaps sometimes only small increases would occur, and sometimes (e.g., when the topic is personally relevant to the receiver) no increase at all, but at least whenever credibility had an effect, it would be in a constant direction, with high-credibility sources being more effective than low-credibility sources.

However plausible such a picture may seem, it is not consistent with the empirical evidence. The direction of credibility's effect is not constant: Several investigations have found that at least sometimes low-credibility communicators are significantly more effective than high-credibility communicators (e.g., Bock & Saine, 1975; Chebat, Filiatrault, Laroche, & Watson, 1988; Dholakia, 1987; Harmon & Coney, 1982; Sternthal et al., 1978). This finding is not easily impeached, as these results have been obtained by different investigators, using various topics, with different participant populations, and with good evidence for the success of the credibility manipulations employed.

The critical factor determining the direction of credibility's effects (that is, determining when a low-credibility source will be more effective than a high-credibility communicator, as opposed to when the high-credibility source will have the advantage) appears to be the nature of the position advocated by the message—specifically, whether the message advocates a position initially opposed by the receiver (a counterattitudinal message) or advocates a position toward which the receiver initially feels at least somewhat favorable (a proattitudinal message). With a counterattitudinal message, the high-credibility communicator will tend to have a persuasive advantage over the low-credibility source; with a proattitudinal message, however, the low-credibility communicator appears to enjoy greater persuasive success than the high-credibility source.

The most direct evidence of this relationship comes from investigations that have varied the counter- or proattitudinal stance of the message (under conditions of low topic relevance and with communicators identified prior to messages). Under these conditions, high-credibility communicators are more effective than low-credibility communicators with counterattitudinal messages, but this advantage diminishes as the advocated position gets closer and closer to the receiver's position, to the point that with proattitudinal messages, the low-credibility communicator is often more effective than the high-credibility source (Bergin, 1962; Bochner & Insko, 1966; Chebat et al., 1988; Harmon & Coney, 1982; McGinnies, 1973; Sternthal et al., 1978, Study 2).

Perhaps one way of understanding this effect is to consider the degree to which the receiver might be stimulated to think about arguments and evidence supporting the advocated view. When receivers hear their views defended by a high-credibility source, they may well be inclined to presume that the communicator will do a perfectly good job of advocacy, will defend the viewpoint adequately, will present the best arguments, and so forth—and so they sit back and let the source do the work. But when the source is low in credibility, receivers might be more inclined to help the communicator in defending their common viewpoint, and hence they might be led to think more extensively about supporting arguments—thereby ending up being more persuaded than if they had listened to a higher-credibility source. (Expressed in ELM terms, a proattitudinal message may provoke more favorable elaboration when it comes from a low-credibility communicator than when it comes from a high-credibility communicator; for some evidence consistent with such an account, see Sternthal et al., 1978).

Greater success of low- (as opposed to high-) credibility communicators should not be expected in every case of proattitudinal messages, however, nor should one expect that high-credibility communicators will have an edge whenever counterattitudinal messages are employed. Rather, one should find such effects only when the conditions promote credibility's having a substantial effect (e.g., only when the topic is not especially personally relevant and the communicator is identified prior to the message). That is, it is important to consider jointly (simultaneously) the factors influencing the magnitude of credibility's effect and the factors influencing the direction of credibility's effect.

Joint Consideration of the Magnitude and Direction of Effects. Taken together, the factors identified as influencing the magnitude of credibility's effects (topic relevance and timing of communicator identification) and the direction of credibility's effects (whether the message is proattitudinal or counterattitudinal for the receiver) appear capable of encompassing the bulk of research findings concerning the effects of source credibility on persuasive outcomes.

In investigations that have manipulated one of the crucial factors, the research findings are largely consistent with this analysis. For example, with a proattitudinal message on a low-relevance topic, a low-credibility source has been found to be more effective than a high-credibility source when both were identified before the message, but this difference was minimized when the communicators were not identified until after the message (Sternthal et al., 1978, Study 1). As another example, several studies have compared the effectiveness of high- and low-credibility communicators using counterattitudinal messages (with the source identified prior to the message) under varying conditions of personal relevance; these investigations find that the persuasive advantage enjoyed by the high-credibility communicator (over the low-credibility source) on low-relevance topics diminishes as topic relevance increases (H. H. Johnson & Scileppi, 1969; Petty, Cacioppo, & Goldman, 1981; Rhine & Severance, 1970).

Most studies comparing high- and low-credibility communicators, however, have not varied topic relevance, the timing of source identification, or the counter- versus proattitudinal character of the message (and hence do not contain the contrasting conditions that are most relevant). Nevertheless, an examination of such investigations finds results that are consistent with this analysis. For example, those investigations that have found high-credibility communicators to be significantly more effective than low-credibility communicators have typically (a) identified the source prior to the message, (b) employed relatively low-relevance topics, and (c) not used messages advocating positions favored by the receivers (for a general review of such studies, see Andersen & Clevenger, 1963). Indeed, when one finds that an investigation has *not* found high-credibility communicators to enjoy an advantage over low-credibility sources, usually one or more of these conditions has not obtained. For instance, some investigations that did not find persuasive advantages for higher credibility sources (even with a counterattitudinal message and with the communicator identified prior to the message) apparently used high-relevance topics (e.g., Benoit, 1987; McGarry & Hendrick, 1974; Plax & Rosenfeld, 1980; Stainback & Rogers, 1983). Other investigations that found lower-credibility sources to enjoy greater persuasive success than high-credibility communicators (with the source identified prior to the message and a low-relevance topic) have used proattitudinal messages (as in Sternthal et al., 1978, Study 1).

The general point to be emphasized is that understanding the effects of communicator credibility requires attending simultaneously to factors influencing the magnitude of credibility's effects and to considerations that bear on the direction of credibility's effects. Just what difference communicator credibility might make in a given persuasive effort can vary a great deal, depending on the particulars of the circumstance; with variations in the relationship between the receiver's initial position and the position advocated by the message, with variations in the degree of the personal relevance that the topic has for the receiver, or with variations in the timing of communicator identification, different patterns of effect are possible.[16]

▨ LIKING

The General Rule

Perhaps it comes as no surprise that a number of investigations have found support for the general principle that on the whole, liked communicators are more effective influence agents than are disliked communicators (e.g., Eagly & Chaiken, 1975; Giffen & Ehrlich, 1963; Sampson & Insko, 1964). But the general principle that liked persuaders are more successful can be misleading. Important exceptions and limiting conditions on that principle are discussed in the following section.

Some Exceptions and Limiting Conditions

Extant research evidence suggests at least three important caveats concerning the effects of liking for the communicator on persuasive outcomes: The effects of liking can apparently be overridden by credibility, the superiority of liked over disliked communicators is minimized as the topic becomes more personally relevant to the receiver, and disliked communicators can at least sometimes be significantly more effective persuaders than can liked communicators. (For indications of additional possible limiting conditions, see Chebat, Laroche, Baddoura, & Filiatrault, 1992; Roskos-Ewoldsen & Fazio, 1992.)

Liking and Credibility. The effects of liking on persuasive outcomes appear to be weaker than the effects of credibility (e.g., Lupia & McCubbins, 1998, pp. 196-199; Simons, Berkowitz, & Moyer, 1970); thus when the receiver's judgment of the source's credibility conflicts with the receiver's liking for the source, the effects of liking may be overridden by the effects of credibility. This may be exemplified by the results of an investigation in which participants were asked to make a judgment about the size of the monetary award to be given in a personal injury damage suit. Each participant heard a persuasive message from a source who advocated either a relatively small or a relatively large monetary award; the source was portrayed either as cold and stingy or as warm and generous. Although the warm, generous source was liked better than was the cold, stingy communicator, the stingy source was nevertheless sometimes a more effective persuader, namely, when the stingy source was arguing for a relatively large award. Indeed, of the four source-message combinations, the two most effective combinations were the stingy source arguing for a large award and the generous source arguing for a small award (Wachtler & Counselman, 1981). Both these combinations, of course, represent sources who are (given their personalities) advocating an unexpected position and who thus may well have been perceived as relatively higher in credibility. Of particular interest is that the communicator who was disliked and (presumably) high in credibility (the stingy source advocating the large award) was significantly more effective than the communicator who was liked and (presumably) low in credibility (the generous source advocating the large award), thus suggesting that the effects of liking for the communicator are weaker than the effects of communicator credibility.

Liking and Topic Relevance. The effects of liking on persuasive out-comes are minimized as the topic becomes more personally relevant to the receiver. Thus although better-liked sources may enjoy some general per-suasive advantage, that advantage is reduced when the issue is personally relevant to the receiver (Chaiken, 1980). This result is, of course, compati-ble with the image offered by the ELM (discussed in Chapter 6). When re-ceivers find the topic personally relevant, they are more likely to engage in systematic active processing of message contents and to minimize reliance on peripheral cues such as whether they happen to like the communication source. But when personal relevance is low, receivers are more likely to rely on simplifying heuristics emphasizing cues such as liking ("I like this per-son, so I'll agree").

Greater Effectiveness of Disliked Communicators. At least sometimes disliked communicators can be more effective persuaders than liked com-municators—even when the communicators are comparable in other char-acteristics (such as credibility). A demonstration of this possibility was pro-vided by an investigation in which participants were induced to eat fried grasshoppers. In one condition, the communicator acted snobbish, cold, bossy, tactless, and hostile (the disliked communicator); the liked com-municator displayed none of these characteristics. The two communica-tors were roughly equally successful in inducing participants to eat the fried grasshoppers, but that is not the result of interest. What is of inter-est is how, among participants who did eat the grasshoppers, their atti-tudes toward eating grasshoppers changed. As one might predict from dissonance-theoretic considerations, among those who ate the grasshop-pers, the disliked communicator was much more effective in changing attitudes in the desired direction than was the liked communicator: The person who ate the grasshoppers under the influence of the disliked com-municator presumably experienced more dissonance—and thus exhibited more attitude change—than did the person induced to eat by the liked source (Zimbardo, Weisenberg, Firestone, & Levy, 1965).

This, of course, is the familiar induced-compliance counterattitudinal action circumstance (as discussed in Chapter 4). But similar results have been obtained in straightforward persuasive communication situations (J. Cooper, Darley, & Henderson, 1974; Himmelfarb & Arazi, 1974; R. A. Jones & Brehm, 1967; cf. Eagly & Chaiken, 1975). A notable clarifi-cation of this effect was provided by an investigation that manipulated both the receiver's liking for the communicator and the recipient's choice about listening to the communication; in the high-choice condition, receivers volunteered to listen to the message, whereas in the no-choice condition, receivers were seemingly accidentally exposed to the message (by hearing it playing in an adjacent room). When receivers had not chosen to listen to the communication, the liked communicator was more effective than the disliked communicator, but when receivers had freely chosen to listen to the message, the disliked communicator was more effective than the liked communicator (R. A. Jones & Brehm, 1967).

Indeed, when other investigations have found disliked communicators to be more successful persuaders than liked communicators, the circumstances appear consistently to have involved the receivers' having freely chosen to listen to the message (J. Cooper et al., 1974; Himmelfarb & Arazi, 1974). For example, in J. Cooper et al.'s (1974) investigation, suburban householders received a counterattitudinal communication (i.e., one opposed to the receiver's views) from either a deviant-appearing communicator (a long-haired hippie) or a conventional-appearing communicator; the deviant-appearing communicator was significantly more effective than the conventionally dressed communicator in persuading these suburbanites, but the message recipients all had freely chosen to receive the communication (and indeed had had two opportunities to decline to receive the communication).

If one remembers that dissonance effects are expected in induced-compliance circumstances only when the person has freely chosen to engage in the discrepant action, the finding that disliked communicators can be more successful than liked communicators only under conditions of choice is perhaps not surprising. Receivers who freely choose to listen to (what turns out to be) an unlikable communicator presumably face a dissonance reduction task that is not faced by receivers who find themselves (through no fault of their own) listening to an unlikable source. Hence the greater success of disliked (as opposed to liked) communicators is, as the research evidence suggests, obtained only when the receiver has chosen to listen to the message.

OTHER SOURCE FACTORS

Beyond credibility and liking, a large number of other source factors have received at least some research attention as possible influences on persuasive outcomes. This section focuses on two additional source factors—similarity and physical attractiveness—but concludes with a more general discussion of other source characteristics.

Similarity

It seems common and natural to assume that to the degree that receivers perceive similarities between themselves and a persuader, to that same degree the persuader's effectiveness will be enhanced. The belief that "greater similarity means greater effectiveness" is an attractive one and is commonly reflected in recommendations that persuaders emphasize commonalities between themselves and the audience.

But the relationship of similarity to persuasive effectiveness is much more complex than this common assumption indicates. Indeed, the research evidence suggests that this common assumption is misleading in important ways; to be sure, some research findings indicate that persuasive effectiveness can be enhanced by similarity (e.g., Brock, 1965; Woodside & Davenport, 1974), but other findings suggest that persuasive effectiveness can be reduced by similarity (e.g., Infante, 1978; S. W. King & Sereno, 1973; Leavitt & Kaigler-Evans, 1975), and still other studies indicate that similarity has no effect on persuasive outcomes (e.g., Klock & Traylor, 1983; Wagner, 1984).

Two initial clarifications will be helpful in untangling these complexities. First, there is "an infinite number of possible dimensions" of similarity-dissimilarity (Simons et al., 1970, p. 3). One might perceive oneself to be similar or dissimilar to another person in age, occupation, attitudes, physique, income, education, speech dialect, personality, ethnicity, political affiliation, interpersonal style, clothing preferences, and on and on. Thus there is not likely to be any truly general relationship between similarity and persuasive effectiveness, or indeed between similarity and *any* other variable. Different particular similarities or dissimilarities will have different effects, making impossible any sound generalization about similarity.

Second, as emphasized by Simons et al. (1970) and R. G. Hass (1981), similarities most likely do not influence persuasive effectiveness directly. Rather, similarities influence persuasive outcomes indirectly, especially by affecting the receiver's liking for the communicator and the receiver's perception of the communicator's credibility (expertise and trustworthiness). Because the effects of similarities may not be identical for liking, perceived expertise, and perceived trustworthiness, the relationship of similarities to each of these needs separate attention.

Similarity and Liking. Given the infinite varieties of possible similarities, any general relationship is unlikely between perceived similarity and liking for another person. That is, "there is no singular 'similarity' effect" on liking but rather "a multiplicity of effects that depend on both content and context" (Huston & Levinger, 1978, p. 126). The effect on liking of one particular sort of similarity, however—attitudinal similarity—has received a good deal of empirical attention. Attitudinal similarity is having similar attitudes (similar evaluations of attitude objects)—as opposed to, say, having similar traits, abilities, occupations, or backgrounds.

A fair amount of evidence now indicates that as a general rule, perceived attitudinal similarity engenders greater liking (for reviews, see Berscheid, 1985; Byrne, 1969). Thus to the extent that message recipients perceive that the communicator has attitudes (on matters other than the topic of the influence attempt) that are similar to theirs, those recipients are likely to come to like the communicator more. Hence even when not especially relevant to the topic of the influence attempt, perceived attitudinal similarities (between source and audience) can enhance the audience's liking of the source and so can potentially influence persuasive effectiveness.

A receiver may come to perceive attitudinal similarities through various routes, of course. The communicator might directly express attitudes similar to the attitudes of the audience, or a third party might indicate the presence of attitudinal similarities. But one basis on which a receiver might infer attitudinal similarities is the presence of *other* types of observed similarities (such as similarities in background, personality, occupation, and the like); these other similarities may indirectly influence the receiver's liking for a communicator.

The hypothesis that attitudinal similarities can influence persuasive effectiveness by influencing the receiver's liking for the communicator is bolstered by the results of investigations that have varied both communicator credibility (specifically, expertise) and communicator-receiver attitudinal similarity. As discussed previously, the effects of liking on persuasive effectiveness appear to be weaker than the effects of credibility. Thus if attitudinal similarities influence persuasive effects by influencing liking for the communicator, then the effect of attitudinal similarities on persuasive effectiveness should be smaller than the effect of credibility. Indeed, several studies have found persuasive success to be more influenced by the communicator's expertise than by the communicator's attitudinal similarity (Wagner, 1984; Woodside & Davenport, 1974).

But enhanced liking of a communicator will not always mean enhanced persuasive effectiveness; as discussed earlier, greater liking for a communicator may enhance, reduce, or have no effect on persuasive effectiveness. Correspondingly, greater perceived attitudinal similarities may (through their influence on the receiver's liking for the communicator) enhance, reduce, or have no influence on persuasive effectiveness. Thus one should not assume that with greater perceived attitudinal similarity comes greater persuasive effectiveness. Rather, with greater perceived attitudinal similarity comes greater liking, which may or may not mean greater effectiveness.

Similarity and Credibility: Expertise Judgments. It is unquestionably the case that perceived similarities (or dissimilarities) between source and audience can influence the audience's judgment of the source's expertise. But there are two noteworthy features of this relationship.

First, the similarity-dissimilarity must be relevant to the influence attempt if it is likely to influence judgments of expertise. For example, a communicator seeking to influence a receiver's judgment of the president's budget policy will probably not obtain enhanced expertise judgments by pointing out that the communicator and recipient are wearing the same color shirt. In a study that varied the communicator's occupational similarity (student vs. nonstudent, for an audience of students) in advertisements for several consumer products, receivers' judgments of the source's expertise were found to be unrelated to judgments of perceived similarity (Swartz, 1984); presumably, the variations in similarity were not relevant to the persuasive issues involved. Only relevant similarities (or dissimilarities) are likely to influence judgments of the communicator's expertise.

Second, not all relevant similarities will enhance perceived expertise, and not all relevant dissimilarities will damage perceived expertise. Different sorts of relevant similarities will have different effects on perceived expertise, depending on the circumstance, and hence no simple generalization can suffice concerning the effects of relevant similarities on perceptions of expertise.

For example, a perceived similarity in relevant training and experience may reduce the perceived expertise of a communicator (because the receiver may be thinking, "I know as much about this topic as the speaker does"). A perceived dissimilarity in relevant training and experience, on the other hand, might either enhance or damage perceived expertise, depending on the direction of the dissimilarity: If the receiver thinks that the communicator is dissimilar because the communicator has *better* training and experience, then presumably enhanced judgments of the communicator's expertise will be likely, but if the receiver thinks that the communicator is dissimilar because the communicator has *poorer* training and experience, then most likely the communicator's perceived expertise will suffer.

A demonstration of this sort of complexity was provided by a study of speech dialect similarity, in which persons who spoke a general American dialect heard one of two versions of a message from a speaker using either a general American dialect or a Southern dialect; the message concerned a well-known Southern governor (who enjoyed some popularity in the South but not elsewhere), with one version offering a favorable view of the governor and the other an unfavorable view. Regardless of the position advocated, the speaker with the Southern (dissimilar) speech dialect was perceived as more expert than the speaker with the general American (similar) dialect, presumably because the Southern speaker could be assumed to have better access to relevant information than would the general American speaker (Delia, 1975; for related investigations, see Houck & Bowers, 1969; Schenck-Hamlin, 1978).

Thus similarities should have varying effects on perceived expertise, depending on the particulars of the circumstances. One should not be surprised that the research literature indicates that similar others are sometimes seen as more expert than dissimilar others (e.g., Mills & Kimble, 1973), sometimes as less expert (e.g., Delia, 1975), and sometimes as not differing in expertise (e.g., Atkinson, Winzelberg, & Holland, 1985; Swartz, 1984). The effects of perceived similarities and dissimilarities on judgments of communicator expertise depend on whether, and how, the receiver perceives these as relevant to the issue at hand.

Similarity and Credibility: Trustworthiness Judgments. The relationship between similarities and judgments of the communicator's trustworthiness appears to be complex as well. As previously mentioned, certain sorts of similarities—specifically, perceived attitudinal similarities—can influence the receiver's liking for the communicator, and enhanced liking for the communicator is commonly accompanied by enhanced judgments of the communicator's trustworthiness. One would thus expect that perceived attitudinal similarities might (through their influence on liking) exert some effect on perceptions of the communicator's trustworthiness.

But this cannot be the whole story. The just described speech dialect investigation (Delia, 1975) also included assessments of the communicator's trustworthiness. Greater trustworthiness was ascribed to the progovernor speaker using the similar (general American) dialect and to the antigovernor speaker using the dissimilar (Southern) dialect. This effect is, of course, readily understandable: The Southern speaker arguing against the Southern governor and the non-Southern speaker supporting that governor could each have been seen as offering views that ran against the tide of regional opinion—and hence seen as speakers who must be especially sincere and honest in their expressions of their opinions.

But notice the complexity of these results regarding similarity: Sometimes similarity enhanced perceptions of trustworthiness, but sometimes it diminished such perceptions, depending on the position advocated. And (to round things out) other investigators have found that sometimes similarities will have no effect on trustworthiness judgments. Atkinson et al. (1985), for example, found that ethnic similarity-dissimilarity did not dependably influence the perceived trustworthiness of pregnancy counselors for Mexican American or Anglo clients.

Summary: The Effects of Similarity. Perhaps it is now clear just how inadequate is a generalization such as "greater similarity leads to greater persuasive effectiveness." The effects of similarity on persuasive outcomes are complex and indirect, and no single easy generalization will encompass those varied effects. Indeed, in several instances, similarities have been found in a single investigation to enhance persuasive effectiveness under some conditions but to inhibit persuasive effectiveness under other circumstances (e.g., Goethals & Nelson, 1973; S. W. King & Sereno, 1973; Mills & Kimble, 1973).

So consider, as an example, the effects of salient similarities or dissimilarities in group membership ("Ah, this communicator is a student at my university") on persuasion. Such group membership similarities might provide bases for inferences about likely attitudinal similarities between receiver and communicator or more generally might provide bases for inferences about likability or credibility. Hence (following ELM-like reasoning) on topics that are not especially personally relevant to the receiver, such similarities might serve as peripheral cues (that engage corresponding heuristics) and thus enhance the persuasiveness of messages from similar communicators (those sharing group membership with the receiver). By contrast, on topics of greater personal relevance (for which greater message scrutiny is likely), these peripheral cue effects of group membership similarities may be diminished. On such personally relevant topics, however, group membership similarity might encourage closer scrutiny of messages from similar communicators (such that receivers pay more attention to the messages that come from sources with whom they share a group membership than to other messages); such closer scrutiny might enhance or inhibit persuasion, depending on such factors as the quality of the message's arguments. (For some relevant empirical work and general discussions, see M. A. Fleming & Petty, 2000; Mackie, Gastardo-Conaco, & Skelly, 1992; Mackie & Queller, 2000; Mackie, Worth, & Asuncion, 1990.)

Such complexities might lead one to wonder about the common practice of using peers (of the target audience) in health education programs on such topics as smoking and unsafe sex; this practice can be seen to reflect a generalized belief in the persuasive power of similarity. Given the observed complexities of similarity's roles and effects in persuasion, however, perhaps it should not be surprising that a review of peer-based health interventions has found them to be not dependably more successful than programs without such peer bases (Posavac, Kattapong, & Dew, 1999).[17]

In sum, if there is a general conclusion to be drawn about source-receiver similarities in persuasion, it surely is that simple generalizations will not do: To say, for example, that "receivers are more likely to be persuaded by communicators they perceive as similar to themselves" is to overlook the complexities of the effects that similarities have on persuasive outcomes.

Physical Attractiveness

The effects of physical attractiveness on persuasive outcomes—like the effects of similarity—are rather varied. For the most part, "existing research does indicate that heightened physical attractiveness generally enhances one's effectiveness as a social influence agent" (Chaiken, 1986, p. 150). But a close look at the research evidence and a consideration of the mechanisms underlying this general effect will underscore the dangers of unqualified reliance on this generalization.

The Research Evidence. A number of investigations have found that physically attractive communicators are more effective persuaders than their less attractive counterparts (e.g., Horai, Naccari, & Fatoullah, 1974; Snyder & Rothbart, 1971; Widgery & Ruch, 1981; for a review, see Chaiken, 1986). For example, Chaiken's (1979) study of messages concerning university dining hall menus found that attractive persuaders induced significantly greater persuasion (on both a verbal and a behavioral index of persuasion) than did unattractive persuaders. But attractive communicators do not always enjoy greater persuasive success; for instance, Maddux and Rogers (1980) found that the persuasiveness of a message arguing that people need only 4 hours of sleep a night was not influenced by the communicator's physical attractiveness (see also Mills & Aronson, 1965). And in some circumstances, attractive communicators have been found to be significantly *less* effective persuaders than their unattractive counterparts (J. Cooper et al., 1974).

An Explanatory Mechanism. What accounts for the observed effects of physical attractiveness on persuasive success? A plausible starting point for an explanation is that the communicator's physical attractiveness influences the recipient's liking for the communicator, which in turn influences persuasive success (see Chaiken, 1986, for a careful elaboration of this idea). After all—and not surprisingly—greater physical attractiveness tends to lead to greater liking (for a review, see Berscheid & Walster, 1974); and, as discussed previously, there is good evidence for the general proposition that on the whole, liked communicators will be more effective persuaders than disliked communicators.

This explanation is also consistent with the results of investigations that have examined the effects of communicator physical attractiveness on both liking for the communicator and persuasive effect. If physical attractiveness influences persuasive outcomes indirectly, through an effect on liking, then (a) whenever physical attractiveness influences persuasive outcomes, it should also influence liking, and (b) the (presumably immediate) effect of physical attractiveness on liking should be larger than the (presumably mediated) effect of physical attractiveness on persuasive outcomes. These are just the sorts of results commonly observed (e.g., Horai et al., 1974; Snyder & Rothbart, 1971).

But if communicator physical attractiveness influences persuasion through its effect on liking for the communicator, then (at least in principle) it should be possible to find empirical results for physical attractiveness that parallel the observed effects of liking. Thus in addition to the generally positive effect of communicator physical attractiveness on persuasive outcomes (paralleling the generally positive effect of liking on persuasion), one should also find that (a) credibility can be a more important determinant of persuasion than physical attractiveness, (b) the effects of physical attractiveness on persuasion are reduced as the personal relevance of the topic to the receiver increases, and (c) physically unattractive communicators will at least sometimes be more effective than physically attractive persuaders.

The research evidence relevant to these expectations is not extensive but is at least largely supportive. Maddux and Rogers (1980), for instance, found source expertise to be a more powerful determinant of persuasion than was communicator physical attractiveness. Although research on the effects of communicator physical attractiveness has generally not systematically varied the personal relevance of the issue, it is nevertheless noteworthy that (as Chaiken, 1986, has emphasized) studies that have found significant effects of communicator physical attractiveness on persuasion overwhelmingly have used what appear to be low-relevance topics. And, as discussed earlier, researchers have found that at least under some circumstances, a deviant-appearing communicator will be a more successful persuader than a conventional-appearing source (J. Cooper et al., 1974).

All told, then, an attractive case can be made for supposing that many of the effects of communicator physical attractiveness on persuasive outcomes can best be explained by the hypothesis that "physical attractiveness affects social influence via its more direct impact on liking for the social influence agent" (Chaiken, 1986, p. 151).

But what of the possibility that communicator physical attractiveness might influence persuasion by influencing perceptions of the communicator's credibility? This alternative has some merit, but the pattern of empirical results suggests that this is not a competitor to (but instead a natural companion of) the explanation that emphasizes effects of attractiveness on liking. To bring this out, however, requires separate consideration of the expertise and trustworthiness dimensions of credibility.

Consider first the possibility that judgments of the communicator's expertise mediate the effects of communicator physical attractiveness. Investigations that have found physically attractive persuaders to be more successful than unattractive persuaders have typically not found the attractive communicators to be rated higher in expertise (e.g., Chaiken, 1979; Horai et al., 1974; Snyder & Rothbart, 1971; see also R. Norman, 1976; Widgery, 1974; cf. Patzer, 1983). Thus it is not plausible to suppose that differential judgments of the communicator's expertise generally mediate the effect of communicator physical attractiveness on persuasive outcomes.[18]

But physical attractiveness may (at least indirectly) influence judgments of the communicator's trustworthiness. As noted earlier, physical attractiveness influences liking for the communicator; and, as discussed earlier, there is at least some indirect evidence that the receiver's liking for the communicator can influence the receiver's judgment of communicator trustworthiness. But this roundabout path of influence is likely to mean that physical attractiveness will have only weak effects on trustworthiness judgments: If the effect of communicator physical attractiveness on trustworthiness judgments is mediated by the receiver's liking for the communicator, then (given that liking for the communicator can be influenced by many other things besides physical attractiveness) one should expect that the effect of attractiveness on trustworthiness will be less strong than the effect of attractiveness on liking (as was found by Patzer, 1983) and indeed will typically be comparatively small, even negligible; Maddux and Rogers (1980), for example, found that physically attractive persuaders were indeed better liked but were not rated as significantly more sincere or honest than were their physically unattractive counterparts (for related results, see Snyder & Rothbart, 1971).

In any event, an understanding of the role that communicator physical attractiveness plays in influencing persuasive outcomes seems to require that central emphasis be given the influence of physical attractiveness on liking. Physical attractiveness appears to affect persuasive outcomes not directly but rather indirectly, especially by means of its influence on the receiver's liking for the communicator.

About Additional Source Characteristics

This discussion of the persuasive effects of communicator-receiver similarity and communicator physical attractiveness has focused on how those factors might influence credibility and liking, because the research evidence in hand is consistent with the supposition that similarity and physical attractiveness often influence persuasive outcomes indirectly, through their effects on credibility and liking. Indeed (given the relatively extensive direct evidence concerning the persuasive effects of variation in communicator credibility and liking), in thinking about the effects of any given additional source characteristic on persuasion, one useful avenue to illuminating that characteristic's effects can be a consideration of how that characteristic might influence credibility or liking (and thereby indirectly influence persuasive outcomes).

Such an approach will reveal considerable complexities in how a given factor might eventually influence persuasive effects. Consider, as an example, the question of the comparative persuasive success of communicators varying in ethnicity (e.g., a Latino communicator and an Anglo communicator) in influencing receivers who also vary in ethnicity. The answer to this question almost certainly varies from case to case, depending on the particulars involved. With one topic, the Latino communicator may be perceived (by all receivers, no matter their ethnicity) to be more credible than the Anglo communicator; with a different topic, the Anglo communicator may be perceived as more credible (no matter the receiver's ethnicity); with yet another topic, there may be no credibility differences associated with the ethnicity of the communicator; or the credibility judgments may depend not just on the topic addressed but also on the position advocated (as in the previously discussed study of speech dialects, which had a topic on which regional differences in knowledge and attitude were likely). But (to add to the complexity here) these credibility judgments may not influence persuasive outcomes substantially because variations in credibility are not always associated with variations in effects; even when variations in these credibility judgments *are* associated with variations in outcomes, sometimes the lower-credibility communicator will be more effective than the higher-credibility source. When one adds the complex relationship between ethnicity and credibility to the complex relationship between credibility and persuasive outcomes, the result is a rococo set of possibilities for the relationship between ethnicity and persuasive effects. (And notice: The discussion of this example has focused only on the direct ethnicity-credibility relationship; the picture of ethnicity's effects becomes even more complex when one considers in addition the ethnicity-liking relationship or the role of perceived ethnic similarity.)

But a still larger complexity is to be borne in mind here, namely, that (as suggested by the ELM; see Chapter 6) a variable can play many roles in persuasion. Consider, for instance, that—apart from whatever influence credibility might otherwise have on the persuasiveness of a message—the communicator's credibility may affect whether the communicator has access to the audience (e.g., editors may provide space on the op-ed pages of a newspaper only to persons who appear to have relevant expertise) and whether the audience pays much attention to the message (that is, credibility may influence message scrutiny).

▧ CONCLUSION

Source characteristics can have complicated relationships with each other and can have various direct and indirect effects on persuasive outcomes. Researchers are still some distance from a clear understanding of all the ways in which source characteristics affect persuasion, but it is already plain that the picture is rather more complex than might once have been supposed.

▧ NOTES

1. Not all the factors that in the research literature have been labeled "trustworthiness" (or "character," "safety," or the like) contain many of the items that here are identified as assessing trustworthiness (e.g., McCroskey, 1966). An important source of confusion is the apparent empirical association between a receiver's liking for a communicator and the receiver's judgment of the communicator's trustworthiness; this covariation is reflected in factor analyses that have found items such as honest-dishonest, trustworthy-untrustworthy, and fair-unfair to load on the same factor with items such as friendly-unfriendly, pleasant-unpleasant, nice-not nice, and valuable-worthless (see, e.g., Applbaum & Anatol, 1972; Bowers & Phillips, 1967; Falcione, 1974; McCroskey, 1966; Pearce & Brommel, 1972). This pattern can plausibly be interpreted as reflecting the effects of liking on trustworthiness judgments (receivers being inclined to ascribe greater trustworthiness to persons they like). But such empirical association should not obscure the conceptual distinction between trustworthiness and liking, especially because the empirical association is imperfect; see Delia's (1976, pp. 374-375) discussion of Whitehead's (1968) results, or consider the stereotypical used car salesman who is likable but untrustworthy. In this chapter, investigations are treated as bearing on judgments of trustworthiness only when it appears that trustworthiness (and not liking) has been assessed.

2. This treatment offers a general discussion of factors influencing perceived credibility. For reviews of research concerning factors affecting credibility in specific persuasion contexts, see Hoyt (1996) and G. R. Miller and Burgoon (1982).

3. This does not mean that researchers should never investigate the effect of a complex of behavioral features. To the contrary, such studies can be useful in the early stages of research (when one is casting one's research net widely) or in the later stages of research (when one already knows the effects of individual behavioral features studied in isolation and now wishes to see the effects of combinations of

factors). But such studies obviously cannot provide all the information necessary for understanding the effects of individual behavioral features.

4. A number of investigations that are commonly cited as indicating significant effects of speaking rate on credibility judgments involve not judgments of expertise (is the communicator informed, trained, qualified, intelligent, expert?) or trustworthiness (is the communicator honest, trustworthy, open-minded, fair?) but rather judgments of other characteristics (e.g., Apple, Streeter, & Krauss, 1979; B. L. Brown, Strong, & Rencher, 1973, 1974; B. L. Smith, Brown, Strong, & Rencher, 1975; Street & Brady, 1982). For example, what B. L. Smith et al. (1975) labeled as a "competence" judgment consisted of judgments of whether the speaker was strong, active, ambitious, intelligent, good-looking, and confident; what was labeled a "benevolence" dimension consisted of judgments of whether the speaker was polite, just, religious, kind, sincere, happy, likable, dependable, and sociable. It would be imprudent to assume that these straightforwardly correspond to the sorts of expertise and trustworthiness judgments of interest here.

5. This finding (that citation of evidence sources can enhance perceptions of the communicator's expertise and trustworthiness) may be seen to have implications for the ELM (see Chapter 6). Although source and message variables are not partitioned by the ELM as having intrinsically different roles to play in persuasion, it is clear that message materials might have implications for perceptions of source characteristics (as when advocacy of an unexpected position enhances perceptions of communicator trustworthiness and thereby engenders reduced message scrutiny; Priester & Petty, 1995). The finding under discussion points specifically to the possibility that variations in argumentative message content may alter impressions of the communicator's credibility (see Slater & Rouner, 1996). (As an aside: Compared with premessage identification, postmessage identification of communicators has often been seen to yield more positive impressions of credibility [Ward & McGinnies, 1973]. This result might easily be understood as a consequence of participants' larger reliance on message materials—which commonly appear to have been of good quality—as a basis for credibility judgments in conditions in which identification follows the message as compared with those in which it precedes the message.) In the context of the ELM, this implies that variations in argument strength might affect persuasive outcomes by providing what amounts to credibility-related cue information. The existence of such a pathway, in turn, invites reconsideration of the commonly observed enhanced effect that argument strength manipulations have (on persuasive outcomes) under conditions of high personal relevance; that effect could come about through the use of a credibility-related heuristic (and not through anything such as genuinely thoughtful consideration of substantive arguments), as long as there was sufficiently close message scrutiny to permit receivers to notice whatever message elements are used as a basis for inferences about credibility. The point here is not that this pathway provides an entirely satisfactory account of the accumulated findings on this matter but only that the possibility of this pathway points to some complexities in untangling what lies behind the effects observed in ELM research.

6. To put the point somewhat differently, communicators who advocate views that advance the communicator's self-interest may naturally be perceived as less credible than communicators whose advocated views do not advance their own interests. For instance, physicians find their colleagues more believable sources of drug information than they do advertisements or salespeople (Beltramini & Sirsi, 1992), and retail salespeople who flatter customers before a sale are perceived as less sincere than those who do so afterward (M. C. Campbell & Kirmani, 2000).

7. The mean effect (across 18 studies) corresponds to a correlation of .16 (O'Keefe, 1999a). Notably, the credibility-enhancing effect (of mentioning opposing considerations without refuting them) that obtains in consumer advertising messages is not found in other messages (e.g., those concerning public policy issues). It may simply be that skepticism about consumer advertising is substantially greater than that about public policy advocacy—and hence nonrefutational acknowledgment of potential counterarguments is more surprising when it occurs in consumer advertisements than when it occurs in other messages.

8. A similar effect on persuasive outcomes was observed by Weinberger and Dillon (1980). Consumers were provided with unfavorable information about a product, attributed to one of three sources: a trade and professional association (whose self-interest would presumably run counter to disclosure of the negative information), a local consumer panel, and an independent testing agency. The unfavorable information had more impact on purchase intentions when it came from unbiased sources (the consumer panel or testing agency) than when it was presumably "reluctant" testimony from the trade association.

9. For results consistent with this expectation, see Marquart, O'Keefe, and Gunther (1995), who found that perceived attitudinal similarity (which is known to influence liking; see, e.g., Berscheid, 1985) influenced ratings of sources' trustworthiness but not expertise.

10. Some experimental manipulations do appear to be especially targeted to influencing perceptions of expertise (e.g., by providing background information about occupation and training), and it can be tempting to interpret such studies as speaking specifically to questions about the effects of variations in perceived expertise. But a manipulation of apparent expertise may also affect perceptions of trustworthiness, and thus the results of such a study should not necessarily be interpreted as reflecting distinctly expertise effects. (Indeed, at least in some domains, perceptions of expertise, trustworthiness, and attractiveness are sufficiently highly correlated that some recommend collecting these under a single global credibility construct; see Hoyt, 1996.) One way of protecting against this problem can be to assess perceptions of both expertise and trustworthiness and to examine the effects of the manipulation on each. (It will not be sufficient to show that the experimental manipulation significantly influenced expertise perceptions but not trustworthiness perceptions. Such a finding would not necessarily mean that the manipulation influenced expertise perceptions significantly more than it influenced trustworthiness perceptions.) But when the research question of interest concerns the relationship between perceived expertise (or perceived trustworthiness) and persuasive outcomes, analyzing data by examining the relationship

between persuasive outcomes and the experimental manipulation fails to provide relevant information; with such a research question, the relationship between the perceptual state (e.g., perceived expertise) and persuasive outcomes should be examined directly.

11. E. J. Wilson and Sherrell's (1993) review reported that expertise manipulations appear to have larger effects on persuasive outcomes than do trustworthiness manipulations. But (as discussed in the preceding note) this does not speak to the question of the relative influence (on persuasive effects) of perceived expertise and perceived trustworthiness. Concerning perceived therapist credibility specifically, Hoyt's (1996) review found (with a relatively small number of effect sizes) no reason to suppose that perceived expertise and perceived trustworthiness were differentially related to therapist influence, but the generality of such a result is an open question.

12. For example, on Neimeyer, Guy, and Metzler's (1989) 7-point credibility scale (with a midpoint of 4), the mean rating for the low-credibility communicator was 4.3; that for the high-credibility communicator was 4.9. In Sternthal et al.'s (1978) investigation, the credibility index (six summed credibility items) could range from 6 to 42, with a midpoint of 24; the low-credibility communicator's mean rating was 20.57 (not significantly different from the scale midpoint), and the high-credibility communicator's was 28.86. For the 12-item credibility index employed by Ward and McGinnies (1974), overall scores could range from 12 to 60 with a midpoint of 36; the mean rating for the low-credibility communicator was 34.95, whereas that for the high-credibility communicator was 41.58. Such results are common (e.g., Bochner & Insko, 1966; Greenberg & Miller, 1966, Experiment 1; H. H. Johnson & Scileppi, 1969).

13. This difficulty is consistent with studies of the ratings given to "ideal" high- and low-credibility communicators, which have found that when respondents are asked to indicate where a perfectly credible and a perfectly noncredible communicator would be rated on expertise and trustworthiness scales, the ratings are not at the absolute extremes (R. A. Clark, Stewart, & Marston, 1972; see also J. K. Burgoon, 1976).

14. As discussed in Chapter 6 (concerning the ELM), a good deal of research concerning variations in personal relevance has used the term "involvement" as a label for this variable (and so the point under discussion would be phased as a matter of credibility's impact declining as the receiver's involvement with the issue increases). But the term "involvement" has also been used to cover other variations in the relationship that receivers have to the message topic and so, in interests of clarity, is avoided here.

15. As discussed in Chapter 6, the ELM actually proposes a slightly more specific version of this generalization (about the decline of credibility's effect on persuasive outcomes as personal relevance increases); it stresses that as elaboration declines (e.g., as topic relevance declines), credibility plays less of a role *as a peripheral cue* but may still influence persuasion through other mechanisms. But when (for instance) credibility influences persuasion through influencing the degree of message scrutiny, then (given that increasing or reducing message scrutiny might

lead to either greater or lesser persuasion, depending on the outcomes of greater message scrutiny) credibility's apparent relationship with persuasive outcomes will presumably also appear to weaken. On the one hand, there is the observed empirical regularity (as personal relevance increases, the simple apparent relationship between credibility variations and persuasive effects weakens), and on the other, an ELM-based explanation of that observed regularity (viz., that credibility has a lessened role as a peripheral cue but might serve in other roles that also would naturally make for a weaker apparent relationship); one presumably does not want to confuse these.

16. Moreover, any observed effects might arise through (and so be explained by) any number of pathways. For example (to employ ELM-based reasoning), when a higher-credibility communicator is observed to be more persuasive than a lower-credibility communicator, this might have occurred because the communicator's apparent credibility served as a cue (and so engaged a credibility-based heuristic), because the higher-credibility communicator engendered greater message scrutiny than did the lower-credibility communicator (in a circumstance in which the message had strong arguments), because the higher-credibility communicator engendered less message scrutiny than did the lower-credibility communicator (in a circumstance in which the message had weak arguments), or because the higher-credibility communicator more or less directly biased (influenced the evaluative direction of) elaboration in a way favorable to the advocated view.

17. The mean difference in effectiveness, across 25 cases, corresponds to a correlation of .01 (Posavac et al., 1999).

18. In certain specific circumstances, the communicator's physical attractiveness might influence judgments of expertise—namely, when the topic of influence is related to physical attractiveness in relevant ways. For example, physically attractive sources might enjoy greater perceived expertise in the realm of beauty products. But generally speaking, the effect of the source's physical attractiveness on persuasive outcomes appears not to be achieved through enhanced perceptions of the source's expertise.

Message Factors

9

This chapter reviews research concerning the effects that selected message variations have on persuasion. The message factors discussed are grouped into three broad categories: message structure, message content, and sequential-request strategies.

MESSAGE STRUCTURE

Three structural features of persuasive messages that have been investigated for their possible effects on persuasive outcomes are discussed here. One concerns the order of arguments in the message; a second concerns whether the message's conclusion should be explicitly stated; the third concerns the degree of specificity with which the communicator's advocated action is described.

Climax Versus Anticlimax Order of Arguments

Where should a persuader put the message's most important arguments? One possibility is to save them for last, thereby building to a strong finish. Another possibility is to put the most important arguments first, to be sure that they are not missed. There have been several studies of the relative effectiveness of these two ways of ordering arguments in a message—the climax order (most important arguments last) and the anticlimax order (most important arguments first). In these investigations, the relative importance of different arguments was assessed in pretests (by obtaining ratings of argument importance), and the experimental messages devoted relatively more time or space to the more important arguments than to less important ones.

As it turns out, the choice between these two ways of arranging the arguments in a message seems to be of little consequence; varying the order makes little difference indeed to overall persuasive effectiveness (Gilkinson, Paulson, & Sikkink, 1954; Gulley & Berlo, 1956; Sikkink, 1956; Sponberg, 1946; for a related study, see Cromwell, 1950, Experiment 2). In the one report of a statistically significant difference between the two orders (Gilkinson et al., 1954, Experiment 2), the climax order was more persuasive; when nonsignificant differences have been found, the direction of effect has generally (but not always) favored the climax order, but in every case the observed differences seem small. A thorough systematic review remains to be done, but perhaps the most sensible conclusion to draw at present is that there might, on average, be some benefit from arranging arguments in a climax order, although likely so small as to be negligible.

The particulars of a persuasive circumstance, however, may suggest that one or another way of arranging arguments should be preferred. Consider, for example, appellate oral argument in U.S. courts (e.g., the Supreme Court). An attorney will commonly have a specified time (perhaps 20 or 30 minutes) in which to present arguments. However, the judges are free to break in at any time with questions and counterarguments, and experienced attorneys know that they are not likely to be able to make an uninterrupted presentation. As should be plain, an attorney who plans on saving the most important arguments for last may never get the chance to present those arguments. In this setting, then, an advocate should employ an anticlimax order—placing one's most important arguments at the beginning of the presentation—rather than a climax order. (This exemplifies a general point about the practical application of persuasion research generalizations, namely, that such application needs to be sensitive to the particulars of persuasion circumstances.)

Conclusion Omission

Obviously, persuasive messages have some point—some opinion or belief that the communicator hopes the audience will accept, some recommended action that the communicator wishes to have adopted. But should the message explicitly make that point—explicitly state the conclusion or recommendation—or should the message leave the point implicit and let receivers figure the conclusion out themselves?[1]

Intuitively, there look to be good reasons for each alternative. For instance, one might think that making the conclusion explicit would be superior because receivers would then be less likely to misunderstand the point of the message. On the other hand, it might be that if the communicator simply supplies the premises, and the audience reasons its own way to the conclusion, then perhaps the audience will be more persuaded than if the communicator had presented the desired conclusion (more persuaded, because they reached the conclusion on their own).

There have been a number of investigations of this question, in which an explicit conclusion is either included in or omitted from the message. For example, Struckman-Johnson and Struckman-Johnson (1996) compared AIDS public service announcements with and without an explicit recommendation to use condoms. In such studies, the overwhelmingly predominant finding is that messages that include explicit conclusions or recommendations are more persuasive than messages without such elements (e.g., Biddle, 1966; Cope & Richardson, 1972; Feingold & Knapp, 1977; Fine, 1957; Hovland & Mandell, 1952; Struckman-Johnson & Struckman-Johnson, 1996; for a review, see O'Keefe, 1997).[2]

There has often been speculation that the apparent advantage of explicit conclusions may be moderated by factors involving the hearer's ability and willingness to draw the appropriate conclusion when left unstated. Hence variables such as the receiver's intelligence (which bears on ability) and initial opinion (which bears on willingness) have often been mentioned as possible moderators (e.g., Hovland & Mandell, 1952; McGuire, 1985; Perloff, 1993). The expectation has been that explicit conclusions may not be necessary to, and might even impair, persuasive success for intellectually more capable audiences and for audiences initially favorable to the advocated view (because such audiences should be able and willing to reason to the advocated conclusion). What little relevant empirical evidence exists, however, gives no support to these speculations. For example, in several studies, the audience was comparatively intelligent and well educated (college students), and even so, there was a significant advantage for messages with explicit recommendations or conclusions (e.g., Fine, 1957; Hewitt, 1972).

One possible explanation for the persuasive advantage of explicitly stated conclusions is that when the conclusion is omitted, assimilation and contrast effects are encouraged. Assimilation and contrast effects are perceptual distortions concerning what position is being advocated by a message (C. W. Sherif et al., 1965; M. Sherif & Hovland, 1961): An assimilation effect occurs when a receiver perceives the message to advocate a view closer to his or her own than it actually does; a contrast effect occurs when a receiver perceives the message to advocate a position more discrepant from his or her own than it actually does. Both assimilation and contrast effects reduce persuasive effectiveness—contrast effects because they make the message appear to urge an even more unacceptable viewpoint, assimilation effects because they reduce the amount of change apparently sought by the message. Notably, relatively ambiguous messages (that is, messages ambiguous about what position is being advocated) appear especially susceptible to assimilation and contrast effects (Granberg & Campbell, 1977; C. W. Sherif et al., 1965, p. 153; M. Sherif & Hovland, 1961, p. 153). Thus the reduced persuasive success of messages omitting explicit conclusions may arise because such messages are relatively more subject to assimilation and contrast effects.

In any case, the research evidence suggests that persuaders commonly have little to gain (and much to lose) by leaving the message's conclusion implicit. Ordinarily, messages containing explicit statements of the conclusion will be more effective than messages that omit such statements.[3]

Recommendation Specificity

When the communicator is urging some particular action, the message can vary in the specificity with which the advocated action is described. The contrast here is between messages that provide only a general description of the advocate's recommended action and messages that provide a more specific (detailed) recommendation. Both messages thus contain an explicitly stated conclusion (in the form of an explicitly identified desired action), but one conclusion is more detailed than the other. For example, Leventhal, Jones, and Trembly (1966) compared persuasive messages recommending that students get tetanus shots at the student health clinic with messages providing a more detailed description of the recommended action (e.g., mentioning the location and hours of the clinic—although students were already familiar with such information). Similarly, Evans, Rozelle, Lasater, Dembroski, and Allen (1970) compared messages giving relatively general and unelaborated dental care recommendations with messages giving more detailed, specific recommendations. Such studies have commonly found that messages with more specific descriptions of the recommended action are more persuasive than those providing general, nonspecific recommendations (e.g., Evans et al., 1970; Frantz, 1994; Leventhal et al., 1966; Nova, 1990; Tanner, Day, & Crask, 1989; cf. Greene, Rubin, & Hale, 1995; for a review, see O'Keefe, 1997).[4]

It is not yet clear what might explain this effect, but one possibility is that more specific descriptions of the recommended action enhance the receiver's behavioral self-efficacy (perceived behavioral control). As discussed in Chapter 5, the theory of planned behavior (Ajzen, 1991) suggests that one factor influencing a person's behavioral intention is the individual's belief in his or her ability to engage in the behavior (perceived behavioral control). For example, people who do not think that they have the ability to engage in a regular exercise program (because they lack the time, the equipment, and so forth) are unlikely to undertake such behavior, even if they have positive attitudes toward exercising. It may be that—akin to the enhanced self-efficacy that can arise from seeing another person perform the action—receivers who encounter a detailed description of the recommended action may become more convinced of their ability to perform the behavior.[5]

▨ MESSAGE CONTENT

This section reviews research concerning the persuasive effects of certain variations in the contents of messages. Literally dozens of content variables have received at least some empirical attention; this review focuses mainly on selected message content factors for which the empirical evidence is relatively more extensive.

One-Sided Versus Two-Sided Messages

In many circumstances, a persuader will be aware of potential arguments supporting an opposing view. How should a persuader handle such arguments? One possibility is simply to ignore the opposing arguments, to not mention or acknowledge them in any way; the persuader would offer only constructive (supporting) arguments, that is, arguments supporting the persuader's advocated view. Alternatively, the persuader might not ignore opposing arguments but rather discuss them explicitly (while also presenting supporting arguments). This basic contrast—ignoring or discussing opposing arguments—has commonly been captured in persuasion research as the difference between a one-sided message (which presents supporting arguments but ignores opposing ones) and a two-sided message (which discusses both supporting and opposing arguments). (The most recent review is O'Keefe, 1999a; for other reviews and discussions, see Allen, 1991, 1993, 1998; Crowley & Hoyer, 1994; O'Keefe, 1993a; Pechmann, 1990.)

There appears to be no general difference in persuasiveness between one-sided and two-sided messages. That is, there is no general persuasive advantage gained either by ignoring or by discussing opposing arguments. Previous discussions of sidedness effects have mentioned many possible moderating factors that might influence the relative persuasiveness of one-sided and two-sided messages, including the audience's level of education, the availability of counterarguments to the audience (sometimes represented as the audience's familiarity with the topic), and the audience's initial opinion on the topic (see, e.g., Chu, 1967; R. G. Hass & Linder, 1972; Hovland, Lumsdaine, & Sheffield, 1949). None of these factors, however, appears to moderate this effect; for example, the relative persuasiveness of one- and two-sided messages does not vary as a function of whether the audience initially favors or opposes the advocated view (O'Keefe, 1999a).

A more complex picture emerges, however, if one distinguishes two varieties of two-sided messages, corresponding to two ways in which a message might discuss opposing arguments. A *refutational* two-sided message attempts to refute opposing arguments; this might involve criticizing the reasoning of an opposing argument, offering evidence to undermine an opposing claim, and so forth. A *nonrefutational* two-sided message acknowledges opposing considerations but does not attempt to refute them directly; it might suggest that the supporting arguments outweigh the opposing ones, but it does not directly attack the opposing considerations. One way of expressing the difference is to say that refutational two-sided messages characteristically attempt to undermine opposing arguments (by refuting them directly), whereas nonrefutational two-sided messages characteristically attempt to overwhelm opposing arguments (using supportive ones).

These two types of two-sided message have dramatically different persuasive effects when compared with one-sided messages. Specifically, refutational two-sided messages are dependably *more* persuasive than one-sided messages; nonrefutational two-sided messages, on the other hand, are significantly *less* persuasive than their one-sided counterparts.[6] That is, acknowledging opposing arguments without refuting them generally makes messages less persuasive (compared with ignoring opposing arguments), whereas refuting opposing arguments enhances persuasiveness.[7] As with the overall contrast between one-sided and two-sided messages, this pattern of effects seems largely unaffected by commonly proposed moderator factors such as audience education or initial attitude, although the research evidence is often sketchy (O'Keefe, 1999a).

One additional complexity is worth noting: Nonrefutational two-sided messages appear to have different effects in consumer advertising messages than in other persuasive messages (messages concerning political questions, public policy issues, and the like). In nonadvertising messages, nonrefutational two-sided messages are dependably less persuasive than their one-sided counterparts, but in consumer advertisements, nonrefutational two-sided messages are neither more nor less persuasive than one-sided advertisements (O'Keefe, 1999a).[8] Put differently: Nonrefutational two-sided advertising messages do not seem to suffer the same negative persuasion consequences that parallel nonadvertising messages do.

Some light might be shed on this by considering the effects of nonrefutational two-sided messages on credibility perceptions. The credibility of consumer advertising is boosted by the use of nonrefutational two-sided messages, but nonrefutational two-sided messages on other persuasive topics do not produce the same enhancement of credibility (O'Keefe, 1999a). It may be that receivers' initial skepticism about consumer advertising leads receivers to expect that advertisers will provide a one-sided depiction of the advertised product—and thus when an advertisement freely acknowledges (and does not refute) opposing considerations, the advertiser's credibility is enhanced (akin to the credibility enhancement effects obtained when communicators advocate positions opposed to their apparent self-interest, as discussed in Chapter 8; see, e.g., Wood & Eagly, 1981).

This enhanced credibility for advertisements, in turn, could have varying effects. It might boost the believability of both the supportive arguments and the acknowledged counterarguments (with these effects canceling each other out), it might enhance the counterarguments more than the supportive arguments (making the ad less persuasive), or it might enhance the supportive arguments more than the counterarguments (making the ad more persuasive). Across a number of nonrefutational two-sided ads, then, one might expect to find no dependable overall difference in persuasiveness—which is precisely the observed effect.

In sum, persuaders are best advised to meet opposing arguments head-on, by refuting them, rather than ignoring or (worse still) merely mentioning such counterarguments—save, perhaps, in the case of consumer advertising, where nonrefutational acknowledgment of opposing arguments promises to be about as persuasive as ignoring opposing considerations.

Discrepancy

In many circumstances, persuaders have some latitude in just how much opinion change they seek. A persuader might advocate a position only slightly discrepant from (different from) the receiver's viewpoint or might advocate a highly discrepant position (or, of course, might advocate some moderately discrepant view). So, for example, if a given audience believes that a 5% increase in state taxes is desirable, a persuader seeking a still larger increase might advocate a 7% increase, a 15% increase, or a 30% increase—with these various positions representing views successively more discrepant from the audience's initial position.

A number of investigations have examined the question of how such variations in discrepancy—the difference between the receiver's position and the position advocated by the message—influence persuasive outcomes. In a way, this research question can be seen as a matter of the relationship between the amount of change *sought* by the message (with greater discrepancy, more change is asked of the audience) and the amount of change *obtained* by the message.[9]

At a minimum, one can confidently say that the relationship between discrepancy and persuasive effectiveness is not simple. Some investigations have found that—at least under some conditions—greater discrepancies are associated with greater effectiveness (i.e., a positive relationship between discrepancy and attitude change; e.g., A. R. Cohen, 1959; Hovland & Pritzker, 1957). But other studies have reported that—at least in some circumstances—with increasing discrepancy, persuasive effectiveness is reduced (a negative relationship; e.g., A. R. Cohen, 1959; Hovland, Harvey, & Sherif, 1957).

The most plausible general image of the relationship of discrepancy and effectiveness is that of an inverted U-shaped curve, such that relatively little change is obtained with extremely small or extremely large discrepancies, and maximum effectiveness is to be found with moderate levels of discrepancy (for a general discussion of this view, see Whittaker, 1967; for findings of such curvilinearity—at least under some conditions—see, e.g., E. Aronson, Turner, & Carlsmith, 1963; Freedman, 1964; Sakaki, 1980; M. J. Smith, 1978; Whittaker, 1963, 1965). That is, with increasing discrepancy, there is increasing attitude change—up to a point (the peak of the curve); beyond that point, increases in discrepancy are associated with decreases in attitude change. This general curvilinear model can accommodate otherwise inconsistent findings of positive and negative relationships. For instance, if a given experiment has only relatively small levels of discrepancy, the results might well seem to suggest that increasing discrepancy leads to increasing attitude change (because there was not a sufficiently large discrepancy used in the research). Similarly, an experiment using only relatively large discrepancies might yield results indicating that increases in discrepancy lead to lessened effectiveness.

But even this curvilinear conception of the discrepancy-effectiveness relationship requires some complications. It is unlikely that just one curve describes the relationship; rather, it is likely that there is a family of curves—all having the same general inverted U shape, but with the point of inflection in the curve (the peak, the point at which the curve turns back down) coming at different discrepancies. In some circumstances, that is, the point of maximum effectiveness may come at a relatively small discrepancy, but in another situation, the point of maximum effectiveness may be at some larger discrepancy. Thus it is not enough to know that the general shape of the discrepancy-effectiveness relationship is that of an inverted U. What is crucial is knowing what factors influence the location of the point of inflection in that curve—knowing the circumstances under which the point of maximum effectiveness occurs at relatively small discrepancies and those under which it occurs at relatively large ones.

A number of factors appear to influence the point of inflection in the discrepancy-effectiveness curve. One is communicator credibility. The peak of the curve appears to occur at smaller discrepancies for low-credibility communicators than it does for high-credibility communicators (see, e.g., E. Aronson et al., 1963; Bergin, 1962; Bochner & Insko, 1966). That is, the optimal level of discrepancy is likely to be somewhat greater for a high-credibility communicator than for a low-credibility communicator; high-credibility sources can safely advocate somewhat more discrepant positions than can low-credibility sources.

A second apparent influence is the personal relevance or importance of the topic for the receiver. Some research evidence indicates that for relatively more important or relevant issues, the peak of the curve occurs at lower levels of discrepancy, whereas on less relevant issues, the curve peaks at some larger discrepancy (see, e.g., Freedman, 1964; Rhine & Severance 1970; Sakaki, 1980). In a sense, then, as the issue becomes more personally important to the receiver, discrepancy becomes less tolerable.

A third factor is whether the advocated view is proattitudinal or counterattitudinal for the receiver. Several studies suggest that proattitudinal discrepancies are more likely to be favorably received than are counterattitudinal discrepancies (Fishbein & Lange, 1990; Lange & Fishbein, 1983; Nemeth & Endicott, 1976). Imagine, for example, a receiver who believes that state taxes should be increased 2%. A communication urging an 8% increase and a communication supporting a 4% decrease are in a sense equally discrepant from that receiver's view (each advocates a change that is six percentage points different from the receiver's view)—but the communication proposing a tax increase is at least on the "right" side of the issue for this receiver (and is, in that sense, proattitudinal) and hence may get a more favorable reception than the message proposing a decrease. The suggestion thus is that it is not simply the sheer amount of discrepancy that matters but also whether the advocated view and the receiver's view fall on the same side of the neutral point (the same side of the issue).

Fear Appeals

The use of fear as a persuasive technique is an altogether common one. "If you don't do what I recommend," the communicator suggests, "then these terrible, fearful consequences will befall you." For example, high school driver education programs may show films depicting gruesome traffic accidents in an effort to discourage dangerous driving practices (such as drinking and driving), antismoking messages may display the horrors of lung cancer, and dental hygiene messages may emphasize the ravages of gum disease.

The effectiveness of such fear appeal messages has been extensively studied. The central question that researchers have addressed concerns just how strong the fear appeal should be: Are stronger fear appeals more effective than weaker ones, or vice versa, or is there perhaps no general difference between them?

Defining Fear Appeal Variations. In thinking about this research question, it is crucial to be clear about how strong and weak (or high and low) fear appeals are to be defined. Unfortunately, there are two fundamentally different—and easily confused—ways of conceiving of the variation in fear appeals. One way of defining variations in the strength of fear appeals is by reference to the properties of the communication. That is, a high fear appeal message is one containing explicit, vivid depictions of negative consequences, and a low fear appeal message is a tamer, toned-down version. This way of defining fear appeal variations, however, makes no reference to the actual arousal of fear in the audience. By this definition, a high fear appeal message and a low fear appeal message might evoke the same degree of fear.

The second way of defining fear appeal variations is by reference to the degree of fear aroused in the audience. In this conception, a high fear appeal message is a message that evokes comparatively greater fear or anxiety in receivers, and a low fear appeal message is one that elicits relatively less fear. This way of defining fear appeal variations makes no reference to the intrinsic characteristics of the message but instead uses the degree of aroused fear as the index for fear appeal variations.

Obviously, these two ways of conceiving of high versus low fear appeals are different. A message might be a high fear appeal by the first definition (because it contains gruesome contents) but not by the second (if it fails to actually arouse fear). Equally obviously, there is a potential for great confusion in thinking about a research question such as "Are high fear appeals more effective than low fear appeals?" This question might be interpreted either as "Are messages with stronger contents more effective than those with weaker contents?" or as "Are messages that arouse greater fear more effective than those arousing lesser fear?" Because these are different questions, it is plainly important to distinguish them.

The Research Evidence. Research concerning fear appeals is extensive and complex, but an overview of the findings can be expressed in four broad conclusions. First, messages with more intense contents do generally arouse greater fear. To be sure, the relationship between fear appeal message variations and aroused fear is not perfect (expressed as a correlation, estimates of the mean effect range between .30 and .40), suggesting that influencing the audience's level of fear is not necessarily something easily accomplished (for reviews, see Boster & Mongeau, 1984; Mongeau, 1998; Witte & Allen, 2000).[10] On reflection, of course, this may not be too surprising. A persuader may be mistaken about what will be fearful (for instance, it would be wrong to assume that death is the most fearful possible outcome one can invoke; see Ditto, Druley, Moore, Danks, & Smucker, 1996), and what one person finds extremely fearful may be only mildly worrisome to another person. Still, in general, stronger fear appeal contents do arouse greater fear.[11]

Second, messages with stronger fear appeal contents also are more persuasive (in changing attitudes, intentions, and actions) than those with weaker contents, although this effect is smaller than the effect of message fear appeal variations on aroused fear (expressed as correlations, the effects average between .10 and .20; for reviews, see Boster & Mongeau, 1984; Mongeau, 1998; Sutton, 1982; Witte & Allen, 2000). This weaker effect on persuasive outcomes is consistent with the idea that fear (the aroused emotional state) mediates the effect of fear appeal message manipulations on persuasive outcomes. That is, the invited image is that varying the message contents produces variations in aroused fear, which in turn are related to changes in attitudes, intentions, and actions (and thus the relationship between message manipulations and persuasive outcomes would be expected to be weaker than the relationship between message manipulations and fear).[12]

Third (and a natural corollary of the first two), messages that successfully arouse greater fear are also generally more persuasive. That is, in studies with messages that have been shown to arouse dependably different amounts of fear, the messages that arouse greater fear are more persuasive than the messages that arouse lesser fear (for reviews, see Sutton, 1982; Witte & Allen, 2000).

Fourth, there is little evidence of any curvilinearity in these relationships. It has sometimes been thought that perhaps as message materials become very intense, then less fear might be aroused (and persuasive effects will weaken). That is, the thought has been that a persuader might "go too far" in using fear appeals. But the evidence in hand gives little indication of any such curvilinear effects (see Boster & Mongeau, 1984; Mongeau, 1998; Sutton, 1992; Witte & Allen, 2000).

Explaining Fear Appeal Effects. At present, there are competing explanations for the observed fear appeal effects, and it is not clear which is the best (for discussion of some alternatives, see Dillard, 1994; Eagly & Chaiken, 1993, pp. 431-447; Girandola, 2000; Witte, 1998). But a sense of some of the issues can be had by considering one especially well studied explanatory framework: protection motivation theory (PMT; Rogers, 1975, 1983; Rogers & Prentice-Dunn, 1997).

As a starting point, it may be helpful to notice that a fear appeal message employs what amounts to a problem-solution message format: It identifies a potential (fear-inducing) problem and recommends a solution (the advocated action). PMT offers an analysis of each part of this format. Protection motivation refers to persons' motivations to adopt protective behaviors in the face of possible threats. PMT identifies two broad mediating processes behind protection motivation, namely, threat appraisal and coping appraisal (corresponding to assessment of the problem and assessment of the solution). Each of these, however, is further unpacked.

Threat appraisal is said to depend on threat severity (that is, the perceived severity of the problem) and threat vulnerability (one's perception of the likelihood that one will encounter or be susceptible to the threat); as persons perceive the threat to be more severe and as they perceive themselves to be more vulnerable to the threat, persons are expected to have higher protection motivation. Coping appraisal is said to depend on response efficacy (the degree to which the recommended action is perceived to be effective in dealing with the problem) and on self-efficacy (one's perceived ability to adopt or perform the protective action); as the perceived efficaciousness of the response increases and as perceived ability to perform the action increases, persons are expected to have greater protection motivation.[13]

For example, imagine someone contemplating adopting an exercise program to prevent heart disease who thinks that heart disease is not all that serious a problem (low threat severity) and, in any case, perceives herself to be relatively unlikely to have heart disease because no one in her family has had it (low threat vulnerability); moreover, she is not convinced that exercise will really prevent heart disease (low response efficacy), and she does not think that she has the discipline to stick with an exercise program (low self-efficacy). Such a person presumably will have relatively low protection motivation, as reflected in corresponding actions (namely, not exercising) and intentions (not intending to exercise).

Experimental tests of this model have commonly involved manipulating some message feature in an effort to influence the theoretically important mediating states. For instance, to influence threat severity, participants would receive either a message suggesting that the consequences are extremely negative or one suggesting that they are minor; to influence response efficacy, the message either would depict the recommended action as highly effective in dealing with the threat or would describe it as an inconsistent or unreliable means of coping with the threat. (For some examples, see Brouwers & Sorrentino, 1993; Fruin, Pratt, & Owen, 1991; Rippetoe & Rogers, 1987.)[14] Such experimental message variations have been found to have the anticipated effects on the corresponding mediating states (e.g., messages varying in their depictions of response efficacy produce corresponding variations in perceived response efficacy; for reviews, see Milne, Sheeran, & Orbell, 2000; Witte & Allen, 2000; see also Mongeau, 1998, p. 62, n. 4) and have been found to have parallel (but weaker) effects on relevant persuasive outcome variables such as attitudes, intentions, and behavior (for reviews, see Floyd, Prentice-Dunn, & Rogers, 2000; Witte & Allen, 2000).[15] These findings indicate that PMT has identified some important influences on protective intentions and actions and thus suggest that PMT-based assessments can be useful in identifying potential foci for influence efforts. For example, PMT-based assessments may indicate whether to focus on threat severity, threat vulnerability, response efficacy, or self-efficacy (see, e.g., Greening, 1997; Melamed, Rabinowitz, Feiner, Weisberg, & Ribak, 1996; Plotnikoff & Higginbotham, 1995).[16]

But PMT's analysis does not emphasize the emotion of fear. It depicts protection-motivated intentions and actions as influenced by various cognitive assessments (threat appraisal and coping appraisal); the emotion of fear is not given a direct causal role to play in fear appeal effects but instead is treated as a by-product (arising from perceptions of threat severity and vulnerability). One central way in which fear appeal explanations differ is precisely whether the key factor at work is taken to be an emotional reaction (fear) or a cognitive reaction (e.g., a judgment of the seriousness of the problem being depicted). Some theoretical accounts have a causal role for fear (e.g., Hovland, Janis, & Kelley, 1953; Witte, 1992), whereas others—such as PMT—place much greater emphasis on cognitive processes (e.g., Beck & Frankel, 1981; Sutton, 1982).

Both sorts of account are consistent with the broad patterns of fear appeal research findings mentioned earlier. For example, the finding that messages that successfully arouse greater fear are also generally more persuasive does not necessarily mean that fear has a causal (mediating) role. A given message might induce more fear in receivers than does another—but that message may also be more successful in leading receivers to believe that the fearful consequences are severe (harmful, noxious, disadvantageous). The real force at work behind the message's effectiveness might be the change in those beliefs, not the arousal of fear. Thus greater aroused fear can be associated with greater persuasive effectiveness not because greater fear causes greater effectiveness but because both fear and effectiveness are caused by the same underlying factor (namely, the cognitive reactions to the message).

In sorting out such matters, one important general question is whether fear has some effect on persuasive outcomes over and above the effects of accompanying cognitive changes. If fear does have such effects, then presumably a good explanation will need to give some causal role to the emotional reaction; if fear does not have such effects, then a purely cognitive explanation might be sufficient. There is less research evidence on this issue than one might like (see, e.g., Sutton & Eiser, 1984; Sutton & Hallett, 1988, 1989), and hence conclusions are probably premature. In any case, one ought not to assume that the apparent covariation of induced fear and persuasive effectiveness means that fear causes effectiveness.

Beyond Fear Appeals. Fear is perhaps the best studied of the various emotions that persuasive appeals might try to engage, although there has also been some work on other emotions such as pride (Aaker & Williams, 1998); disgust (Nabi, 1998); and especially guilt (e.g., Coulter & Pinto, 1995; Ruth & Faber, 1988; for reviews, see O'Keefe, 2000, in press). These lines of work have a common underlying idea, namely, that one avenue to persuasion involves the arousal of an emotional state (such as fear or guilt), with the advocated action providing a means for the receiver to deal with those aroused feelings.[17] (For some general treatments of emotions and persuasion, see Breckler, 1993; Jorgensen, 1998; Nabi, 1999.)

There is another broad way, however, in which emotions might figure in persuasion, namely, through the anticipation of emotional states. Anticipated emotions plainly shape intentions and actions (for example, people often avoid actions that they think would make them feel guilty; Birkimer et al., 1993), and such anticipations can be influenced (e.g., Grasmick et al., 1991). This research is discussed more extensively in Chapter 5 (concerning theories of behavioral intention) in the context of considering how inclusion of anticipated affective states might enhance the predictability of intentions beyond that afforded by the theory of planned behavior. The point to be noticed here is simply that emotional considerations might play a role in persuasive messages either through the actual arousal of emotions or through the invocation of expected emotional states.

Examples Versus Statistical Summaries

A number of studies have examined the persuasive effects of two forms of information: the example (or case history), which describes some instance in detail, and the statistical summary, which provides a quantitative summary of a large number of instances (in the form of averages, percentages, etc.). This research thus compares information about one (or a few) cases (individuals, objects, or events) and equivalent, summarized statistical information about many cases.

Despite the seemingly greater informativeness of statistical information, it is clear that a single example can be more persuasive than parallel statistical summary information. For example, Koballa (1986) provided preservice high school teachers with favorable information about a particular type of science curriculum. In one condition, the information was presented as the report of a single teacher who had used the curriculum; the teacher discussed how much more interested the students were, how much more the students learned, and how student performance improved in related areas (such as math and writing). In the other condition, the same points were made (about students being more interested, learning more, and improving in related areas), but the information was presented as a statistical summary of the findings of a dozen or so uses of this curriculum. The case study report was much more persuasive than the statistical summary report (although, obviously, the statistical summary was based on the experience of many teachers, not just one). Other investigators have also reported finding that examples or case histories are more influential than statistical information or other data summaries (for a review, see S. E. Taylor & Thompson, 1982).

But this is not a consistent result. Some studies have found no dependable difference in persuasiveness between examples and statistical summaries (e.g., Krupat, Smith, Leach, & Jackson, 1997), and some have found statistical summaries to be more persuasive than examples (e.g., Baesler & Burgoon, 1994; Hoeken, 1999). That is, there appears to be no reason to suppose any general persuasive advantage of one of these information forms over the other, and yet the observed differences in persuasiveness are sometimes large (suggesting the potential importance of this variation). Thus a great deal is yet to be learned on this subject; the mechanisms underlying the various observed effects (and the conditions that encourage one or another effect) remain to be identified.[18]

◼ SEQUENTIAL-REQUEST STRATEGIES

Substantial research has been conducted concerning the effectiveness of two sequential-request influence strategies, the foot-in-the-door (FITD) strategy and the door-in-the-face (DITF) strategy. In each strategy, the request that the communicator is primarily interested in (the target request) is preceded by some other request; the question of interest is how compliance with the target request is affected by the presence of the preceding request.[19]

Foot-in-the-Door

The Strategy. The FITD strategy consists of initially making a small request of the receiver, which the receiver grants, and then making the (larger) target request. The hope is that having gotten one's foot in the door, the second (target) request will be looked on more favorably by the receiver. The question thus is whether receivers will be more likely to grant a second request if they have already granted an initial, smaller request.

The Research Evidence. The research evidence suggests that this FITD strategy can enhance compliance with the second (target) request. For example, in Freedman and Fraser's (1966, Experiment 2) FITD condition, homeowners were initially approached by a member of the "Community Committee for Traffic Safety" or the "Keep California Beautiful Committee." The requester either asked that the receiver display a small sign in their front window ("Be a safe driver" or "Keep California beautiful") or asked that they sign a petition supporting appropriate legislation (legislation that would promote either safer driving or keeping California beautiful). Two weeks later, a different requester (from "Citizens for Safe Driving") approached the receiver, asking if the receiver would be willing to have a large, unattractive "Drive Carefully" sign installed in the front yard for a week. In the control condition, in which receivers heard only the large request, fewer than 20% agreed to put the sign in the yard. But in the FITD conditions, more than 55% agreed.[20] This effect was obtained no matter whether the same topic was involved in the two requests (safe driving or beautification), and no matter whether the same action was involved (displaying a sign or signing a petition): Even receivers who initially signed the "Keep California beautiful" petition were more likely to agree to display the large safe driving yard sign. As these results suggest, the FITD strategy can be quite successful.

Several factors that influence the strategy's effectiveness (i.e., the size of the effect that the strategy has) have been identified. First, if the FITD strategy is to be successful, there must be no obvious external justification for complying with the initial request (for reviews, see Burger, 1999; Dillard, Hunter, & Burgoon, 1984). For example, if receivers are given some financial reward in exchange for complying with the first request, then the FITD strategy is not very successful. Second, the larger the first request (presuming it is agreed to by the receiver), the more successful the FITD strategy (see the review by Fern, Monroe, & Avila, 1986). Third, the FITD strategy appears to be more successful if the receiver actually performs the action requested in the initial request, as opposed to simply agreeing to perform the action (for reviews, see Beaman, Cole, Preston, Klentz, & Steblay, 1983; Burger, 1999; Fern et al., 1986; cf. Dillard et al., 1984). Fourth, the FITD strategy is more effective when the requests are prosocial requests (that is, requests from institutions that might provide some benefit to the community at large, such as civic or environmental groups) as opposed to nonprosocial requests (from profit-seeking organizations such as marketing firms; Dillard et al., 1984).[21]

Notably, several factors apparently do not affect the success of the FITD strategy. The time interval between the two requests does not make a difference (Beaman et al., 1983; Burger, 1999; Dillard et al., 1984; Fern et al., 1986); for example, Cann, Sherman, and Elkes (1975) obtained equivalent FITD effects with no delay between the two requests and with a delay of 710 days. Similarly, it does not appear to matter whether the same person makes the two requests (Fern et al., 1986).[22]

Explaining FITD Effects. The most widely accepted explanation for FITD effects has been based on self-perception processes (for a brief statement, see Freedman & Fraser, 1966; a more extensive discussion is provided by DeJong, 1979). Briefly, the explanation is that compliance with the first request leads receivers to make inferences about themselves; in particular, initial compliance is taken to enhance receivers' conceptions of their helpfulness, cooperativeness, and the like. These enhanced self-perceptions, in turn, are thought to increase the probability of the receiver's agreeing to the second request.

In some ways, the observed moderating factors are consistent with this self-perception explanation. For example, the presence of an external justification for initial compliance obviously undermines enhancement of the relevant self-perceptions: If one is paid money in exchange for agreeing to the initial request, it is more difficult to conclude that one is especially cooperative and helpful just because one agreed. Similarly, the larger the request initially agreed to, the more one's self-perceptions of helpfulness and cooperativeness should be enhanced ("If I'm going along with this big request, without any obvious external justification, then I must really be a pretty nice person, the kind of person who does this sort of thing"). And it's easier to think of oneself as a helpful, socially minded person when one agrees to requests from civic groups (as opposed to marketing firms) or when one actually performs the requested action (as opposed to merely agreeing to perform it).[23]

As attractive as the self-perception account is (given its ability to accommodate the observed moderator variable effects), there are at least two reasons to doubt its adequacy. First, as several commentators have remarked, it is implausible to suppose that self-perceptions of helpfulness would be deeply affected by compliance with small requests of the sort used in FITD research (Rittle, 1981, p. 435; Gorassini & Olson, 1995, p. 102). Presumably, persons' beliefs about their helpfulness rest on some large number of relevant experiences, and it seems unlikely that such beliefs would be significantly altered by consenting to a single small request.

Second, the explanation has fared poorly in studies that have included direct assessments of participants' self-perceptions of helpfulness (e.g., Rittle, 1981; C. A. Scott, 1977). For instance, Gorassini and Olson (1995) found that the self-perception changes attendant to various FITD manipulations were not related to target-request compliance. The failure to obtain confirming evidence in these studies is especially worrisome because these studies directly assess the hypothesized mediating state; such studies provide better evidence about an FITD explanation than do studies that manipulate some independent variable that is expected (on the basis of the explanation) to influence FITD effects (see Dillard, 1991).

At present, however, alternatives to the self-perception explanation are rather sketchy and not extensively studied. One common theme in several proposed alternatives is the suggestion that first-request compliance activates "powerful attitudes that already exist in the self" (Gorassini & Olson, 1995, p. 103), which then affect compliance with the target request. Depending on the particular situation, a number of sorts of attitudes may be relevant, including attitudes toward a general issue domain (e.g., environmental protection), attitudes about the self and self-appearance (e.g., a desire to be or appear compassionate), and so forth (see Ahluwalia & Burnkrant, 1993; Dillard, 1990, 1991; Gorassini & Olson, 1995). But these accounts have yet to receive the conceptual and empirical articulation required to yield an entirely satisfying explanation of the accumulated FITD research findings. In short, the self-perception account is on shaky ground, but no fully developed alternative is yet available.

Door-in-the-Face

The Strategy. The DITF strategy turns the FITD strategy on its head. The DITF strategy consists of initially making a large request, which the receiver turns down, and then making the smaller target request. The question is whether initially having (metaphorically) closed the door in the requester's face will enhance the receiver's compliance with the second request.

The Research Evidence. Studies of the DITF strategy have found that it can indeed enhance compliance. That is, receivers will at least sometimes be more likely to agree to a second smaller request if they have initially turned down a larger first request. For example, in a study reported by Cialdini et al. (1975, Experiment 1), individuals on campus sidewalks were approached by a student who indicated that he or she represented the county youth counseling program. In the DITF condition, persons were initially asked to volunteer to spend 2 hours a week for a minimum of 2 years as an unpaid counselor at a local juvenile detention center; no one agreed to this request. The requester then asked if the person would volunteer to chaperone a group of juveniles from the detention center on a 2-hour trip to the zoo. Among those in the control condition, who received only the target request, only 17% agreed to chaperone the zoo trip, but among those in the DITF condition, who initially turned down the large request, 50% agreed.

The research evidence also suggests that various factors moderate the success of the DITF strategy. DITF effects are larger if the two requests are made by the same person as opposed to by different persons (for relevant reviews, see Fern et al., 1986; O'Keefe & Hale, 1998, 2001); if the two requests have the same beneficiary as opposed to benefiting different persons (O'Keefe & Hale, 1998, 2001); if there is no delay between the requests (Dillard et al., 1984; Fern et al., 1986; O'Keefe & Hale, 1998, 2001); if the requests come from prosocial rather than nonprosocial organizations (Dillard et al., 1984; O'Keefe & Hale, 1998, 2001); and if the requests are made face-to-face as opposed to by telephone (O'Keefe & Hale, 1998, 2001).[24]

Explaining DITF Effects. The best-known explanation of DITF effects has been the reciprocal concessions explanation (see Cialdini et al., 1975). This explanation proposes that the successive requests make the situation appear to be one involving bargaining or negotiation—that is, a situation in which a concession by one side is supposed to be reciprocated by the other. This explanation suggests that the smaller second request represents a concession by the requester—and so the receiver reciprocates ("OK, you gave in a little bit by making a smaller request, so I'll also make a concession and agree with that request"). Some of the observed moderator variable effects are nicely explained by this account. For example, given this analysis, it makes sense that DITF effects should be smaller if different persons make the requests; if different persons make the requests, then no concession has been made (and hence there is no pressure to reciprocate a concession).

But for several reasons, one might doubt whether the reciprocal concessions explanation is entirely satisfactory. First, some moderator variable effects are not so obviously accommodated by the explanation. For example, it is not clear why having a different beneficiary for the second request should reduce the strategy's effectiveness.

Second, several meta-analytic reviews have found that DITF effects are not influenced by the size of the concession made (Fern et al., 1986; O'Keefe & Hale, 1998, 2001), and this seems inconsistent with the reciprocal concessions account. The reciprocal concessions account appears to predict that larger concessions will make the DITF strategy more effective (by putting greater pressure on the receiver), and hence the failure to find such an effect seemingly indicates some weakness in the explanation. The explanation might be defended against this criticism, however, by suggesting that any concession merely needs to be large enough to trigger the reciprocal concessions norm; so long as the concession surpasses this threshold, the reciprocal concessions mechanism will be engaged (and thus increasing the size of the concession beyond that threshold would not affect the strategy's effectiveness).[25]

Third, DITF effects do not appear to be influenced by emphasizing or deemphasizing the concession. For example, stressing that the second request represents a concession does not enhance the strategy's effectiveness, and deemphasizing the fact of a concession does not weaken the strategy (see, e.g., Goldman, McVeigh, & Richterkessing, 1984; R. L. Miller, Seligman, Clark, & Bush, 1976; for a review, see O'Keefe, 1999b).

Finally, direct assessments of (what look to be) relevant perceptions offer little encouragement for this explanation. The reciprocal concessions account suggests that the request sequence makes the situation seem like bargaining or negotiation (and thus a circumstance in which reciprocation of concessions is normative). But Tusing and Dillard (2000) have reported that DITF situations are commonly perceived as more similar to helping situations than to bargaining situations.

An alternative account suggests that guilt arousal underlies DITF effects (O'Keefe & Figge, 1997). The general idea is that first-request refusal arouses feelings of guilt, which then motivate target-request compliance. This account appears capable of accommodating the observed moderator variable effects. For example, declining prosocial requests probably generates greater guilt than does declining nonprosocial requests, thus making the strategy more effective for prosocial organizations. Similarly, one might expect greater reduction of guilt if one can consent to a second request that comes from the same requester (or that has the same benefi-ciary) as the first request. (For more detailed discussion of the relationship of observed moderator variable effects and a guilt-based account, see O'Keefe & Hale, 1998.) Some direct evidence suggests that even if target-request compliance does not actually reduce persons' guilt, DITF com-pliance can be motivated by the expectation of reduced guilt (O'Keefe & Figge, 1999).

▧ CONCLUSION

Researchers have investigated a number of message characteristics as possi-ble influences on persuasive effectiveness. These message factors are varied, ranging from the details of internal message organization (climax versus anticlimax argument order) to the sequencing of multiple messages (as in the FITD and DITF strategies). Indeed, this discussion can do no more than provide a sampling of the message features that have been studied.

Visual aspects of persuasive messages, however, have received relatively little systematic research attention (for a general treatment, see Messaris, 1997). Surely, this reflects the better articulation of the conceptual frame-works for describing verbal variation than the corresponding frameworks for describing imagery in persuasive messages (not to mention schemes for describing the interplay of images and verbal materials). But the promi-nence of visual images in persuasive messages suggests that this is likely to be an increasingly significant focus for research.

▧ NOTES

1. This variation (stating or omitting the message's overall conclusion) thus is different from varying whether the message states the conclusions to its individual supporting arguments (e.g., Gutteling, 1993; Kardes, 1988). Both have been glossed as "conclusion omission" manipulations but are plainly distinguishable variations.

2. The observed mean effect size (across 14 such studies) corresponds to a cor-relation of .12 (O'Keefe, 1997). Cruz's (1998) review offers a different view but omits a number of relevant studies (e.g., Feingold & Knapp, 1977; Leventhal, Watts, & Pagano, 1967) and includes an irrelevant case (Kardes, 1988).

3. It may be that in social influence settings such as psychotherapy, or perhaps in unusual persuasive message circumstances (see, e.g., Linder & Worchel, 1970), there can be some benefit to letting the receiver draw the conclusion, but in ordi-nary persuasive message contexts, the evidence indicates that such benefits are, as a rule, unlikely to obtain. It will plainly be useful for future research to obtain a prin-cipled description of the circumstances in which explicit conclusions might impair persuasive success (see, e.g., Sawyer & Howard, 1991).

4. Across 18 such studies, the mean effect size corresponds to a correlation of .10 (O'Keefe, 1997).

5. One might also consider the possibility that a message with a more specific description of the recommended action makes it easier for receivers to imagine themselves performing that action. This possibility is worth noticing because at least under some conditions, imagining performing a hypothetical future behavior can lead to increased (perceived and actual) likelihood of performing that behavior (C. A. Anderson, 1983; Gregory, Cialdini, & Carpenter, 1982; R. T. Sherman & Anderson, 1987). This obviously supplies another possible explanation for the enhanced persuasiveness of messages with more specific descriptions of the advocated action. But this imagined behavior account might not be inconsistent with a self-efficacy-based explanation because the mechanism by which imagined behavior has effects on future behavior is not yet clear. One possibility is that imagining behavioral performance makes reasons for performing the behavior more salient (see R. T. Sherman & Anderson, 1987), thereby enhancing the likelihood of subsequent behavior. But alternatively (or in addition), the effect might arise by influencing perceived behavioral control. That is, imagining oneself performing a behavior might enhance one's belief in one's ability to do so.

6. The average persuasive advantage of refutational two-sided messages over one-sided messages (across 42 studies) corresponds to a correlation of .08. The average persuasive disadvantage of nonrefutational two-sided messages compared with one-sided messages (across 65 studies) corresponds to a correlation of −.05 (O'Keefe, 1999a).

7. Both kinds of two-sided messages are perceived as more credible than one-sided messages. For refutational two-sided messages, the effect corresponds to a correlation of .11 (across 20 studies); for nonrefutational two-sided messages, the correlation is .08 (across 36 cases; O'Keefe, 1999a).

8. Refutational two-sided messages appear to enjoy a persuasive advantage (over one-sided messages) in both advertising (mean effect corresponding to a correlation of .07, across 9 cases) and nonadvertising (mean effect corresponding to a correlation of .08, across 33 cases) messages, although there are too few studies of refutational two-sided advertisements to permit one to be confident of this effect (see O'Keefe, 1999a).

9. This research question is perhaps more difficult to investigate than one might initially suppose. For instance, if a given experiment uses a single message and so generates varying degrees of discrepancy by using receivers whose initial positions vary, then the degree of discrepancy is confounded with initial position, creating difficulties in interpreting the experimental results. For a nice (if brief) discussion of subtleties here, see Insko (1967, pp. 69-70); for some related discussion, see Kaplowitz and Fink (1997) and Kaplowitz, Fink, Mulcrone, Atkin, and Dabil (1991).

10. Even these estimates may be misleading. For example, the most extensive and recent review (Witte & Allen, 2000) reported a mean correlation of .30 between fear appeal message manipulations and aroused fear (across 51 cases). But this figure was inflated by (a) the exclusion of studies with a failed manipulation

check (studies in which there was not a dependable difference in aroused fear between message conditions) and (b) the correction of individual effect sizes, before being analyzed, for factors such as range restriction (thereby increasing the size of the individual effects). An analysis that included all studies and used uncorrected correlations would presumably yield a smaller mean effect.

11. There has been regrettably little attention to describing the particulars of fear appeal message variations. The meta-analytic treatments of this literature commonly simply rely on the primary research categories (e.g., "strong" and "weak" fear appeal) and do not consider what specific message features might have been experimentally varied. The consequence is that we know rather less than we might about what particular message variations might produce the observed effects (but also notice that protection motivation theory, to be discussed shortly, contains some suggestions about how fear appeal message contents might be analyzed).

12. Unfortunately, fear appeal research results are often reported in ways that do not permit full examination of the relationships of interest. For example, it is common that a researcher will create two message variations (high and low fear appeal contents), check that they arouse different levels of fear (in a manipulation check), and then report the contrast between the two message conditions for the persuasion-outcome dependent variables (such as attitude and intention)—leaving unreported the direct relationship between the presumed mediating state (fear) and the persuasion outcome variables.

This is actually a rather widespread problem in persuasion research. It appears not only in fear appeal research and in research on other emotional appeals (such as guilt; O'Keefe, 2000, p. 93, n. 7) but also in research on such topics as credibility (see Hoyt, 1996, p. 431) and (in a slightly different form) argument quality. A complete analysis of this problem cannot be given here, but the primary suspect, I think, is training in experimental analysis of variance (ANOVA)-based data analysis methods. Such methods naturally encourage thinking in factorial experimental designs in which variables are unambiguously classified as independent or dependent; such designs can make it difficult for investigators to see exactly what data analyses are relevant to assessing the claims of interest (because the standard analysis of the usual experimental design has no place for examination of the relationship between a possible mediating state and an outcome). A brief way of putting the problem is to say that assessments of intervening states, rather than being understood (and analyzed) as assessing mediating states, have instead been seen (and analyzed) as providing manipulation checks for independent variables.

13. PMT is actually a bit more complex than this. Threat appraisal is said to depend not just on threat severity and threat vulnerability but also on the rewards of adopting a maladaptive response (e.g., the perceived rewards of not adopting the protective behavior); coping appraisal is said to depend not just on response efficacy and self-efficacy but also on response costs (perceived costs of taking the protective response, such as money, time, and so forth). But maladaptive rewards and response costs have received less research attention than the other four elements, and the simpler version presented here suffices to introduce the relevant general issues. (Moreover, the relation between self-efficacy and response costs is

not lucid. After all, one reason why I might think that I can't actually carry out a protective behavior such as an exercise program [low self-efficacy] is that it takes too much time [high response cost]. But PMT treats these separately.)

14. For ethical reasons, when the message topic concerns a real (as opposed to fabricated) threat, the experimental conditions often involve contrasts between (for instance) a high-vulnerability message and a no-message control condition (e.g., Boer & Seydel, 1996; Yzer et al., 1998).

15. Expressed as correlations, the mean effects of message manipulations (of threat severity, threat vulnerability, response efficacy, and self-efficacy) on corresponding perceptions (perceived threat severity, perceived threat vulnerability, and so forth) range from roughly .30 to .45 (Witte & Allen, 2000); Milne et al. (2000) reported mean effects ranging from about .25 to .65 but analyzed a much smaller set of studies. The mean effects (expressed as correlations) of these message manipulations on persuasive outcomes (attitudes, intentions, and behaviors) were reported by Witte and Allen (2000) to be in the neighborhood of .10 to .20; Floyd et al. (2000), reviewing a different (and usually smaller) set of studies, reported mean effects corresponding to correlations roughly in a range from .20 to .40. The mean correlations between PMT-related perceptions (perceived threat severity and so on) and persuasive outcomes (intentions and behaviors) were reported by Milne et al. (2000) to range roughly from .05 to .35, although relatively few cases were available for analysis.

16. It is not yet clear exactly how these elements combine to produce protective intentions and actions, however. Some versions of PMT have suggested that the elements combine in some multiplicative way (for example, one possibility is that perceived severity and perceived vulnerability combine multiplicatively to yield threat appraisal, that perceived response efficacy and perceived self-efficacy similarly combine to yield coping appraisal, and that threat appraisal and coping appraisal then combine multiplicatively to yield protection motivation), although at least some multiplicative models seem not to have fared well empirically (for illustrative studies, see Maddux & Rogers, 1983; Mulilis & Lippa, 1990; Rogers & Mewborn, 1976; for some discussion, see Eagly & Chaiken, 1993, pp. 441-447; Rogers, 1975, 1983; Weinstein, 2000).

Any number of alternatives are possible. For example, the extended parallel process model (EPPM; Witte, 1992, 1994, 1998) suggests that threat appraisal occurs first (and reflects threat severity and threat vulnerability, combined additively rather than multiplicatively). If the threat is taken to be low, then no protection motivations are activated (given the lack of a threat, coping appraisal is irrelevant and no change in intention or behavior is needed). But if the threat is perceived to be high, then coping appraisal is initiated (and reflects, additively, response efficacy and self-efficacy). If coping capability is taken to be sufficiently high given the level of threat, then "danger control" processes are engaged, in which people adopt the recommended actions to control the apparent danger. If coping capability is taken to be insufficient, however, then "fear control" processes take over, and persons may engage in denial or defensive avoidance (seeking to manage their feelings of fear rather than thinking about the threat). (For some applications of the EPPM, see McMahan, Witte, & Meyer, 1998; Roberto, Meyer, Johnson, & Atkin, 2000; Witte, Berkowitz, Cameron, & McKeon, 1998; Witte et al., 1993; Witte & Morrison, 1995.) As an example of another possibility, the relationships of these variables may change depending on whether the recommended action is designed to prevent the threat (as in the use of condoms to prevent HIV infection) or to detect the threat (as in screening procedures such as HIV tests or mammography); see Girandola (2000) and Millar and Millar (1996b).

17. These various lines of research also commonly focus on a single emotional reaction (fear, guilt, and so on). Although research is only beginning to untangle the complexities here, there is good reason to think that messages influence multiple emotions and that the interplay of evoked emotions may be important in influencing message effects (Dillard & Peck, 2001; Dillard, Plotnick, Godbold, Freimuth, & Edgar, 1996; Stout & Sego, 1994).

18. A thorough review of the relevant research has yet to be done. Allen and Preiss's (1997) review includes studies that do not compare the persuasive effectiveness of examples and parallel quantitative summaries (e.g., Harte, 1976) and does not include studies that do contain such comparisons (e.g., Rook, 1986). Zillmann and Brosius (2000) discuss a good deal of relevant work, although their focus is the use of examples in news reports.

19. Other compliance techniques have also received some research attention. Notable among these are the "that's-not-all" technique, in which before any response is given to the initial request, the communicator makes the offer more attractive (see, e.g., Burger, 1986; Burger, Reed, DeCesare, Rauner, & Rozolis, 1999); the "low-ball" technique, in which the communicator initially obtains the receiver's commitment to an action and then increases the cost of performing the action (see, e.g., Cialdini, Cacioppo, Bassett, & Miller, 1978; Katzev & Brownstein, 1989); and the "even-a-penny-helps" technique, in which fundraisers explicitly legitimize small contributions (see, e.g., Cialdini & Schroeder, 1976; Reeves & Saucer, 1993). Cialdini and Trost (1998, pp. 168-180) provide a useful general discussion of compliance techniques.

20. The reported compliance rate in the FITD conditions (55%) does not represent a "pure" FITD effect because all participants who heard the first request (regardless of whether they agreed to it) were included as FITD participants in Freedman and Fraser's (1966) data analysis. But if those who declined the initial request had been excluded from the analysis, then a higher target-request compliance rate in the FITD condition might have been explained as an artifact of having excluded dispositionally uncooperative persons (those generally unwilling to accede to requests) from the FITD condition denominator but not the control condition denominator (or, alternatively expressed, as an artifact of having dispositionally cooperative persons overrepresented in the FITD condition by virtue of having passed through what amounted to the screening procedure of the initial request).

21. The average effect size in FITD studies is roughly equivalent to a correlation of between .10 and .15, with larger effects under optimal conditions (Beaman et al., 1983; Dillard et al., 1984; Fern et al., 1986).

22. Chartrand, Pinckert, and Burger (1999) found that if the same person makes both requests with no delay between them, the FITD technique may backfire. But even this effect is apparently not general. Burger's (1999) review reported an advantage for FITD conditions over control conditions when the same person made both requests without a delay (mean effect corresponding to a correlation of .05 across 24 studies); when the same person made the requests but with a delay between them (mean correlation of .07, seven studies); when different persons made the requests without a delay (mean correlation of .11, five studies); and when different persons made the requests with a delay (mean correlation of .12, 28 studies). On the face of things, these reported mean effects underwrite (a) a conclusion that FITD effects are unaffected by delay and (b) a suspicion that FITD effects perhaps might be larger when different persons make the requests than when the same person makes them (but in the absence of appropriate statistical analyses—comparing the differences between the relevant mean effects—this can be only a suspicion).

23. The lack of an effect for the time interval between the requests is sometimes seen as inconsistent with the self-perception explanation (e.g., Dillard et al., 1984). But it is not clear what predictions the self-perception explanation would make here. On the one hand, it might be expected that with increasing delay between the two requests, the FITD effect would weaken (because there would be many opportunities, during the interval, for other events to undermine the self-attributions of helpfulness and cooperativeness). On the other hand, it might be predicted that with increasing delay between the requests, the FITD effect would become stronger (because it takes time for receivers to reflect on the causes of their behavior, and so to make the required self-attributions). Or (as Beaman et al., 1983, note) it might be that both these processes are at work and cancel each other out.

24. The average effect size in DITF studies is equivalent to a correlation of between .07 and .10; under optimal conditions, larger effects (averaging .15) are observed (Dillard et al., 1984; Fern et al., 1986; O'Keefe & Hale, 1998, 2001).

25. This defense is certainly adequate as far as it goes, but consider that if larger concessions had been found to be associated with greater DITF effectiveness, such a result surely would have been counted as evidence supporting the reciprocal concessions explanation. Thus the failure to find such effects requires at a minimum some revision in the account (such as represented by the articulation of a threshold model version of the explanation).

Receiver and Context Factors

10

This chapter reviews research concerning the effects that various recipient characteristics and contextual factors have on persuasive outcomes. The discussion is organized around three main topics: natural or enduring receiver characteristics (such as sex and personality traits), induced receiver factors (induced states that may influence persuasive effects), and contextual factors.

▨ NATURAL RECEIVER CHARACTERISTICS

General Persuasibility

Persuasibility refers to how easily someone is persuaded in general (that is, across topics, sources, settings, other receiver characteristics, and so on). It is an open question whether there is some general persuasibility difference among persons (whether there really is some such persuasibility factor, something that makes some people generally more easily persuaded than others).

Some indirect evidence indicates the existence of such persuasibility differences. This evidence comes from research designs in which persons receive multiple persuasive messages on various topics; with such designs, one can look for evidence of intraindividual consistency in the amount of attitude change displayed. This evidence does suggest that there may indeed be some differences between persons in how easily they are persuaded, but these differences look to be rather small (Janis & Field, 1956; McGuire, 1969, p. 242). That is, even if one person is (in general) more easily persuaded than another, the difference in ease of persuasion is not great.

But there is not yet any entirely well established procedure that permits advance identification of persuadable persons, and there is not good evidence about the correlates of general persuasibility.[1] The research concerning a general persuasibility factor thus remains tantalizingly incomplete.

Sex Differences in Persuasibility

One much studied question has been whether there are any reliable sex-related differences in persuasibility: Are women more easily persuaded than men (in general, or in specifiable circumstances), or men more easily persuaded than women?[2]

Several reviews have concluded that the research literature does contain dependable sex differences in persuasibility, with women being more easily persuaded than men (Becker, 1986; Eagly & Carli, 1981). These differences, however, are not especially large.[3] Moreover, it is not clear whether this observed difference reflects some genuinely general sex difference in persuasibility, as opposed to being a spurious difference attributable to other factors. Two other factors have been suggested as possibly underlying the observed persuasibility differences.

One concerns the topics of the persuasive messages used in research. Broadly put, the suggestion is that message topics are (stereotypically) sex linked in important ways; for some topics, men may commonly be more knowledgeable and interested, whereas for other topics, women will typically be more knowledgeable and interested. And (this reasoning runs) persons will be more likely to let themselves be influenced on topics in which they are not especially knowledgeable or interested. Hence the apparent greater persuasibility of women might reflect nothing more than a preponderance of male-oriented topics among studies of persuasive messages.

The research evidence does not give much support to this explanation. Eagly and Carli (1981) did find that sex differences in topic interest and knowledgeability were indeed associated with sex differences in persuasibility: The topics with greater male interest and knowledgeability were the topics on which women tended to show greater persuasibility (and vice versa). But Eagly and Carli also found that male-oriented topics were not overrepresented in the research literature (if anything, the persuasion topics tended to be slightly more interesting to women than to men). Because masculine topics have not predominated in the research literature, the observed sex differences in persuasibility are unlikely to be attributable to a generalized use of male-biased contents.

The other factor that has been proposed as potentially underlying the observed sex difference in persuasibility is the sex of the investigator. One review has reported evidence suggesting that although female researchers tended to find no sex differences in persuasibility, male researchers tended to find women to be more easily persuaded than men (Eagly & Carli, 1981). This evidence is not uncontroversial, and other analyses of the research literature seem not to have confirmed this influence of the researcher's sex on the findings (Becker, 1986). Perhaps the most that can be said at present is that the investigator's sex may explain the observed sex differences in persuasibility, but the issue is very much an open one.[4]

If the observed sex differences in persuasibility are not largely attributable to artifacts such as the nature of the topic or the sex of the researcher, then some other explanation needs to be found (for a careful discussion of some possibilities, see Eagly & Wood, 1985). Perhaps the most obvious explanations focus on cultural training and socialization. For example, it might be that whereas men have typically been encouraged to be analytical, critical, independent thinkers, women may have been commonly encouraged to preserve social harmony and express support for others—thereby creating conditions that foster the appearance of sex differences in persuasibility. If this is the relevant explanation, then to the extent that the relevant socialization patterns change, so will apparent sex differences in persuasibility.[5]

Other Individual Differences

Besides sex, a number of other individual-difference receiver characteristics have been examined for their possible relationships to persuasibility. For most such characteristics, the research evidence is commonly not extensive, and dependable generalizations seem hard to come by. (For some illustrative studies, see Alden & Crowley, 1995b; DeBono & Klein, 1993; DeBono & McDermott, 1994; Fleshler et al., 1974; Helweg-Larsen & Howell, 2000; Kowert & Homer, 1993; Kruglanski, Wenster, & Klem, 1993.)

For at least two characteristics, however—self-esteem and intelligence—there appears to be sufficient research evidence to permit some general conclusions. There is some indication that persuasibility may be maximized at intermediate levels of self-esteem and at lower levels of intelligence (for reviews, see Rhodes & Wood, 1992).[6] Explanations for these differences are at present somewhat speculative, but the most plausible accounts look to the possible influence of these personality characteristics on various aspects of persuasion processes (see Rhodes & Wood, 1992). Concerning self-esteem, the suggestion has been that persons low in self-esteem are unlikely to pay sufficient attention to the message (by virtue of being withdrawn or distracted), and those high in self-esteem are likely to be confident in the correctness of their current opinions (and so, perhaps, be more likely to counterargue), thus making each group less likely to be persuaded than those of moderate levels of self-esteem. With regard to intelligence, it may be that the greater knowledgeability commonly associated with greater intelligence enables more critical scrutiny of messages.

These proposed explanations (of the observed effects of self-esteem and intelligence on persuasibility) focus on the influence that these characteristics have on receiver activities such as counterarguing, attending to the message, and the like. This naturally invites consideration of the possibility that a framework such as the elaboration likelihood model (see Chapter 6) might provide a general scheme within which to consider the role of such individual-difference variables. Recall, for example, that the receiver's degree of need for cognition influences elaboration motivation and thereby can affect persuasive outcomes (for a review, see Cacioppo, Petty, et al., 1996); it might be that other individual-difference variables could be fitted within an ELM-like scheme and so to be seen to influence persuasion by affecting such things as elaboration likelihood or sensitivity to particular sorts of cues. For example, a given personality attribute might turn out to be related to elaboration ability generally (across situations, topics, and so forth) and hence produce corresponding effects on persuasive outcomes. Any such unified treatment is some way in the distance but obviously represents one attractive avenue to understanding how individual-difference variables might affect persuasion.

Individual-difference variables may also be associated with topic-specific differences in attitudes, beliefs, values, or behaviors—and hence (where relevant to the topic) such individual differences may be related to persuasive effects.[7] A convenient example is provided by the personality variable of self-monitoring (the degree to which a person regulates self-presentation). As discussed in Chapter 2 (concerning functional approaches to attitude), high and low self-monitors differ in what they tend to value in certain consumer products; for instance, high self-monitors especially favor the image projection attributes of automobiles, whereas low self-monitors are more likely to value characteristics such as reliability. Hence high and low self-monitors are differentially influenced by corresponding persuasive appeals; high self-monitors react more favorably to image-oriented advertisements than to ads focused on product quality, whereas the opposite tendency is found for low self-monitors (e.g., Snyder & DeBono, 1985). To put the relevant point generally, this personality difference serves as a marker of differences in receiver values and hence is related to the success of persuasive appeals that vary in the degree to which those values are engaged.

As another (but slightly different) example, the personality variable of sensation seeking (which concerns preferences for novel, complex, and ambiguous stimuli and situations) appears to be related to susceptibility to adolescent drug use. High sensation seekers appear to use drugs and alcohol more frequently and to begin using them at an earlier age than do low sensation seekers (e.g., Zuckerman, 1979, pp. 278-294). In designing programs aimed at reducing drug use, then, this personality variable provides a means of identifying receivers who are the most important and appropriate targets for persuasive messages (Palmgreen et al., 1995; Stephenson et al., 1999). High and low sensation seekers may also differ in the types of messages to which they are especially susceptible, and hence sensation seeking might provide not only a basis for identifying members of the target audience but also a means of adapting appeals to that audience (see Donohew, Lorch, & Palmgreen, 1991; Everett & Palmgreen, 1995; Lorch et al., 1994).

Other receiver individual differences (that is, other than receiver personality characteristics—self-esteem, sensation seeking, and so on) may affect persuasion in similar ways. Consider, for example, that variations in receiver age can sometimes serve as a marker of topic-specific variations in persuasion-relevant beliefs and attitudes. For instance, the motivations underlying volunteering appear to characteristically differ for persons of different ages; older adults seem to be motivated more by community obligation concerns than by the interpersonal relationships that can come from volunteering, whereas the opposite is more likely to be the case for younger adults (Omoto, Snyder, & Martino, 2000). Thus when seeking to encourage volunteering, presumably one would want to use different types of persuasive appeals for receivers varying in age—not because age per se is important but because age serves as a proxy for the relevant value differences.

As another example, differences in receivers' cultural backgrounds might serve to index various topic-specific differences relevant to persuasion. For instance, cultural variation may be associated with value differences and hence with differential effectiveness of corresponding persuasive appeals (e.g., Han & Shavitt, 1994; Zhang & Gelb, 1996; for some complexities, see Aaker & Williams, 1998). Or receivers of varying cultural backgrounds might typically have different salient beliefs on a given topic, suggesting correspondingly different persuasive approaches (see, e.g., G. Marin, Marin, Perez-Stable, Sabogal, & Otero-Sabogal, 1990).

Perhaps it is clear why research on the effects of receiver individual differences in persuasion has so often yielded complex results. A given individual difference such as receiver age might potentially be related to general persuasibility differences (Krosnick & Alwin, 1989), to dispositional differences in information-processing inclinations (Spotts, 1994; Yoon, 1997), and to topic-specific differences in persuasion-relevant beliefs and attitudes (as in the observed age-related differences in evaluations of volunteering outcomes; Omoto et al., 2000). It is likely to take some time to sort out completely the different pathways by which various individual-difference variables exert their influence on persuasive effects.

▧ INDUCED RECEIVER FACTORS

The preceding section discussed the role played in persuasion by natural, enduring receiver states or characteristics (such as personality traits). In this section, induced recipient characteristics are considered.

Inoculation

It's all very well to persuade someone to one's point of view—but once persuaded, the person may be exposed to counterpersuasion, that is, persuasive messages advocating some opposing viewpoint. The question that naturally arises is how receivers might be made resistant to such persuasive efforts (recognizing that making receivers resistant to counterpersuasion may involve something different from persuading them in the first place). Illuminating research concerning this question has been stimulated by inoculation theory, which focuses on the processes by which persons can be made resistant to persuasion (for a classic treatment, see McGuire, 1964; for recent general reviews, see Eagly & Chaiken, 1993, pp. 561-568; Pfau, 1997; Szabo & Pfau, in press).[8]

The Biological Metaphor. The fundamental ideas of inoculation theory can be usefully displayed through a biological metaphor. Consider the question of how persons can be made resistant to a disease virus (such as smallpox). One possibility is what might be called "supportive" treatments—making sure that people get adequate rest, a good diet, sufficient exercise, necessary vitamin supplements, and so on. The hope, obviously, is that this treatment will make it less likely that the disease will be contracted. But another approach to inducing resistance is inoculation (as with smallpox vaccines). An inoculation treatment consists of exposing persons to small doses of the disease virus. The dose is small (to avoid bringing on the disease itself) but is sufficient to stimulate and build the body's defenses so that any later massive attack (e.g., a smallpox epidemic) can be defeated.

These ideas probably already suggest the fundamental approach that inoculation theory recommends for inducing resistance to persuasion (namely, giving people inoculatory treatments involving exposure to "small doses" of the opposing view). But the biological metaphor can be elaborated yet another step, by noticing the sorts of circumstances that commonly make people especially susceptible to disease viruses. Perhaps understandably, infants who are raised in a germ-free (aseptic) environment are often quite vulnerable when exposed to large doses of a disease virus. After all, their bodies have not had the opportunities to develop resistance to the various viruses (having never been exposed to them). So (to consider the parallel) the beliefs that should be especially susceptible to attack are ones that have been maintained in a "germ-free" social environment, not exposed to attack; these beliefs are called cultural truisms.

Cultural Truisms. A cultural truism is a belief that (within a given culture, a given social environment) is rarely, if ever, attacked. These beliefs thus are truisms in one's culture: Everybody holds these beliefs, and no one criticizes them. Examples of cultural truisms that have been used in research include "It's a good idea to brush after every meal if possible" and "Mental illness is not contagious."

Inoculation theory suggests that cultural truisms are especially vulnerable to attack, for two reasons. First, the believer has no practice in defending the belief. The belief is never attacked, so there is never any opportunity (or need) to defend the belief. Second, the believer is unmotivated to undertake the necessary practice (because the belief is regarded as unassailable). For example, one can easily imagine that in idle moments one might mentally rehearse arguments that support one's position on a controversial issue such as abortion, but it is unlikely that one would ever mentally rehearse arguments in favor of brushing after every meal. That is, there is no motivation to rehearse arguments in defense of cultural truisms.

Consistent with this analysis, cultural truisms have been found to indeed be especially susceptible to persuasive attack (e.g., McGuire & Papageorgis, 1961; see, relatedly, Maio & Olson, 1998). Plausible-sounding attacking messages can substantially reduce receivers' beliefs in truisms. The question, then, is how one might go about making truisms more resistant to persuasion.

Supportive and Refutational Treatments. Researchers have compared the effectiveness of various treatments for inducing resistance to persuasion on cultural truisms. In the general design of this research, receivers are initially exposed to some treatment designed to induce resistance to persuasion on a given truism. Receivers are then exposed to an attack on that truism to see whether the treatment has made them resistant to the attack.[9]

Following the biological metaphor, researchers have studied two treatments. The supportive treatment consists of giving receivers arguments supporting the truism; this treatment parallels the supportive medical treatment (good diet, adequate rest, etc.). The refutational treatment consists of first showing receivers a weak attack on the truism and then refuting that attack; this refutational treatment is intended as a conceptual parallel to medical inoculation (in that receivers are exposed to weak doses of the opposing view, which are then overturned). For example, on the toothbrushing truism, the refutational treatment might consist of showing receivers a poorly argued message suggesting that excessive brushing will wear away the enamel on one's teeth and then giving receivers a refutation of that attack.

As one might expect from the biological metaphor, the refutational treatment is more effective in conferring resistance to persuasion than is the supportive treatment (see, e.g., McGuire, 1961b; McGuire & Papageorgis, 1961). Inoculating the receiver through exposure to refutation of antitruism arguments is a better way of inducing resistance to subsequent antitruism messages than is simply providing protruism (supportive) material.

Moreover, the refutational treatment does not simply immunize receivers against the one particular antitruism argument that receivers see refuted. Rather, the refutational treatment confers resistance to other antitruism arguments as well (e.g., Papageorgis & McGuire, 1961). That is, the refutational treatment does not simply convince receivers that "this one antitruism argument is defective" but actually stimulates the receivers' defenses against other (novel) antitruism arguments.

The combination of supportive and refutational treatments has also been studied for its effectiveness in conferring resistance. The combination is more effective in inducing resistance than is the refutational treatment alone (e.g., McGuire, 1961a). Why does adding a supportive treatment to the refutational treatment enhance resistance (given that the supportive treatment by itself has little effect on resistance)? By itself, the supportive material may seem to be useless (who needs arguments and evidence in favor of toothbrushing?)—but once the refutational treatment shows the truism to be potentially vulnerable to attack, there is a natural motivation for the bolstering material provided by the supportive treatment.

Nontruisms. The inoculation research discussed thus far has concerned inducing resistance to persuasion for cultural truisms. Truisms were a theoretically important focus of inoculation research (because the theory suggests that truisms will be especially vulnerable to attack), but it is obviously important to consider the induction of resistance to persuasion for nontruisms (i.e., more controversial beliefs and attitudes). Research on inoculation for nontruisms points to several general conclusions.

First, refutational treatments can be effective in conferring resistance to persuasion on nontruism topics but are not strikingly more effective than supportive treatments (see, e.g., Adams & Beatty, 1977; Benoit, 1991; M. Burgoon & Chase, 1973; Easley, Bearden, & Teel, 1995; Pfau, Holbert, Zubric, Pasha, & Lin, 2000; B. Pryor & Steinfatt, 1978; Szybillo & Heslin, 1973). Because the issue is not a cultural truism, receivers probably do not assume that their belief is invulnerable; hence the refutational treatment is not needed to underscore the usefulness of the supporting materials.

As with cultural truisms, however, the resistance produced by refutational treatments does appear to generalize to novel arguments (e.g., Pfau & Burgoon, 1988; Pfau, Kenski, Nitz, & Sorenson, 1990; Pfau et al., 1997; B. Pryor & Steinfatt, 1978; Szybillo & Heslin, 1973). That is, the refutational treatment not only makes persons resistant to the particular argument that is refuted but makes them resistant to additional arguments as well.

Finally, for nontruisms, the combination of supportive and refutational treatments seems to confer greater resistance than do supportive treatments alone (e.g., Koehler, 1972; McCroskey, Young, & Scott, 1972; Szybillo & Heslin, 1973), just as for truisms. The combination of supportive and refutational treatments amounts to creating a refutational two-sided persuasive message (as discussed in Chapter 9), that is, a message that both gives arguments supporting the communicator's view and gives refutations of counterarguments. Thus this last finding can be expressed in terms of message sidedness: Refutational two-sided messages appear to be more effective in conferring resistance to persuasion than are one-sided messages.

Explaining Inoculation Effects. Although it is plain that refutational treatments (inoculation) can create resistance to persuasion, there has been little systematic investigation of the mechanisms by which inoculation induces resistance. Given that the resistance created by refutational treatments generalizes to novel arguments (both for truisms and nontruisms), the underlying mechanism is unlikely to involve receivers simply acquiring the particular contents of the refutation to which they are exposed; obviously, something more general happens (something that makes receivers resistant to even novel attacks on their views).

It certainly seems plausible that in one way or another, one important element contributing to resistance induction is the receiver's perception that the current attitude may be vulnerable to attack (as suggested by McGuire, 1964). But the idea of perceived vulnerability has not yet been entirely carefully specified. For example, does the receiver need to think that an attack message is actually about to be encountered? Or only that it might plausibly occur at some time in the future? Or perhaps merely that in the abstract, somebody somewhere might believe differently (never mind whether an actual attack is expected)? Is it necessary that the receiver think that the attack message (or the imagined interlocutor) has good reasons for the opposing view (reasons that might form the basis of good arguments against the receiver's opinion)? Or perhaps is the mere recognition of the possibility of opposition (whether or not well-founded) sufficient?

Even given some specification of the idea of vulnerability, the issue will then become explaining exactly how and why perceived vulnerability leads to resistance. Perhaps it stimulates counterarguing, or possibly it simply inclines the receiver to reject the opposing view out of hand without thinking about it very much.[10] (For some discussion of alternative means of resistance, see Ahluwalia, 2000; Blumberg, 2000.) In short, much remains to be learned about how inoculation creates resistance to persuasion.

Warning

If (as inoculation theory suggests) one's awareness that a belief is vulnerable to attack can be sufficient to lead one to bolster one's defense of that belief (and thereby reduce the effectiveness of attacks on it), then presumably simply warning a person of an impending counterattitudinal message will decrease the effectiveness of the attack once it is presented. A fair amount of research has been conducted concerning the effects of such warning on resistance to persuasion on nontruism topics.[11]

Two sorts of warnings have been studied (as noticed by Papageorgis, 1968). One type simply warns receivers that they will hear a message intended to persuade them, without providing any information about the topic of the message, the viewpoint to be advocated, and so on; this sort of warning, then, merely warns of the persuasive intent of an impending communication. The other type of warning tells receivers the topic and position of the message (that is, the issue that the message is about and the position that the message advocates on that issue).

Both sorts of warning can confer resistance to persuasion and appear to do so by stimulating counterarguing in the audience (e.g., Petty & Cacioppo, 1977, 1979a; cf. Jacks & Devine, 2000).[12] Topic-position warnings make it possible for receivers to engage in anticipatory counterarguing (that is, counterarguing before the message is received) because the audience knows the issue to be discussed and the view to be advocated. Thus as the time interval between the topic-position warning and the onset of the message increases (up to a point, anyway), there is more opportunity for the audience to engage in counterarguing (and hence greater resistance can be built up). For example, in one study, high school students were shown messages arguing that teenagers should not be allowed to drive. Students received a warning of the topic and position of the impending message, but the interval between the warning and the message varied (no delay between warning and message, a 2-minute delay, or a 10-minute delay). With increasing delay, there was increasing resistance to persuasion (Freedman & Sears, 1965b).

Persuasive-intent warnings, of course, do not permit anticipatory counterarguing because the receivers do not know the subject of the message; consequently, variations in the time interval between a persuasive-intent warning and the communication have little effect on resistance (e.g., R. G. Hass & Grady, 1975). But persuasive-intent warnings do apparently stimulate greater counterarguing during the persuasive message, thereby reducing receivers' susceptibility to persuasion.

Because warning creates resistance by encouraging counterarguing, the effectiveness of warnings is influenced by factors that affect receivers' motivation and ability to counterargue. When receivers are not motivated to counterargue (e.g., because the issue is insufficiently important to them) or are unable to counterargue (e.g., because accompanying distraction prevents them from doing so), then the resistance-inducing effects of warning are reduced (see, e.g., H. C. Chen, Reardon, Rea, & Moore, 1992; Neimeyer et al., 1991; Petty & Cacioppo, 1979a; Romero, Agnew, & Insko, 1996).[13]

Refusal Skills Training

Another approach to creating resistance to persuasion focuses on training the receiver in skills for refusing unwanted offers. The central idea is that in some circumstances, the key to resistance is being able to refuse offers or requests made by an influence agent. In particular, it has often been supposed that children and adolescents are commonly unable to resist offers of illegal drugs, alcohol, or tobacco and hence end up using these substances—even if they have negative attitudes about such substances.

Hence it has been thought that one avenue to preventing substance use (or abuse) might be to provide training in how to refuse such offers.

Refusal skills training is a different approach to resistance induction from inoculation (or its corollary, warning). Inoculation-based approaches seek to provide the receiver with certain sorts of cognitive defenses; inoculation and warning attempt to create resistance to persuasion by hardening the initial attitude, preparing the receiver's attitudinal defenses, and encouraging mental counterarguing. In contrast, refusal skills training aims at equipping the receiver with certain communicative abilities.

A good deal of research has explored refusal skills induction in the context of preventing children and adolescents from using or misusing drugs, alcohol, and tobacco. Three broad conclusions may be drawn from this research. First, it is possible to teach such refusal skills. Studies have found that resistance skills training does improve the quality of role-played refusals, participants' perceived self-efficacy for refusing offers, and the like (see, e.g., Hops et al., 1986; Langlois, Petosa, & Hallam, 1999; Sallis et al., 1990; Wynn, Schulenberg, Maggs, & Zucker, 2000).

Second, the programs that are most effective at teaching refusal skills commonly involve rehearsal with directed feedback (that is, opportunities for participants to practice their refusal skills and to receive systematic evaluation of their performance). Simply encouraging participants to refuse offers or providing information about refusal skills seems less effective in developing such skills than is providing guided practice (see, e.g., Corbin, Jones, & Schulman, 1993; R. T. Jones, McDonald, Fiore, Arrington, & Randall, 1990; Turner et al., 1993).

Third, refusal skills programs are generally not very effective in preventing or reducing drug, alcohol, or tobacco use/misuse. Evaluations of such programs commonly find that refusal skills (or refusal skills self-efficacy or exposure to refusal skills training) are unrelated to substance use or abuse (for examples and reviews, see Donaldson, Graham, & Hansen, 1994; Elder, Sallis, Woodruff, & Wildey, 1993; Gorman, 1995; Wynn et al., 2000). Some successes have been reported (e.g., Donaldson, Graham, Piccinin, & Hansen, 1995; Ellickson & Hays, 1991), but in a few circumstances, boomerang effects—where refusal skills training has outcomes that appear to encourage substance use—have also been observed (Biglan et al., 1987; Donaldson et al., 1995; S. Kim, McLeod, & Shantzis, 1989).[14]

The lack of effectiveness of these refusal skills training programs may simply reflect that the key to preventing substance use/misuse is not found in the ability to refuse offers but rather lies somewhere else. (One possibility is that descriptive norms—the perceived prevalence of substance use among one's peers—are a more important determinant of use than are refusal skills; see, e.g., Donaldson et al., 1994; Wynn et al., 2000.) That is, the apparent relative ineffectiveness of the refusal skills programs aimed at preventing (or reducing) substance misuse does not mean that the general refusal skills induction strategy is somehow intrinsically defective as a mechanism for creating resistance to persuasion. These results show only that this approach seems inappropriate for these particular applications. It may be that in other circumstances, induction of relevant discourse skills will be more helpful.[15]

▨ CONTEXTUAL FACTORS

This section discusses research concerning the influence that features of the persuasion context have on persuasive outcomes. Three general areas of research are discussed: primacy-recency effects (which involve successive communications on an issue), communication medium effects, and the persistence of persuasive effects.

Primacy-Recency

Some persuasion contexts involve a debatelike setting, in which two communicators defend different sides of a given issue. A simplified debate setting—in which each communicator gives only one message (with no rebuttals or follow-up messages)—has been the focus of substantial research aimed at addressing the question of whether there is any advantage associated with either speaking position. Is there some intrinsic advantage to being the first of two speakers in such a setting, or to being the second? If the first communication enjoys some advantage over the second, a primacy effect is said to occur; if the second position is more advantageous, a recency effect is said to occur.

The research evidence clearly shows that there is no general advantage to either position (for more detailed reviews of this work, see Insko, 1967, pp. 49-61; Rosnow, 1966; Rosnow & Robinson, 1967). That is, there is no general primacy effect or recency effect. In varying circumstances, both primacy effects (e.g., Lund, 1925) and recency effects (e.g., Cromwell, 1950) have been obtained.

There is some indication, however, that primacy effects are more likely to be found with interesting, controversial, and familiar topics; conversely, recency effects are more common with topics that are relatively uninteresting, noncontroversial, or unfamiliar (see Rosnow, 1966). These effects may reflect differences in elaboration. Haugtvedt and Wegener (1994) suggested that primacy effects may be more likely to occur when elaboration is high (because then the first message can produce attitudes that are relatively more resistant to persuasion), whereas recency effects may be more likely to obtain when elaboration is low (because then whatever is heard last is more prominent in memory). This analysis, however, assumes that the messages contain strong arguments (in the ELM sense). For example, the occurrence of a primacy effect under conditions of high elaboration depends on the initial message's establishing a relatively strong (specifically, persistent) attitude, an outcome that presumably requires strong arguments (and, indeed, only strong arguments were used in the experiments reported by Haugtvedt & Wegener, 1994). The implication is that any effects of variation in speaking position might be altered if one side's arguments are stronger than the other's (see Cromwell, 1950, Experiment 1); indeed, it may be that the side with the stronger arguments will have the advantage, whichever speaking position it occupies (Rosnow & Robinson, 1967, p. 102).

Thus persuaders who find themselves in the position of choosing whether to speak first or second might well base the choice on the likelihood of elaboration (and so, for example, choose the first position when the topic is relatively more controversial, interesting, and familiar). But whatever advantage this confers may be sufficiently slight that persuaders who lose the coin flip should not suppose that all is lost.[16]

Medium

Persuasion can be pursued through any number of communication media: face-to-face interaction, telephone interaction, television, radio, computers (including via the Web, CD-ROMs, and so on), and written messages (including traditional print media—books, magazines, newspapers, brochures, and such mass media—but also personal letters). It might well be supposed that variations in the medium of communication will affect persuasive outcomes.

But surprisingly little research has concerned the effects of variations in communication medium on persuasive outcomes. In part, surely, this reflects the difficulties in undertaking useful research in this area.

Untangling the Effects of Communication Media. A central barrier to understanding medium effects is the nature of communication media. The common communication media represent bundles of different attributes, and it is not easy to untangle just which attribute (or set of attributes) is responsible for any observed differences between media.

As a simple example, imagine that a company finds that its advertising messages are more effective in television than in radio. One possible explanation for this differential effectiveness might be that television is an audio-visual medium, whereas radio is an audio-only medium, and it might be that this difference in information channel (audio plus visual information, as opposed to only audio information) made the company's advertising more effective. But it is also possible that the television advertising and the radio advertising reached different audiences (i.e., one group of people saw the television advertising, and a different group heard the radio advertising); it could be that this company's target audience was more likely to watch the television programs on which the company's advertising appeared than it was to hear the radio programs on which the company advertised—and so the television advertising was superior.

Or imagine that a business finds that face-to-face communication is more effective (in selling the company's products) than radio advertising. Once again, there is a difference in the information channels involved (audiovisual information in face-to-face interaction, audio-only in radio), and that might account for the difference in effectiveness. But radio advertising is a noninteractive medium, whereas face-to-face interaction is interactive. Interactive communication media make it possible for participants to adjust moment by moment to the other's reactions, whereas noninteractive media do not. It is possible that the face-to-face messages were more successful than the radio advertising because the company's communicators were skilled at using the interactive resources provided by face-to-face conversation.

It should be plain that unraveling the bases of difference between communication media will involve sorting out a large number of factors that distinguish media (different channels of information, different audiences reached, differences between interactive and noninteractive media, and so on). Of course, comparisons among common communication media can be of considerable practical value. For instance, it may be useful to know, on a given subject, whether different media are seen as having differential credibility as sources of information, or whether people prefer to receive information through one or another channel (for some examples of research on such questions, see S. L. Hammond, 1987; J. D. Johnson & Meishcke, 1992; McCallum, Hammond, & Covello, 1991). But plainly, a great deal of careful work will be required before one can hope to obtain a clear picture of just how and why variations in communication media influence persuasive outcomes.

Written Versus Audiotaped Versus Videotaped Messages. Some informative research, however, concerns a set of comparisons among written, audiotaped, and videotaped messages (that is, comparing the persuasiveness of a message presented in these three formats). These comparisons are simplified in the sense that there is typically no effort to exploit any of the special properties of these media (e.g., no effort to include visual images with the written message or to create special audio or visual effects for the audiotaped and videotaped messages). Receivers either watch a video-tape of the communicator delivering the message, hear the corresponding audio-only message, or read the corresponding written message (the text).

There does not seem to be any general advantage associated with one or another of these forms; it is not true that messages are typically more persuasive in (say) videotaped form than in written form. There appears to be heightened impact of source characteristics on persuasive outcomes, however, as one moves from written to audiotaped to videotaped messages (e.g., Booth-Butterfield & Gutowski, 1993; Pfau et al., 2000; J. R. Sparks, Areni, & Cox, 1998; cf. E. J. Wilson & Sherrell, 1993). For example, credibility variations and likability variations make more difference in videotaped messages than they do in written messages (Andreoli & Worchel, 1978; Chaiken & Eagly, 1983; Worchel et al., 1975).

It is not entirely clear what might explain such differences. Compared with the written format, the audiotape and videotape formats provide more information about the communicator (voice and appearance) and may make the communicator appear more "present" or more "real"; this might naturally give the communicator's characteristics a greater role in influencing persuasive outcomes. Alternatively (or in addition), the written format affords receivers the opportunity to reread all or part of the message; any such rereading might enhance the impact of any message content variation (making readers more sensitive to, say, argument quality) and dampen the relative influence of communicator characteristics.

Whatever account is given will want to be sensitive to related findings concerning differences in recall of message content. As long as the message material is sufficiently difficult, message content is commonly better remembered from written messages than from audiotaped or videotaped messages (e.g., Chaiken & Eagly, 1976; Furnham, Benson, & Gunter, 1987; Furnham, Proctor, & Gunter, 1988; Furnham & Williams, 1987).[17] These differences in recall might reflect that receivers can easily reread printed (but not audiotaped or videotaped) messages or might result from an absence of distracting visual or auditory information in printed (but not audiotaped or videotaped) messages (see Corston & Colman, 1997). Message recall is not necessarily an index of persuasive effect (receivers might remember very well a message with which they strongly disagreed, for instance), but the point is that even the apparently simple comparison of written, audiotaped, and videotaped messages displays the considerable challenges of understanding the effects of variations in communication medium.

Computer-Mediated Communication. Dependable generalizations about media and persuasion are especially difficult to come by in the case of computer-mediated communication. In part, this reflects the variety of forms that such communication can take (Web sites, CD-ROMs, e-mail messages, videoconferencing, instant messaging, and so forth). And in part, it reflects the relative recency of widespread access to computing; the personal computer was introduced in the 1980s, and the first Web browser appeared in 1993. Correspondingly, relatively little empirical evidence exists concerning computer-mediated persuasion.

Obviously, however, the widespread penetration of computer-based communicative forms gives rise to research questions concerning persuasion and computer-mediated communication. For example: What makes expert systems (computer-based reasoning systems that model human expert problem solving) persuasive to users? (See J. J. Dijkstra, Liebrand, & Timminga, 1998; Jiang, Klein, & Vedder, 2000.) What elements make interactive or Web-based advertisements effective? (See Bezjian-Avery, Calder, & Iacobucci, 1998; Li & Bukovac, 1999.) How might the physical properties of computer-mediated communication systems influence persuasion processes? (See Moon, 1999.) At present, such questions are only beginning to be investigated.

One feature of computer-based communication that may be especially relevant for persuasion is the possibility of the easy tailoring of persuasive messages to particular receivers. For example, a health care provider can enter individualizing information about a patient, and then the hospital's computer program can provide a customized diet—accompanied by persuasive appeals tailored to the patient's characteristics (using different appeals for a pregnant woman than for an older man, for instance). For some illustrative studies and reviews, see Brug, Campbell, and van Assema (1999); M. K. Campbell et al. (1999); A. Dijkstra and De Vries (1999); A. Dijkstra, De Vries, and Roijackers (1998); Kreuter, Farrell, Olevitch, and Brennan (1999); and Strecher (1999).

Summary. Untangling the properties of communication media is a tall order and yet crucial to examining their influence on persuasion. We are still some distance from having a satisfactory general understanding of the roles of communication media in persuasive effects—in good measure because we are some way from having a good grasp of the character of communication media themselves.

The Persistence of Persuasion

Persuaders are sometimes interested in obtaining success at some specific point of decision or action—getting the voter to cast a favorable ballot on election day, getting a person to make a charitable donation on the spot, and so on. At other times, there is no specific point in the future at which the persuader desires success; product advertising, for example, hopes to be successful at some indeterminate time in the future (whenever the receiver has occasion to be in a position to make the relevant purchase). In either case, questions of the persistence of persuasive effects arise. For instance, depending on how long-lasting a message's effects are, a persuader may be able to forgo subsequent persuasive efforts (e.g., an advertiser may not need to purchase so much advertising time).

The Decay of Message Effects. A well-established empirical generalization concerns the persistence of persuasion: On the whole, persuasive effects tend to dissipate over time (for a general review, see Cook & Flay, 1978). Perhaps they decay slowly, perhaps rapidly, and sometimes they may not decay at all. But generally speaking, one should expect that persuasive effects will evaporate as time passes. Old habits and attitudes can return, competing persuasive messages can be received, and hence the impact of a given persuasive effort is likely to diminish over time.

There is, thus, a corresponding rule of thumb concerning the temporal placement of persuasive messages: For maximum effect, persuasive messages should be delivered temporally close to the point of decision or action. For example, in political campaigns, candidates should (everything else being equal) buy more advertising time for the period just before election day than for time slots well in advance of the election.[18]

Influences on the Decay of Effects. Of course, not all persuasive effects will decay at the same rate, and the question arises of what factors might influence the rate of decay. There is less direct evidence on this matter than one might like; research is rather scattered, and secure generalizations have seemed elusive (for a general discussion, see Eagly & Chaiken, 1993, pp. 608-621).

The elaboration likelihood model (Chapter 6), however, provides an attractive general framework for understanding at least some of the research evidence concerning the persistence of persuasion. Broadly put, the ELM suggests that persuasion achieved under conditions of high elaboration (central route processes) is more likely to be enduring than that obtained under conditions of low elaboration (peripheral route processes). That is, persistent effects are more likely when persuasion is the result of thoughtful consideration of issues and arguments as opposed to the result of reliance on heuristics.

This analysis can encompass a variety of more particular findings. For example, persuasion has been found to be relatively more persistent for receivers high in need for cognition (persons who tend to enjoy and engage in thinking) than in those low in need for cognition (e.g., Verplanken, 1991), presumably because greater need for cognition is associated with greater elaboration motivation. Greater persuasion persistence has been observed on topics of greater personal relevance (compared with less personally relevant topics), again consistent with the idea that elaboration-induced persuasion is relatively more persistent (Haugtvedt & Strathman, 1990). Similarly, when receivers expect to have to discuss the message topic (a circumstance presumably likely to encourage elaboration), greater persuasion persistence has been found (compared with conditions in which receivers had no such expectation; see, e.g., Boninger, Brock, Cook, Gruder, & Romer, 1990). (For a general discussion of elaboration and persuasion persistence, see Petty et al., 1995.)

But the question now arises of how and why elaboration-based persuasion produces greater persistence. One might naturally be inclined to suppose that central route persuasion produces attitudes that are in some sense "stronger" than the attitudes produced by peripheral route persuasion— but then the challenge becomes one of spelling out just what properties constitute attitude strength.[19] Although it is not yet clear what specifiable property (or properties) of attitude gives rise to persistence, several plausible suggestions have been advanced, including attitude accessibility (the degree to which the attitude is easily activated from memory), the internal structure of the attitude (e.g., the degree of evaluative consistency in the underlying beliefs), the degree to which the attitude is embedded in a larger attitudinal structure (linkages between the attitude and other attitudes, for instance), and so forth (e.g., Chaiken, Pomerantz, & Giner-Sorolla, 1995; Eagly & Chaiken, 1995; Fazio, 1995; Petty et al., 1995; Wood et al., 1995; Zanna, Fazio, & Ross, 1994). There is a good deal of empirical and conceptual uncertainty about how such properties are related to each other and about how these (and other) candidates will fare either as specifications of attitude strength generally or as explanations of persuasion persistence specifically; progress on these matters will be welcome.

Sleeper Effect. Do persuasive effects inevitably decay through time, or is it possible that some might increase with the passage of time? No small effort has been devoted to tracking down the possibility of a "sleeper effect" in persuasion (defined as an increase in persuasive effectiveness over time).[20] There has often been substantial confusion over this question, in good measure because of definitional problems.[21]

It is now clear, however, that it is possible, under specifiable circumstances, to find a sleeper effect—to find an increase in the persuasive effectiveness of a message over time. The relevant conditions are these:

Receivers attend to high-quality arguments in a message (for example, by being told to underline them or because the topic is personally relevant), but then, following the message, receivers are given a strong "discounting cue" indicating that the information in the message (or the message's conclusion) is false (e.g., Lariscy & Tinkham, 1999; Pratkanis & Greenwald, 1985; Pratkanis, Greenwald, Leippe, & Baumgardner, 1988; Priester, Wegener, Petty, & Fabrigar, 1999). It appears that the discounting cue's strong effect initially suppresses the otherwise favorable impact of the message's arguments; over time, however, the effect of the discounting cue fades, and the effect of the receiver's examination of the message's arguments emerges. Indeed, as Pratkanis and Greenwald (1985) pointed out, this observed sleeper effect is not actually an exception to the general idea of decay of effect. The relevant experimental situation has two sources of effect—the message and the discounting cue—with differential rates of decay. The discounting cue has a strong initial (negative) effect that dissipates more quickly than does the (positive) effect of the message, thus yielding the observed sleeper effect.

▧ CONCLUSION

As the research reviewed in this chapter makes plain, persuasive effects are often dependent on receiver characteristics and contextual factors. Although researchers are well along in studying various receiver attributes as influences on persuasion, only a few features of the communication context have gotten much research attention thus far.

▧ NOTES

1. Some research has aimed at developing items to assess the degree to which persons are susceptible to certain kinds of interpersonal influence in consumer purchases (e.g., the degree to which the approval of others is important to them, or the extent to which they rely on information from others, in making such purchases; see Bearden, Netemeyer, & Teel, 1989, 1990); this work can be seen as naturally related to research on such factors as self-monitoring (which is associated with susceptibility to certain sorts of normative appeals; see Bazzini & Shaffer, 1995; DeBono, 1987) but is different from assessing general persuasibility.

2. The question of interest here is thus different from two other (related) questions. First, the question here concerns sex differences in persuasibility specifically, not in influenceability generally. Various sorts of influence situations have been examined for possible sex differences in influenceability; studies of influence through persuasive messages (as opposed to, say, studies of conformity to group pressure) are of interest here. The distinction is important because it appears that the size and nature of sex differences in influenceability vary depending on the

type of influence situation studied (see, e.g., Eagly & Carli, 1981). Second, the question under discussion concerns persuasibility differences, as opposed to possible information-processing differences (see, e.g., Meyers-Levy & Maheswaran, 1991; Meyers-Levy & Sternthal, 1991); notice, however, that any sex-related message-processing differences might provide a basis for explaining sex-related differences in persuasibility.

3. Expressed as a correlation, the association between sex and persuasibility has been estimated as in the neighborhood of .05 to .08 (Becker, 1986, p. 195; Eagly & Carli, 1981, p. 7), based on from 33 to 61 cases. Although in absolute terms this is plainly not a large effect, it is also not entirely uncharacteristic of the magnitudes commonly observed in persuasion effects research.

4. Becker's (1986) best-fitting model for explaining sex differences in persuasibility did not include the sex of the researcher. There are several relevant differences, however, between Becker's procedure and that of Eagly and Carli (1981). For example, Becker used a more defensible means of investigating the relationship between authorship and study outcome than did Eagly and Carli (see Becker, 1986, p. 189). But Becker's analysis apparently used percentage of male authors as the predictor of outcome, whereas Eagly and Carli used a dichotomized authorship variable as the predictor (because, they indicated, percentage of male authors was a highly skewed variable). Moreover, Becker's report does not give details on just what her analysis revealed concerning the relevant association (see p. 196). The upshot of all this is that one cannot confidently offer conclusions on this issue.

5. Persuasion effects researchers often report (or have) information concerning sex differences in persuasibility even if that is not their research focus. Given the time that has passed—and the not inconsiderable amount of persuasion effects research conducted—since the last reviews on this subject, new reviews (in addition to examining the general effect and possible artifacts) might be able to examine specifically the potential change through time in the size of any genuine sex-related difference in persuasibility.

6. Rhodes and Wood (1992) reviewed both self-esteem and intelligence effects on persuasibility. Their mean reported persuasibility difference between low and medium levels of self-esteem corresponds to a correlation of .12 (across nine cases), indicating greater persuasibility at medium levels; the difference between medium and high levels of self-esteem corresponds to a correlation of −.06 (across nine cases), again indicating greater persuasibility at medium levels. The mean persuasibility difference between low and high levels of intelligence corresponds to a correlation of −.14 (across seven cases), indicating greater persuasibility at lower levels.

7. This possibility (that individual-difference variables may be associated with topic-specific differences in persuasion-relevant attitudes, beliefs, values, or behaviors) can be fitted within something like an ELM-based treatment (in which individual differences are seen to affect such things as elaboration likelihood). For instance, for a given persuasive message, personality-related differences in values might lead to corresponding personality-related differences in elaboration valence.

8. The question taken up in this section concerns how an existing attitude can be made resistant to change—that is, what interventions (treatments, messages) might make an attitude resistant to influence. This is different from (but of course related to) the question of what naturally occurring circumstances or features make attitudes resistant to change (see, e.g., Eagly & Chaiken, 1995; Zuwerink & Devine, 1996).

9. One matter of some delicacy that is not treated here concerns the definition of resistance to persuasion, which poses more difficulties than one might initially suppose; a useful (if incomplete) discussion of this topic has been provided by B. Pryor and Steinfatt (1978, pp. 220-221).

10. One might think that refutational treatments would create resistance by encouraging counterarguing (in response to subsequent attack messages), but what little evidence exists on this matter appears not to be encouraging (see, e.g., Benoit, 1991; Pfau et al., 2000; Pfau et al., 1997).

11. For cultural truisms, it appears that warning is even less successful than supportive treatments in conferring resistance to persuasion (e.g., McGuire & Papageorgis, 1962).

12. A review of some warning studies reported that expressed as a correlation, the mean persuasion-inhibiting effect of warnings was .18 across 12 studies (Benoit, 1998).

13. A number of complexities in the research literature on warning are passed over here. For example, on topics that are not especially personally relevant to receivers, topic-position warnings sometimes seem to initially produce opinion change *toward* the to-be-advocated position (e.g., J. Cooper & Jones, 1970), but this change is apparently merely a strategic anticipatory shift toward neutrality (which disappears when the expectation of the impending message is canceled); for further discussion, see Cialdini and Petty (1981). As another example of complexity, at least some prosocial solicitations appear to be made more persuasive if preceded by a warning (Kennedy, 1982); this, however, might reflect processes engaged when warning of an impending *proattitudinal* communication (for example, such a warning, instead of eliciting the counterarguing engendered by warnings of counterattitudinal messages, might encourage supportive argumentation).

14. In the United States, Drug Abuse Resistance Education (DARE) has been a particularly prominent refusal skills training program; the program is aimed at children and adolescents and features police officers as influence agents. The traditional DARE curriculum has many elements, but its core is focused on teaching students skills for recognizing and resisting pressures to use drugs and alcohol. Despite widespread implementation, there is strikingly little evidence that DARE dependably reduces substance use (e.g., Lynam et al., 1999; for a review, see Ennett, Tobler, Ringwald, & Flowelling, 1994).

15. An illustration of the potential of this strategy may be provided by the case of a U.S. long-distance telephone company that had been losing business; its customers were being called up by a rival, whose sales pitch convinced many customers to switch long-distance providers on the spot (an oral agreement was all that was needed to change providers). The original company responded by running a series

of advertisements suggesting that when called, customers should ask to "get it in writing" from the rival. This provided customers with a way of responding to the rival's pitch without having to agree with it and without having to risk sounding rude by flatly refusing it. The company's strategy was not to enhance their customers' existing positive attitudes toward the company nor to inoculate receivers against the rival's offers (for example, by refuting some of the rival's claims) but rather to inculcate certain discourse skills in their customers.

16. The research bearing on primacy-recency effects simply presents two opposing messages in different orders (half of the participants hear message A and then message B; the other half hear message B and then message A). This provides a test of the simple position effect but obviously does not reflect the tailoring possibilities that inhere in each position. For example, in an actual two-message setting, the initial message might seek to frame the overall discussion in ways congenial to the first communicator's advocated view (thus exploiting that potential advantage of the first position), and the second message might undertake explicit rebuttal of the specific arguments advanced in the first message (thereby exploiting an advantage of the second position).

17. This gloss overlooks some potentially complicating considerations. At least some of this research does not involve entirely simple experimental contrasts of the sort previously mentioned (e.g., between a printed text and a "talking head" videotape using the same text) but instead involves such comparisons as between a television ad and a printed transcript of the ad's voice-over material (e.g., Furnham et al., 1987) or between television and print ads for the same product (e.g., Furnham & Williams, 1987).

18. This generalization (about political campaigns) is too simple, because the time of action (voting) can be different from the time of decision. Indeed, for quite some time, studies of political campaigns have found it useful to distinguish "early deciders" (who make up their minds well before election day) from "late deciders" (see, e.g., Nimmo, 1970, pp. 24-25). Obviously, for early deciders, advertising that appears just before election day may come too late to influence their decision (it may influence whether they implement their decision, that is, whether they actually vote, but that is another matter). So if there are a great many late deciders in a given election, then a last-minute advertising blitz may well be an appropriate strategy; as the proportion of early deciders increases (as it well might for, say, high-visibility elections that spark considerable voter interest), then last-minute advertising becomes a less attractive persuasive approach. (Even this analysis, however, underrepresents the complexities in time-related aspects of voter decisions; see Chaffee & Rimal, 1996.)

19. One danger is that if attitude strength is *defined* as (inter alia) persistence (as suggested by Krosnick & Petty, 1995), then attitude strength variations will provide only the appearance of an explanation of persistence effects. That is, if it is true by definition that stronger attitudes are more persistent, then saying "high-elaboration-induced attitudes are persistent because they are strong" amounts to saying "high-elaboration-induced attitudes are persistent because they are persistent."

20. This is sometimes called an absolute sleeper effect, as distinct from a relative sleeper effect, which involves only different rates of decay through time under different conditions. For discussion, see Gruder et al. (1978).

21. For a time, the phrase "sleeper effect" was used to refer specifically to "a delayed increase in the persuasive impact of a communication *from a source low in credibility*" (italics added; Gillig & Greenwald, 1974, p. 132; see also, e.g., Allen & Stiff, 1989). But the application of the phrase has shifted with time, such that it has become common to define a sleeper effect as "a delayed increase in the impact of a persuasive message" (Pratkanis et al., 1988, p. 203)—never mind whether the source is low in credibility. Thus the narrower question of whether low-credibility sources specifically might exhibit delayed effectiveness has been replaced by the broader question of delayed effectiveness generally.

References

Aaker, J. L., & Williams, P. (1998). Empathy versus pride: The influence of emotional appeals across cultures. *Journal of Consumer Research, 25,* 241-261.

Aarts, H., Paulussen, T., & Schaalma, H. (1997). Physical exercise habit: On the conceptualization and formation of habitual health behaviours. *Health Education Research, 12,* 363-374.

Abelson, R. P. (1986). Beliefs are like possessions. *Journal for the Theory of Social Behavior, 16,* 223-250.

Abelson, R. P. (1997). A retrospective on the significance test ban of 1999 (if there were no significance tests, they would be invented). In L. L. Harlow, S. A. Mulaik, & J. H. Steiger (Eds.), *What if there were no significance tests?* (pp. 117-141). Mahwah, NJ: Lawrence Erlbaum.

Abelson, R. P., Kinder, D. R., Peters, M. D., & Fiske, S. T. (1982). Affective and semantic components in political person perception. *Journal of Personality and Social Psychology, 42,* 619-630.

Abelson, R. P., & Prentice, D. A. (1989). Beliefs as possessions: A functional perspective. In A. R. Pratkanis, S. J. Breckler, & A. G. Greenwald (Eds.), *Attitude structure and function* (pp. 361-381). Hillsdale, NJ: Lawrence Erlbaum.

Abraham, C., Sheeran, P., Norman, P., Conner, M., de Vries, N., & Otten, W. (1999). When good intentions are not enough: Modeling postdecisional cognitive correlates of condom use. *Journal of Applied Social Psychology, 29,* 2591-2612.

Adams, W. C., & Beatty, M. J. (1977). Dogmatism, need for social approval, and the resistance to persuasion. *Communication Monographs, 44,* 321-325.

Addington, D. W. (1971). The effect of vocal variations on ratings of source credibility. *Speech Monographs, 38,* 242-247.

Agnew, C. R. (1998). Modal versus individually-derived beliefs about condom use: Measuring the cognitive underpinnings of the theory of reasoned action. *Psychology and Health, 13,* 271-287.

Ahluwalia, R. (2000). Examination of psychological processes underlying resistance to persuasion. *Journal of Consumer Research, 27,* 217-232.

Ahluwalia, R., & Burnkrant, R. E. (1993). A framework for explaining multiple request effectiveness: The role of attitude toward the request. *Advances in Consumer Research, 20,* 620-624.

Aitken, C. K., McMahon, T. A., Wearing, A. J., & Finlayson, B. L. (1994). Residential water use: Predicting and reducing consumption. *Journal of Applied Social Psychology, 24,* 136-158.

Ajzen, I. (1971). Attitudinal versus normative messages: An investigation of the differential effects of persuasive communication on behavior. *Sociometry, 34,* 263-280.

Ajzen, I. (1985). From intentions to actions: A theory of planned behavior. In J. Kuhl & J. Beckmann (Eds.), *Action control: From cognition to behavior* (pp. 11-39). Berlin: Springer-Verlag.

Ajzen, I. (1991). The theory of planned behavior. *Organizational Behavior and Human Decision Processes, 50,* 179-211.

Ajzen, I. (1999). Dual-mode processing in the pursuit of insight is no vice. *Psychological Inquiry, 10,* 110-112.

Ajzen, I., & Fishbein, M. (1972). Attitudes and normative beliefs as factors influencing behavioral intentions. *Journal of Personality and Social Psychology, 21,* 1-9.

Ajzen, I., & Fishbein, M. (1977). Attitude-behavior relations: A theoretical analysis and review of empirical research. *Psychological Bulletin, 84,* 888-918.

Ajzen, I., & Fishbein, M. (1980). *Understanding attitudes and predicting social behavior.* Englewood Cliffs, NJ: Prentice Hall.

Ajzen, I., & Madden, T. J. (1986). Prediction of goal-directed behavior: Attitudes, intentions, and perceived behavioral control. *Journal of Experimental Social Psychology, 22,* 453-474.

Ajzen, I., Nichols, A. J., III, & Driver, B. L. (1995). Identifying salient beliefs about leisure activities: Frequency of elicitation versus response latency. *Journal of Applied Social Psychology, 25,* 1391-1410.

Ajzen, I., & Sexton, J. (1999). Depth of processing, belief congruence, and attitude-behavior correspondence. In S. Chaiken & Y. Trope (Eds.), *Dual-process models in social psychology* (pp. 117-138). New York: Guilford.

Ajzen, I., Timko, C., & White, J. B. (1982). Self-monitoring and the attitude-behavior relation. *Journal of Personality and Social Psychology, 42,* 426-435.

Albarracin, D., Johnson, B. T., Fishbein, M., & Muellerleile, P. A. (2001). Theories of reasoned action and planned behavior as models of condom use: A meta-analysis. *Psychological Bulletin, 127,* 142-161.

Alden, D. L., & Crowley, A. E. (1995a). Improving the effectiveness of condom advertising: A research note. *Health Marketing Quarterly, 12*(4), 25-38.

Alden, D. L., & Crowley, A. E. (1995b). Sex guilt and receptivity to condom advertising. *Journal of Applied Social Psychology, 25,* 1446-1463.

Allen, M. (1991). Meta-analysis comparing the persuasiveness of one-sided and two-sided messages. *Western Journal of Speech Communication, 55,* 390-404.

Allen, M. (1993). Determining the persuasiveness of message sidedness: A prudent note about utilizing research summaries. *Western Journal of Communication, 57,* 98-103.

Allen, M. (1998). Comparing the persuasive effectiveness of one- and two-sided messages. In M. Allen & R. W. Preiss (Eds.), *Persuasion: Advances through meta-analysis* (pp. 87-98). Cresskill, NJ: Hampton.

Allen, M., & Preiss, R. W. (1997). Comparing the persuasiveness of narrative and statistical evidence using meta-analysis. *Communication Research Reports, 14,* 125-131.

Allen, M., & Preiss, R. W. (Eds.). (1998). *Persuasion: Advances through meta-analysis.* Cresskill, NJ: Hampton.

Allen, M., & Stiff, J. B. (1989). Testing three models for the sleeper effect. *Western Journal of Speech Communication, 53,* 411-426.

Allport, G. W. (1935). Attitudes. In C. Murchison (Ed.), *A handbook of social psychology* (pp. 798-844). Worcester, MA: Clark University Press.

Alwin, D. F. (1997). Feeling thermometers versus 7-point scales: Which are better? *Sociological Methods and Research, 25,* 318-340.

Andersen, K. E. (1961). An experimental study of the interaction of artistic and nonartistic ethos in persuasion (Doctoral dissertation, University of Wisconsin-Madison, 1961). *Dissertation Abstracts, 22* (1961), 940. (University Microfilms No. AAI-6103079)

Andersen, K. E., & Clevenger, T., Jr. (1963). A summary of experimental research in ethos. *Speech Monographs, 30,* 59-78.

Anderson, C. A. (1983). Imagination and expectation: The effect of imaging behavioral scripts on personal intentions. *Journal of Personality and Social Psychology, 45,* 293-305.

Anderson, D. S., & Kristiansen, C. M. (1990). Measuring attitude functions. *Journal of Social Psychology, 130,* 419-421.

Anderson, L. (1970). An experimental study of reluctant and biased authority-based assertions. *Journal of the American Forensic Association, 7,* 79-84.

Anderson, L. R. (1970). Prediction of negative attitude from congruity, summation, and logarithm formulae for the evaluation of complex stimuli. *Journal of Social Psychology, 81,* 37-48.

Anderson, N. H. (1965). Averaging versus adding as a stimulus-combination rule in impression formation. *Journal of Experimental Psychology, 70,* 394-400.

Anderson, N. H. (1971). Integration theory and attitude change. *Psychological Review, 78,* 171-206.

Anderson, N. H. (1981a). *Foundations of information integration theory.* New York: Academic Press.

Anderson, N. H. (1981b). Integration theory applied to cognitive responses and attitudes. In R. E. Petty, T. M. Ostrom, & T. C. Brock (Eds.), *Cognitive responses in persuasion* (pp. 361-397). Hillsdale, NJ: Lawrence Erlbaum.

Anderson, N. H. (Ed.). (1991). *Contributions to information integration theory* (Vols. 1-3). Hillsdale, NJ: Lawrence Erlbaum.

Anderson, R. B. (1995). Cognitive appraisal of performance capability in the prevention of drunken driving: A test of self-efficacy theory. *Journal of Public Relations Research, 7,* 205-229.

Anderson, R. B. (2000). Vicarious and persuasive influences on efficacy expectations and intentions to perform breast self-examination. *Public Relations Review, 26,* 97-114.

Anderson, R. B., & McMillion, P. Y. (1995). Effects of similar and diversified modeling on African American women's efficacy expectations and intentions to perform breast self-examination. *Health Communication, 7,* 327-343.

Andreoli, V., & Worchel, S. (1978). Effects of media, communicator, and message position on attitude change. *Public Opinion Quarterly, 42,* 59-70.

Andrews, J. C., & Shimp, T. A. (1990). Effects of involvement, argument strength, and source characteristics on central and peripheral processing of advertising. *Psychology and Marketing, 7,* 195-214.

Andrews, L. W., & Gutkin, T. B. (1994). Influencing attitudes regarding special class placement using a psychoeducational report: An investigation of the elaboration likelihood model. *Journal of School Psychology, 32,* 321-337.

Applbaum, R. L., & Anatol, K. W. E. (1972). The factor structure of source credibility as a function of the speaking situation. *Speech Monographs, 39,* 216-222.

Applbaum, R. L., & Anatol, K. W. E. (1973). Dimensions of source credibility: A test for reproducibility. *Speech Monographs, 40,* 231-237.

Apple, W., Streeter, L. A., & Krauss, R. M. (1979). Effects of pitch and speech rate on personal attributions. *Journal of Personality and Social Psychology, 37,* 715-727.

Apsler, R., & Sears, D. O. (1968). Warning, personal involvement, and attitude change. *Journal of Personality and Social Psychology, 9,* 162-166.

Areni, C. S., & Lutz, R. J. (1988). The role of argument quality in the elaboration likelihood model. *Advances in Consumer Research, 15,* 197-203.

Armitage, C. J., & Conner, M. (1999a). Distinguishing perceptions of control from self-efficacy: Predicting consumption of a low-fat diet using the theory of planned behavior. *Journal of Applied Social Psychology, 29,* 72-90.

Armitage, C. J., & Conner, M. (1999b). Predictive validity of the theory of planned behaviour: The role of questionnaire format and social desirability. *Journal of Community and Applied Social Psychology, 9,* 261-272.

Armitage, C. J., & Conner, M. (1999c). The theory of planned behaviour: Assessment of predictive validity and "perceived control." *British Journal of Social Psychology, 38,* 35-54.

Armitage, C. J., Conner, M., & Norman, P. (1999). Differential effects of mood on information processing: Evidence from the theories of reasoned action and planned behaviour. *European Journal of Social Psychology, 29,* 419-433.

Arnold, W. E., & McCroskey, J. C. (1967). The credibility of reluctant testimony. *Central States Speech Journal, 18,* 97-103.

Aronson, E. (1968). Dissonance theory: Progress and problems. In R. P. Abelson, E. Aronson, W. J. McGuire, T. M. Newcomb, M. J. Rosenberg, & P. H. Tannenbaum (Eds.), *Theories of cognitive consistency: A sourcebook* (pp. 5-27). Chicago: Rand McNally.

Aronson, E. (1992). The return of the repressed: Dissonance theory makes a comeback. *Psychological Inquiry, 3,* 303-311.

Aronson, E. (1999). Dissonance, hypocrisy, and the self-concept. In E. Harmon-Jones & J. Mills (Eds.), *Cognitive dissonance: Progress on a pivotal theory in social psychology* (pp. 103-126). Washington, DC: American Psychological Association.

Aronson, E., & Carlsmith, J. M. (1963). Effect of the severity of threat on the devaluation of forbidden behavior. *Journal of Abnormal and Social Psychology, 66,* 584-588.

Aronson, E., Fried, C., & Stone, J. (1991). Overcoming denial and increasing the intention to use condoms through the induction of hypocrisy. *American Journal of Public Health, 81,* 1636-1638.

Aronson, E., Turner, J. A., & Carlsmith, J. M. (1963). Communicator credibility and communication discrepancy as determinants of opinion change. *Journal of Abnormal and Social Psychology, 67,* 31-36.

Aronson, J., Cohen, G., & Nail, P. R. (1999). Self-affirmation theory: An update and appraisal. In E. Harmon-Jones & J. Mills (Eds.), *Cognitive dissonance: Progress on a pivotal theory in social psychology* (pp. 127-147). Washington, DC: American Psychological Association.

Atkinson, D. R., Winzelberg, A., & Holland, A. (1985). Ethnicity, locus of control for family planning, and pregnancy counselor credibility. *Journal of Counseling Psychology, 32,* 417-421.

Audi, R. (1972). On the conception and measurement of attitudes in contemporary Anglo-American psychology. *Journal for the Theory of Social Behavior, 2,* 179-203.

Axsom, D., Yates, S., & Chaiken, S. (1987). Audience response as a heuristic cue in persuasion. *Journal of Personality and Social Psychology, 53,* 30-40.

Babrow, A. S., & O'Keefe, D. J. (1984). Construct differentiation as a moderator of attitude-behavior consistency: A failure to confirm. *Central States Speech Journal, 35,* 160-165.

Baesler, E. J., & Burgoon, J. K. (1994). The temporal effects of story and statistical evidence on belief change. *Communication Research, 21,* 582-602.

Bagozzi, R. P. (1982). A field investigation of causal relations among cognitions, affect, intentions, and behavior. *Journal of Marketing Research, 19,* 562-584.

Bagozzi, R. P. (1984). Expectancy-value attitude models: An analysis of critical measurement issues. *International Journal of Research in Marketing, 1,* 295-310.

Bagozzi, R. P. (1985). Expectancy-value attitude models: An analysis of critical theoretical issues. *International Journal of Research in Marketing, 2,* 43-60.

Bagozzi, R. P. (1992). The self-regulation of attitudes, intentions, and behavior. *Social Psychology Quarterly, 55,* 178-204.

Bagozzi, R. P., Baumgartner, H., & Pieters, R. (1998). Goal-directed emotions. *Cognition and Emotion, 12,* 1-26.

Bagozzi, R. P., Baumgartner, H., & Yi, Y. (1992). State versus action orientation and the theory of reasoned action: An application to coupon usage. *Journal of Consumer Research, 18,* 505-518.

Bagozzi, R. P., & Warshaw, P. R. (1990). Trying to consume. *Journal of Consumer Research, 17,* 127-140.

Bagozzi, R. P., Yi, Y., & Baumgartner, J. (1990). The level of effort required for behaviour as a moderator of the attitude-behaviour relation. *European Journal of Social Psychology, 20,* 45-59.

Bandura, A. (1977). Self-efficacy: Toward a unifying theory of behavioral change. *Psychological Review, 84,* 191-215.

Bandura, A. (1986). *Social foundations of thought and action: A social cognitive theory.* Englewood Cliffs, NJ: Prentice Hall.

Bandura, A. (1997). *Self-efficacy: The exercise of control.* New York: Freeman.

Baron, R. S., Baron, P. H., & Miller, N. (1973). The relation between distraction and persuasion. *Psychological Bulletin, 80,* 310-323.

Basen-Engquist, K., & Parcel, G. S. (1992). Attitudes, norms, and self-efficacy: A model of adolescents' HIV-related sexual risk behavior. *Health Education Quarterly, 19,* 263-277.

Bassili, J. N. (1996). Meta-judgmental versus operative indexes of psychological attributes: The case of measures of attitude strength. *Journal of Personality and Social Psychology, 71,* 637-653.

Baudhuin, E. S., & Davis, M. K. (1972). Scales for the measurement of ethos: Another attempt. *Speech Monographs, 39,* 296-301.

Baumeister, R. F., Reis, H. T., & Delespaul, P. A. E. G. (1995). Subjective and experiential correlates of guilt in daily life. *Personality and Social Psychology Bulletin, 21,* 1256-1268.

Bazzini, D. G., & Shaffer, D. R. (1995). Investigating the social-adjustive and value-expressive functions of well-grounded attitudes: Implications for change and for subsequent behavior. *Motivation and Emotion, 19,* 279-305.

Beaman, A. L., Cole, C. M., Preston, M., Klentz, B., & Steblay, N. M. (1983). Fifteen years of foot-in-the-door research: A meta-analysis. *Personality and Social Psychology Bulletin, 9,* 181-196.

Bearden, W. O., & Crockett, M. (1981). Self-monitoring, norms, and attitudes as influences on consumer complaining. *Journal of Business Research, 9,* 255-266.

Bearden, W. O., Netemeyer, R. G., & Teel, J. E. (1989). Measurement of consumer susceptibility to interpersonal influence. *Journal of Consumer Research,* 15, 473-481.

Bearden, W. O., Netemeyer, R. G., & Teel, J. E. (1990). Further validation of the consumer susceptibility to interpersonal influence scale. *Advances in Consumer Research, 17,* 770-776.

Bearden, W. O., Shuptrine, F. K., & Teel, J. E. (1989). Self-monitoring and reactions to image appeals and claims about product quality. *Advances in Consumer Research, 16,* 703-710.

Beatty, M. J., & Behnke, R. R. (1980). Teacher credibility as a function of verbal content and paralinguistic cues. *Communication Quarterly, 28(1),* 55-59.

Beatty, M. J., & Kruger, M. W. (1978). The effects of heckling on speaker credibility and attitude change. *Communication Quarterly, 26(2),* 46-50.

Beauvois, J.-L., & Joule, R.-V. (1996). *A radical dissonance theory.* London: Taylor & Francis.

Beauvois, J.-L., & Joule, R.-V. (1999). A radical point of view on dissonance theory. In E. Harmon-Jones & J. Mills (Eds.), *Cognitive dissonance: Progress on a pivotal theory in social psychology* (pp. 43-70). Washington, DC: American Psychological Association.

Beck, K. H., & Frankel, A. (1981). A conceptualization of threat communications and protective health behavior. *Social Psychology Quarterly, 44,* 204-217.

Becker, B. J. (1986). Influence again: An examination of reviews and studies of gender differences in social influence. In J. S. Hyde & M. C. Linn (Eds.), *The psychology of gender: Advances through meta-analysis* (pp. 178-209). Baltimore: Johns Hopkins University Press.

Beisecker, T. D., & Parson, D. W. (1972). Introduction. In T. D. Beisecker & D. W. Parson (Eds.), *The process of social influence* (pp. 1-6). Englewood Cliffs, NJ: Prentice Hall.

Belch, G. E., & Belch, M. A. (1987). The application of an expectancy value operationalization of function theory to examine attitudes of boycotters and nonboycotters of a consumer product. *Advances in Consumer Research, 14,* 232-236.

Bell, R. A., Zahn, C. J., & Hopper, R. (1984). Disclaiming: A test of two competing views. *Communication Quarterly, 32,* 28-36.

Beltramini, R. F., & Sirsi, A. K. (1992). Physician information acquisition and believability. *Journal of Health Care Marketing, 12(4),* 52-59.

Bem, D. J. (1972). Self-perception theory. In L. Berkowitz (Ed.), *Advances in experimental social psychology* (Vol. 6, pp. 1-62). New York: Academic Press.

Benoit, W. L. (1987). Argumentation and credibility appeals in persuasion. *Southern Speech Communication Journal, 52,* 181-197.

Benoit, W. L. (1991). Two tests of the mechanism of inoculation theory. *Southern Communication Journal, 56,* 219-229.

Benoit, W. L. (1998). Forewarning and persuasion. In M. Allen & R. W. Preiss (Eds.), *Persuasion: Advances through meta-analysis* (pp. 139-154). Cresskill, NJ: Hampton.

Bentler, P. M., & Speckart, G. (1979). Models of attitude-behavior relations. *Psychological Bulletin, 86,* 452-464.

Bergin, A. E. (1962). The effect of dissonant persuasive communications upon changes in a self-referring attitude. *Journal of Personality, 30,* 423-438.

Berlo, D. K., Lemert, J. B., & Mertz, R. J. (1969). Dimensions for evaluating the acceptability of message sources. *Public Opinion Quarterly, 33,* 563-576.

Berscheid, E. (1985). Interpersonal attraction. In G. Lindzey & E. Aronson (Eds.), *Handbook of social psychology* (3rd ed., Vol. 2, pp. 413-484). New York: Random House.

Berscheid, E., & Walster, E. (1974). Physical attractiveness. In L. Berkowitz (Ed.), *Advances in experimental social psychology* (Vol. 7, pp. 157-215). New York: Academic Press.

Bertrand, J. T. (1979). Selective avoidance on health topics: A field test. *Communication Research, 6,* 271-294.

Bettman, J. R., Capon, N., & Lutz, R. J. (1975). Cognitive algebra in multiattribute attitude models. *Journal of Marketing Research, 12,* 151-164.

Bezjian-Avery, A., Calder, B., & Iacobucci, D. (1998). New media interactive advertising vs. traditional advertising. *Journal of Advertising Research, 38*(4), 23-32.

Biddle, P. R. (1966). An experimental study of ethos and appeal for overt behavior in persuasion (Doctoral dissertation, University of Illinois at Urbana-Champaign, 1966). *Dissertation Abstracts, 27* (1967), 3963A. (University Microfilms No. AAC-6706558)

Biek, M., Wood, W., & Chaiken, S. (1996). Working knowledge, cognitive processing, and attitudes: On the determinants of bias. *Personality and Social Psychology Bulletin, 22,* 547-556.

Biglan, A., Glasgow, R., Ary, D., Thompson, R., Severson, H., Lichtenstein, E., Weissman, W., Faller, C., & Gallison, C. (1987). How generalizable are the effects of smoking prevention programs? Refusal skills training and parent messages in a teacher-administered program. *Journal of Behavioral Medicine, 10,* 613-628.

Bineham, J. L. (1988). A historical account of the hypodermic model in mass communication. *Communication Monographs, 55,* 230-246.

Birkimer, J. C., Johnston, P. L., & Berry, M. M. (1993). Guilt and help from friends: Variables related to healthy behavior. *Journal of Social Psychology, 133,* 683-692.

Bless, H., Bohner, G., Schwarz, N., & Strack, F. (1990). Mood and persuasion: A cognitive response analysis. *Personality and Social Psychology Bulletin, 16,* 331-345.

Bless, H., Mackie, D. M., & Schwarz, N. (1992). Mood effects on attitude judgments: Independent effects of mood before and after message elaboration. *Journal of Personality and Social Psychology, 63,* 585-595.

Bless, H., & Schwarz, N. (1999). Sufficient and necessary conditions in dual-process models: The case of mood and information processing. In S. Chaiken &

Y. Trope (Eds.), *Dual-process models in social psychology* (pp. 423-440). New York: Guilford.

Blue, C. L. (1995). The predictive capacity of the theory of reasoned action and the theory of planned behavior in exercise research: An integrated literature review. *Research in Nursing and Health, 18,* 105-121.

Blumberg, S. J. (2000). Guarding against threatening HIV prevention messages: An information-processing model. *Health Education and Behavior, 27,* 780-795.

Blumler, J. G., & Gurevitch, M. (1982). The political effects of mass communication. In M. Gurevitch, T. Bennett, J. Curran, & J. Woollacott (Eds.), *Culture, society, and the media* (pp. 236-267). London: Methuen.

Bochner, S., & Insko, C. A. (1966). Communicator discrepancy, source credibility, and opinion change. *Journal of Personality and Social Psychology, 4,* 614-621.

Bock, D. G., & Saine, T. J. (1975). The impact of source credibility, attitude valence, and task sensitivity on trait errors in speech evaluation. *Speech Monographs, 42,* 229-236.

Bodur, H. O., Brinberg, D., & Coupey, E. (2000). Belief, affect, and attitude: Alternative models of the determinants of attitude. *Journal of Consumer Psychology, 9,* 17-28.

Boer, H., & Seydel, E. R. (1996). Protection motivation theory. In M. Conner & P. Norman (Eds.), *Predicting health behaviour: Research and practice with social cognition models* (pp. 95-120). Buckingham, UK: Open University Press.

Bohner, G., Chaiken, S., & Hunyadi, P. (1994). The role of mood and message ambiguity in the interplay of heuristic and systematic processing. *European Journal of Social Psychology, 24,* 207-221.

Bohner, G., Crow, K., Erb, H.-P., & Schwarz, N. (1992). Affect and persuasion: Mood effects on the processing of message content and context cues and on subsequent behaviour. *European Journal of Social Psychology, 22,* 511-530.

Boller, G. W., Swasy, J. L., & Munch, J. M. (1990). Conceptualizing argument quality via argument structure. *Advances in Consumer Research, 17,* 321-328.

Bolton, G. M. (1974). The lost letter technique as a measure of community attitudes toward a major social issue. *Sociological Quarterly, 15,* 567-570.

Boninger, D. S., Brock, T. C., Cook, T. D., Gruder, C. L., & Romer, D. (1990). Discovery of reliable attitude change persistence resulting from a transmitter tuning set. *Psychological Science, 1,* 268-271.

Booth-Butterfield, S., Cooke, P., Andrighetti, A., Casteel, B., Lang, T., Pearson, D., & Rodriquez, B. (1994). Simultaneous versus exclusive processing of persuasive arguments and cues. *Communication Quarterly, 42,* 21-35.

Booth-Butterfield, S., & Gutowski, C. (1993). Message modality and source credibility can interact to affect argument processing. *Communication Quarterly, 41,* 77-89.

Borgida, E., & Campbell, B. (1982). Belief relevance and attitude-behavior consistency: The moderating role of personal experience. *Journal of Personality and Social Psychology, 42,* 239-247.

Boster, F. J., & Mongeau, P. (1984). Fear-arousing persuasive messages. *Communication Yearbook, 8,* 330-375.

Bowers, J. W. (1965). The influence of delivery on attitudes toward concepts and speakers. *Speech Monographs, 32,* 154-158.

Bowers, J. W., & Phillips, W. A. (1967). A note on the generality of source-credibility scales. *Speech Monographs, 34,* 185-186.

Bowman, C. H., & Fishbein, M. (1978). Understanding public reaction to energy proposals: An application of the Fishbein model. *Journal of Applied Social Psychology, 8,* 319-340.

Bradac, J. J. (1983). On generalizing cabbages, messages, kings, and several other things: The virtues of multiplicity. *Human Communication Research, 9,* 181-187.

Bradac, J. J. (1986). Threats to generalization in the use of elicited, purloined, and contrived messages in human communication research. *Communication Quarterly, 34,* 55-65.

Bradac, J. J., Bowers, J. W., & Courtright, J. A. (1980). Lexical variations in intensity, immediacy, and diversity: An axiomatic theory and causal model. In R. N. St. Clair & H. Giles (Eds.), *The social and psychological contexts of language* (pp. 193-223). Hillsdale, NJ: Lawrence Erlbaum.

Bradley, P. H. (1981). The folk-linguistics of women's speech: An empirical examination. *Communication Monographs, 48,* 73-90.

Brannon, L. A., & Brock, T. C. (1994). Test of schema correspondence theory of persuasion: Effects of matching an appeal to actual, ideal, and product "selves." In E. M. Clark, T. C. Brock, & D. W. Stewart (Eds.), *Attention, attitude, and affect in response to advertising* (pp. 169-188). Hillsdale, NJ: Lawrence Erlbaum.

Brashers, D. E., & Jackson, S. (1999). Changing conceptions of "message effects": A 24-year overview. *Human Communication Research, 25,* 457-477.

Breckler, S. J. (1993). Emotion and attitude change. In M. Lewis & J. M. Haviland (Eds.), *Handbook of emotions* (pp. 461-473). New York: Guilford.

Breckler, S. J. (1994). A comparison of numerical indexes for measuring attitudinal ambivalence. *Educational and Psychological Measurement, 54,* 350-365.

Breckler, S. J., & Wiggins, E. C. (1989). On defining attitude and attitude theory: Once more with feeling. In A. R. Pratkanis, S. J. Breckler, & A. G. Greenwald (Eds.), *Attitude structure and function* (pp. 407-427). Hillsdale, NJ: Lawrence Erlbaum.

Brehm, J. W. (1956). Postdecision changes in the desirability of alternatives. *Journal of Abnormal and Social Psychology, 52,* 384-389.

Brenes, G. A., Strube, M. J, & Storandt, M. (1998). An application of the theory of planned behavior to exercise among older adults. *Journal of Applied Social Psychology, 28,* 2274-2290.

Brinberg, D., & Durand, J. (1983). Eating at fast-food restaurants: An analysis using two behavioral intention models. *Journal of Applied Social Psychology, 13,* 459-472.

Brock, T. C. (1965). Communicator-recipient similarity and decision change. *Journal of Personality and Social Psychology, 1*, 650-654.

Bromer, P. (1998). Ambivalent attitudes and information processing. *Swiss Journal of Psychology, 57*, 225-234.

Brouwers, M. C., & Sorrentino, R. M. (1993). Uncertainty orientation and protection motivation theory: The role of individual differences in health compliance. *Journal of Personality and Social Psychology, 65*, 102-112.

Brown, B. L., Strong, W. J., & Rencher, A. C. (1973). Perceptions of personality from speech: Effects of manipulations of acoustical parameters. *Journal of the Acoustical Society of America, 54*, 29-35.

Brown, B. L., Strong, W. J., & Rencher, A. C. (1974). Fifty-four voices from two: The effects of simultaneous manipulations of rate, mean fundamental frequency, and variance of fundamental frequency on ratings of personality from speech. *Journal of the Acoustical Society of America, 55*, 313-318.

Brown, S. P., Cron, W. L., & Slocum, J. W., Jr. (1997). Effects of goal-directed emotions on salesperson volitions, behavior, and performance: A longitudinal study. *Journal of Marketing, 61*(1), 39-50.

Brown, S. P., & Stayman, D. M. (1992). Antecedents and consequences of attitude toward the ad: A meta-analysis. *Journal of Consumer Research, 19*, 34-51.

Browne, B. A., & Kaldenberg, D. O. (1997). Self-monitoring and image appeals in advertising. *Psychological Reports, 81*, 1267-1275.

Brubaker, R. G., & Fowler, C. (1990). Encouraging college males to perform testicular self-examination: Evaluation of a persuasive message based on the revised theory of reasoned action. *Journal of Applied Social Psychology, 20*, 1411-1422.

Brubaker, R. G., & Wickersham, D. (1990). Encouraging the practice of testicular self-examination: A field application of the theory of reasoned action. *Health Psychology, 9*, 154-163.

Brug, J., Campbell, M., & van Assema, P. (1999). The application and impact of computer-generated personalized nutrition education: A review of the literature. *Patient Education and Counseling, 36*, 145-156.

Bryan, A. D., Aiken, L. S., & West, S. G. (1996). Increasing condom use: Evaluation of a theory-based intervention to prevent sexually transmitted diseases in young women. *Health Psychology, 15*, 371-382.

Bryant, J., Brown, D., Silberberg, A. R., & Elliott, S. M. (1981). Effects of humorous illustrations in college textbooks. *Human Communication Research, 8*, 43-57.

Budd, R. J. (1986). Predicting cigarette use: The need to incorporate measures of salience in the theory of reasoned action. *Journal of Applied Social Psychology, 16*, 663-685.

Budd, R. J., North, D., & Spencer, C. (1984). Understanding seat-belt use: A test of Bentler and Speckart's extension of the "theory of reasoned action." *European Journal of Social Psychology, 14*, 69-78.

Budd, R. J., & Spencer, C. (1984a). Latitude of rejection, centrality, and certainty: Variables affecting the relationship between attitudes, norms, and behavioural intentions. *British Journal of Social Psychology, 23*, 1-8.

Budd, R. J., & Spencer, C. P. (1984b). Predicting undergraduates' intentions to drink. *Journal of Studies on Alcohol, 45,* 179-183.

Buller, D. B. (1986). Distraction during persuasive communication: A meta-analytic review. *Communication Monographs, 53,* 91-114.

Buller, D. B., & Hall, J. R. (1998). The effects of distraction during persuasion. In M. Allen & R. W. Preiss (Eds.), *Persuasion: Advances through meta-analysis* (pp. 155-173). Cresskill, NJ: Hampton.

Burger, J. M. (1986). Increasing compliance by improving the deal: The that's-not-all technique. *Journal of Personality and Social Psychology, 51,* 277-283.

Burger, J. M. (1999). The foot-in-the-door compliance procedure: A multiple-process analysis and review. *Personality and Social Psychology Review, 3,* 303-325.

Burger, J. M., Reed, M., DeCesare, K., Rauner, S., & Rozolis, J. (1999). The effects of initial request size on compliance: More about the that's-not-all technique. *Basic and Applied Social Psychology, 21,* 243-249.

Burgoon, J. K. (1976). The ideal source: A reexamination of source credibility measurement. *Central States Speech Journal, 27,* 200-206.

Burgoon, J. K., Birk, T., & Pfau, M. (1990). Nonverbal behaviors, persuasion, and credibility. *Human Communication Research, 17,* 140-169.

Burgoon, M., & Chase, L. J. (1973). The effects of differential linguistic patterns in messages attempting to induce resistance to persuasion. *Speech Monographs, 40,* 1-7.

Burgoon, M., Hall, J., & Pfau, M. (1991). A test of the "messages-as-fixed-effect fallacy" argument: Empirical and theoretical implications of design choices. *Communication Quarterly, 39,* 18-34.

Burgoon, M., Jones, S. B., & Stewart, D. (1975). Toward a message-centered theory of persuasion: Three empirical investigations of language intensity. *Human Communication Research, 1,* 240-256.

Burnell, P., & Reeve, A. (1984). Persuasion as a political concept. *British Journal of Political Science, 14,* 393-410.

Burnkrant, R. E., & Howard, D. J. (1984). Effects of the use of introductory rhetorical questions versus statements on information processing. *Journal of Personality and Social Psychology, 47,* 1218-1230.

Byrne, D. (1969). Attitudes and attraction. In L. Berkowitz (Ed.), *Advances in experimental social psychology* (Vol. 4, pp. 35-89). New York: Academic Press.

Cacioppo, J. T., Bush, L. K., & Tassinary, L. G. (1992). Microexpressive facial actions as a function of affective stimuli: Replication and extension. *Personality and Social Psychology Bulletin, 18,* 515-526.

Cacioppo, J. T., Crites, S. L., Jr., & Gardner, W. L. (1996). Attitudes to the right: Evaluative processing is associated with lateralized late positive event-related brain potentials. *Personality and Social Psychology Bulletin, 22,* 1205-1219.

Cacioppo, J. T., Crites, S. L., Jr., Gardner, W. L., & Berntson, G. G. (1994). Bioelectrical echoes from evaluative categorizations: I. A late positive brain potential that varies as a function of trait negativity and extremity. *Journal of Personality and Social Psychology, 67,* 115-125.

Cacioppo, J. T., Harkins, S. G., & Petty, R. E. (1981). The nature of attitudes and cognitive responses and their relationships to behavior. In R. E. Petty, T. M. Ostrom, & T. C. Brock (Eds.), *Cognitive responses in persuasion* (pp. 31-54). Hillsdale, NJ: Lawrence Erlbaum.

Cacioppo, J. T., & Petty, R. E. (1982). The need for cognition. *Journal of Personality and Social Psychology, 42,* 116-131.

Cacioppo, J. T., & Petty, R. E. (1984). The elaboration likelihood model of persuasion. *Advances in Consumer Research, 11,* 673-675.

Cacioppo, J. T., & Petty, R. E. (1985). Central and peripheral routes to persuasion: The role of message repetition. In L. F. Alwitt & A. A. Mitchell (Eds.), *Psychological processes and advertising effects: Theory, research, and application* (pp. 91-111). Hillsdale, NJ: Lawrence Erlbaum.

Cacioppo, J. T., Petty, R. E., Feinstein, J. A., & Jarvis, W. B. G. (1996). Dispositional differences in cognitive motivation: The life and times of individuals varying in need for cognition. *Psychological Bulletin, 119,* 197-253.

Cacioppo, J. T., Petty, R. E., & Geen, T. R. (1989). Attitude structure and function: From the tripartite to the homeostasis model of attitudes. In A. R. Pratkanis, S. J. Breckler, & A. G. Greenwald (Eds.), *Attitude structure and function* (pp. 275-309). Hillsdale, NJ: Lawrence Erlbaum.

Cacioppo, J. T., Petty, R. E., Kao, C. F., & Rodriguez, R. (1986). Central and peripheral routes to persuasion: An individual difference perspective. *Journal of Personality and Social Psychology, 51,* 1032-1043.

Cacioppo, J. T., Petty, R. E., Losch, M. E., & Kim, H. S. (1986). Electromyographic activity over facial muscle regions can differentiate the valence and intensity of affective reactions. *Journal of Personality and Social Psychology, 50,* 260-268.

Cacioppo, J. T., Petty, R. E., & Morris, K. J. (1983). Effects of need for cognition on message evaluation, recall, and persuasion. *Journal of Personality and Social Psychology, 45,* 805-818.

Cacioppo, J. T., Petty, R. E., & Sidera, J. A. (1982). The effects of a salient self-schema on the evaluation of proattitudinal editorials: Top-down versus bottom-up message processing. *Journal of Experimental Social Psychology, 18,* 324-338.

Cacioppo, J. T., Petty, R. E., & Stoltenberg, C. D. (1985). Processes of social influence: The elaboration likelihood model of persuasion. In P. C. Kendall (Ed.), *Advances in cognitive-behavioral research and therapy* (Vol. 4, pp. 215-274). New York: Academic Press.

Cacioppo, J. T., & Sandman, C. A. (1981). Psychophysical functioning, cognitive responding, and attitudes. In R. E. Petty, T. M. Ostrom, & T. C. Brock (Eds.), *Cognitive responses in persuasion* (pp. 81-103). Hillsdale, NJ: Lawrence Erlbaum.

Cacioppo, J. T., von Hippel, W., & Ernst, J. M. (1997). Mapping cognitive structures and processes through verbal content: The thought-listing technique. *Journal of Consulting and Clinical Psychology, 65,* 928-940.

Campbell, M. C., & Kirmani, A. (2000). Consumers' use of persuasion knowledge: The effects of accessibility and cognitive capacity on perceptions of an influence agent. *Journal of Consumer Research, 27,* 69-83.

Campbell, M. K., Bernhardt, J. M., Waldmiller, M., Jackson, B., Potenziani, D., Weathers, B., & Demissie, S. (1999). Varying the message source in computer-tailored nutrition education. *Patient Education and Counseling, 36,* 157-169.

Cann, A., Sherman, S. J., & Elkes, R. (1975). Effects of initial request size and timing of a second request on compliance: The foot in the door and the door in the face. *Journal of Personality and Social Psychology, 32,* 774-782.

Cardenas, M. P., & Simons-Morton, B. G. (1993). The effect of anticipatory guidance on mothers' self-efficacy and behavioral intentions to prevent burns caused by hot tap water. *Patient Education and Counseling, 21,* 117-123.

Carlsmith, J. M., Collins, B. E., & Helmreich, R. L. (1966). Studies in forced compliance: I. The effect of pressure for compliance on attitude change produced by face-to-face role playing and anonymous essay writing. *Journal of Personality and Social Psychology, 4,* 1-13.

Carlson, E. R. (1956). Attitude change through modification of attitude structure. *Journal of Abnormal and Social Psychology, 52,* 256-261.

Celuch, K., & Slama, M. (1995). "Getting along" and "getting ahead" as motives for self-presentation: Their impact on advertising effectiveness. *Journal of Applied Social Psychology, 25,* 1700-1713.

Chaffee, S. H., & Hochheimer, J. L. (1985). The beginnings of political communication research in the United States: Origins of the "limited effects" model. In E. M. Rogers & F. Balle (Eds.), *The media revolution in America and western Europe* (pp. 267-296). Norwood, NJ: Ablex.

Chaffee, S. H., & Miyo, Y. (1983). Selective exposure and the reinforcement hypothesis: An intergenerational panel study of the 1980 presidential campaign. *Communication Research, 10,* 3-36.

Chaffee, S. H., & Rimal, R. N. (1996). Time of vote decision and openness to persuasion. In D. C. Mutz, P. M. Sniderman, & R. A. Brody (Eds.), *Political persuasion and attitude change* (pp. 267-291). Ann Arbor: University of Michigan Press.

Chaiken, S. (1979). Communicator physical attractiveness and persuasion. *Journal of Personality and Social Psychology, 37,* 1387-1397.

Chaiken, S. (1980). Heuristic versus systematic information processing and the use of source versus message cues in persuasion. *Journal of Personality and Social Psychology, 39,* 752-766.

Chaiken, S. (1986). Physical appearance and social influence. In C. P. Herman, M. P. Zanna, & E. T. Higgins (Eds.), *Physical appearance, stigma, and social behavior: The Ontario Symposium, vol. 3* (pp. 143-177). Hillsdale, NJ: Lawrence Erlbaum.

Chaiken, S. (1987). The heuristic model of persuasion. In M. P. Zanna, J. M. Olson, & C. P. Herman (Eds.), *Social influence: The Ontario Symposium, vol. 5* (pp. 3-39). Hillsdale, NJ: Lawrence Erlbaum.

Chaiken, S., Duckworth, K. L., & Darke, P. (1999). When parsimony fails . . . *Psychological Inquiry, 10,* 118-123.

Chaiken, S., & Eagly, A. H. (1976). Communication modality as a determinant of message persuasiveness and message comprehensibility. *Journal of Personality and Social Psychology, 34,* 605-614.

Chaiken, S., & Eagly, A. H. (1983). Communication modality as a determinant of persuasion: The role of communicator salience. *Journal of Personality and Social Psychology, 45,* 241-256.

Chaiken, S., & Maheswaran, D. (1994). Heuristic processing can bias systematic processing: Effects of source credibility, argument ambiguity, and task importance on attitude judgment. *Journal of Personality and Social Psychology, 66,* 460-473.

Chaiken, S., Pomerantz, E. M., & Giner-Sorolla, R. (1995). Structural consistency and attitude strength. In R. E. Petty & J. A. Krosnick (Eds.), *Attitude strength: Antecedents and consequences* (pp. 387-412). Mahwah, NJ: Lawrence Erlbaum.

Chaiken, S., & Stangor, C. (1987). Attitudes and attitude change. *Annual Review of Psychology, 38,* 575-630.

Chaiken, S., & Trope, Y. (Eds.). (1999). *Dual-process theories in social psychology.* New York: Guilford.

Chaiken, S., Wood, W., & Eagly, A. H. (1996). Principles of persuasion. In E. T. Higgins & A. W. Kruglanski (Eds.), *Social psychology: Handbook of basic principles* (pp. 702-742). New York: Guilford.

Chang, M.-J., & Gruner, C. R. (1981). Audience reaction to self-disparaging humor. *Southern Speech Communication Journal, 46,* 419-426.

Chartrand, T., Pinckert, S., & Burger, J. M. (1999). When manipulation backfires: The effects of time delay and requester on the foot-in-the-door technique. *Journal of Applied Social Psychology, 29,* 211-221.

Chassin, L., Corty, E., Presson, C. C., Olshavsky, R. W., Bensenberg, M., & Sherman, S. J. (1981). Predicting adolescents' intentions to smoke cigarettes. *Journal of Health and Social Behavior, 22,* 445-455.

Chebat, J.-C., Filiatrault, P., Laroche, M., & Watson, C. (1988). Compensatory effects of cognitive characteristics of the source, the message, and the receiver upon attitude change. *Journal of Psychology, 122,* 609-621.

Chebat, J.-C., Laroche, M., Baddoura, D., & Filiatrault, P. (1992). Effects of source likability on attitude change through message repetition. *Advances in Consumer Research, 19,* 353-358.

Chen, H. C., Reardon, R., Rea, C., & Moore, D. J. (1992). Forewarning of content and involvement: Consequences for persuasion and resistance to persuasion. *Journal of Experimental Social Psychology, 28,* 523-541.

Chen, S., & Chaiken, S. (1999). The heuristic-systematic model in its broader context. In S. Chaiken & Y. Trope (Eds.), *Dual-process theories in social psychology* (pp. 73-96). New York: Guilford.

Cheung, S. F., Chan, D. K.-S., & Wong, Z. S.-Y. (1999). Reexamining the theory of planned behavior in understanding wastepaper recycling. *Environment and Behavior, 31,* 587-612.

Chu, G. C. (1967). Prior familiarity, perceived bias, and one-sided versus two-sided communications. *Journal of Experimental Social Psychology, 3,* 243-254.

Cialdini, R. B. (1984). *Influence: How and why people agree to things.* New York: William Morrow.

Cialdini, R. B. (1987). Compliance principles of compliance professionals: Psychologists of necessity. In M. P. Zanna, J. M. Olson, & C. P. Herman (Eds.), *Social influence: The Ontario Symposium, vol. 5* (pp. 165-184). Hillsdale, NJ: Lawrence Erlbaum.

Cialdini, R. B., Cacioppo, J. T., Bassett, R., & Miller, J. A. (1978). Low-ball procedure for producing compliance: Commitment then cost. *Journal of Personality and Social Psychology, 36,* 463-476.

Cialdini, R. B., Kallgren, C. A., & Reno, R. R. (1991). A focus theory of normative conduct: A theoretical refinement and reevaluation of the role of norms in human behavior. In M. P. Zanna (Ed.), *Advances in experimental social psychology* (Vol. 24, pp. 201-234). New York: Academic Press.

Cialdini, R. B., & Petty, R. E. (1981). Anticipatory opinion effects. In R. E. Petty, T. M. Ostrom, & T. C. Brock (Eds.), *Cognitive responses in persuasion* (pp. 217-235). Hillsdale, NJ: Lawrence Erlbaum.

Cialdini, R. B., & Schroeder, D. A. (1976). Increasing compliance by legitimizing paltry contributions: When even a penny helps. *Journal of Personality and Social Psychology, 34,* 599-604.

Cialdini, R. B., & Trost, M. R. (1998). Social influence: Social norms, conformity, and compliance. In D. T. Gilbert, S. T. Fiske, & G. T. Lindzey (Eds.), *Handbook of social psychology* (4th ed., Vol. 2, pp. 151-192). Boston: McGraw-Hill.

Cialdini, R. B., Vincent, J. E., Lewis, S. K., Catalan, J., Wheeler, D., & Darby, B. L. (1975). Reciprocal concessions procedure for inducing compliance: The door-in-the-face technique. *Journal of Personality and Social Psychology, 31,* 206-215.

Clark, H. H. (1973). The language-as-fixed-effect fallacy: A critique of language statistics in psychological research. *Journal of Verbal Learning and Verbal Behavior, 12,* 335-359.

Clark, R. A., Stewart, R., & Marston, A. (1972). Scale values for highest and lowest levels of credibility. *Central States Speech Journal, 23,* 193-196.

Clary, E. G., & Snyder, M. (1991). A functional analysis of altruism and prosocial behavior: The case of volunteerism. In M. S. Clark (Ed.), *Prosocial behavior* (pp. 119-148). Newbury Park, CA: Sage.

Clary, E. G., Snyder, M., Ridge, R. D., Copeland, J., Stukas, A. A., Haugen, J., & Miene, P. (1998). Understanding and assessing the motivations of volunteers: A functional approach. *Journal of Personality and Social Psychology, 74,* 1516-1530.

Clary, E. G., Snyder, M., Ridge, R. D., Miene, P. K., & Haugen, J. A. (1994). Matching messages to motives in persuasion: A functional approach to promoting volunteerism. *Journal of Applied Social Psychology, 24,* 1129-1149.

Cochran, S. D., Mays, V. M., Ciarletta, J., Caruso, C., & Mallon, D. (1992). Efficacy of the theory of reasoned action in predicting AIDS-related sexual risk reduction among gay men. *Journal of Applied Social Psychology, 22,* 1481-1501.

Cohen, A. R. (1959). Communication discrepancy and attitude change: A dissonance theory approach. *Journal of Personality, 27,* 386-396.

Cohen, A. R. (1964). *Attitude change and social influence.* New York: Basic Books.

Cohen, J. (1990). Things I have learned (so far). *American Psychologist, 45,* 1304-1312.

Cohen, J. (1994). The earth is round *(p < .05). American Psychologist, 49,* 997-1002.

Cohen, J. B., Fishbein, M., & Ahtola, O. T. (1972). The nature and uses of expectancy-value models in consumer attitude research. *Journal of Marketing Research, 9,* 456-460.

Collins, R. L., Taylor, S. E., Wood, J. V., & Thompson, S. C. (1988). The vividness effect: Elusive or illusory? *Journal of Experimental Social Psychology, 24,* 1-18.

Conner, M., & Armitage, C. J. (1998). Extending the theory of planned behavior: A review and avenues for further research. *Journal of Applied Social Psychology, 28,* 1429-1464.

Conner, M., Graham, S., & Moore, B. (1999). Alcohol and intentions to use condoms: Applying the theory of planned behaviour. *Psychology and Health, 14,* 795-812.

Conner, M., & McMillan, B. (1999). Interaction effects in the theory of planned behaviour: Studying cannabis use. *British Journal of Social Psychology, 38,* 195-222.

Conner, M., & Sparks, P. (1996). The theory of planned behaviour and health behaviours. In M. Conner & P. Norman (Eds.), *Predicting health behaviour: Research and practice with social cognition models* (pp. 121-162). Buckingham, UK: Open University Press.

Conner, M., Warren, R., Close, S., & Sparks, P. (1999). Alcohol consumption and the theory of planned behavior: An examination of the cognitive mediation of past behavior. *Journal of Applied Social Psychology, 29,* 1676-1704.

Converse, J., Jr., & Cooper, J. (1979). The importance of decisions and free-choice attitude change: A curvilinear finding. *Journal of Experimental Social Psychology, 15,* 48-61.

Cook, T. D., & Flay, B. R. (1978). The persistence of experimentally induced attitude change. In L. Berkowitz (Ed.), *Advances in experimental social psychology* (Vol. 11, pp. 1-57). New York: Academic Press.

Cooper, H., & Hedges, L. V. (Eds.). (1994). *The handbook of research synthesis.* New York: Russell Sage.

Cooper, J. (1998). Unlearning cognitive dissonance: Toward an understanding of the development of dissonance. *Journal of Experimental Social Psychology, 34,* 562-575.

Cooper, J. (1999). Unwanted consequences and the self: In search of the motivation for dissonance reduction. In E. Harmon-Jones & J. Mills (Eds.), *Cognitive dissonance: Progress on a pivotal theory in social psychology* (pp. 149-173). Washington, DC: American Psychological Association.

Cooper, J., Darley, J. M., & Henderson, J. E. (1974). On the effectiveness of deviant- and conventional-appearing communicators: A field experiment. *Journal of Personality and Social Psychology, 29,* 752-757.

Cooper, J., & Fazio, R. H. (1984). A new look at dissonance theory. In L. Berkowitz (Ed.), *Advances in experimental social psychology* (Vol. 17, pp. 229-266). New York: Academic Press.

Cooper, J., & Jones, R. A. (1970). Self-esteem and consistency as determinants of anticipatory opinion change. *Journal of Personality and Social Psychology, 14,* 312-320.

Cope, F., & Richardson, D. (1972). The effects of reassuring recommendations in a fear-arousing speech. *Speech Monographs, 39,* 148-150.

Corbin, S. K. T., Jones, R. T., & Schulman, R. S. (1993). Drug refusal behavior: The relative efficacy of skills-based and information-based treatment. *Journal of Pediatric Psychology, 18,* 769-784.

Corby, N. H., Enguidanos, S. M., & Kay, L. S. (1996). Development and use of role model stories in a community level HIV risk reduction intervention. *Public Health Reports, 111*(Suppl. 1), 54-58.

Corston, R., & Colman, A. M. (1997). Modality of communication and recall of health-related information. *Journal of Health Psychology, 2,* 185-194.

Cotton, J. L. (1985). Cognitive dissonance in selective exposure. In D. Zillmann & J. Bryant (Eds.), *Selective exposure to communication* (pp. 11-33). Hillsdale, NJ: Lawrence Erlbaum.

Cotton, J. L., & Hieser, R. A. (1980). Selective exposure to information and cognitive dissonance. *Journal of Research in Personality, 14,* 518-527.

Coulter, R. H., & Pinto, M. B. (1995). Guilt appeals in advertising: What are their effects? *Journal of Applied Psychology, 80,* 697-705.

Courneya, K. S. (1994). Predicting repeated behavior from intention: The issue of scale correspondence. *Journal of Applied Social Psychology, 24,* 580-594.

Courneya, K. S. (1995). Understanding readiness for regular physical activity in older individuals: An application of the theory of planned behavior. *Health Psychology, 14,* 80-87.

Crandall, C. S., Glor, J., & Britt, T. W. (1997). AIDS-related stigmatization: Instrumental and symbolic attitudes. *Journal of Applied Social Psychology, 27,* 95-123.

Crano, W. D., & Prislin, R. (1995). Components of vested interest and attitude-behavior consistency. *Basic and Applied Social Psychology, 17,* 1-21.

Crawley, F. E., III (1990). Intentions of science teachers to use investigative teaching methods: A test of the theory of planned behavior. *Journal of Research in Science Teaching, 27,* 685-698.

Crawley, F. E., III, & Coe, A. S. (1990). Determinants of middle school students' intention to enroll in a high school science course: An application of the theory of reasoned action. *Journal of Research in Science Teaching, 27,* 461-476.

Crawley, F. E., & Koballa, T. R., Jr. (1992). Hispanic-American students' attitudes toward enrolling in high school chemistry: A study of planned behavior and belief-based change. *Hispanic Journal of Behavioral Sciences, 14,* 469-486.

Crites, S. L., Jr., Fabrigar, L. R., & Petty, R. E. (1994). Measuring the affective and cognitive properties of attitudes: Conceptual and methodological issues. *Personality and Social Psychology Bulletin, 20,* 619-634.

Crockett, W. H. (1982). Balance, agreement, and positivity in the cognition of small social structures. In L. Berkowitz (Ed.), *Advances in experimental social psychology* (Vol. 15, pp. 1-57). New York: Academic Press.

Cromwell, H. (1950). The relative effect on audience attitude of the first versus the second argumentative speech of a series. *Speech Monographs, 17,* 105-122.

Cronen, V. E., & Conville, R. L. (1975). Fishbein's conception of belief strength: A theoretical, methodological, and experimental critique. *Speech Monographs, 42,* 143-150.

Cronkhite, G., & Liska, J. (1976). A critique of factor analytic approaches to the study of credibility. *Communication Monographs, 43,* 91-107.

Crowley, A. E., & Hoyer, W. D. (1994). An integrative framework for understanding two-sided persuasion. *Journal of Consumer Research, 20,* 561-574.

Cruz, M. G. (1998). Explicit and implicit conclusions in persuasive messages. In M. Allen & R. W. Preiss (Eds.), *Persuasion: Advances through meta-analysis* (pp. 217-230). Cresskill, NJ: Hampton.

Darke, P. R., Chaiken, S., Bohner, G., Einwiller, S., Erb, H.-P., & Hazlewood, J. D. (1998). Accuracy motivation, consensus information, and the law of large numbers: Effects on attitude judgment in the absence of argumentation. *Personality and Social Psychology Bulletin, 24,* 1205-1215.

Darley, S. A., & Cooper, J. (1972). Cognitive consequences of forced noncompliance. *Journal of Personality and Social Psychology, 24,* 321-326.

Davis, M. H., & Runge, T. E. (1981). Beliefs and attitudes in a gubernatorial primary: Some limitations on the Fishbein model. *Journal of Applied Social Psychology, 11,* 93-113.

Davis, S., Inman, J. J., & McAlister, L. (1992). Promotion has a negative effect on brand evaluations—or does it? Additional disconfirming evidence. *Journal of Marketing Research, 29,* 143-148.

Dawes, R. M., & Smith, T. L. (1985). Attitude and opinion measurement. In G. Lindzey & E. Aronson (Eds.), *Handbook of social psychology* (3rd ed., Vol. 1, pp. 509-566). New York: Random House.

DeBono, K. G. (1987). Investigating the social-adjustive and value-expressive functions of attitudes: Implications for persuasion processes. *Journal of Personality and Social Psychology, 52,* 279-287.

DeBono, K. G. (1992). Pleasant scents and persuasion: An information processing approach. *Journal of Applied Social Psychology, 22,* 910-919.

DeBono, K. G., & Harnish, R. J. (1988). Source expertise, source attractiveness, and the processing of persuasive information: A functional approach. *Journal of Personality and Social Psychology, 55,* 541-546.

DeBono, K. G., & Klein, C. (1993). Source expertise and persuasion: The moderating role of recipient dogmatism. *Personality and Social Psychology Bulletin, 19,* 166-172.

DeBono, K. G., & McDermott, J. B. (1994). Trait anxiety and persuasion: Individual differences in information processing strategies. *Journal of Research in Personality, 28,* 395-407.

DeBono, K. G., & Omoto, A. M. (1993). Individual differences in predicting behavioral intentions from attitude and subjective norm. *Journal of Social Psychology, 133,* 825-831.

DeBono, K. G., & Packer, M. (1991). The effects of advertising appeal on perceptions of product quality. *Personality and Social Psychology Bulletin, 17,* 194-200.

DeBono, K. G., & Snyder, M. (1989). Understanding consumer decision-making processes: The role of form and function in product evaluation. *Journal of Applied Social Psychology, 19,* 416-424.

DeBono, K. G., & Telesca, C. (1990). The influence of source physical attractiveness on advertising effectiveness: A functional perspective. *Journal of Applied Social Psychology, 20,* 1383-1395.

DeFleur, M. L., & Ball-Rokeach, S. (1982). *Theories of mass communication* (4th ed.). New York: Longman.

DeJong, W. (1979). An examination of self-perception mediation of the foot-in-the-door effect. *Journal of Personality and Social Psychology, 37,* 2221-2239.

DeJong, W., & Oopnik, A. J. (1992). Effect of legitimizing small contributions and labeling potential donors as "helpers" on responses to a direct mail solicitation for charity. *Psychological Reports, 71,* 923-928.

Delia, J. G. (1975). Regional dialect, message acceptance, and perceptions of the speaker. *Central States Speech Journal, 26,* 188-194.

Delia, J. G. (1976). A constructivist analysis of the concept of credibility. *Quarterly Journal of Speech, 62,* 361-375.

Delia, J. G. (1987). Communication research: A history. In C. R. Berger & S. H. Chaffee (Eds.), *Handbook of communication science* (pp. 20-98). Newbury Park, CA: Sage.

Delia, J. G., Crockett, W. H., Press, A. N., & O'Keefe, D. J. (1975). The dependency of interpersonal evaluations on context-relevant beliefs about the other. *Speech Monographs, 42,* 10-19.

DeVries, D. L., & Ajzen, I. (1971). The relationship of attitudes and normative beliefs to cheating in college. *Journal of Social Psychology, 83,* 199-207.

De Wit, J. B. F., Stroebe, W., De Vroome, E. M. M., Sandfort, T. G. M., & van Griensven, G. J. P. (2000). Understanding AIDS preventive behavior with casual and primary partners in homosexual men: The theory of planned behavior and the information-motivation-behavioral-skills model. *Psychology and Health, 15,* 325-340.

De Young, R. (1989). Exploring the difference between recyclers and non-recyclers: The role of information. *Journal of Environmental Systems, 18,* 341-351.

Dholakia, R. R. (1987). Source credibility effects: A test of behavioral persistence. *Advances in Consumer Research, 14,* 426-430.

Dickerson, C. A., Thibodeau, R., Aronson, E., & Miller, D. (1992). Using cognitive dissonance to encourage water conservation. *Journal of Applied Social Psychology, 22,* 841-854.

Dijkstra, A., & De Vries, H. (1999). The development of computer-generated tailored interventions. *Patient Education and Counseling, 36,* 193-203.

Dijkstra, A., De Vries, H., & Roijackers, J. (1998). Computerized tailored feedback to change cognitive determinants of smoking: A Dutch field experiment. *Health Education Research, 13,* 197-206.

Dijkstra, J. J., Liebrand, W. B. G., & Timminga, E. (1998). Persuasiveness of expert systems. *Behaviour and Information Technology, 17,* 155-163.

Dillard, J. P. (1990). Self-inference and the foot-in-the-door technique: Quantity of behavior and attitudinal mediation. *Human Communication Research, 16,* 422-447.

Dillard, J. P. (1991). The current status of research on sequential-request compliance techniques. *Personality and Social Psychology Bulletin, 17,* 283-288.

Dillard, J. P. (1994). Rethinking the study of fear appeals: An emotional perspective. *Communication Theory, 4,* 295-323.

Dillard, J. P., Hunter, J. E., & Burgoon, M. (1984). Sequential-request persuasive strategies: Meta-analysis of foot-in-the-door and door-in-the-face. *Human Communication Research, 10,* 461-488.

Dillard, J. P., & Peck, E. (2000). Affect and persuasion: Emotional responses to public service announcements. *Communication Research, 27,* 461-495.

Dillard, J. P., & Peck, E. (2001). Persuasion and the structure of affect: Dual systems and discrete emotions as complementary models. *Human Communication Research, 27,* 38-68.

Dillard, J. P., Plotnick, C. A., Godbold, L. C., Freimuth, V. S., & Edgar, T. (1996). The multiple affective outcomes of AIDS PSAs: Fear appeals do more than scare people. *Communication Research, 23,* 44-72.

Dillman, D. A., Singer, E., Clark, J. R., & Treat, J. B. (1996). Effects of benefits appeals, mandatory appeals, and variations in statements of confidentiality on completion rates for census questionnaires. *Public Opinion Quarterly, 60,* 376-389.

Ditto, P. H., Druley, J. A., Moore, K. A., Danks, J. H., & Smucker, W. D. (1996). Fates worse than death: The role of valued life activities in health-state evaluations. *Health Psychology, 15,* 332-343.

DiVesta, F. J., & Merwin, J. C. (1960). The effects of need-oriented communications on attitude change. *Journal of Abnormal and Social Psychology, 60,* 80-85.

Doll, J., & Ajzen, I. (1992). Accessibility and stability of predictors in the theory of planned behavior. *Journal of Personality and Social Psychology, 63,* 754-765.

Doll, J., Ajzen, I., & Madden, T. J. (1991). Optimale skalierung und urteilsbildung in unterschiedlichen einstellungsbereichen: Eine reanalyse [Optimal scaling and judgment in different attitude domains: A reanalysis]. *Zeitschrift für Sozialpsychologie, 22,* 102-111.

Doll, J., & Mallu, R. (1990). Individuierte einstellungsformation, einstellungsstruktur und einstellungs-verhalten-konsistenz [Individuated attitude-formation, attitude structure and attitude-behavior consistency]. *Zeitschrift für Sozialpsychologie, 21,* 2-14.

Doll, J., & Orth, B. (1993). The Fishbein and Ajzen theory of reasoned action applied to contraceptive behavior: Model variants and meaningfulness. *Journal of Applied Social Psychology, 23,* 395-415.

Donaldson, S. I., Graham, J. W., & Hansen, W. B. (1994). Testing the generalizability of intervening mechanism theories: Understanding the effects of adolescent drug use prevention interventions. *Journal of Behavioral Medicine, 17,* 195-216.

Donaldson, S. I., Graham, J. W., Piccinin, A. M., & Hansen, W. B. (1995). Resistance-skills training and onset of alcohol use: Evidence for beneficial and potentially harmful effects in public schools and in private Catholic schools. *Health Psychology, 14,* 291-300.

Donnelly, J. H., Jr., & Ivancevich, J. M. (1970). Post-purchase reinforcement and back-out behavior. *Journal of Marketing Research, 7,* 399-400.

Donohew, L., Lorch, E., & Palmgreen, P. (1991). Sensation seeking and targeting of televised anti-drug PSAs. In L. Donohew, H. E. Sypher, & W. J. Bukoski (Eds.), *Persuasive communication and drug abuse prevention* (pp. 209-226). Hillsdale, NJ: Lawrence Erlbaum.

Doob, A. N., Carlsmith, J. M., Freedman, J. L., Landauer, T. K., & Tom, S., Jr. (1969). Effect of initial selling price on subsequent sales. *Journal of Personality and Social Psychology, 11,* 345-350.

Duncan, T. E., Duncan, S. C., Beauchamp, N., Wells, J., & Ary, D. V. (2000). Development and evaluation of an interactive CD-ROM refusal skills program to prevent youth substance use: "Refuse to Use." *Journal of Behavioral Medicine, 23,* 59-72.

Eagly, A. H. (1999). The processing of nested persuasive messages. *Psychological Inquiry, 10,* 123-127.

Eagly, A. H., & Carli, L. L. (1981). Sex of researchers and sex-typed communications as determinants of sex differences in influenceability: A meta-analysis of social influence studies. *Psychological Bulletin, 90,* 1-20.

Eagly, A. H., & Chaiken, S. (1975). An attribution analysis of the effect of communicator characteristics on opinion change: The case of communicator attractiveness. *Journal of Personality and Social Psychology, 32,* 136-144.

Eagly, A. H., & Chaiken, S. (1984). Cognitive theories of persuasion. In L. Berkowitz (Ed.), *Advances in experimental social psychology* (Vol. 17, pp. 267-359). New York: Academic Press.

Eagly, A. H., & Chaiken, S. (1993). *The psychology of attitudes.* Fort Worth, TX: Harcourt Brace Jovanovich.

Eagly, A. H., & Chaiken, S. (1995). Attitude strength, attitude structure, and resistance to change. In R. E. Petty & J. A. Krosnick (Eds.), *Attitude strength: Antecedents and consequences* (pp. 413-432). Mahwah, NJ: Lawrence Erlbaum.

Eagly, A. H., & Chaiken, S. (1998). Attitude structure and function. In D. T. Gilbert, S. T. Fiske, & G. Lindzey (Eds.), *Handbook of social psychology* (4th ed., Vol. 1, pp. 269-322). Boston: McGraw-Hill.

Eagly, A. H., Mladinic, A., & Otto, S. (1994). Cognitive and affective bases of attitudes toward social groups and social policies. *Journal of Experimental Social Psychology, 30,* 113-137.

Eagly, A. H., & Wood, W. (1985). Gender and influenceability: Stereotype versus behavior. In V. E. O'Leary, R. K. Unger, & B. S. Wallston (Eds.), *Women, gender, and social psychology* (pp. 225-256). Hillsdale, NJ: Lawrence Erlbaum.

Eagly, A. H., Wood, W., & Chaiken, S. (1978). Causal inferences about communicators and their effect on opinion change. *Journal of Personality and Social Psychology, 36,* 424-435.

Eagly, A. H., Wood, W., & Chaiken, S. (1981). An attribution analysis of persuasion. In J. H. Harvey, W. Ickes, & R. F. Kidd (Eds.), *New directions in attribution research* (Vol. 3, pp. 37-62). Hillsdale, NJ: Lawrence Erlbaum.

Easley, R. W., Bearden, W. O., & Teel, J. E. (1995). Testing predictions derived from inoculation theory and the effectiveness of self-disclosure communications strategies. *Journal of Business Research, 34,* 93-105.

Eayrs, C. B., & Ellis, N. (1990). Charity advertising: For or against people with a mental handicap? *British Journal of Social Psychology, 29,* 349-366.

Eckes, T., & Six, B. (1994). Fakten und fiktionen in der einstellungs-verhaltensforschung: Eine meta-analyse [Fact and fiction in attitude-behavior research: A meta-analysis]. *Zeitschrift für Sozialpsychologie, 25,* 253-271.

Eden, D., & Kinnar, J. (1991). Modeling Galatea: Boosting self-efficacy to increase volunteering. *Journal of Applied Psychology, 76,* 770-780.

Edgar, T., Freimuth, V. S., Hammond, S. L., McDonald, D. A., & Fink, E. L. (1992). Strategic sexual communication: Condom use resistance and response. *Health Communication, 4,* 83-104.

Edwards, K. (1990). The interplay of affect and cognition in attitude formation and change. *Journal of Personality and Social Psychology, 59,* 202-216.

Elder, J. P., Sallis, J. F., Woodruff, S. I., & Wildey, M. B. (1993). Tobacco-refusal skills and tobacco use among high-risk adolescents. *Journal of Behavioral Medicine, 16,* 629-642.

Ellickson, P. L., & Hays, R. D. (1991). Beliefs about resistance self-efficacy and drug prevalence: Do they really affect drug use? *International Journal of the Addictions, 25,* 1353-1378.

Elliott, R., Jobber, D., & Sharp, J. (1995). Using the theory of reasoned action to understand organizational behaviour: The role of belief salience. *British Journal of Social Psychology, 34,* 161-172.

Elms, A. C. (Ed.). (1969). *Role playing, reward, and attitude change.* New York: Van Nostrand Reinhold.

Engstrom, E. (1994). Effects of nonfluencies on speaker's credibility in newscast settings. *Perceptual and Motor Skills, 78,* 739-743.

Ennett, S. T., Tobler, N. S., Ringwald, C. L. , & Flowelling, R. L. (1994). How effective is drug abuse resistance education? A meta-analysis of Project DARE outcome evaluations. *American Journal of Public Health, 84,* 1394-1401.

Ennis, R., & Zanna, M. P. (1993). Attitudes, advertising, and automobiles: A functional approach. *Advances in Consumer Research, 20,* 662-666.

Ennis, R., & Zanna, M. P. (2000). Attitude function and the automobile. In G. R. Maio & J. M. Olson (Eds.), *Why we evaluate: Functions of attitudes* (pp. 395-415). Mahwah, NJ: Lawrence Erlbaum.

Erez, A., Bloom, M. C., & Wells, M. T. (1996). Using random rather than fixed effects models in meta-analysis: Implications for situational specificity and validity generalization. *Personnel Psychology, 49,* 275-306.

Esses, V. M., Haddock, G., & Zanna, M. P. (1993). Values, stereotypes, and emotions as determinants of intergroup attitudes. In D. M. Mackie & D. L. Hamilton (Eds.), *Affect, cognition, and stereotyping: Interactive processes in group perception* (pp. 137-166). San Diego, CA: Academic Press.

Estabrooks, P., & Carron, A. V. (1998). The conceptualization and effect of control beliefs on exercise attendance in the elderly. *Journal of Aging and Health, 10,* 441-457.

Evans, R. I., Rozelle, R. M., Lasater, T. M., Dembroski, T. M., & Allen, B. P. (1970). Fear arousal, persuasion, and actual versus implied behavioral change: New perspective utilizing a real-life dental hygiene program. *Journal of Personality and Social Psychology, 16,* 220-227.

Everett, M. W., & Palmgreen, P. (1995). Influences of sensation seeking, message sensation value, and program context on effectiveness of anticocaine public service announcements. *Health Communication, 7,* 225-248.

Faber, R. J., Karlen, S., & Christenson, G. A. (1993). Differential preference for advertising appeals among compulsive and non-compulsive buyers. In E. Thorson (Ed.), *Proceedings of the 1993 conference of the American Academy of Advertising* (pp. 216-224). Columbia, MO: American Academy of Advertising.

Fabrigar, L. R., & Petty, R. E. (1999). The role of the affective and cognitive bases of attitudes in susceptibility to affectively and cognitively based persuasion. *Personality and Social Psychology Bulletin, 25,* 363-381.

Falcione, R. L. (1974). The factor structure of source credibility scales for immediate superiors in the organizational context. *Central States Speech Journal, 25,* 63-66.

Farley, J. U., Lehmann, D. R., & Ryan, M. J. (1981). Generalizing from "imperfect" replication. *Journal of Business, 54,* 597-610.

Fazio, R. H. (1995). Attitudes as object-evaluation associations: Determinants, consequences, and correlates of attitude accessibility. In R. E. Petty & J. A. Krosnick (Eds.), *Attitude strength: Antecedents and consequences* (pp. 247-282). Mahwah, NJ: Lawrence Erlbaum.

Fazio, R. H., Powell, M. C., & Williams, C. J. (1989). The role of attitude accessibility in the attitude-to-behavior process. *Journal of Consumer Research, 16,* 280-288.

Fazio, R. H., & Towles-Schwen, T. (1999). The MODE model of attitude-behavior processes. In S. Chaiken & Y. Trope (Eds.), *Dual-process models in social psychology* (pp. 97-116). New York: Guilford.

Fazio, R. H., & Zanna, M. P. (1978). Attitudinal qualities relating to the strength of the attitude-behavior relationship. *Journal of Experimental Social Psychology, 14,* 398-408.

Fazio, R. H., & Zanna, M. P. (1981). Direct experience and attitude-behavior consistency. In L. Berkowitz (Ed.), *Advances in experimental social psychology* (Vol. 14, pp. 161-202). New York: Academic Press.

Fazio, R. H., Zanna, M. P., & Cooper, J. (1977). Dissonance and self-perception: An integrative view of each theory's proper domain of application. *Journal of Experimental Social Psychology, 13,* 464-479.

Fein, S., & Spencer, S. J. (1997). Prejudice as self-image maintenance: Affirming the self through derogating others. *Journal of Personality and Social Psychology, 73,* 31-44.

Feingold, P. C., & Knapp, M. L. (1977). Anti-drug abuse commercials. *Journal of Communication, 27*(1), 20-28.

Fern, E. F., Monroe, K. B., & Avila, R. A. (1986). Effectiveness of multiple request strategies: A synthesis of research results. *Journal of Marketing Research, 23,* 144-152.

Festinger, L. (1957). *A theory of cognitive dissonance.* Stanford, CA: Stanford University Press.

Festinger, L., & Carlsmith, J. M. (1959). Cognitive consequences of forced compliance. *Journal of Abnormal and Social Psychology, 58,* 203-210.

Festinger, L., & Walster, E. (1964). Post-decision regret and decision reversal. In L. Festinger (Ed.), *Conflict, decision, and dissonance* (pp. 100-110). Stanford, CA: Stanford University Press.

Festinger, L. (Ed.). (1964). *Conflict, decision, and dissonance.* Stanford, CA: Stanford University Press.

Fine, B. J. (1957). Conclusion-drawing, communicator credibility, and anxiety as factors in opinion change. *Journal of Abnormal and Social Psychology, 54,* 369-374.

Fishbein, M. (1967a). Attitude and the prediction of behavior. In M. Fishbein (Ed.), *Readings in attitude theory and measurement* (pp. 477-492). New York: John Wiley.

Fishbein, M. (1967b). A behavior theory approach to the relations between beliefs about an object and the attitude toward the object. In M. Fishbein (Ed.), *Readings in attitude theory and measurement* (pp. 389-400). New York: John Wiley.

Fishbein, M. (1967c). A consideration of beliefs, and their role in attitude measurement. In M. Fishbein (Ed.), *Readings in attitude theory and measurement* (pp. 257-266). New York: John Wiley.

Fishbein, M., & Ajzen, I. (1974). Attitudes towards objects as predictors of single and multiple behavioral criteria. *Psychological Review, 81,* 59-74.

Fishbein, M., & Ajzen, I. (1975). *Belief, attitude, intention, and behavior.* Reading, MA: Addison-Wesley.

Fishbein, M., & Ajzen, I. (1980). Predicting and understanding consumer behavior: Attitude-behavior correspondence. In I. Ajzen & M. Fishbein (Eds.), *Understanding attitudes and predicting social behavior* (pp. 148-172). Englewood Cliffs, NJ: Prentice Hall.

Fishbein, M., & Ajzen, I. (1981a). Attitudes and voting behaviour: An application of the theory of reasoned action. In G. M. Stephenson & J. M. Davis (Eds.), *Progress in applied social psychology* (Vol. 1, pp. 253-313). New York: John Wiley.

Fishbein, M., & Ajzen, I. (1981b). On construct validity: A critique of Miniard and Cohen's paper. *Journal of Experimental Social Psychology, 17,* 340-350.

Fishbein, M., Ajzen, I., & Hinkle, R. (1980). Predicting and understanding voting in American elections: Effects of external variables. In I. Ajzen & M. Fishbein

(Eds.), *Understanding attitudes and predicting social behavior* (pp. 173-195). Englewood Cliffs, NJ: Prentice Hall.

Fishbein, M., Ajzen, I., & McArdle, J. (1980). Changing the behavior of alcoholics: Effects of persuasive communication. In I. Ajzen & M. Fishbein (Eds.), *Understanding attitudes and predicting social behavior* (pp. 217-242). Englewood Cliffs, NJ: Prentice Hall.

Fishbein, M., Bowman, C. H., Thomas, K., Jaccard, J. J., & Ajzen, I. (1980). Predicting and understanding voting in British elections and American referenda: Illustrations of the theory's generality. In I. Ajzen & M. Fishbein (Eds.), *Understanding attitudes and predicting social behavior* (pp. 196-216). Englewood Cliffs, NJ: Prentice Hall.

Fishbein, M., & Hunter, R. (1964). Summation versus balance in attitude organization and change. *Journal of Abnormal and Social Psychology, 69,* 505-510.

Fishbein, M., Jaccard, J. J., Davidson, A. R., Ajzen, I., & Loken, B. (1980). Predicting and understanding family planning behaviors: Beliefs, attitudes, and intentions. In I. Ajzen & M. Fishbein (Eds.), *Understanding attitudes and predicting social behavior* (pp. 130-147). Englewood Cliffs, NJ: Prentice Hall.

Fishbein, M., & Lange, R. (1990). The effects of crossing the midpoint on belief change: A replication and extension. *Personality and Social Psychology Bulletin, 16,* 189-199.

Fishbein, M., & Middlestadt, S. (1995). Noncognitive effects on attitude formation and change: Fact or artifact? *Journal of Consumer Psychology, 4,* 181-202.

Fishbein, M., & Middlestadt, S. E. (1997). A striking lack of evidence for non-belief-based attitude formation and change: A response to five commentaries. *Journal of Consumer Psychology, 6,* 107-115.

Fishbein, M., & Raven, B. H. (1962). The AB scales: An operational definition of belief and attitude. *Human Relations, 15,* 35-44.

Fishbein, M., & Stasson, M. (1990). The role of desires, self-predictions, and perceived control in the prediction of training session attendance. *Journal of Applied Social Psychology, 20,* 173-198.

Fisher, J. D., Fisher, W. A., Misovich, S. J., Kimble, D. L., & Malloy, T. E. (1996). Changing AIDS-risk behavior: Effects of an intervention emphasizing AIDS risk reduction information, motivation, and behavioral skills in a college student population. *Health Psychology, 15,* 114-123.

Flay, B. R., McFall, S., Burton, D., Cook, T. D., & Warnecke, R. B. (1993). Health behavior changes through television: The roles of de facto and motivated selection processes. *Journal of Health and Social Behavior, 34,* 322-335.

Fleming, D. (1967). Attitude: The history of a concept. *Perspectives in American History, 1,* 287-365.

Fleming, M. A., & Petty, R. E. (2000). Identity and persuasion: An elaboration likelihood approach. In D. J. Terry & M. A. Hogg (Eds.), *Attitudes, behavior, and social context: The role of norms and group membership* (pp. 171-199). Mahwah, NJ: Lawrence Erlbaum.

Fleshler, H., Ilardo, J., & Demoretcky, J. (1974). The influence of field dependence, speaker credibility set, and message documentation on evaluations of speaker and message credibility. *Southern Speech Communication Journal, 39,* 389-402.

Floyd, D. L., Prentice-Dunn, S., & Rogers, R. W. (2000). A meta-analysis of research on protection motivation theory. *Journal of Applied Social Psychology, 30,* 407-429.

Fontenelle, G. A., Phillips, A. P., & Lane, D. M. (1985). Generalizing across stimuli as well as subjects: A neglected aspect of external validity. *Journal of Applied Psychology, 70,* 101-107.

Frantz, J. P. (1994). Effect of location and procedural explicitness on user processing of and compliance with product warnings. *Human Factors, 36,* 532-546.

Freedman, J. L. (1964). Involvement, discrepancy, and change. *Journal of Abnormal and Social Psychology, 69,* 290-295.

Freedman, J. L. (1965). Preference for dissonant information. *Journal of Personality and Social Psychology, 2,* 287-289.

Freedman, J. L., & Fraser, S. C. (1966). Compliance without pressure: The foot-in-the-door technique. *Journal of Personality and Social Psychology, 4,* 195-202.

Freedman, J. L., & Sears, D. O. (1965a). Selective exposure. In L. Berkowitz (Ed.), *Advances in experimental social psychology* (Vol. 2, pp. 57-97). New York: Academic Press.

Freedman, J. L., & Sears, D. O. (1965b). Warning, distraction, and resistance to influence. *Journal of Personality and Social Psychology, 1,* 262-266.

Frewer, L. J., Howard, C., Hedderley, D., & Shepherd, R. (1996). What determines trust in information about food-related risks? Underlying psychological constructs. *Risk Analysis, 16,* 473-486.

Frey, D. (1986). Recent research on selective exposure to information. In L. Berkowitz (Ed.), *Advances in experimental social psychology* (Vol. 19, pp. 41-80). New York: Academic Press.

Fried, C. B. (1998). Hypocrisy and identification with transgressions: A case of undetected dissonance. *Basic and Applied Social Psychology, 20,* 145-154.

Fried, C. B., & Aronson, E. (1995). Hypocrisy, misattribution, and dissonance reduction. *Personality and Social Psychology Bulletin, 21,* 925-933.

Friestad, M., & Wright, P. (1994). The persuasion knowledge model: How people cope with persuasion attempts. *Journal of Consumer Research, 21,* 1-31.

Fruin, D. J., Pratt, C., & Owen, N. (1991). Protection motivation theory and adolescents' perceptions of exercise. *Journal of Applied Social Psychology, 22,* 55-69.

Furnham, A., Benson, I., & Gunter, B. (1987). Memory for television commercials as a function of the channel of communication. *Social Behaviour, 2,* 105-112.

Furnham, A., Proctor, E., & Gunter, B. (1988). Memory for material presented in the media: The superiority of written communication. *Psychological Reports, 63,* 935-938.

Furnham, A., & Williams, C. (1987). Remembering commercials presented in different media. *Journal of Educational Television, 13,* 115-124.

Gagne, C., & Godin, G. (2000). The theory of planned behavior: Some measurement issues concerning belief-based variables. *Journal of Applied Social Psychology, 30,* 2173-2193.

Gallois, C., Terry, D., Timmins, P., Kashima, Y., & McCamish, M. (1994). Safe sexual intentions and behavior among heterosexuals and homosexual men: Testing the theory of reasoned action. *Psychology and Health, 10,* 1-16.

Gangestad, S. W., & Snyder, M. (2000). Self-monitoring: Appraisal and reappraisal. *Psychological Bulletin, 126,* 530-555.

Gardner, M. P. (1985). Does attitude toward the ad affect brand attitude under a brand evaluation set? *Journal of Marketing Research, 22,* 192-198.

Garramone, G. M. (1984). Voter responses to negative political ads. *Journalism Quarterly, 61,* 250-259.

Gastil, J. (1992). Why we believe in democracy: Testing theories of attitude functions and democracy. *Journal of Applied Social Psychology, 22,* 423-450.

Gatch, C. L., & Kendzierski, D. (1990). Predicting exercise intentions: The theory of planned behavior. *Research Quarterly for Exercise and Sport, 61,* 100-102.

Gaziano, C., & McGrath, K. (1986). Measuring the concept of credibility. *Journalism Quarterly, 63,* 451-462.

Gerber, R. W., Newman, I. M., & Martin, G. L. (1988). Applying the theory of reasoned action to early adolescent tobacco chewing. *Journal of School Health, 58,* 410-413.

Gibbon, P., & Durkin, K. (1995). The third person effect: Social distance and perceived media bias. *European Journal of Social Psychology, 25,* 597-602.

Giffen, K., & Ehrlich, L. (1963). Attitudinal effects of a group discussion on a proposed change in company policy. *Speech Monographs, 30,* 377-379.

Giles, M., & Cairns, E. (1995). Blood donation and Ajzen's theory of planned behaviour: An examination of perceived behavioural control. *British Journal of Social Psychology, 34,* 173-188.

Gilham, S. A., Lucas, W. L., & Sivewright, D. (1997). The impact of drug education and prevention programs: Disparity between impressionistic and empirical assessments. *Evaluation Review, 21,* 589-613.

Gilkinson, H., Paulson, S. F., & Sikkink, D. E. (1954). Effects of order and authority in an argumentative speech. *Quarterly Journal of Speech, 40,* 183-192.

Gillig, P. M., & Greenwald, A. G. (1974). Is it time to lay the sleeper effect to rest? *Journal of Personality and Social Psychology, 29,* 132-139.

Girandola, F. (2000). Peur et persuasion: Presentations des recherches (1953-1998) et d'une nouvelle lecture [Fear and persuasion: Review and re-analysis of the literature (1953-1998)]. *L'Année Psychologique, 100,* 333-376.

Gist, M. E., Schwoerer, C., & Rosen, B. (1989). Effects of alternative training methods on self-efficacy and performance in computer software training. *Journal of Applied Psychology, 74,* 884-891.

Godin, G., & Kok, G. (1996). The theory of planned behavior: A review of its applications to health-related behaviors. *American Journal of Health Promotion, 11,* 87-98.

Godin, G., Maticka-Tyndale, E., Adrien, A., Manson-Singer, S., Willms, D., & Cappon, P. (1996). Cross-cultural testing of three social cognitive theories: An application to condom use. *Journal of Applied Social Psychology, 26,* 1556-1586.

Godin, G., Valois, P., & Lepage, L. (1993). The pattern of influence of perceived behavioral control upon exercising behavior: An application of Ajzen's theory of planned behavior. *Journal of Behavioral Medicine, 16,* 81-102.

Goethals, G. R., & Nelson, R. E. (1973). Similarity in the influence process: The belief-value distinction. *Journal of Personality and Social Psychology, 25,* 117-122.

Goldman, M., McVeigh, J. F., & Richterkessing, J. L. (1984). Door-in-the-face procedure: Reciprocal concession, perceptual contrast, or worthy person. *Journal of Social Psychology, 123,* 245-251.

Gollwitzer, P. M., & Brandstatter, V. (1997). Implementation intentions and effective goal pursuit. *Journal of Personality and Social Psychology, 73,* 186-199.

Gorassini, D. R., & Olson, J. M. (1995). Does self-perception change explain the foot-in-the-door effect? *Journal of Personality and Social Psychology, 69,* 91-105.

Gorman, D. R. (1995). Are school-based resistance skills training programs effective in preventing alcohol misuse? *Journal of Alcohol and Drug Education, 41,* 74-98.

Gorsuch, R. L., & Ortberg, J. (1983). Moral obligation and attitudes: Their relation to behavioral intentions. *Journal of Personality and Social Psychology, 44,* 1025-1028.

Gottleib, N. H., Gingiss, P. L., & Weinstein, R. P. (1992). Attitudes, subjective norms and models of use for smokeless tobacco among college athletes: Implications for prevention and cessation programming. *Health Education Research, 7,* 359-368.

Gould, S. J. (1991). *Bully for brontosaurus: Reflections in natural history.* New York: Norton.

Gould, S. J. (1993). *Eight little piggies: Reflections in natural history.* New York: Norton.

Granberg, D., & Campbell, K. E. (1977). Effect of communication discrepancy and ambiguity on placement and opinion shift. *European Journal of Social Psychology, 7,* 137-150.

Granberg, D., & Holmberg, S. (1990). The intention-behavior relationship among U.S. and Swedish voters. *Social Psychology Quarterly, 53,* 44-54.

Grasmick, H. G., Bursik, R. J., Jr., & Kinsey, K. A. (1991). Shame and embarrassment as deterrents to noncompliance with the law: The case of an antilittering campaign. *Environment and Behavior, 23,* 233-251.

Grasmick, H. G., & Scott, W. J. (1982). Tax evasion and mechanisms of social control: A comparison with grand and petty theft. *Journal of Economic Psychology, 2,* 213-230.

Green, B. F. (1954). Attitude measurement. In G. Lindzey (Ed.), *Handbook of social psychology* (Vol. 1, pp. 335-369). Reading, MA: Addison-Wesley.

Greenberg, B. S., & Miller, G. R. (1966). The effects of low-credible sources on message acceptance. *Speech Monographs, 33,* 127-136.

Greenberg, B. S., & Tannenbaum, P. H. (1961). The effects of bylines on attitude change. *Journalism Quarterly, 38,* 535-537.

Greene, K., Rubin, D. L., & Hale, J. L. (1995). Egocentrism, message explicitness, and AIDS messages directed toward adolescents: An application of the theory of reasoned action. *Journal of Social Behavior and Personality, 10,* 547-570.

Greening, L. (1997). Adolescents' cognitive appraisals of cigarette smoking: An application of the protection motivation theory. *Journal of Applied Social Psychology, 27,* 1972-1985.

Gregory, W. L., Cialdini, R. B., & Carpenter, K. M. (1982). Self-relevant scenarios as mediators of likelihood estimates and compliance: Does imagining make it so? *Journal of Personality and Social Psychology, 43,* 89-99.

Gruder, C. L., Cook, T. D., Hennigan, K. M., Flay, B. R., Alessis, C., & Halamaj, J. (1978). Empirical tests of the absolute sleeper effect predicted from the discounting cue hypothesis. *Journal of Personality and Social Psychology, 36,* 1061-1074.

Gruner, C. R. (1967). Effect of humor on speaker ethos and audience information gain. *Journal of Communication, 17,* 228-233.

Gruner, C. R. (1970). The effect of humor in dull and interesting informative speeches. *Central States Speech Journal, 21,* 160-166.

Gruner, C. R., & Lampton, W. E. (1972). Effects of including humorous material in a persuasive sermon. *Southern Speech Communication Journal, 38,* 188-196.

Gulley, H. E., & Berlo, D. K. (1956). Effect of intercellular and intracellular speech structure on attitude change and learning. *Speech Monographs, 23,* 288-297.

Gundersen, D. F., & Hopper, R. (1976). Relationships between speech delivery and speech effectiveness. *Communication Monographs, 43,* 158-165.

Gur-Arie, O., Durand, R. M., & Bearden, W. O. (1979). Attitudinal and normative dimensions of opinion leaders and nonleaders. *Journal of Psychology, 101,* 305-312.

Gutteling, J. M. (1993). A field experiment in communicating a new risk: Effects of the source and a message containing explicit conclusions. *Basic and Applied Social Psychology, 14,* 295-316.

Hackman, J. R., & Anderson, L. R. (1968). The strength, relevance, and source of beliefs about an object in Fishbein's attitude theory. *Journal of Social Psychology, 76,* 55-67.

Haddock, G., & Zanna, M. P. (1998). Assessing the impact of affective and cognitive information in predicting attitudes toward capital punishment. *Law and Human Behavior, 22,* 325-339.

Hagen, K. M., Gutkin, T. B., Wilson, C. P., & Oats, R. G. (1998). Using vicarious experience and verbal persuasion to enhance self-efficacy in pre-service teachers: "Priming the pump" for consultation. *School Psychology Quarterly, 13,* 169-178.

Haines, M., & Spear, S. F. (1996). Changing the perception of the norm: A strategy to decrease binge drinking among college students. *Journal of American College Health, 45,* 134-140.

Hamid, P. N., & Cheng, S.-T. (1995). Predicting antipollution behavior: The role of molar behavioral intentions, past behavior, and locus of control. *Environment and Behavior, 27,* 679-698.

Hammond, K. R. (1948). Measuring attitudes by error-choice: An indirect method. *Journal of Abnormal and Social Psychology, 43,* 38-48.

Hammond, S. L. (1987). Health advertising: The credibility of organizational sources. *Communication Yearbook, 10,* 613-628.

Han, S., & Shavitt, S. (1994). Persuasion and culture: Advertising appeals in individualistic and collectivistic societies. *Journal of Experimental Social Psychology, 30,* 326-350.

Harkins, S. G., & Petty, R. E. (1987). Information utility and the multiple source effect. *Journal of Personality and Social Psychology, 52,* 260-268.

Harland, P., Staats, H., & Wilke, H. A. M. (1999). Explaining proenvironmental intention and behavior by personal norms and the theory of planned behavior. *Journal of Applied Social Psychology, 29,* 2505-2528.

Harmon, R. R., & Coney, K. A. (1982). The persuasive effects of source credibility in buy and lease situations. *Journal of Marketing Research, 19,* 255-260.

Harmon-Jones, E. (1999). Toward an understanding of the motivation underlying dissonance effects: Is the production of aversive consequences necessary? In E. Harmon-Jones & J. Mills (Eds.), *Cognitive dissonance: Progress on a pivotal theory in social psychology* (pp. 71-99). Washington, DC: American Psychological Association.

Harmon-Jones, E. (in press). A cognitive dissonance theory perspective on persuasion. In J. P. Dillard & M. Pfau (Eds.), *The persuasion handbook: Developments in theory and practice.* Thousand Oaks, CA: Sage.

Harmon-Jones, E., Brehm, J. W., Greenberg, J., Simon, L., & Nelson, D. E. (1996). Evidence that the production of aversive consequences is not necessary to create cognitive dissonance. *Journal of Personality and Social Psychology, 70,* 5-16.

Harte, T. (1976). The effects of evidence in persuasive communication. *Central States Speech Journal, 27,* 42-46.

Hass, J. W., Bagley, G. S., & Rogers, R. W. (1975). Coping with the energy crisis: Effects of fear appeals upon attitudes toward energy consumption. *Journal of Applied Psychology, 60,* 754-756.

Hass, R. G. (1981). Effects of source characteristics on cognitive responses and persuasion. In R. E. Petty, T. M. Ostrom, & T. C. Brock (Eds.), *Cognitive responses in persuasion* (pp. 141-172). Hillsdale, NJ: Lawrence Erlbaum.

Hass, R. G., & Grady, K. (1975). Temporal delay, type of forewarning, and resistance to influence. *Journal of Experimental Social Psychology, 11,* 459-469.

Hass, R. G., & Linder, D. E. (1972). Counterargument availability and the effects of message structure on persuasion. *Journal of Personality and Social Psychology, 23,* 219-233.

Haugtvedt, C., Petty, R. E., Cacioppo, J. T., & Steidley, T. (1988). Personality and ad effectiveness: Exploring the utility of need for cognition. *Advances in Consumer Research, 15,* 209-212.

Haugtvedt, C. P., & Strathman, A. J. (1990). Situational product relevance and attitude persistence. *Advances in Consumer Research, 17,* 766-769.

Haugtvedt, C. P., & Wegener, D. T. (1994). Message order effects in persuasion: An attitude strength perspective. *Journal of Consumer Research, 21,* 205-218.

Hausenblas, H. A., Carron, A. V., & Mack, D. E. (1997). Application of the theories of reasoned action and planned behavior to exercise behavior: A meta-analysis. *Journal of Sport and Exercise Psychology, 19,* 36-51.

Hausknecht, D. R., & Moore, D. L. (1986). The effects of time compressed advertising on brand attitude judgments. *Advances in Consumer Research, 13,* 105-110.

Hedeker, D., Flay, B. R., & Petraitis, J. (1996). Estimating individual influences of behavioral intentions: An application of random-effects modeling to the theory of reasoned action. *Journal of Consulting and Clinical Psychology, 64,* 109-120.

Hedges, L. V., & Olkin, I. (1985). *Statistical methods for meta-analysis.* New York: Academic Press.

Hedges, L. V., & Vevea, J. L. (1998). Fixed- and random-effects models in meta-analysis. *Psychological Methods, 3,* 486-504.

Heesacker, M., Petty, R. E., & Cacioppo, J. T. (1983). Field dependence and attitude change: Source credibility can alter persuasion by affecting message-relevant thinking. *Journal of Personality, 51,* 653-666.

Heider, F. (1946). Attitudes and cognitive organization. *Journal of Psychology, 21,* 107-112.

Heider, F. (1958). *The psychology of interpersonal relations.* New York: John Wiley.

Helweg-Larsen, M., & Howell, C. (2000). Effects of erotophobia on the persuasiveness of condom advertisements containing strong or weak arguments. *Basic and Applied Social Psychology, 22,* 111-117.

Hensley, W. E. (1974). A criticism of "Dimensions of source credibility: A test for reproducibility." *Speech Monographs, 41,* 293-294.

Herek, G. M. (1986). The instrumentality of attitudes: Toward a neofunctional theory. *Journal of Social Issues, 42,* 99-114.

Herek, G. M. (1987). Can functions be measured? A new perspective on the functional approach to attitudes. *Social Psychology Quarterly, 50,* 285-303.

Herek, G. M. (2000). The social construction of attitudes: Functional consensus and divergence in the U.S. public's reactions to AIDS. In G. R. Maio & J. M. Olson (Eds.), *Why we evaluate: Functions of attitudes* (pp. 325-364). Mahwah, NJ: Lawrence Erlbaum.

Herek, G. M., & Capitanio, J. P. (1998). Symbolic prejudice or fear of infection? A functional analysis of AIDS-related stigma among heterosexual adults. *Basic and Applied Social Psychology, 20,* 230-241.

Herr, P. M. (1995). Whither fact, artifact, and attitude: Reflections on the theory of reasoned action. *Journal of Consumer Psychology, 4,* 371-380.

Hetts, J. J., Boninger, D. S., Armor, D. A., Gleicher, F., & Nathanson, A. (2000). The influence of anticipated counterfactual regret on behavior. *Psychology and Marketing, 17,* 345-368.

Hewes, D. E. (1983). Confessions of a methodological puritan: A response to Jackson and Jacobs. *Human Communication Research, 9,* 187-191.

Hewgill, M. A., & Miller, G. R. (1965). Source credibility and response to fear-arousing communications. *Speech Monographs, 32,* 95-101.

Hewitt, D. (1972). Conceptual complexity, environmental complexity, communication salience and attitude change. *European Journal of Social Psychology, 2,* 285-306.

Hewstone, M., & Young, L. (1988). Expectancy-value models of attitude: Measurement and combination of evaluations and beliefs. *Journal of Applied Social Psychology, 18,* 958-971.

Hickson, M., III, Powell, L., Hill, S. R., Jr., Holt, G. B., & Flick, H. (1979). Smoking artifacts as indicators of homophily, attraction, and credibility. *Southern Speech Communication Journal, 44,* 191-200.

Himmelfarb, S. (1993). The measurement of attitudes. In A. H. Eagly & S. Chaiken, *The psychology of attitudes* (pp. 23-87). Fort Worth, TX: Harcourt Brace Jovanovich.

Himmelfarb, S., & Arazi, D. (1974). Choice and source attractiveness in exposure to discrepant messages. *Journal of Experimental Social Psychology, 10,* 516-527.

Hines, G. H. (1980). A longitudinal comparative study of nonreactive attitude measurement of controversial topics. *Perceptual and Motor Skills, 51,* 567-574.

Ho, R. (1994). Cigarette advertising and cigarette health warnings: What role do adolescents' motives for smoking play in their assessment? *Australian Psychologist, 29,* 49-56.

Hocking, J., Margreiter, D., & Hylton, C. (1977). Intra-audience effects: A field test. *Human Communication Research, 3,* 243-249.

Hoeken, H. (1999). The perceived and actual persuasiveness of different types of inductive arguments. In F. H. van Eemeren, R. Grootendorst, J. A. Blair, & C. A. Willard (Eds.), *Proceedings of the fourth international conference of the International Society for the Study of Argumentation* (pp. 353-357). Amsterdam: Sic Sat.

Holbrook, M. B. (1977). Comparing multiattribute attitude models by optimal scaling. *Journal of Consumer Research, 4,* 165-171.

Holbrook, M. B. (1978). Beyond attitude structure: Toward the informational determinants of attitude. *Journal of Marketing Research, 15,* 545-556.

Holbrook, M. B., & Hulbert, J. M. (1975). Multi-attribute attitude models: A comparative analysis. *Advances in Consumer Research, 2,* 375-388.

Hoogstraten, J., de Haan, W., & ter Horst, G. (1985). Stimulating the demand for dental care: An application of Ajzen and Fishbein's theory of reasoned action. *European Journal of Social Psychology, 15,* 401-414.

Hops, H., Weissman, W., Biglan, A., Thompson, R., Faller, C., & Severson, H. H. (1986). A taped situation test of cigarette refusal skill among adolescents. *Behavioral Assessment, 8,* 145-154.

Horai, J., Naccari, N., & Fatoullah, E. (1974). The effects of expertise and physical attractiveness upon opinion agreement and liking. *Sociometry, 37,* 601-606.

Houck, C. L., & Bowers, J. W. (1969). Dialect and identification in persuasive messages. *Language and Speech, 12,* 180-186.

Hovland, C. I., Harvey, O. J., & Sherif, M. (1957). Assimilation and contrast effects in reactions to communication and attitude change. *Journal of Abnormal and Social Psychology, 55,* 244-252.

Hovland, C. I., Janis, I. L., & Kelley, H. H. (1953). *Communication and persuasion.* New Haven, CT: Yale University Press.

Hovland, C. I., Lumsdaine, A. A., & Sheffield, F. D. (1949). *Experiments on mass communication.* Princeton, NJ: Princeton University Press.

Hovland, C. I., & Mandell, W. (1952). An experimental comparison of conclusion-drawing by the communicator and by the audience. *Journal of Abnormal and Social Psychology, 47,* 581-588.

Hovland, C. I., & Pritzker, H. A. (1957). Extent of opinion change as a function of amount of change advocated. *Journal of Abnormal and Social Psychology, 54,* 257-261.

Hoyt, W. T. (1996). Antecedents and effects of perceived therapist credibility: A meta-analysis. *Journal of Counseling Psychology, 43,* 430-447.

Hughes, G. D. (1971). *Attitude measurement for marketing strategies.* Glenview, IL: Scott, Foresman.

Huhmann, B. A., & Brotherton, T. P. (1997). A content analysis of guilt appeals in popular magazine advertisements. *Journal of Advertising, 26*(2), 35-45.

Hunt, J. M., Smith, M. F., & Kernan, J. B. (1985). The effects of expectancy disconfirmation and argument strength on message processing level: An application to personal selling. *Advances in Consumer Research, 12,* 450-454.

Hunter, J. E. (1997). Needed: A ban on the significance test. *Psychological Science, 8,* 3-7.

Hunter, J. E., & Hamilton, M. A. (1998). Meta-analysis of controlled message designs. In M. Allen & R. W. Preiss (Eds.), *Persuasion: Advances through meta-analysis* (pp. 29-52). Cresskill, NJ: Hampton.

Hunter, J. E., Hamilton, M., & Allen, M. (1989). The design and analysis of language experiments in communication. *Communication Monographs, 56,* 341-363.

Hurwitz, S. D., Miron, M. S., & Johnson, B. T. (1992). Source credibility and the language of expert testimony. *Journal of Applied Social Psychology, 24,* 1909-1939.

Husek, T. R. (1965). Persuasive impacts of early, late, or no mention of a negative source. *Journal of Personality and Social Psychology, 2,* 125-128.

Huston, T. L., & Levinger, G. (1978). Interpersonal attraction and relationships. *Annual Review of Psychology, 29,* 115-156.

Hylton, C. (1971). Intra-audience effects: Observable audience response. *Journal of Communication, 21,* 253-265.

Infante, D. A. (1971). Predicting attitude from desirability and likelihood ratings of rhetorical propositions. *Speech Monographs, 38,* 321-326.

Infante, D. A. (1972). Cognitive structure as a predictor of post speech attitude and attitude change. *Speech Monographs, 39,* 55-61.

Infante, D. A. (1973). The perceived importance of cognitive structure components: An adaptation of Fishbein's theory. *Speech Monographs, 40,* 8-16.

Infante, D. A. (1975). Differential function of desirable and undesirable consequences in predicting attitude and attitude change toward proposals. *Speech Monographs, 42,* 115-134.

Infante, D. A. (1978). Similarity between advocate and receiver: The role of instrumentality. *Central States Speech Journal, 29,* 187-193.

Infante, D. A. (1980). The construct validity of semantic differential scales for the measurement of source credibility. *Communication Quarterly, 28*(2), 19-26.

Insko, C. A. (1967). *Theories of attitude change.* New York: Appleton-Century-Crofts.

Jaccard, J., Brinberg, D., & Ackerman, L. J. (1986). Assessing attribute importance: A comparison of six methods. *Journal of Consumer Research, 12,* 463-468.

Jaccard, J. J., & Davidson, A. R. (1972). Toward an understanding of family planning behaviors: An initial investigation. *Journal of Applied Social Psychology, 2,* 228-235.

Jaccard, J., Radecki, C., Wilson, T., & Dittus, P. (1995). Methods for identifying consequential beliefs: Implications for understanding attitude strength. In R. E. Petty & J. A. Krosnick (Eds.), *Attitude strength: Antecedents and consequences* (pp. 337-359). Mahwah, NJ: Lawrence Erlbaum.

Jaccard, J., & Sheng, D. (1984). A comparison of six methods for assessing the importance of perceived consequences in behavioral decisions: Applications from attitude research. *Journal of Experimental Social Psychology, 20,* 1-28.

Jacks, J. Z., & Devine, P. G. (2000). Attitude importance, forewarning of message content, and resistance to persuasion. *Basic and Applied Social Psychology, 22,* 19-29.

Jackson, S. (1991). Meta-analysis for primary and secondary data analysis: The super-experiment metaphor. *Communication Monographs, 58,* 449-462.

Jackson, S. (1992). *Message effects research: Principles of design and analysis.* New York: Guilford.

Jackson, S. (1993). How to do things to words: The experimental manipulation of message variables. *Southern Communication Journal, 58,* 103-114.

Jackson, S., & Brashers, D. (1994). M > 1: Analysis of treatment x replication designs. *Human Communication Research, 20,* 356-389.

Jackson, S., Brashers, D. E., & Massey, J. E. (1992). Statistical testing in treatment by replication designs: Three options reconsidered. *Communication Quarterly, 40,* 211-227.

Jackson, S., & Jacobs, S. (1983). Generalizing about messages: Suggestions for design and analysis of experiments. *Human Communication Research, 9,* 169-181.

Jackson, S., O'Keefe, D. J., & Brashers, D. (1994). The messages replication factor: Methods tailored to messages as objects of study. *Journalism Quarterly, 71,* 984-996.

Jackson, S., O'Keefe, D. J., & Jacobs, S. (1988). The search for reliable generalizations about messages: A comparison of research strategies. *Human Communication Research, 15,* 127-142.

Jackson, S., O'Keefe, D. J., Jacobs, S., & Brashers, D. E. (1989). Messages as replications: Toward a message-centered design strategy. *Communication Monographs, 56,* 364-384.

Janis, I. L., & Field, P. B. (1956). A behavioral assessment of persuasibility: Consistency of individual differences. *Sociometry, 19,* 241-259.

Jemmott, L. S., & Jemmott, J. B., III. (1991). Applying the theory of reasoned action to AIDS risk behavior: Condom use among black women. *Nursing Research, 40,* 228-234.

Jepson, C., & Chaiken, S. (1990). Chronic issue-specific fear inhibits systematic processing of persuasive communications. *Journal of Social Behavior and Personality, 5*(2), 61-84.

Jiang, J. J., Klein, G., & Vedder, R. G. (2000). Persuasive expert systems: The influence of confidence and discrepancy. *Computers in Human Behavior, 16,* 99-109.

Johnson, B. T. (1994). Effects of outcome-relevant involvement and prior information on persuasion. *Journal of Experimental Social Psychology, 30,* 556-579.

Johnson, B. T., & Eagly, A. H. (1989). Effects of involvement on persuasion: A meta-analysis. *Psychological Bulletin, 106,* 290-314.

Johnson, B. T., & Eagly, A. H. (1990). Involvement and persuasion: Types, traditions, and the evidence. *Psychological Bulletin, 107,* 375-384.

Johnson, B. T., Mullen, B., & Salas, E. (1995). Comparison of three major meta-analytic approaches. *Journal of Applied Psychology, 80,* 94-106.

Johnson, H. H., & Scileppi, J. A. (1969). Effects of ego-involvement conditions on attitude change to high and low credibility communicators. *Journal of Personality and Social Psychology, 13,* 31-36.

Johnson, J. D., & Meishcke, H. (1992). Differences in evaluations of communication channels for cancer-related information. *Journal of Behavioral Medicine, 15,* 429-445.

Johnson, R. W., Kelly, R. J., & LeBlanc, B. A. (1995). Motivational basis of dissonance: Aversive consequences or inconsistency. *Personality and Social Psychology Bulletin, 21,* 850-855. (Erratum notice: *Personality and Social Psychology Bulletin, 22,* 222)

Jones, R. A., & Brehm, J. W. (1967). Attitudinal effects of communicator attractiveness when one chooses to listen. *Journal of Personality and Social Psychology, 6,* 64-70.

Jones, R. E. (1990). Understanding paper recycling in an institutionally supportive setting: An application of the theory of reasoned action. *Journal of Environmental Systems, 19,* 307-321.

Jones, R. T., McDonald, D. W., Fiore, M. F., Arrington, T., & Randall, J. (1990). A primary preventive approach to children's drug refusal behavior: The impact of rehearsal-plus. *Journal of Pediatric Psychology, 15,* 211-223.

Jorgensen, P. F. (1998). Affect, persuasion, and communication processes. In P. A. Andersen & L. K. Guerrero (Eds.), *Handbook of communication and emotion: Research, theory, applications, and contexts* (pp. 403-422). San Diego, CA: Academic Press.

Jourdan, P. (1999). Creation and validation of an advertising scale based on the individual perception of the emotional or informational intent of the advertisement. *Advances in Consumer Research, 26,* 504-512.

Kamins, M. A., & Assael, H. (1987a). Moderating disconfirmation of expectations through the use of two-sided appeals: A longitudinal approach. *Journal of Economic Psychology, 8,* 237-254.

Kamins, M. A., & Assael, H. (1987b). Two-sided versus one-sided appeals: A cognitive perspective on argumentation, source derogation, and the effect of disconfirming trial on belief change. *Journal of Marketing Research, 24,* 29-39.

Kamins, M. A., & Marks, L. J. (1987). Advertising puffery: The impact of using two-sided claims on product attitude and purchase intention. *Journal of Advertising, 16*(4), 6-15.

Kamins, M. A., & Marks, L. J. (1988). An examination into the effectiveness of two-sided comparative price appeals. *Journal of the Academy of Marketing Science, 16*(2), 64-71.

Kantola, S. J., Syme, G. J., & Campbell, N. A. (1982). The role of individual differences and external variables in a test of the sufficiency of Fishbein's model to explain behavioral intentions to conserve water. *Journal of Applied Social Psychology, 12,* 70-83.

Kantola, S. J., Syme, G. J., & Campbell, N. A. (1984). Cognitive dissonance and energy conservation. *Journal of Applied Psychology, 69,* 416-421.

Kaplan, K. J. (1972). On the ambivalence-indifference problem in attitude theory and measurement: A suggested modification of the semantic differential technique. *Psychological Bulletin, 77,* 361-372.

Kaplan, K. J., & Fishbein, M. (1969). The source of beliefs, their saliency, and prediction of attitude. *Journal of Social Psychology, 78,* 63-74.

Kaplowitz, S. A., & Fink, E. L. (1997). Message discrepancy and persuasion. In G. A. Barnett & F. J. Boster (Eds.), *Progress in communication sciences: Vol. 13. Advances in persuasion* (pp. 75-106). Greenwich, CT: Ablex.

Kaplowitz, S. A., Fink, E. L., Mulcrone, J., Atkin, D., & Dabil, S. (1991). Disentangling the effects of discrepant and disconfirming information. *Social Psychology Quarterly, 54,* 191-207.

Kardes, F. R. (1988). Spontaneous inference processes in advertising: The effects of conclusion omission and involvement on persuasion. *Journal of Consumer Research, 15,* 225-233.

Kasprzyk, D., Montano, D. E., & Fishbein, M. (1998). Application of an integrated behavioral model to predict condom use: A prospective study among high HIV risk groups. *Journal of Applied Social Psychology, 28,* 1557-1583.

Katz, D. (1960). The functional approach to the study of attitudes. *Public Opinion Quarterly, 24,* 163-204.

Katz, D., McClintock, C., & Sarnoff, I. (1957). The measurement of ego defense as related to attitude change. *Journal of Personality, 25,* 465-474.

Katzev, R., & Brownstein, R. (1989). The influence of enlightenment on compliance. *Journal of Social Psychology, 129,* 335-347.

Kelly, J. A., St. Lawrence, J. S., Stevenson, Y., Hauth, A. C., Kalichman, S. C., Diaz, Y. E., Brasfield, T. L., Koob, J. J., & Morgan, M. G. (1992). Community AIDS/HIV risk reduction: The effects of endorsements by popular people in three cities. *American Journal of Public Health, 82,* 1483-1489.

Kelman, H. C. (1961). Processes of opinion change. *Public Opinion Quarterly, 25,* 57-78.

Keltner, D., & Buswell, B. N. (1996). Evidence for the distinctness of embarrassment, shame, and guilt: A study of recalled antecedents and facial expressions of emotion. *Cognition and Emotion, 10,* 155-171.

Kendzierski, D. (1990). Decision making versus decision implementation: An action control approach to exercise adoption and adherence. *Journal of Applied Social Psychology, 20,* 27-45.

Kendzierski, D., & Whitaker, D. J. (1997). The role of self-schema in linking intentions with behavior. *Personality and Social Psychology Bulletin, 23,* 139-147.

Kennedy, N. B. (1982). Contact donors before making solicitations. *Fund Raising Management, 13*(9), 16-17.

Kettlewell, N. M., & Evans, L. (1991). Optimizing letter design for donation requests. *Psychological Reports, 68,* 579-584.

Kidder, L. H., & Campbell, D. T. (1970). The indirect testing of social attitudes. In G. F. Summers (Ed.), *Attitude measurement* (pp. 333-385). Chicago: Rand McNally.

Kiesler, C. A., Collins, B. E., & Miller, N. (1969). *Attitude change: A critical analysis of theoretical approaches.* New York: John Wiley.

Kiesler, S. B., & Mathog, R. B. (1968). Distraction hypothesis in attitude change: Effects of effectiveness. *Psychological Reports, 23,* 1123-1133.

Kim, M.-S., & Hunter, J. E. (1993a). Attitude-behavior relations: A meta-analysis of attitudinal relevance and topic. *Journal of Communication, 43*(1), 101-142.

Kim, M.-S., & Hunter, J. E. (1993b). Relationships among attitudes, behavioral intentions, and behavior: A meta-analysis of past research, part 2. *Communication Research, 20,* 331-364.

Kim, S., McLeod, J. H., & Shantzis, C. (1989). An outcome evaluation of refusal skills program as a drug abuse prevention strategy. *Journal of Drug Education, 19,* 363-371.

Kinder, D. R., & Sears, D. O. (1981). Prejudice and politics: Symbolic racism versus racial threats to the good life. *Journal of Personality and Social Psychology, 40,* 414-431.

King, G. W. (1975). An analysis of attitudinal and normative variables as predictors of intentions and behavior. *Speech Monographs, 42,* 237-244.

King, S. W. (1976). Reconstructing the concept of source perceptions: Toward a paradigm of source appropriateness. *Western Speech Communication, 40,* 216-225.

King, S. W., & Sereno, K. K. (1973). Attitude change as a function of degree and type of interpersonal similarity and message type. *Western Speech, 37,* 218-232.

Klock, S. J., & Traylor, M. B. (1983). Older and younger models in advertising to older consumers: An advertising effectiveness experiment. *Akron Business and Economic Review, 14*(4), 48-52.

Koballa, T. R., Jr. (1986). Persuading teachers to reexamine the innovative elementary science programs of yesterday: The effect of anecdotal versus data-summary communications. *Journal of Research in Science Teaching, 23,* 437-449.

Koehler, J. W. (1972). Effects on audience opinion of one-sided and two-sided speeches supporting and opposing a proposition. In T. D. Beisecker & D. W. Parson (Eds.), *The process of social influence* (pp. 351-369). Englewood Cliffs, NJ: Prentice Hall.

Kohn, P. (1969). Attitude change as a function of changes in belief and the evaluative aspects of belief. *Canadian Journal of Behavioural Science, 1,* 87-97.

Kokkinaki, F., & Lunt, P. (1997). The relationship between involvement, attitude accessibility and attitude-behaviour consistency. *British Journal of Social Psychology, 36,* 497-509.

Kowert, D. W., & Homer, P. M. (1993). Targeting consumers through birth order: A match-up hypothesis explanation. In E. Thorson (Ed.), *Proceedings of the 1993 conference of the American Academy of Advertising* (pp. 225-235). Columbia, MO: American Academy of Advertising.

Kraus, S. J. (1995). Attitudes and the prediction of behavior: A meta-analysis of the empirical literature. *Personality and Social Psychology Bulletin, 21,* 58-75.

Kreuter, M., Farrell, D., Olevitch, L., & Brennan, L. (1999). *Tailoring health messages: Customizing communication with computer technology.* Mahwah, NJ: Lawrence Erlbaum.

Krosnick, J. A., & Alwin, D. F. (1989). Aging and susceptibility to attitude change. *Journal of Personality and Social Psychology, 57,* 416-425.

Krosnick, J. A., & Petty, R. E. (1995). Attitude strength: An overview. In R. E. Petty & J. A. Krosnick (Eds.), *Attitude strength: Antecedents and consequences* (pp. 1-24). Mahwah, NJ: Lawrence Erlbaum.

Kruglanski, A. W., & Thompson, E. P. (1999a). The illusory second mode or, the cue is the message. *Psychological Inquiry, 10,* 182-193.

Kruglanski, A. W., & Thompson, E. P. (1999b). Persuasion by a single route: A view from the unimodel. *Psychological Inquiry, 10,* 83-109.

Kruglanski, A. W., Thompson, E. P., & Spiegel, S. (1999). Separate or equal? Bimodal notions of persuasion and a single-process "unimodel." In S. Chaiken

& Y. Trope (Eds.), *Dual-process models in social psychology* (pp. 293-313). New York: Guilford.

Kruglanski, A. W., Wenster, D. M., & Klem, A. (1993). Motivated resistance and openness to persuasion in the presence or absence of prior information. *Journal of Personality and Social Psychology, 65,* 861-876.

Krupat, E., Smith, R. H., Leach, C. W., & Jackson, M. A. (1997). Generalizing from atypical cases: How general a tendency? *Basic and Applied Social Psychology, 19,* 345-361.

Kurland, N. B. (1995). Ethical intentions and the theories of reasoned action and planned behavior. *Journal of Applied Social Psychology, 25,* 297-313.

Laczniak, R. N., Muehling, D. D., & Carlson, L. (1991). Effects of motivation and ability on ad-induced cognitive processing. In R. Holman (Ed.), *Proceedings of the 1991 conference of the American Academy of Advertising* (pp. 81-87). New York: D'Arcy Masius Benton & Bowles.

Lagace, R. R., & Gassenheimer, J. B. (1991). An exploratory study of trust and suspicion toward salespeople: Scale validation and replication. In T. L. Childers, S. B. MacKenzie, T. W. Leigh, S. Skinner, J. G. Lynch, Jr., S. Heckler, H. Gatignon, R. P. Fisk, & J. L. Graham (Eds.), *1991 AMA winter educators' conference: Marketing theory and applications* (pp. 121-127). Chicago: American Marketing Association.

Lam, S.-P. (1999). Predicting intentions to conserve water from the theory of planned behavior, perceived moral obligation, and perceived water right. *Journal of Applied Social Psychology, 29,* 1058-1071.

Lambert, B. L., Salmon, J. W., Stubbings, J., Gilomen-Study, G., Valuck, R. J., & Kezlarian, K. (1997). Factors associated with antibiotic prescribing in a managed care setting: An exploratory investigation. *Social Science and Medicine, 45,* 1767-1779.

Landman, J., & Petty, R. (2000). "It could have been you": How states exploit counterfactual thought to market lotteries. *Psychology and Marketing, 17,* 299-321.

Landy, D. (1972). The effects of an overheard audience's reaction and attractiveness on opinion change. *Journal of Experimental Social Psychology, 8,* 276-288.

Lange, R., & Fishbein, M. (1983). Effects of category differences on belief change and agreement with the source of a persuasive communication. *Journal of Personality and Social Psychology, 44,* 933-941.

Langlois, M. A., Petosa, R., & Hallam, J. S. (1999). Why do effective smoking prevention programs work? Student changes in social cognitive theory constructs. *Journal of School Health, 69,* 326-331.

LaPiere, R. T. (1934). Attitudes vs. actions. *Social Forces, 13,* 230-237.

Lariscy, R. A. W., & Tinkham, S. F. (1999). The sleeper effect and negative political advertising. *Journal of Advertising, 28*(4), 13-30.

Lautman, M. R., & Dean, K. J. (1983). Time compression of television advertising. In L. Percy & A. G. Woodside (Eds.), *Advertising and consumer psychology* (pp. 219-236). Lexington, MA: Lexington Books.

Lauver, D., & Knapp, T. R. (1993). Sum-of-products variables: A methodological critique. *Research in Nursing and Health, 16,* 385-391.

Lavine, H., & Snyder, M. (1996). Cognitive processing and the functional matching effect in persuasion: The mediating role of subjective perceptions of message quality. *Journal of Experimental Social Psychology, 32,* 580-604.

Lavine, H., & Snyder, M. (2000). Cognitive processes and the functional matching effect in persuasion: Studies of personality and political behavior. In G. R. Maio & J. M. Olson (Eds.), *Why we evaluate: Functions of attitudes* (pp. 97-131). Mahwah, NJ: Lawrence Erlbaum.

Leavitt, C., & Kaigler-Evans, K. (1975). Mere similarity versus information processing: An exploration of source and message interaction. *Communication Research, 2,* 300-306.

Lechner, L., De Vries, H., & Offermans, N. (1997). Participation in a breast cancer screening program: Influence of past behavior and determinants on future screening participation. *Preventive Medicine, 26,* 473-482.

Leippe, M. R., & Eisenstadt, D. (1999). A self-accountability model of dissonance reduction: Multiple modes on a continuum of elaboration. In E. Harmon-Jones & J. Mills (Eds.), *Cognitive dissonance: Progress on a pivotal theory in social psychology* (pp. 201-232). Washington, DC: American Psychological Association.

Lennon, S. J., Davis, L. L., & Fairhurst, A. (1988). Evaluations of apparel advertising as a function of self-monitoring. *Perceptual and Motor Skills, 66,* 987-996.

Le Poire, B. A. (1994). Attraction toward and nonverbal stigmatization of gay males and persons with AIDS: Evidence of symbolic over instrumental attitudinal structures. *Human Communication Research, 21,* 241-279.

Leventhal, H., Jones, S., & Trembly, G. (1966). Sex differences in attitude and behavior change under conditions of fear and specific instructions. *Journal of Experimental Social Psychology, 2,* 387-399.

Leventhal, H., Watts, J. C., & Pagano, F. (1967). Effects of fear and instructions on how to cope with danger. *Journal of Personality and Social Psychology, 6,* 313-321.

Levin, K. D., Nichols, D. R., & Johnson, B. T. (2000). Involvement and persuasion: Attitude functions for the motivated processor. In G. R. Maio & J. M. Olson (Eds.), *Why we evaluate: Functions of attitudes* (pp. 163-194). Mahwah, NJ: Lawrence Erlbaum.

Levin, P. F. (1999). Test of the Fishbein and Ajzen models as predictors of health care workers' glove use. *Research in Nursing and Health, 22,* 295-307.

Levy, D. A., Collins, B. E., & Nail, P. R. (1998). A new model of interpersonal influence characteristics. *Journal of Social Behavior and Personality, 13,* 715-733.

Lewis, J. J. (1974). A criticism of "The factor structure of source credibility as a function of the speaking situation." *Speech Monographs, 41,* 287-290.

Li, H., & Bukovac, J. L. (1999). Cognitive impact of banner ad characteristics: An experimental study. *Journalism and Mass Communication Quarterly, 76,* 341-353.

Likert, R. (1932). A technique for the measurement of attitudes. *Archives of Psychology, 22*(Whole No. 140), 1-55.

Linder, D. E., Cooper, J., & Jones, E. E. (1967). Decision freedom as a determinant of the role of incentive magnitude in attitude change. *Journal of Personality and Social Psychology, 6,* 245-254.

Linder, D. E., & Worchel, S. (1970). Opinion change as a result of effortfully drawing a counterattitudinal conclusion. *Journal of Experimental Social Psychology, 6,* 432-448.

Linz, D., Fuson, I. A., & Donnerstein, E. (1990). Mitigating the negative effects of sexually violent mass communications through preexposure briefings. *Communication Research, 17,* 641-674.

Liska, J. (1978). Situational and topical variations in credibility criteria. *Communication Monographs, 45,* 85-92.

Lorch, E. P., Palmgreen, P., Donohew, L., Helm, D., Baer, S. A., & Dsilva, M. U. (1994). Program context, sensation seeking, and attention to televised antidrug public service announcements. *Human Communication Research, 20,* 390-412.

Luchok, J. A., & McCroskey, J. C. (1978). The effect of quality of evidence on attitude change and source credibility. *Southern Speech Communication Journal, 43,* 371-383.

Lull, J., & Cappella, J. (1981). Slicing the attitude pie: A new approach to attitude measurement. *Communication Quarterly, 29,* 67-80.

Lund, F. H. (1925). The psychology of belief: A study of its emotional and volitional determinants. *Journal of Abnormal and Social Psychology, 20,* 174-196.

Lupia, A., & McCubbins, M. D. (1998). *The democratic dilemma: Can citizens learn what they need to know?* Cambridge, UK: Cambridge University Press.

Lutz, R. J. (1975a). Changing brand attitudes through modification of cognitive structure. *Journal of Consumer Research, 1*(4), 49-59.

Lutz, R. J. (1975b). First-order and second-order cognitive effects in attitude change. *Communication Research, 2,* 289-299.

Lutz, R. J. (1976). Conceptual and operational issues in the extended Fishbein model. *Advances in Consumer Research, 3,* 469-476.

Lutz, R. J. (1981). A reconceptualization of the functional approach to attitudes. In J. N. Sheth (Ed.), *Research in marketing* (Vol. 5, pp. 165-210). Greenwich, CT: JAI.

Lutz, R. J., MacKenzie, S. B., & Belch, G. E. (1983). Attitude toward the ad as a mediator of advertising effectiveness: Determinants and consequences. *Advances in Consumer Research, 10,* 532-539.

Luzzo, D. A., Hasper, P., Albert, K. A., Bibby, M. A., & Martinelli, E. A., Jr. (1999). Effects of self-efficacy-enhancing interventions on the math/science self-efficacy and career interests, goals, and actions of career undecided college students. *Journal of Consulting Psychology, 46,* 233-243.

Lynam, D. R., Milich, R., Zimmerman, R., Novak, S. P., Logan, T. K., Martin, C., Leukefeld, C., & Clayton, R. (1999). Project DARE: No effects at 10-year follow-up. *Journal of Consulting and Clinical Psychology, 67,* 590-593.

MacKenzie, S. B., Lutz, R. J., & Belch, G. E. (1986). The role of attitude toward the ad as a mediator of advertising effectiveness: A test of competing explanations. *Journal of Marketing Research, 23,* 130-143.

MacKenzie, S. B., & Spreng, R. A. (1992). How does motivation moderate the impact of central and peripheral processing on brand attitudes and intentions? *Journal of Consumer Research, 18,* 519-529.

Mackie, D. M., Gastardo-Conaco, M. C., & Skelly, J. J. (1992). Knowledge of the advocated position and the processing of in-group and out-group persuasive messages. *Personality and Social Psychology Bulletin, 18,* 145-151.

Mackie, D. M., & Queller, S. (2000). The impact of group membership on persuasion: Revisiting "who says what to whom with what effect?" In D. J. Terry & M. A. Hogg (Eds.), *Attitudes, behavior, and social context: The role of norms and group membership* (pp. 135-155). Mahwah, NJ: Lawrence Erlbaum.

Mackie, D. M., Worth, L. T., & Asuncion, A. G. (1990). Processing of persuasive in-group messages. *Journal of Personality and Social Psychology, 58,* 812-822.

MacLachlan, J. (1982). Listener perception of time-compressed spokespersons. *Journal of Advertising Research, 22*(2), 47-51.

Madden, T. J., Ellen, P. S., & Ajzen, I. (1992). A comparison of the theory of planned behavior and the theory of reasoned action. *Personality and Social Psychology Bulletin, 18,* 3-9.

Maddux, J. E., & Rogers, R. W. (1980). Effects of source expertness, physical attractiveness, and supporting arguments on persuasion: A case of brains over beauty. *Journal of Personality and Social Psychology, 39,* 235-244.

Maddux, J. E., & Rogers, R. W. (1983). Protection motivation and self-efficacy: A revised theory of fear appeals and attitude change. *Journal of Experimental Social Psychology, 19,* 469-479.

Mahler, H. I. M., Kulik, J. A., & Hill, M. R. (1993). A preliminary report on the effects of videotape preparations for coronary artery bypass surgery on anxiety and self-efficacy: A simulation and validation with college students. *Basic and Applied Social Psychology, 14,* 437-453.

Maibach, E., & Flora, J. A. (1993). Symbolic modeling and cognitive rehearsal: Using video to promote AIDS prevention self-efficacy. *Communication Research, 20,* 517-545.

Maio, G. R., Bell, D. W., & Esses, V. M. (1996). Ambivalence and persuasion: The processing of messages about immigrant groups. *Journal of Experimental Social Psychology, 32,* 513-536.

Maio, G. R., Esses, V. M., & Bell, D. W. (2000). Examining conflict between components of attitudes: Ambivalence and inconsistency are distinct constructs. *Canadian Journal of Behavioural Science, 32,* 71-83.

Maio, G. R., & Olson, J. M. (1994). Value-attitude-behaviour relations: The moderating role of attitude functions. *British Journal of Social Psychology, 33,* 301-312.

Maio, G. R., & Olson, J. M. (1995). Relations between values, attitudes, and behavioral intentions: The moderating role of attitude function. *Journal of Experimental Social Psychology, 31,* 266-285.

Maio, G. R., & Olson, J. M. (1998). Values as truisms: Evidence and implications. *Journal of Personality and Social Psychology, 74,* 294-311.

Maio, G. R., & Olson, J. M. (2000a). What is a "value-expressive" attitude? In G. R. Maio & J. M. Olson (Eds.), *Why we evaluate: Functions of attitude* (pp. 249-269). Mahwah, NJ: Lawrence Erlbaum.

Maio, G. R., & Olson, J. M. (Eds.). (2000b). *Why we evaluate: Functions of attitude.* Mahwah, NJ: Lawrence Erlbaum.

Mangleburg, T. F., Sirgy, M. J., Grewal, D., Axsom, D., Hatzios, M., Claiborne, C. B., & Bogle, T. (1998). The moderating effect of prior experience in consumers' use of user-image based versus utilitarian cues in brand attitude. *Journal of Business and Psychology, 13,* 101-113.

Manstead, A. S. R. (2000). The role of moral norms in the attitude-behavior relation. In D. J. Terry & M. A. Hogg (Eds.), *Attitudes, behavior, and social context: The role of norms and group membership* (pp. 11-30). Mahwah, NJ: Lawrence Erlbaum.

Manstead, A. S. R., & van der Pligt, J. (1999). One process or two? Quantitative and qualitative distinctions in models of persuasion. *Psychological Inquiry, 10,* 144-149.

Marcus, A. C., Crane, L. A., Kaplan, C. P., Reading, A. E., Savage, E., Gunning, J., Bernstein, G., & Berek, J. S. (1992). Improving adherence to screening follow-up among women with abnormal pap smears: Results from a large clinic-based trial of three intervention strategies. *Medical Care, 30,* 216-230.

Marin, B. V., Marin, G., Perez-Stable, E. J., Otero-Sabogal, R., & Sabogal, F. (1990). Cultural differences in attitudes toward smoking: Developing messages using the theory of reasoned action. *Journal of Applied Social Psychology, 20,* 478-493.

Marin, G., Marin, B. V., Perez-Stable, E. J., Sabogal, F., & Otero-Sabogal, R. (1990). Cultural differences in attitudes and expectancies between Hispanic and non-Hispanic white smokers. *Hispanic Journal of Behavioral Sciences, 12,* 422-436.

Markham, D. (1968). The dimensions of source credibility of television newscasters. *Journal of Communication, 18,* 57-64.

Marquart, J., O'Keefe, G. J., & Gunther, A. C. (1995). Believing in biotech: Farmers' perceptions of the credibility of BGH information sources. *Science Communication, 16,* 388-402.

McCallum, D. B., Hammond, S. L., & Covello, V. T. (1991). Communicating about environmental risks: How the public uses and perceives information sources. *Health Education Quarterly, 18,* 349-361.

McCarty, D. (1981). Changing contraceptive usage intentions: A test of the Fishbein model of intention. *Journal of Applied Social Psychology, 11,* 192-211.

McCarty, D., Morrison, S., & Mills, K. C. (1983). Attitudes, beliefs, and alcohol use: An analysis of relationships. *Journal of Studies on Alcohol, 44,* 328-341.

McCaul, K. D., Glasgow, R. E., & O'Neill, H. K. (1992). The problem of creating habits: Establishing health-protective dental behaviors. *Health Psychology, 11,* 101-110.

McCaul, K. D., Sandgren, A. K., O'Neill, H. K., & Hinsz, V. B. (1993). The value of the theory of planned behavior, perceived control, and self-efficacy expectations for predicting health-protective behaviors. *Basic and Applied Social Psychology, 14,* 231-252.

McConnell, A. R., Niedermeier, K. E., Leibold, J. M., El-Alayli, A. G., Chin, P. P., & Kuiper, N. M. (2000). What if I find it cheaper somewhere else?: Role of prefactual thinking and anticipated regret in consumer behavior. *Psychology and Marketing, 17,* 281-298.

McCroskey, J. C. (1966). Scales for the measurement of ethos. *Speech Monographs, 33,* 65-72.

McCroskey, J. C. (1967). The effects of evidence in persuasive communication. *Western Speech, 31,* 189-199.

McCroskey, J. C. (1969). A summary of experimental research on the effects of evidence in persuasive communication. *Quarterly Journal of Speech, 55,* 169-176.

McCroskey, J. C. (1970). The effects of evidence as an inhibitor of counter-persuasion. *Speech Monographs, 37,* 188-194.

McCroskey, J. C., & Mehrley, R. S. (1969). The effects of disorganization and nonfluency on attitude change and source credibility. *Speech Monographs, 36,* 13-21.

McCroskey, J. C., & Young, T. J. (1981). Ethos and credibility: The construct and its measurement after three decades. *Central States Speech Journal, 32,* 24-34.

McCroskey, J. C., Young, T. J., & Scott, M. D. (1972). The effects of message sidedness and evidence on inoculation against counterpersuasion in small group communication. *Speech Monographs, 39,* 205-212.

McGarry, J., & Hendrick, C. (1974). Communicator credibility and persuasion. *Memory and Cognition, 2,* 82-86.

McGinnies, E. (1973). Initial attitude, source credibility, and involvement as factors in persuasion. *Journal of Experimental Social Psychology, 9,* 285-296.

McGinnies, E., & Ward, C. D. (1980). Better liked than right: Trustworthiness and expertise as factors in credibility. *Personality and Social Psychology Bulletin, 6,* 467-472.

McGuire, W. J. (1961a). The effectiveness of supportive and refutational defenses in immunizing and restoring beliefs against persuasion. *Sociometry, 24,* 184-197.

McGuire, W. J. (1961b). Persistence of the resistance to persuasion induced by various types of prior defenses. *Journal of Abnormal and Social Psychology, 64,* 241-248.

McGuire, W. J. (1964). Inducing resistance to persuasion: Some contemporary approaches. In L. Berkowitz (Ed.), *Advances in experimental social psychology* (Vol. 1, pp. 191-229). New York: Academic Press.

McGuire, W. J. (1969). The nature of attitudes and attitude change. In G. Lindzey & E. Aronson (Eds.), *Handbook of social psychology* (2nd ed., Vol. 3, pp. 136-314). Reading, MA: Addison-Wesley.

McGuire, W. J. (1985). Attitudes and attitude change. In G. Lindzey & E. Aronson (Eds.), *Handbook of social psychology* (3rd ed., Vol. 2, pp. 233-346). New York: Random House.

McGuire, W. J. (1986). The vicissitudes of attitudes and similar representational constructs in twentieth century psychology. *European Journal of Social Psychology, 16,* 89-130.

McGuire, W. J., & Papageorgis, D. (1961). The relative efficacy of various types of prior belief-defense in producing immunity against persuasion. *Journal of Abnormal and Social Psychology, 62,* 327-337.

McGuire, W. J., & Papageorgis, D. (1962). Effectiveness of forewarning in developing resistance to persuasion. *Public Opinion Quarterly, 26,* 24-34.

McLaughlin, M. L. (1975). Recovering the structure of credibility judgments: An alternative to factor analysis. *Speech Monographs, 42,* 221-228.

McMahan, S., Witte, K., & Meyer, J. (1998). The perception of risk messages regarding electromagnetic fields: Extending the extended parallel process model to an unknown risk. *Health Communication, 10,* 247-259.

Melamed, S., Rabinowitz, S., Feiner, M., Weisberg, E., & Ribak, J. (1996). Usefulness of the protection motivation theory in explaining hearing protection device use among male industrial workers. *Health Psychology, 15,* 209-215.

Messaris, P. (1997). *Visual persuasion: The role of images in advertising.* Thousand Oaks, CA: Sage.

Meyers-Levy, J., & Maheswaran, D. (1991). Exploring differences in males' and females' processing strategies. *Journal of Consumer Research, 18,* 63-70.

Meyers-Levy, J., & Sternthal, B. (1991). Gender differences in the use of message cues and judgments. *Journal of Marketing Research, 28,* 84-96.

Miles, E. W., & Leathers, D. G. (1984). The impact of aesthetic and professionally-related objects on credibility in the office setting. *Southern Speech Communication Journal, 49,* 361-379.

Milgram, S., Mann, L., & Harter, S. (1965). The lost-letter technique: A tool of social research. *Public Opinion Quarterly, 29,* 437-438.

Millar, M. G., & Millar, K. U. (1990). Attitude change as a function of attitude type and argument type. *Journal of Personality and Social Psychology, 59,* 217-228.

Millar, M. G., & Millar, K. U. (1996a). The effects of direct and indirect experience on affective and cognitive responses and the attitude-behavior relation. *Journal of Experimental Social Psychology, 32,* 561-579.

Millar, M. G., & Millar, K. U. (1996b). Effects of message anxiety on disease detection and health promotion behaviors. *Basic and Applied Social Psychology, 18,* 61-74.

Millar, M. G., & Millar, K. U. (1998). Effects of prior experience and thought on the attitude-behavior relation. *Social Behavior and Personality, 26,* 105-114.

Miller, D. T., Monin, B., & Prentice, D. A. (2000). Pluralistic ignorance and inconsistency between private attitudes and public behaviors. In D. J. Terry &

M. A. Hogg (Eds.), *Attitudes, behavior, and social context: The role of norms and group membership* (pp. 95-113). Mahwah, NJ: Lawrence Erlbaum.

Miller, G. R., & Baseheart, J. (1969). Source trustworthiness, opinionated statements, and response to persuasive communication. *Speech Monographs, 36,* 1-7.

Miller, G. R., & Burgoon, J. K. (1982). Factors affecting assessments of witness credibility. In N. L. Kerr & R. M. Bray (Eds.), *Psychology of the courtroom* (pp. 169-194). New York: Academic Press.

Miller, G. R., & Hewgill, M. A. (1964). The effect of variations in nonfluency on audience ratings of source credibility. *Quarterly Journal of Speech, 50,* 36-44.

Miller, N., Lee, J., & Carlson, M. (1991). The validity of inferential judgments when used in theory-testing meta-analysis. *Personality and Social Psychology Bulletin, 17,* 335-343.

Miller, N., Maruyama, G., Beaber, R. J., & Valone, K. (1976). Speed of speech and persuasion. *Journal of Personality and Social Psychology, 34,* 615-624.

Miller, N., & Pedersen, W. C. (1999). Assessing process distinctiveness. *Psychological Inquiry, 10,* 150-156.

Miller, R. L., Brickman, P., & Bolen, D. (1975). Attribution versus persuasion as a means for modifying behavior. *Journal of Personality and Social Psychology, 31,* 430-441.

Miller, R. L., Seligman, C., Clark, N. T., & Bush, M. (1976). Perceptual contrast versus reciprocal concession as mediators of induced compliance. *Canadian Journal of Behavioural Science, 8,* 401-409.

Mills, J., & Aronson, E. (1965). Opinion change as a function of the communicator's attractiveness and desire to influence. *Journal of Personality and Social Psychology, 1,* 173-177.

Mills, J., & Harvey, J. (1972). Opinion change as a function of when information about the communicator is received and whether he is attractive or expert. *Journal of Personality and Social Psychology, 21,* 52-55.

Mills, J., & Kimble, C. E. (1973). Opinion change as a function of perceived similarity of the communicator and subjectivity of the issue. *Bulletin of the Psychonomic Society, 2,* 35-36.

Milne, S., Sheeran, P., & Orbell, S. (2000). Prediction and intervention in health-related behavior: A meta-analytic review of protection motivation theory. *Journal of Applied Social Psychology, 30,* 106-143.

Miniard, P. W., & Barone, M. J. (1997). The case for noncognitive determinants of attitude: A critique of Fishbein and Middlestadt. *Journal of Consumer Psychology, 6,* 77-91.

Miniard, P. W., & Cohen, J. B. (1979). Isolating attitudinal and normative influences in behavioral intentions models. *Journal of Marketing Research, 16,* 102-110.

Miniard, P. W., & Cohen, J. B. (1981). An examination of the Fishbein-Ajzen behavioral-intentions model's concepts and measures. *Journal of Experimental Social Psychology, 17,* 309-339.

Miniard, P. W., & Page, T. J., Jr. (1984). Causal relationships in the Fishbein behavioral intention model. *Advances in Consumer Research, 11,* 137-142.

Mishra, S. I., Chavez, L. R., Magana, J. R., Nava, P., Valdez, R. B., & Hubbell, F. A. (1998). Improving breast cancer control among Latinas: Evaluation of a theory-based educational program. *Health Education and Behavior, 25,* 653-670.

Mitchell, A. A. (1986). The effect of verbal and visual components of advertisements on brand attitudes and attitude toward the advertisement. *Journal of Consumer Research, 13,* 12-24.

Mitchell, A. A., & Olson, J. C. (1981). Are product attribute beliefs the only mediator of advertising effects on brand attitude? *Journal of Marketing Research, 18,* 318-332.

Mittal, B. (1990). The relative roles of brand beliefs and attitude toward the ad as mediators of brand attitude: A second look. *Journal of Marketing Research, 27,* 209-219.

Mittal, B., Ratchford, B., & Prabhakar, P. (1990). Functional and expressive attributes as determinants of brand-attitude. In J. N. Sheth (Ed.), *Research in marketing* (Vol. 10, pp. 135-155). Greenwich, CT: JAI.

Mongeau, P. A. (1998). Another look at fear-arousing persuasive appeals. In M. Allen & R. W. Preiss (Eds.), *Persuasion: Advances through meta-analysis* (pp. 53-68). Cresskill, NJ: Hampton.

Moon, Y. (1999). The effects of physical distance and response latency on persuasion in computer-mediated communication and human-computer communication. *Journal of Experimental Psychology: Applied, 5,* 379-392.

Moore, D. J., & Reardon, R. (1987). Source magnification: The role of multiple sources in the processing of advertising appeals. *Journal of Marketing Research, 24,* 412-417.

Moore, E. M., Bearden, W. O., & Teel, J. E. (1985). Use of labeling and assertions of dependency in appeals for consumer support. *Journal of Consumer Research, 12,* 90-96.

Moore, S. M., Barling, N. R., & Hood, B. (1998). Predicting testicular and breast self-examination behaviour: A test of the theory of reasoned action. *Behaviour Change, 15,* 41-49.

Morley, D. D. (1988a). Meta-analytic techniques: When generalizing to message populations is not possible. *Human Communication Research, 15,* 112-126.

Morley, D. D. (1988b). Reply to Jackson, O'Keefe, and Jacobs. *Human Communication Research, 15,* 143-147.

Mowen, J. C., Wiener, J. L., & Joag, S. (1987). An information integration analysis of how trust and expertise combine to influence source credibility and persuasion. *Advances in Consumer Research, 14,* 564.

Mueller, D. J. (1970). Physiological techniques of attitude measurement. In G. F. Summers (Ed.), *Attitude measurement* (pp. 534-552). Chicago: Rand McNally.

Mulaik, S. A., Raju, N. S., & Harshman, R. A. (1997). There is a time and a place for significance testing. In L. L. Harlow, S. A. Mulaik, & J. H. Steiger (Eds.),

What if there were no significance tests? (pp. 65-115). Mahwah, NJ: Lawrence Erlbaum.

Mulilis, J.-P., & Lippa, R. (1990). Behavioral change in earthquake preparedness due to negative threat appeals: A test of protection motivation theory. *Journal of Applied Social Psychology, 20,* 619-638.

Munch, J. M., & Swasy, J. L. (1988). Rhetorical question, summarization frequency, and argument strength effects on recall. *Journal of Consumer Research, 15,* 69-76.

Munn, W. C., & Gruner, C. R. (1981). "Sick" jokes, speaker sex, and informative speech. *Southern Speech Communication Journal, 46,* 411-418.

Myeong, J., & Crawley, F. E. (1993). Predicting and understanding Korean high school students' science-track choice: Testing the theory of reasoned action by structural equation modeling. *Journal of Research in Science Teaching, 30,* 381-400.

Nabi, R. L. (1998). The effect of disgust-eliciting visuals on attitudes toward animal experimentation. *Communication Quarterly, 46,* 472-484.

Nabi, R. L. (1999). A cognitive-functional model for the effects of discrete negative emotions on information processing, attitude change, and recall. *Communication Theory, 9,* 292-320.

Nakanishi, M., & Bettman, J. R. (1974). Attitude models revisited: An individual level analysis. *Journal of Consumer Research, 1*(3), 16-21.

Neimeyer, G. J., Guy, J., & Metzler, A. (1989). Changing attitudes regarding the treatment of disordered eating: An application of the elaboration likelihood model. *Journal of Social and Clinical Psychology, 8,* 70-86.

Neimeyer, G. J., MacNair, R., Metzler, A. E., & Courchaine, K. (1991). Changing personal beliefs: Effects of forewarning, argument quality, prior bias, and personal exploration. *Journal of Social and Clinical Psychology, 10,* 1-20.

Nemeth, C., & Endicott, J. (1976). The midpoint as an anchor: Another look at discrepancy of position and attitude change. *Sociometry, 39,* 11-18.

Netemeyer, R. G., & Burton, S. (1990). Examining the relationships between voting behavior, intention, perceived behavioral control, and expectation. *Journal of Applied Social Psychology, 20,* 661-680.

Ng, J. Y. Y., Tam, S. F., Yew, W. W., & Lam, W. K. (1999). Effects of video modeling on self-efficacy and exercise performance of COPD patients. *Social Behavior and Personality, 27,* 475-486.

Nickerson, R. S. (2000). Null hypothesis significance testing: A review of an old and continuing controversy. *Psychological Methods, 5,* 241-301.

Nimmo, D. (1970). *The political persuaders: The techniques of modern election campaigns.* Englewood Cliffs, NJ: Prentice Hall.

Norman, P., Bennett, P., & Lewis, H. (1998). Understanding binge drinking among young people: An application of the theory of planned behavior. *Health Education Research, 13,* 163-169.

Norman, P., & Smith, L. (1995). The theory of planned behaviour and exercise: An investigation into the role of prior behaviour, behavioural intentions and attitude variability. *European Journal of Social Psychology, 25,* 403-415.

Norman, R. (1975). Affective-cognitive consistency, attitudes, conformity, and behavior. *Journal of Personality and Social Psychology, 32,* 83-91.

Norman, R. (1976). When what is said is important: A comparison of expert and attractive sources. *Journal of Experimental Social Psychology, 12,* 294-300.

Norwich, B., & Duncan, J. (1990). Attitudes, subjective norm, perceived preventive factors, intentions and learning science: Testing a modified theory of reasoned action. *British Journal of Educational Psychology, 60,* 312-321.

Notani, A. S. (1998). Moderators of perceived behavioral control's predictiveness in the theory of planned behavior: A meta-analysis. *Journal of Consumer Psychology, 7,* 247-271.

Nova, C. J. (1990). Persuasive communications and AIDS: The impact of fear arousing communications and coping recommendations on health protective behaviors to prevent the spread of AIDS (Doctoral dissertation, California School of Professional Psychology, 1990). *Dissertation Abstracts International, 51* (1990), 4642B. (University Microfilms No. AAG-9031244)

Ohanian, R. (1990). Construction and validation of a scale to measure celebrity endorsers' perceived expertise, trustworthiness, and attractiveness. *Journal of Advertising, 19*(3), 39-52.

O'Hara, B. S., Netemeyer, R. G., & Burton, S. (1991). An examination of the relative effects of source expertise, trustworthiness, and likability. *Social Behavior and Personality, 19,* 305-314.

O'Keefe, D. J. (1987). The persuasive effects of delaying identification of high- and low-credibility communicators: A meta-analytic review. *Central States Speech Journal, 38,* 63-72.

O'Keefe, D. J. (1991). Extracting dependable generalizations from the persuasion effects literature: Some issues in meta-analytic reviews. *Communication Monographs, 58,* 472-481.

O'Keefe, D. J. (1993a). The persuasive effects of message sidedness variations: A cautionary note concerning Allen's (1991) meta-analysis. *Western Journal of Communication, 57,* 87-97.

O'Keefe, D. J. (1993b). Understanding social influence: Relations between lay and technical perspectives. *Communication Studies, 44,* 228-238.

O'Keefe, D. J. (1997). Standpoint explicitness and persuasive effect: A meta-analytic review of the effects of varying conclusion articulation in persuasive messages. *Argumentation and Advocacy, 34,* 1-12.

O'Keefe, D. J. (1998). Justification explicitness and persuasive effect: A meta-analytic review of the effects of varying support articulation in persuasive messages. *Argumentation and Advocacy, 35,* 61-75.

O'Keefe, D. J. (1999a). How to handle opposing arguments in persuasive messages: A meta-analytic review of the effects of one-sided and two-sided messages. *Communication Yearbook, 22,* 209-249.

O'Keefe, D. J. (1999b). Three reasons for doubting the adequacy of the reciprocal-concessions explanation of door-in-the-face effects. *Communication Studies, 50,* 211-220.

O'Keefe, D. J. (1999c). Variability of persuasive message effects: Meta-analytic evidence and implications. *Document Design, 1,* 87-97.

O'Keefe, D. J. (2000). Guilt and social influence. *Communication Yearbook, 23,* 67-101.

O'Keefe, D. J. (in press). Guilt as a mechanism of persuasion. In J. P. Dillard & M. Pfau (Eds.), *The persuasion handbook: Developments in theory and practice.* Thousand Oaks, CA: Sage.

O'Keefe, D. J., & Figge, M. (1997). A guilt-based explanation of the door-in-the-face influence strategy. *Human Communication Research, 24,* 64-81.

O'Keefe, D. J., & Figge, M. (1999). Guilt and expected guilt in the door-in-the-face technique. *Communication Monographs, 66,* 312-324.

O'Keefe, D. J., & Hale, S. L. (1998). The door-in-the-face influence strategy: A random-effects meta-analytic review. *Communication Yearbook, 21,* 1-33.

O'Keefe, D. J., & Hale, S. L. (2001). An odds-ratio-based meta-analysis of research on the door-in-the-face influence strategy. *Communication Reports, 14,* 31-38.

O'Keefe, D. J., & Jackson, S. (1995). Argument quality and persuasive effects: A review of current approaches. In S. Jackson (Ed.), *Argumentation and values: Proceedings of the ninth Alta conference on argumentation* (pp. 88-92). Annandale, VA: Speech Communication Association.

O'Keefe, D. J., Jackson, S., & Jacobs, S. (1988). Reply to Morley. *Human Communication Research, 15,* 148-151.

O'Keefe, D. J., & Shepherd, G. J. (1982). Interpersonal construct differentiation, attitudinal confidence, and the attitude-behavior relationship. *Central States Speech Journal, 33,* 416-423.

Oliver, R. L., & Bearden, W. O. (1985). Crossover effects in the theory of reasoned action: A moderating influence attempt. *Journal of Consumer Research, 12,* 324-340.

Olson, J. M., & Zanna, M. P. (1979). A new look at selective exposure. *Journal of Experimental Social Psychology, 15,* 1-15.

Omoto, A. M., Snyder, M., & Martino, S. C. (2000). Volunteerism and the life course: Investigating age-related agendas for action. *Basic and Applied Social Psychology, 22,* 181-197. (Erratum notice: *Basic and Applied Social Psychology, 23,* 73)

Orbell, S., Hodgkins, S., & Sheeran, P. (1997). Implementation intentions and the theory of planned behavior. *Personality and Social Psychology Bulletin, 23,* 945-954.

Orbell, S., & Sheeran, P. (2000). Motivational and volitional processes in action initiation: A field study of the role of implementation intentions. *Journal of Applied Social Psychology, 30,* 780-797.

Osgood, C. E., Suci, G. J., & Tannenbaum, P. H. (1957). *The measurement of meaning.* Urbana: University of Illinois Press.

Osgood, C. E., & Tannenbaum, P. H. (1955). The principle of congruity in the prediction of attitude change. *Psychological Review, 62,* 42-55.

Oskamp, S., Harrington, M. J., Edwards, T. C., Sherwood, D. L., Okuda, S. M., & Swanson, D. C. (1991). Factors influencing household recycling behavior. *Environment and Behavior, 23,* 494-519.

Ostermeier, T. H. (1967). Effects of type and frequency of reference upon perceived source credibility and attitude change. *Speech Monographs, 34,* 137-144.

Ouellette, J. A., & Wood, W. (1998). Habit and intention in everyday life: The multiple processes by which past behavior predicts future behavior. *Psychological Bulletin, 124,* 54-74.

Palmgreen, P., Lorch, E. P., Donohew, L., Harrington, N. G., Dsilva, M., & Helm, D. (1995). Reaching at-risk populations in a mass media drug abuse prevention campaign: Sensation seeking as a targeting variable. *Drugs and Society, 8*(3/4), 29-45.

Papageorgis, D. (1968). Warning and persuasion. *Psychological Bulletin, 70,* 271-282.

Papageorgis, D., & McGuire, W. J. (1961). The generality of immunity to persuasion produced by pre-exposure to weakened counterarguments. *Journal of Abnormal and Social Psychology, 62,* 475-481.

Park, C. W., & Mittal, B. (1985). A theory of involvement in consumer behavior: Problems and issues. In J. N. Sheth (Ed.), *Research in consumer behavior* (Vol. 1, pp. 201-231). Greenwich, CT: JAI.

Parker, D., Manstead, A. S. R., & Stradling, S. G. (1995). Extending the theory of planned behaviour: The role of personal norm. *British Journal of Social Psychology, 34,* 127-137.

Parker, D., Manstead, A. S. R., Stradling, S. G., Reason, J. T., & Baxter, J. S. (1992). Intention to commit driving violations: An application of the theory of planned behavior. *Journal of Applied Psychology, 77,* 94-101.

Parker, D., Stradling, S. G., & Manstead, A. S. R. (1996). Modifying beliefs and attitudes to exceeding the speed limit: An intervention study based on the theory of planned behavior. *Journal of Applied Social Psychology, 26,* 1-19.

Patzer, G. L. (1983). Source credibility as a function of communicator physical attractiveness. *Journal of Business Research, 11,* 229-241.

Peak, H. (1955). Attitude and motivation. In M. R. Jones (Ed.), *Nebraska Symposium on Motivation* (Vol. 3, pp. 149-188). Lincoln: University of Nebraska Press.

Pearce, W. B. (1971). The effect of vocal cues on credibility and attitude change. *Western Speech, 35,* 176-184.

Pearce, W. B., & Brommel, B. J. (1972). Vocalic communication in persuasion. *Quarterly Journal of Speech, 58,* 298-306.

Pearce, W. B., & Conklin, F. (1971). Nonverbal vocalic communication and perceptions of a speaker. *Speech Monographs, 38,* 235-241.

Peay, M. Y. (1980). Changes in attitudes and beliefs in two-person interaction situations. *European Journal of Social Psychology, 10,* 367-377.

Pechmann, C. (1990). How do consumer inferences moderate the effectiveness of two-sided messages? *Advances in Consumer Research, 17,* 337-341.

Pechmann, C. (1992). Predicting when two-sided ads will be more effective than one-sided ads: The role of correlational and correspondent inferences. *Journal of Marketing Research, 29,* 441-453.

Perkins, H. W., Meilman, P. W., Leichliter, J. S., Cashin, J. R., & Presley, C. A. (1999). Misperceptions of the norms for the frequency of alcohol and other drug use on college campuses. *Journal of American College Health, 47,* 253-258.

Perloff, R. M. (1993). *The dynamics of persuasion.* Hillsdale, NJ: Lawrence Erlbaum.

Peters, R. G., Covello, V. T., & McCallum, D. B. (1997). The determinants of trust and credibility in environmental risk communication: An empirical study. *Risk Analysis, 17,* 43-54.

Petkova, K. G., Ajzen, I., & Driver, B. L. (1995). Salience of anti-abortion beliefs and commitment to an attitudinal position: On the strength, structure, and predictive validity of anti-abortion attitudes. *Journal of Applied Social Psychology, 25,* 463-483.

Petty, R. E., & Brock, T. C. (1981). Thought disruption and persuasion: Assessing the validity of attitude change experiments. In R. E. Petty, T. M. Ostrom, & T. C. Brock (Eds.), *Cognitive responses in persuasion* (pp. 55-79). Hillsdale, NJ: Lawrence Erlbaum.

Petty, R. E., & Cacioppo, J. T. (1977). Forewarning, cognitive responding, and resistance to persuasion. *Journal of Personality and Social Psychology, 35,* 645-655.

Petty, R. E., & Cacioppo, J. T. (1979a). Effects of forewarning of persuasive intent and involvement on cognitive responses and persuasion. *Personality and Social Psychology Bulletin, 5,* 173-176.

Petty, R. E., & Cacioppo, J. T. (1979b). Issue involvement can increase or decrease persuasion by enhancing message-relevant cognitive responses. *Journal of Personality and Social Psychology, 37,* 1915-1926.

Petty, R. E., & Cacioppo, J. T. (1981). Issue involvement as a moderator of the effects on attitude of advertising content and context. *Advances in Consumer Research, 8,* 20-24.

Petty, R. E., & Cacioppo, J. T. (1983). The role of bodily responses in attitude measurement and change. In J. T. Cacioppo & R. E. Petty (Eds.), *Social psychophysiology: A sourcebook* (pp. 51-101). New York: Guilford.

Petty, R. E., & Cacioppo, J. T. (1984). The effects of involvement on responses to argument quantity and quality: Central and peripheral routes to persuasion. *Journal of Personality and Social Psychology, 46,* 69-81.

Petty, R. E., & Cacioppo, J. T. (1986a). *Communication and persuasion: Central and peripheral routes to attitude change.* New York: Springer-Verlag.

Petty, R. E., & Cacioppo, J. T. (1986b). The elaboration likelihood model of persuasion. In L. Berkowitz (Ed.), *Advances in experimental social psychology* (Vol. 19, pp. 123-205). New York: Academic Press.

Petty, R. E., & Cacioppo, J. T. (1990). Involvement and persuasion: Tradition versus integration. *Psychological Bulletin, 107,* 367-374.

Petty, R. E., Cacioppo, J. T., & Goldman, R. (1981). Personal involvement as a determinant of argument-based persuasion. *Journal of Personality and Social Psychology, 41,* 847-855.

Petty, R. E., Cacioppo, J. T., & Heesacker, M. (1981). Effects of rhetorical questions on persuasion: A cognitive response analysis. *Journal of Personality and Social Psychology, 40,* 432-440.

Petty, R. E., Cacioppo, J. T., Kasmer, J. A., & Haugtvedt, C. P. (1987). A reply to Stiff and Boster. *Communication Monographs, 54,* 257-262.

Petty, R. E., Cacioppo, J. T., & Schumann, D. (1983). Central and peripheral routes to advertising effectiveness: The moderating role of involvement. *Journal of Consumer Research, 10,* 135-146.

Petty, R. E., Haugtvedt, C. P., & Smith, S. M. (1995). Elaboration as a determinant of attitude strength: Creating attitudes that are persistent, resistant, and predictive of behavior. In R. E. Petty & J. A. Krosnick (Eds.), *Attitude strength: Antecedents and consequences* (pp. 93-130). Mahwah, NJ: Lawrence Erlbaum.

Petty, R. E., Kasmer, J. A., Haugtvedt, C. P., & Cacioppo, J. T. (1987). Source and message factors in persuasion: A reply to Stiff's critique of the elaboration likelihood model. *Communication Monographs, 54,* 233-249.

Petty, R. E., & Krosnick, J. A. (Eds.). (1995). *Attitude strength: Antecedents and consequences.* Mahwah, NJ: Lawrence Erlbaum.

Petty, R. E., Schumann, D. W., Richman, S. A., & Strathman, A. J. (1993). Positive mood and persuasion: Different roles for affect under high- and low-elaboration conditions. *Journal of Personality and Social Psychology, 64,* 5-20.

Petty, R. E., & Wegener, D. T. (1998a). Attitude change: Multiple roles for persuasion variables. In D. T. Gilbert, S. T. Fiske, & G. Lindzey (Eds.), *Handbook of social psychology* (4th ed., Vol. 1, pp. 323-390). Boston: McGraw-Hill.

Petty, R. E., & Wegener, D. T. (1998b). Matching versus mismatching attitude functions: Implications for scrutiny of persuasive messages. *Personality and Social Psychology Bulletin, 24,* 227-240.

Petty, R. E., & Wegener, D. T. (1999). The elaboration likelihood model: Current status and controversies. In S. Chaiken & Y. Trope (Eds.), *Dual-process theories in social psychology* (pp. 41-72). New York: Guilford.

Petty, R. E., Wegener, D. T., Fabrigar, L. R., Priester, J. R., & Cacioppo, J. T. (1993). Conceptual and methodological issues in the elaboration likelihood model: A reply to the Michigan State critics. *Communication Theory, 3,* 336-362.

Petty, R. E., Wells, G. L., & Brock, T. C. (1976). Distraction can enhance or reduce yielding to propaganda: Thought disruption versus effort justification. *Journal of Personality and Social Psychology, 34,* 874-884.

Petty, R. E., Wells, G. L., Heesacker, M., Brock, T. C., & Cacioppo, J. T. (1983). The effects of recipient posture on persuasion: A cognitive response analysis. *Personality and Social Psychology Bulletin, 9,* 209-222.

Petty, R. E., Wheeler, S. C., & Bizer, G. Y. (1999). Is there one persuasion process or more? Lumping versus splitting in attitude change theories. *Psychological Inquiry, 10,* 156-163.

Petty, R. E., Wheeler, S. C., & Bizer, G. Y. (2000). Attitude functions and persuasion: An elaboration likelihood approach to matched versus mismatched messages. In G. R. Maio & J. M. Olson (Eds.), *Why we evaluate: Functions of attitudes* (pp. 133-162). Mahwah, NJ: Lawrence Erlbaum.

Pfau, M. (1997). The inoculation model of resistance to influence. In G. A. Barnett & F. J. Boster (Eds.), *Progress in communication sciences: Vol. 13. Advances in persuasion* (pp. 133-171). Greenwich, CT: Ablex.

Pfau, M., & Burgoon, M. (1988). Inoculation in political campaign communication. *Human Communication Research, 15,* 91-111.

Pfau, M., Holbert, R. L., Zubric, S. J., Pasha, N. H., & Lin, W.-K. (2000). Role and influence of communication modality in the process of resistance to persuasion. *Media Psychology, 2,* 1-33.

Pfau, M., Kenski, H. C., Nitz, M., & Sorenson, J. (1990). Efficacy of inoculation strategies in promoting resistance to political attack messages: Application to direct mail. *Communication Monographs, 57,* 25-43.

Pfau, M., Tusing, K. J., Koerner, A. F., Lee, W., Godbold, L. C., Penaloza, L. C., Yang, V. S.-H., & Hong, Y.-H. (1997). Enriching the inoculation construct: The role of critical components in the process of resistance. *Human Communication Research, 24,* 187-215.

Piccolino, E. B. (1966). Depicted threat, realism, and specificity: Variables governing safety poster effectiveness (Doctoral dissertation, Illinois Institute of Technology, 1966). *Dissertation Abstracts, 28,* 4330B-4331B. (University Microfilms No. AAG-684473)

Pieters, R. G. M., & Verplanken, B. (1995). Intention-behaviour consistency: Effects of consideration set size, involvement and need for cognition. *European Journal of Social Psychology, 25,* 531-543.

Plax, T. G., & Rosenfeld, L. B. (1980). Individual differences in the credibility and attitude change relationship. *Journal of Social Psychology, 111,* 79-89.

Plotnikoff, R. C., & Higginbotham, N. (1995). Predicting low-fat diet intentions and behaviors for the prevention of coronary heart disease: An application of protection motivation theory among an Australian population. *Psychology and Health, 10,* 397-408.

Posavac, E. J., Kattapong, K. R., & Dew, D. E., Jr. (1999). Peer-based interventions to influence health-related behaviors and attitudes: A meta-analysis. *Psychological Reports, 85,* 1179-1194.

Povey, R., Conner, M., Sparks, P., James, R., & Shepherd, R. (2000a). Application of the theory of planned behaviour to two dietary behaviours: Roles of perceived control and self-efficacy. *British Journal of Health Psychology, 5,* 121-139.

Povey, R., Conner, M., Sparks, P., James, R., & Shepherd, R. (2000b). The theory of planned behaviour and healthy eating: Examining additive and moderating effects of social influence variables. *Psychology and Health, 14,* 991-1006.

Pratkanis, A. R. (2000). Altercasting as an influence tactic. In D. J. Terry & M. A. Hogg (Eds.), *Attitudes, behavior, and social context: The role of norms and group membership* (pp. 201-226). Mahwah, NJ: Lawrence Erlbaum.

Pratkanis, A. R., Breckler, S. J., & Greenwald, A. G. (Eds.). (1989). *Attitude structure and function*. Hillsdale, NJ: Lawrence Erlbaum.

Pratkanis, A. R., & Greenwald, A. G. (1985). A reliable sleeper effect in persuasion: Implications for opinion change theory and research. In L. F. Alwitt & A. A. Mitchell (Eds.), *Psychological processes and advertising effects* (pp. 157-173). Hillsdale, NJ: Lawrence Erlbaum.

Pratkanis, A. R., & Greenwald, A. G. (1989). A sociocognitive model of attitude structure and function. In L. Berkowitz (Ed.), *Advances in experimental social psychology* (Vol. 22, pp. 245-285). New York: Academic Press.

Pratkanis, A. R., Greenwald, A. G., Leippe, M. R., & Baumgardner, M. H. (1988). In search of reliable persuasion effects: III. The sleeper effect is dead. Long live the sleeper effect. *Journal of Personality and Social Psychology, 54,* 203-218.

Pratkanis, A. R., Greenwald, A. G., Ronis, D. L., Leippe, M. R., & Baumgardner, M. H. (1986). Consumer-product and sociopolitical messages for use in studies of persuasion. *Personality and Social Psychology Bulletin, 12,* 536-538.

Prentice, D. A., & Carlsmith, K. M. (2000). Opinions and personality: On the psychological functions of attitudes and other valued possessions. In G. R. Maio & J. M. Olson (Eds.), *Why we evaluate: Functions of attitudes* (pp. 223-248). Mahwah, NJ: Lawrence Erlbaum.

Priester, J. R., & Fleming, M. A. (1997). Artifact or meaningful theoretical constructs?: Examining evidence for nonbelief- and belief-based attitude change processes. *Journal of Consumer Psychology, 6,* 67-76.

Priester, J. R., & Petty, R. E. (1995). Source attributions and persuasion: Perceived honesty as a determinant of message scrutiny. *Personality and Social Psychology Bulletin, 21,* 637-654.

Priester, J. R., & Petty, R. E. (1996). The gradual threshold model of ambivalence: Relating the positive and negative bases of attitudes to subjective ambivalence. *Journal of Personality and Social Psychology, 71,* 431-449.

Priester, J., Wegener, D., Petty, R., & Fabrigar, L. (1999). Examining the psychological process underlying the sleeper effect: The elaboration likelihood model explanation. *Media Psychology, 1,* 27-48.

Prislin, R. (1987). Attitude-behaviour relationship: Attitude relevance and behaviour relevance. *European Journal of Social Psychology, 17,* 483-485.

Pryor, B., & Steinfatt, T. M. (1978). The effects of initial belief level on inoculation theory and its proposed mechanisms. *Human Communication Research, 4,* 217-230.

Pryor, J. B., Reeder, G. D., Vinacco, R., Jr., & Kott, T. L. (1989). The instrumental and symbolic functions of attitudes toward persons with AIDS. *Journal of Applied Social Psychology, 19,* 377-404.

Puckett, J. M., Petty, R. E., Cacioppo, J. T., & Fischer, D. L. (1983). The relative impact of age and attractiveness stereotypes on persuasion. *Journal of Gerontology, 38,* 340-343.

Raaijmakers, J. G. W., Schrijnemakers, J. M. C., & Gremmen, F. (1999). How to deal with "the language-as-fixed-effect fallacy": Common misconceptions and alternative solutions. *Journal of Memory and Language, 41,* 416-426.

Radecki, C. M., & Jaccard, J. (1999). Signing an organ donation letter: The prediction of behavior from behavioral intentions. *Journal of Applied Social Psychology, 29,* 1833-1853.

Raden, D. (1985). Strength-related attitude dimensions. *Social Psychology Quarterly, 48,* 312-330.

Raghubir, P., & Corfman, K. (1999). When do price promotions affect pretrial brand evaluations? *Journal of Marketing Research, 36,* 211-222.

Randall, D. M., & Wolff, J. A. (1994). The time interval in the intention-behaviour relationship: Meta-analysis. *British Journal of Social Psychology, 33,* 405-418.

Ratneshwar, S., & Chaiken, S. (1986). When is the expert source more persuasive? A heuristic processing analysis. In T. A. Shimp, S. Sharma, G. John, J. A. Quelch, J. H. Lindgren Jr., W. Dillon, M. P. Gardner, & R. F. Dyer (Eds.), *1986 AMA educators' proceedings* (p. 86). Chicago: American Marketing Association.

Reeves, R. A., & Saucer, P. R. (1993). A test of commitment in legitimizing paltry contributions. *Journal of Social Behavior and Personality, 8,* 537-544.

Regan, D. T., & Fazio, R. (1977). On the consistency between attitudes and behavior: Look to the method of attitude formation. *Journal of Experimental Social Psychology, 13,* 28-45.

Reinard, J. C. (1988). The empirical study of the persuasive effects of evidence: The status after fifty years of research. *Human Communication Research, 15,* 3-59.

Reinard, J. C. (1998). The persuasive effects of testimonial assertion evidence. In M. Allen & R. W. Preiss (Eds.), *Persuasion: Advances through meta-analysis* (pp. 69-86). Cresskill, NJ: Hampton.

Reingen, P. H. (1982). Test of a list procedure for inducing compliance with a request to donate money. *Journal of Applied Psychology, 67,* 110-118.

Rhine, R. J. (1967). Some problems in dissonance theory research on information selectivity. *Psychological Bulletin, 68,* 21-28.

Rhine, R. J., & Severance, L. J. (1970). Ego-involvement, discrepancy, source credibility, and attitude change. *Journal of Personality and Social Psychology, 16,* 175-190.

Rhodes, N., & Wood, W. (1992). Self-esteem and intelligence affect influenceability: The mediating role of message reception. *Psychological Bulletin, 111,* 156-171.

Richard, R., de Vries, N. K., & van der Pligt, J. (1998). Anticipated regret and precautionary sexual behavior. *Journal of Applied Social Psychology, 28,* 1411-1428.

Richard, R., van der Pligt, J., & de Vries, N. (1995). Anticipated affective reactions and prevention of AIDS. *British Journal of Social Psychology, 34,* 9-21.

Richard, R., van der Pligt, J., & de Vries, N. (1996a). Anticipated affect and behavioral choice. *Basic and Applied Social Psychology, 18,* 111-129.

Richard, R., van der Pligt, J., & de Vries, N. (1996b). Anticipated regret and time perspective: Changing sexual risk-taking behavior. *Journal of Behavioral Decision Making, 9,* 185-199.

Richter, M. L., & Seay, M. B. (1987). ANOVA designs with subjects and stimuli as random effects: Applications to prototype effects on recognition memory. *Journal of Personality and Social Psychology, 53*, 470-480.

Riddle, P. K. (1980). Attitudes, beliefs, behavioral intentions, and behaviors of women and men toward regular jogging. *Research Quarterly for Exercise and Sport, 51*, 663-674.

Rippetoe, P. A., & Rogers, R. W. (1987). Effects of components of protection-motivation theory on adaptive and maladaptive coping with a health threat. *Journal of Personality and Social Psychology, 52*, 596-604.

Rise, J., Astrom, A. N., & Sutton, S. (1998). Predicting intentions and use of dental floss among adolescents: An application of the theory of planned behaviour. *Psychology and Health, 13*, 223-236.

Rittle, R. H. (1981). Changes in helping behavior: Self- versus situational perceptions as mediators of the foot-in-the-door effect. *Personality and Social Psychology Bulletin, 7*, 431-437.

Roberto, A. J., Meyer, G., Johnson, A. J., & Atkin, C. K. (2000). Using the extended parallel process model to prevent firearm injury and death: Field experiment results of a video-based intervention. *Journal of Communication, 50*(4), 157-175.

Rogers, R. W. (1975). A protection motivation theory of fear appeals and attitude change. *Journal of Psychology, 91*, 93-114.

Rogers, R. W. (1983). Cognitive and physiological processes in fear appeals and attitude change: A revised theory of protection motivation. In J. T. Cacioppo & R. E. Petty (Eds.), *Social psychophysiology: A sourcebook* (pp. 153-176). New York: Guilford.

Rogers, R. W., & Mewborn, C. R. (1976). Fear appeals and attitude change: Effects of a threat's noxiousness, probability of occurrence, and the efficacy of coping responses. *Journal of Personality and Social Psychology, 34*, 54-61.

Rogers, R. W., & Prentice-Dunn, S. (1997). Protection motivation theory. In D. Gochman (Ed.), *Handbook of health behavior research: Vol. 1. Personal and social determinants* (pp. 113-132). New York: Plenum.

Romer, D. (1983). Effects of own attitude on polarization of judgment. *Journal of Personality and Social Psychology, 44*, 273-284.

Romero, A. A., Agnew, C. R., & Insko, C. A. (1996). The cognitive mediation hypothesis revisited: An empirical response to methodological and theoretical criticism. *Personality and Social Psychology Bulletin, 22*, 651-665.

Rook, K. S. (1986). Encouraging preventive behavior for distant and proximal health threats: Effects of vivid versus abstract information. *Journal of Gerontology, 41*, 526-534.

Rosen, S. (1961). Postdecision affinity for incompatible information. *Journal of Abnormal and Social Psychology, 63*, 188-190.

Rosenberg, M. J. (1956). Cognitive structure and attitudinal affect. *Journal of Abnormal and Social Psychology, 53*, 367-372.

Rosenberg, M. J. (1965). When dissonance fails: On eliminating evaluation apprehension from attitude measurement. *Journal of Personality and Social Psychology, 1*, 28-42.

Rosenberg, M. J., & Hovland, C. I. (1960). Cognitive, affective, and behavioral components of attitudes. In C. I. Hovland & M. J. Rosenberg (Eds.), *Attitude organization and change: An analysis of consistency among attitude components* (pp. 1-14). New Haven, CT: Yale University Press.

Rosenthal, R. (1991). *Meta-analytic procedures for social research* (2nd ed.). Newbury Park, CA: Sage.

Roskos-Ewoldsen, D. R. (1997). Attitude accessibility and persuasion: Review and a transactive model. *Communication Yearbook, 20,* 185-225.

Roskos-Ewoldsen, D. R., & Fazio, R. H. (1992). The accessibility of source likability as a determinant of persuasion. *Personality and Social Psychology Bulletin, 18,* 19-25.

Roskos-Ewoldsen, D. R., & Fazio, R. H. (1997). The role of belief accessibility in attitude formation. *Southern Communication Journal, 62,* 107-116.

Rosnow, R. L. (1966). Whatever happened to the "law of primacy"? *Journal of Communication, 16,* 10-31.

Rosnow, R. L., & Robinson, E. J. (1967). Primacy-recency. In R. L. Rosnow & E. J. Robinson (Eds.), *Experiments in persuasion* (pp. 99-104). New York: Academic Press.

Rosselli, F., Skelly, J. J., & Mackie, D. M. (1995). Processing rational and emotional messages: The cognitive and affective mediation of persuasion. *Journal of Experimental Social Psychology, 31,* 163-190.

Ruth, J. A., & Faber, R. J. (1988). Guilt: An overlooked advertising appeal. In J. D. Leckenby (Ed.), *The proceedings of the 1988 conference of the American Academy of Advertising* (pp. 83-89). Austin, TX: American Academy of Advertising.

Rutter, D. R., & Bunce, D. J. (1989). The theory of reasoned action of Fishbein and Ajzen: A test of Towriss's amended procedure for measuring beliefs. *British Journal of Social Psychology, 28,* 39-46.

Ryan, M. J. (1982). Behavioral intention formation: The interdependency of attitudinal and social influence variables. *Journal of Consumer Research, 9,* 263-278.

Ryan, M. J., & Bonfield, E. H. (1975). The Fishbein extended model and consumer behavior. *Journal of Consumer Research, 2,* 118-136.

Sakaki, H. (1980). [Communication discrepancy and ego involvement as determinants of attitude change]. *Journal of the Nihon University College of Industrial Technology, 13,* 1-9.

Sallis, J. F., Elder, J. P., Wildey, M. B., de Moor, C., Young, R. L., Shulkin, J. J., & Helme, J. M. (1990). Assessing skills for refusing cigarettes and smokeless tobacco. *Journal of Behavioral Medicine, 13,* 489-503.

Saltzer, E. B. (1981). Cognitive moderators of the relationship between behavioral intentions and behavior. *Journal of Personality and Social Psychology, 41,* 260-271.

Sampson, E. E., & Insko, C. A. (1964). Cognitive consistency and performance in the autokinetic situation. *Journal of Abnormal and Social Psychology, 68,* 184-192.

Sarnoff, I., & Katz, D. (1954). The motivational bases of attitude change. *Journal of Abnormal and Social Psychology, 49,* 115-124.

Sawyer, A. G., & Howard, D. J. (1991). Effects of omitting conclusions in advertisements to involved and uninvolved audiences. *Journal of Marketing Research, 28,* 467-474.

Schenck-Hamlin, W. J. (1978). The effects of dialectical similarity, stereotyping, and message agreement on interpersonal perceptions. *Human Communication Research, 5,* 15-26.

Scher, S. J., & Cooper, J. (1989). Motivational basis of dissonance: The singular role of behavioral consequences. *Journal of Personality and Social Psychology, 56,* 899-906.

Schlegel, R. P., Crawford, C. A., & Sanborn, M. D. (1977). Correspondence and mediational properties of the Fishbein model: An application to adolescent alcohol use. *Journal of Experimental Social Psychology, 13,* 421-430.

Schliesser, H. F. (1968). Information transmission and ethos of a speaker using normal and defective speech. *Central States Speech Journal, 19,* 169-174.

Schmidt, F. L., & Hunter, J. E. (1997). Eight common but false objections to the discontinuation of significance testing in the analysis of research data. In L. L. Harlow, S. A. Mulaik, & J. H. Steiger (Eds.), *What if there were no significance tests?* (pp. 37-64). Mahwah, NJ: Lawrence Erlbaum.

Schmidt, F. L., & Hunter, J. E. (1999). Comparison of three meta-analysis methods revisited: An analysis of Johnson, Mullen, and Salas (1995). *Journal of Applied Psychology, 84,* 144-148.

Schneider, A. L., Snyder-Joy, Z., & Hopper, M. (1993). Rational and symbolic models of attitudes toward AIDS policy. *Social Science Quarterly, 74,* 349-366.

Schwarz, N. (1997). Moods and attitude judgments: A comment on Fishbein and Middlestadt. *Journal of Consumer Psychology, 6,* 93-98.

Schweitzer, D., & Ginsburg, G. P. (1966). Factors of communicator credibility. In C. W. Backman & P. F. Secord (Eds.), *Problems in social psychology* (pp. 94-102). New York: McGraw-Hill.

Scott, C. A. (1977). Modifying socially-conscious behavior: The foot-in-the-door technique. *Journal of Consumer Research, 4,* 156-164.

Scott, W. A. (1969). Attitude measurement. In G. Lindzey & E. Aronson (Eds.), *Handbook of social psychology* (2nd ed., Vol. 2, pp. 204-273). Reading, MA: Addison-Wesley.

Searle, J. R. (1969). *Speech acts.* Cambridge, UK: Cambridge University Press.

Sears, D. O. (1965). Biased indoctrination and selectivity of exposure to new information. *Sociometry, 28,* 363-376.

Sears, D. O., & Freedman, J. L. (1967). Selective exposure to information: A critical review. *Public Opinion Quarterly, 31,* 194-213.

Seligman, C., Hall, D., & Finegan, J. (1983). Predicting home energy consumption: An application of the Fishbein-Ajzen model. *Advances in Consumer Research, 10,* 647-651.

Sengupta, S. (1996). Understanding less educated smokers' intention to quit smoking: Strategies for antismoking communication aimed at less educated smokers. *Health Communication, 8,* 55-72.

Sereno, K. K., & Hawkins, G. J. (1967). The effects of variations in speakers' nonfluency upon audience ratings of attitude toward the speech topic and speakers' credibility. *Speech Monographs, 34,* 58-64.

Settle, R. B., & Mizerski, R. (1974). Differential response to objective and social information in advertisements. In T. V. Greer (Ed.), *1973 combined proceedings: Increasing marketing productivity and conceptual and methodological foundations of marketing* (pp. 250-255). Chicago: American Marketing Association.

Shavitt, S. (1989). Operationalizing functional theories of attitude. In A. R. Pratkanis, S. J. Breckler, & A. G. Greenwald (Eds.), *Attitude structure and function* (pp. 311-337). Hillsdale, NJ: Lawrence Erlbaum.

Shavitt, S. (1990). The role of attitude objects in attitude functions. *Journal of Experimental Social Psychology, 26,* 124-148.

Shavitt, S., & Fazio, R. H. (1990). Effects of attribute salience on the consistency of product evaluations and purchase predictions. *Advances in Consumer Research, 17,* 91-97.

Shavitt, S., & Lowrey, T. M. (1992). Attitude functions in advertising effectiveness: The interactive role of product type and personality type. *Advances in Consumer Research, 19,* 323-328.

Shavitt, S., & Nelson, M. R. (2000). The social-identity function in person perception: Communicated meanings of product preferences. In G. R. Maio & J. M. Olson (Eds.), *Why we evaluate: Functions of attitudes* (pp. 37-57). Mahwah, NJ: Lawrence Erlbaum.

Sheeran, P., Norman, P., & Orbell, S. (1999). Evidence that intentions based on attitudes better predict behaviour than intentions based on subjective norms. *European Journal of Social Psychology, 29,* 403-406.

Sheeran, P., & Orbell, S. (1998). Do intentions predict condom use? Meta-analysis and examination of six moderator variables. *British Journal of Social Psychology, 37,* 231-250.

Sheeran, P., & Orbell, S. (1999a). Augmenting the theory of planned behavior: Roles for anticipated regret and descriptive norms. *Journal of Applied Social Psychology, 29,* 2107-2142.

Sheeran, P., & Orbell, S. (1999b). Implementation intentions and repeated behaviour: Augmenting the predictive validity of the theory of planned behaviour. *European Journal of Social Psychology, 29,* 349-369.

Sheeran, P., & Orbell, S. (2000a). Self-schemas and the theory of planned behaviour. *European Journal of Social Psychology, 30,* 533-550.

Sheeran, P., & Orbell, S. (2000b). Using implementation intentions to increase attendance for cervical cancer screening. *Health Psychology, 19,* 283-289.

Sheeran, P., Orbell, S., & Trafimow, D. (1999). Does the temporal stability of behavioral intentions moderate intention-behavior and past behavior-future behavior relations? *Personality and Social Psychology Bulletin, 25,* 721-730.

Sheeran, P., & Taylor, S. (1999). Predicting intentions to use condoms: A meta-analysis and comparison of the theories of reasoned action and planned behavior. *Journal of Applied Social Psychology, 29,* 1624-1675.

Shepherd, G. J. (1985). Linking attitudes and behavioral criteria. *Human Communication Research, 12,* 275-284. (Erratum notice: *Human Communication Research, 12,* 358)

Shepherd, G. J. (1987). Individual differences in the relationship between attitudinal and normative determinants of behavioral intent. *Communication Monographs, 54,* 221-231.

Shepherd, G. J., & O'Keefe, B. J. (1984). The relationship between the developmental level of persuasive strategies and their effectiveness. *Central States Speech Journal, 35,* 137-152.

Shepherd, G. J., & O'Keefe, D. J. (1984). Separability of attitudinal and normative influences on behavioral intentions in the Fishbein-Ajzen model. *Journal of Social Psychology, 122,* 287-288.

Sheppard, B. H., Hartwick, J., & Warshaw, P. R. (1988). The theory of reasoned action: A meta-analysis of past research with recommendations for modifications and future research. *Journal of Consumer Research, 15,* 325-343.

Sherif, C. W., Sherif, M., & Nebergall, R. E. (1965). *Attitude and attitude change: The social judgment-involvement approach.* Philadelphia: W. B. Saunders.

Sherif, M., & Hovland, C. I. (1961). *Social judgment: Assimilation and contrast effects in communication and attitude change.* New Haven, CT: Yale University Press.

Sherman, R. T., & Anderson, C. A. (1987). Decreasing premature termination from psychotherapy. *Journal of Social and Clinical Psychology, 5,* 298-312.

Sherman, S. J., & Gorkin, L. (1980). Attitude bolstering when behavior is inconsistent with central attitudes. *Journal of Experimental Social Psychology, 16,* 388-403.

Sheth, J. N., & Talarzyk, W. W. (1972). Perceived instrumentality and value importance as determinants of attitudes. *Journal of Marketing Research, 9,* 6-9.

Shimp, T. A., & Kavas, A. (1984). The theory of reasoned action applied to coupon usage. *Journal of Consumer Research, 11,* 795-809.

Shotland, R. L., Berger, W. G., & Forsythe, R. (1970). A validation of the lost-letter technique. *Public Opinion Quarterly, 34,* 278-281.

Sikkink, D. (1956). An experimental study of the effects on the listener of anti-climax order and authority in an argumentative speech. *Southern Speech Journal, 22,* 73-78.

Silverthorne, C. P., & Mazmanian, L. (1975). The effects of heckling and media of presentation on the impact of a persuasive communication. *Journal of Social Psychology, 96,* 229-236.

Simon, L., Greenberg, J., & Brehm, J. (1995). Trivialization: The forgotten mode of dissonance reduction. *Journal of Personality and Social Psychology, 68,* 247-260.

Simons, H. W. (1976). *Persuasion: Understanding, practice, and analysis.* Reading, MA: Addison-Wesley.

Simons, H. W. (1986). *Persuasion: Understanding, practice, and analysis* (2nd ed.). New York: Random House.

Simons, H. W., Berkowitz, N. N., & Moyer, R. J. (1970). Similarity, credibility, and attitude change: A review and a theory. *Psychological Bulletin, 73,* 1-16.

Simonson, I. (1992). The influence of anticipating regret and responsibility on purchase decisions. *Journal of Consumer Research, 19,* 105-118.

Sjoberg, L. (1982). Attitude-behavior correlation, social desirability, and perceived diagnostic value. *British Journal of Social Psychology, 21,* 283-292.

Slater, M. D. (1991). Use of message stimuli in mass communication experiments: A methodological assessment and discussion. *Journalism Quarterly, 68,* 412-421.

Slater, M. D. (1997). Persuasion processes across receiver goals and message genres. *Communication Theory, 7,* 125-148.

Slater, M. D., & Rouner, D. (1996). How message evaluation and source attributes may influence credibility assessment and belief change. *Journalism and Mass Communication Quarterly, 73,* 974-991.

Smith, A. J., & Clark, R. D., III. (1973). The relationship between attitudes and beliefs. *Journal of Personality and Social Psychology, 26,* 321-326.

Smith, B. L., Brown, B. L., Strong, W. J., & Rencher, A. C. (1975). Effects of speech rate on personality perception. *Language and Speech, 18,* 145-152.

Smith, J. L. (1996). Expectancy, value, and attitudinal semantics. *European Journal of Social Psychology, 26,* 501-506.

Smith, M. B., Bruner, J. B., & White, R. W. (1956). *Opinions and personality.* New York: John Wiley.

Smith, M. J. (1978). Discrepancy and the importance of attitudinal freedom. *Human Communication Research, 4,* 308-314.

Smith, R. E., & Hunt, S. D. (1978). Attributional processes and effects in promotional situations. *Journal of Consumer Research, 5,* 149-158.

Smith, R. E., & Swinyard, W. R. (1983). Attitude-behavior consistency: The impact of product trial versus advertising. *Journal of Marketing Research, 20,* 257-267.

Smith, S. M., Haugtvedt, C. P., & Petty, R. E. (1994). Need for cognition and the effects of repeated expression on attitude accessibility and extremity. *Advances in Consumer Research, 21,* 234-237.

Snyder, M. (1974). Self-monitoring of expressive behavior. *Journal of Personality and Social Psychology, 30,* 526-537.

Snyder, M. (1982). When believing means doing: Creating links between attitudes and behavior. In M. P. Zanna, E. T. Higgins, & C. P. Herman (Eds.), *Consistency in social behavior: The Ontario Symposium, vol. 2* (pp. 105-130). Hillsdale, NJ: Lawrence Erlbaum.

Snyder, M., Clary, E. G., & Stukas, A. A. (2000). The functional approach to volunteerism. In G. R. Maio & J. M. Olson (Eds.), *Why we evaluate: Functions of attitudes* (pp. 365-393). Mahwah, NJ: Lawrence Erlbaum.

Snyder, M., & DeBono, K. G. (1985). Appeals to image and claims about quality: Understanding the psychology of advertising. *Journal of Personality and Social Psychology, 49,* 586-597.

Snyder, M., & DeBono, K. G. (1987). A functional approach to attitudes and persuasion. In M. P. Zanna, J. M. Olson, & C. P. Herman (Eds.), *Social influence: The Ontario Symposium, vol. 5* (pp. 107-125). Hillsdale, NJ: Lawrence Erlbaum.

Snyder, M., & DeBono, K. G. (1989). Understanding the functions of attitudes: Lessons from personality and social behavior. In A. R. Pratkanis, S. J. Breckler, & A. G. Greenwald (Eds.), *Attitude structure and function* (pp. 339-359). Hillsdale, NJ: Lawrence Erlbaum.

Snyder, M., & Gangestad, S. (1986). On the nature of self-monitoring: Matters of assessment, matters of validity. *Journal of Personality and Social Psychology, 51,* 125-139.

Snyder, M., & Kendzierski, D. (1982). Acting on one's attitudes: Procedures for linking attitude and behavior. *Journal of Experimental Social Psychology, 18,* 165-183.

Snyder, M., & Rothbart, M. (1971). Communicator attractiveness and opinion change. *Canadian Journal of Behavioural Science, 3,* 377-387.

Soley, L. C. (1986). Copy length and industrial advertising readership. *Industrial Marketing Management, 15,* 245-251.

Solomon, S., Greenberg, J., Psyczynski, T., & Pryzbylinski, J. (1995). The effects of mortality salience on personally-relevant persuasive appeals. *Social Behavior and Personality, 23,* 177-190.

Sorrentino, R. M., Bobocel, D. R., Gitta, M. Z., Olson, J. M., & Hewitt, E. C. (1988). Uncertainty orientation and persuasion: Individual differences in the effects of personal relevance on social judgments. *Journal of Personality and Social Psychology, 55,* 357-371.

Sparks, J. R., Areni, C. S., & Cox, K. C. (1998). An investigation of the effects of language style and communication modality on persuasion. *Communication Monographs, 65,* 108-125.

Sparks, P., & Guthrie, C. A. (1998). Self-identity and the theory of planned behavior: A useful addition or an unhelpful artifice? *Journal of Applied Social Psychology, 28,* 1393-1410.

Sparks, P., Guthrie, C. A., & Shepherd, R. (1997). The dimensional structure of the perceived behavioral control construct. *Journal of Applied Social Psychology, 27,* 418-438.

Sparks, P., Hedderley, D., & Shepherd, R. (1991). Expectancy-value models of attitude: A note on the relationship between theory and methodology. *European Journal of Social Psychology, 21,* 261-271.

Sparks, P., & Shepherd, R. (1992). Self-identity and the theory of planned behavior: Assessing the role of identification with "green consumerism." *Social Psychology Quarterly, 55,* 388-399.

Sperber, B. M., Fishbein, M., & Ajzen, I. (1980). Predicting and understanding women's occupational orientations: Factors underlying choice intentions. In

I. Ajzen & M. Fishbein (Eds.), *Understanding attitudes and predicting social behavior* (pp. 113-129). Englewood Cliffs, NJ: Prentice Hall.

Sponberg, H. (1946). A study of the relative effectiveness of climax and anticlimax order in an argumentative speech. *Speech Monographs, 13,* 35-44.

Spotts, H. (1994). Evidence of a relationship between need for cognition and chronological age: Implications for persuasion in consumer research. *Advances in Consumer Research, 21,* 238-243.

Stainback, R. D., & Rogers, R. W. (1983). Identifying effective components of alcohol abuse prevention programs: Effects of fear appeals, message style, and source expertise. *International Journal of the Addictions, 18,* 393-405.

Steele, C. M. (1988). The psychology of self-affirmation: Sustaining the integrity of the self. In L. Berkowitz (Ed.), *Advances in experimental social psychology* (Vol. 21, pp. 261-302). San Diego, CA: Academic Press.

Steele, C. M., & Liu, T. J. (1983). Dissonance processes as self-affirmation. *Journal of Personality and Social Psychology, 45,* 5-19.

Steele, C. M., & Spencer, S. J. (1992). The primacy of self-integrity. *Psychological Inquiry, 3,* 345-346.

Steffen, V. J., & Gruber, V. A. (1991). Direct experience with a cancer self-exam: Effects on cognitions and behavior. *Journal of Social Psychology, 13,* 165-177.

Steffen, V. J., Sternberg, L., Teegarden, L. A., & Shepherd, K. (1994). Practice and persuasive frame: Effects on beliefs, intention, and performance of a cancer self-examination. *Journal of Applied Social Psychology, 24,* 897-925.

Steffian, G. (1999). Correction of normative misperceptions: An alcohol abuse prevention program. *Journal of Drug Education, 29,* 115-138.

Steinfatt, T. M. (1974). A criticism of "Dimensions of source credibility: A test for reproducibility." *Speech Monographs, 41,* 291-292.

Steinfatt, T. M. (1977). Measurement, transformations, and the real world: Do the numbers represent the concept? *Et Cetera, 34,* 277-289.

Stephenson, M. T., Palmgreen, P., Hoyle, R. H., Donohew, L., Lorch, E. P., & Colon, S. E. (1999). Short-term effects of an anti-marijuana media campaign targeting high sensation seeking adolescents. *Journal of Applied Communication Research, 27,* 175-195.

Stern, S. E., & Faber, J. E. (1997). The lost e-mail method: Milgram's lost-letter technique in the age of the Internet. *Behavior Research Methods, Instruments, and Computers, 29,* 260-263.

Sternthal, B., Dholakia, R., & Leavitt, C. (1978). The persuasive effect of source credibility: Tests of cognitive response. *Journal of Consumer Research, 4,* 252-260.

Stiff, J. B. (1986). Cognitive processing of persuasive message cues: A meta-analytic review of the effects of supporting information on attitudes. *Communication Monographs, 53,* 75-89.

Stiff, J. B., & Boster, F. J. (1987). Cognitive processing: Additional thoughts and a reply to Petty, Kasmer, Haugtvedt, and Cacioppo. *Communication Monographs, 54,* 250-256.

St. Lawrence, J. S., Brasfield, T. L., Diaz, Y. E., Jefferson, K. W., Reynolds, M. T., & Leonard, M. O. (1994). Three-year follow-up of an HIV risk-reduction intervention that used popular peers. *American Journal of Public Health, 84,* 2027-2028.

Stone, J. (1999). What exactly have I done? The role of self-attribute accessibility in dissonance. In E. Harmon-Jones & J. Mills (Eds.), *Cognitive dissonance: Progress on a pivotal theory in social psychology* (pp. 175-200). Washington, DC: American Psychological Association.

Stone, J., Aronson, E., Crain, A. L., Winslow, M. P., & Fried, C. B. (1994). Inducing hypocrisy as a means of encouraging young adults to use condoms. *Personality and Social Psychology Bulletin, 20,* 116-128.

Stone, J., Wiegand, A. W., Cooper, J., & Aronson, E. (1997). When exemplification fails: Hypocrisy and the motive for self-integrity. *Journal of Personality and Social Psychology, 72,* 54-65.

Stout, P. A., & Sego, T. (1994). Emotions elicited by threat appeals and their impact on persuasion. In K. W. King (Ed.), *Proceedings of the 1994 conference of the American Academy of Advertising* (pp. 8-16). Athens, GA: American Academy of Advertising.

Strader, M. K., & Katz, B. M. (1990). Effects of a persuasive communication on beliefs, attitudes, and career choice. *Journal of Social Psychology, 130,* 141-150.

Strecher, V. J. (1999). Computer-tailored smoking cessation materials: A review and discussion. *Patient Education and Counseling, 36,* 107-117.

Street, R. L., Jr., & Brady, R. M. (1982). Speech rate acceptance ranges as a function of evaluative domain, listener speech rate, and communication context. *Communication Monographs, 49,* 290-308.

Stroebe, W. (1999). The return of the one-track mind. *Psychological Inquiry, 10,* 173-176.

Struckman-Johnson, C. J., Gilliland, R. C., Struckman-Johnson, D. L., & North, T. C. (1990). The effects of fear of AIDS and gender on responses to fear-arousing condom advertisements. *Journal of Applied Social Psychology, 20,* 1396-1410.

Struckman-Johnson, D., & Struckman-Johnson, C. (1996). Can you say condom? It makes a difference in fear-arousing AIDS prevention public service announcements. *Journal of Applied Social Psychology, 26,* 1068-1083.

Stutman, R. K., & Newell, S. E. (1984). Beliefs versus values: Salient beliefs in designing a persuasive message. *Western Journal of Speech Communication, 48,* 362-372.

Sutton, S. R. (1982). Fear-arousing communications: A critical examination of theory and research. In J. R. Eiser (Ed.), *Social psychology and behavioral medicine* (pp. 303-337). New York: John Wiley.

Sutton, S. (1992). Shock tactics and the myth of the inverted U. *British Journal of Addiction, 87,* 517-519.

Sutton, S. (1998). Predicting and explaining intentions and behavior: How well are we doing? *Journal of Applied Social Psychology, 28,* 1317-1338.

Sutton, S. R., & Eiser, J. R. (1984). The effect of fear-arousing communications on cigarette smoking: An expectancy-value approach. *Journal of Behavioral Medicine, 7,* 13-33.

Sutton, S., & Hallett, R. (1988). Understanding the effects of fear-arousing communications: The role of cognitive factors and amount of fear aroused. *Journal of Behavioral Medicine, 11,* 353-360.

Sutton, S., & Hallett, R. (1989). The contribution of fear and cognitive factors in mediating the effects of fear-arousing communications. *Social Behavior, 4,* 83-98.

Sutton, S., McVey, D., & Glanz, A. (1999). A comparative test of the theory of reasoned action and the theory of planned behavior in the prediction of condom use intentions in a national sample of English young people. *Health Psychology, 18,* 72-81.

Swanson, D. L. (1976). Information utility: An alternative perspective in political communication. *Central States Speech Journal, 27,* 95-101.

Swartz, T. A. (1984). Relationship between source expertise and source similarity in an advertising context. *Journal of Advertising, 13*(2), 49-55.

Swasy, J. L., & Munch, J. M. (1985). Examining the target of receiver elaborations: Rhetorical question effects on source processing and persuasion. *Journal of Consumer Research, 11,* 877-886.

Swenson, R. A., Nash, D. L., & Roos, D. C. (1984). Source credibility and perceived expertness of testimony in a simulated child-custody case. *Professional Psychology, 15,* 891-898.

Szabo, E. A., & Pfau, M. (in press). Nuances in inoculation: Theory and application. In J. P. Dillard & M. Pfau (Eds.), *The persuasion handbook: Developments in theory and practice.* Thousand Oaks, CA: Sage.

Szybillo, G. J., & Heslin, R. (1973). Resistance to persuasion: Inoculation theory in a marketing context. *Journal of Marketing Research, 10,* 396-403.

Tamborini, R., & Zillmann, D. (1981). College students' perceptions of lecturers using humor. *Perceptual and Motor Skills, 52,* 427-432.

Tangney, J. P. (1992). Situational determinants of shame and guilt in young adulthood. *Personality and Social Psychology Bulletin, 18,* 199-206.

Tanner, J. F., Jr., Day, E., & Crask, M. R. (1989). Protection motivation theory: An extension of fear appeals theory in communication. *Journal of Business Research, 19,* 267-276.

Taylor, P. M. (1974). An experimental study of humor and ethos. *Southern Speech Communication Journal, 39,* 359-366.

Taylor, S. E., & Thompson, S. C. (1982). Stalking the elusive "vividness" effect. *Psychological Review, 89,* 155-181.

Tedesco, L. A., Keffer, M. A., Davis, E. L., & Christersson, L. A. (1993). Self-efficacy and reasoned action: Predicting oral health status and behaviour at one, three, and six month intervals. *Psychology and Health, 8,* 105-121.

Tedesco, L. A., Keffer, M. A., & Fleck-Kandath, C. (1991). Self-efficacy, reasoned action, and oral health behavior reports: A social cognitive approach to compliance. *Journal of Behavioral Medicine, 14,* 341-355.

Terry, D. J., Galligan, R. F., & Conway, V. J. (1993). The prediction of safe sex behaviour: The role of intentions, attitudes, norms and control beliefs. *Psychology and Health, 8,* 355-368.

Terry, D. J., & Hogg, M. A. (1996). Group norms and the attitude-behavior relationship: A role for group identification. *Personality and Social Psychology Bulletin, 22,* 776-793.

Terry, D. J., Hogg, M. A., & White, K. M. (1999). The theory of planned behaviour: Self-identity, social identity and group norms. *British Journal of Social Psychology, 38,* 225-244.

Terry, D. J., & O'Leary, J. E. (1995). The theory of planned behaviour: The effects of perceived behavioural control and self-efficacy. *British Journal of Social Psychology, 34,* 199-220.

Theodorakis, Y. (1994). Planned behavior, attitude strength, role identity, and the prediction of exercise behavior. *Sport Psychologist, 8,* 149-165.

Thompson, E. P., Kruglanski, A. W., & Spiegel, S. (2000). Attitudes as knowledge structures and persuasion as a specific case of subjective knowledge acquisition. In G. R. Maio & J. M. Olson (Eds.), *Why we evaluate: Functions of attitudes* (pp. 59-95). Mahwah, NJ: Lawrence Erlbaum.

Thompson, M. M., Zanna, M. P., & Griffin, D. W. (1995). Let's not be indifferent about (attitudinal) ambivalence. In R. E. Petty & J. A. Krosnick (Eds.), *Attitude strength: Antecedents and consequences* (pp. 361-386). Mahwah, NJ: Lawrence Erlbaum.

Thomsen, C. J., Borgida, E., & Lavine, H. (1995). The causes and consequences of personal involvement. In R. E. Petty & J. A. Krosnick (Eds.), *Attitude strength: Antecedents and consequences* (pp. 191-214). Mahwah, NJ: Lawrence Erlbaum.

Thornton, B., Kirchner, G., & Jacobs, J. (1991). Influence of a photograph on a charitable appeal: A picture may be worth a thousand words when it has to speak for itself. *Journal of Applied Social Psychology, 21,* 433-445.

Thuen, F., & Rise, J. (1994). Young adolescents' intention to use seat belts: The role of attitudinal and normative beliefs. *Health Education Research, 9,* 215-223.

Thurman, Q. C., St. John, C., & Riggs, L. (1984). Neutralization and tax evasion: How effective would a moral appeal be in improving compliance to tax laws? *Law and Policy, 6,* 309-327.

Thurstone, L. L. (1931). The measurement of social attitudes. *Journal of Abnormal and Social Psychology, 26,* 249-269.

Thurstone, L. L., & Chave, E. J. (1929). *The measurement of attitude.* Chicago: University of Chicago Press.

Trafimow, D. (1998). Attitudinal and normative processes in health behavior. *Psychology and Health, 13,* 307-317.

Trafimow, D. (2000). A theory of attitudes, subjective norms, and private versus collective self-concepts. In D. J. Terry & M. A. Hogg (Eds.), *Attitudes, behavior, and social context: The role of norms and group membership* (pp. 47-65). Mahwah, NJ: Lawrence Erlbaum.

Trafimow, D., & Duran, A. (1998). Some tests of the distinction between attitude and perceived behavioural control. *British Journal of Social Psychology, 37*, 1-14.

Trafimow, D., & Finlay, K. A. (1996). The importance of subjective norms for a minority of people: Between-subject and within-subject analyses. *Personality and Social Psychology Bulletin, 22*, 820-828.

Trafimow, D., & Fishbein, M. (1994a). The importance of risk in determining the extent to which attitudes affect intentions to wear seat belts. *Journal of Applied Social Psychology, 24*, 1-11.

Trafimow, D., & Fishbein, M. (1994b). The moderating effect of behavior type on the subjective norm-behavior relationship. *Journal of Social Psychology, 134*, 755-763.

Trafimow, D., & Sheeran, P. (1998). Some tests of the distinction between cognitive and affective beliefs. *Journal of Experimental Social Psychology, 34*, 378-397.

Triandis, H. C. (1980). Values, attitudes, and interpersonal behavior. In M. M. Page (Ed.), *Nebraska Symposium on Motivation 1979: Beliefs, attitudes, and values* (pp. 195-259). Lincoln: University of Nebraska Press.

Trumbo, C. W. (1999). Heuristic-systematic information processing and risk judgment. *Risk Analysis, 19*, 391-400.

Tucker, R. K. (1971). On the McCroskey scales for the measurement of ethos. *Central States Speech Journal, 22*, 127-129.

Tufte, E. R. (1997). *Visual explanations: Images and quantities, evidence and narrative.* Cheshire, CT: Graphics Press.

Tuppen, C. J. S. (1974). Dimensions of communicator credibility: An oblique solution. *Speech Monographs, 41*, 253-260.

Turner, G. E., Burciaga, C., Sussman, S., Klein-Selski, E., Craig, S., Dent, C. W., Mason, H. R. C., Burton, D., & Flay, B. (1993). Which lesson components mediate refusal assertion skill improvement in school-based adolescent tobacco use prevention? *International Journal of the Addictions, 28*, 749-766.

Tusing, K. J., & Dillard, J. P. (2000). The psychological reality of the door-in-the-face: It's helping, not bargaining. *Journal of Language and Social Psychology, 19*, 5-25.

Valiquette, C. A. M., Valois, P., Desharnais, R., & Godin, G. (1988). An item-analytic investigation of the Fishbein and Ajzen multiplicative scale: The problem of a simultaneous negative evaluation of belief and outcome. *Psychological Reports, 63*, 723-728.

Valois, P., Desharnais, R., Godin, G., Perron, J., & LeComte, C. (1993). Psychometric properties of a perceived behavioral control multiplicative scale developed according to Ajzen's theory of planned behavior. *Psychological Reports, 72*, 1079-1083.

Valois, P., & Godin, G. (1991). The importance of selecting appropriate adjective pairs for measuring attitude based on the semantic differential method. *Quality and Quantity, 25*, 57-68.

van der Pligt, J., & de Vries, N. K. (1998a). Belief importance in expectancy-value models of attitudes. *Journal of Applied Social Psychology, 28*, 1339-1354.

van der Pligt, J., & de Vries, N. K. (1998b). Expectancy-value models of health behaviour: The role of salience and anticipated affect. *Psychology and Health, 13,* 289-305.

van der Pligt, J., de Vries, N. K., Manstead, A. S. R., & van Harreveld, F. (2000). The importance of being selective: Weighing the role of attribute importance in attitudinal judgment. In M. P. Zanna (Ed.), *Advances in experimental social psychology* (Vol. 32, pp. 135-200). San Diego, CA: Academic Press.

van der Pligt, J., & Eiser, J. R. (1984). Dimensional salience, judgment, and attitudes. In J. R. Eiser (Ed.), *Attitudinal judgment* (pp. 161-177). New York: Springer-Verlag.

van Harreveld, F., van der Pligt, J., & de Vries, N. K. (1999). Attitudes towards smoking and the subjective importance of attributes: Implications for changing risk-benefit ratios. *Swiss Journal of Psychology, 58,* 65-72.

Venkatraman, M. P., Marlino, D., Kardes, F. R., & Sklar, K. B. (1990). The interactive effects of message appeals and individual differences on information processing and persuasion. *Psychology and Marketing, 7,* 85-96.

Verplanken, B. (1991). Persuasive communication of risk information: A test of cue versus message processing effects in a field experiment. *Personality and Social Psychology Bulletin, 17,* 188-193.

Verplanken, B., Hofstee, G., & Janssen, H. J. W. (1998). Accessibility of affective versus cognitive components of attitudes. *European Journal of Social Psychology, 28,* 23-35.

Wachtler, J., & Counselman, E. (1981). When increased liking for a communicator decreases opinion change: An attribution analysis of attractiveness. *Journal of Experimental Social Psychology, 17,* 386-395.

Wagner, W. (1984). Social comparison of opinions: Similarity, ability, and the value-fact distinction. *Journal of Psychology, 117,* 197-202.

Wall, A.-M., Hinson, R. E., & McKee, S. A. (1998). Alcohol outcome expectancies, attitudes toward drinking and the theory of planned behavior. *Journal of Studies on Alcohol, 59,* 409-419.

Walster, E. (1964). The temporal sequence of post-decision processes. In L. Festinger (Ed.), *Conflict, decision, and dissonance* (pp. 112-127). Stanford, CA: Stanford University Press.

Walster, E., Aronson, E., & Abrahams, D. (1966). On increasing the persuasiveness of a low prestige communicator. *Journal of Experimental Social Psychology, 2,* 325-342.

Warburton, J., & Terry, D. J. (2000). Volunteer decision making by older people: A test of a revised theory of planned behavior. *Basic and Applied Social Psychology, 22,* 245-258.

Ward, C. D., & McGinnies, E. (1973). Perception of communicator's credibility as a function of when he is identified. *Psychological Record, 23,* 561-562.

Ward, C. D., & McGinnies, E. (1974). Persuasive effects of early and late mention of credible and noncredible sources. *Journal of Psychology, 86,* 17-23.

Warren, I. D. (1969). The effect of credibility in sources of testimony on audience attitudes toward speaker and message. *Speech Monographs, 36,* 456-458.

Warshaw, P. R. (1980). A new model for predicting behavioral intentions: An alternative to Fishbein. *Journal of Marketing Research, 17,* 153-172.

Wartella, E. (1996). The history reconsidered. In E. E. Dennis & E. Wartella (Eds.), *American communication research: The remembered history* (pp. 169-180). Mahwah, NJ: Lawrence Erlbaum.

Wartella, E., & Reeves, B. (1985). Historical trends in research on children and the media: 1900-1960. *Journal of Communication, 35*(2), 118-133.

Wechsler, H., & Kuo, M. (2000). College students define binge drinking and estimate its prevalence: Results of a national survey. *Journal of American College Health, 49,* 57-64.

Weeks, K., Levy, S. R., Zhu, C., Perhats, C., Handler, A., & Flay, B. R. (1995). Impact of a school-based AIDS prevention program on young adolescents' self-efficacy skills. *Health Education Research, 10,* 329-344.

Wegener, D. T., & Claypool, H. M. (1999). The elaboration continuum by any other name does not smell as sweet. *Psychological Inquiry, 10,* 176-181.

Weigel, R. H., & Newman, L. S. (1976). Increasing attitude-behavior correspondence by broadening the scope of the behavioral measure. *Journal of Personality and Social Psychology, 33,* 793-802.

Weinberger, M. G., & Dillon, W. R. (1980). The effects of unfavorable product rating information. *Advances in Consumer Research, 7,* 528-532.

Weinstein, N. D. (2000). Perceived probability, perceived severity, and health-protective behavior. *Health Psychology, 19,* 65-74.

Weisse, C. S., Turbiasz, A. A., & Whitney, D. J. (1995). Behavioral training and AIDS risk reduction: Overcoming barriers to condom use. *AIDS Education and Prevention, 7,* 50-59.

Wells, G. L., & Windschitl, P. D. (1999). Stimulus sampling and social psychological experimentation. *Personality and Social Psychology Bulletin, 25,* 1115-1125.

Wells, W. D. (Ed.). (1997). *Measuring advertising effectiveness.* Mahwah, NJ: Lawrence Erlbaum.

Werch, C. E., Pappas, D. M., Carlson, J. M., DiClemente, C. C., Chally, P. S., & Sinder, J. A. (2000). Results of a social norm intervention to prevent binge drinking among first-year residential college students. *Journal of American College Health, 49,* 85-92.

West, M. D. (1994). Validating a scale for the measurement of credibility: A covariance structure modeling approach. *Journalism Quarterly, 71,* 159-168.

Wheeless, L. R. (1971). Some effects of time-compressed speech on persuasion. *Journal of Broadcasting, 15,* 415-420.

White, G. L., & Gerard, H. B. (1981). Postdecision evaluation of choice alternatives as a function of valence of alternatives, choice, and expected delay of choice consequences. *Journal of Research in Personality, 15,* 371-382.

White, K. M., Terry, D. J., & Hogg, M. A. (1994). Safer sex behavior: The role of attitudes, norms, and control factors. *Journal of Applied Social Psychology, 24,* 2164-2192.

Whitehead, J. L., Jr. (1968). Factors of source credibility. *Quarterly Journal of Speech, 54,* 59-63.

Whitehead, J. L., Jr. (1971). Effects of authority-based assertion on attitude and credibility. *Speech Monographs, 38,* 311-315.

Whittaker, J. O. (1963). Opinion change as a function of communication-attitude discrepancy. *Psychological Reports, 13,* 763-772.

Whittaker, J. O. (1965). Attitude change and communication-attitude discrepancy. *Journal of Social Psychology, 65,* 141-147.

Whittaker, J. O. (1967). Resolution of the communication discrepancy issue in attitude change. In C. W. Sherif & M. Sherif (Eds.), *Attitude, ego-involvement, and change* (pp. 159-177). New York: John Wiley.

Wicker, A. W. (1969). Attitudes versus actions: The relationship of verbal and overt behavioral responses to attitude objects. *Journal of Social Issues, 25*(4), 41-78.

Wicklund, R. A., & Brehm, J. W. (1976). *Perspectives on cognitive dissonance.* Hillsdale, NJ: Lawrence Erlbaum.

Widgery, R. N. (1974). Sex of receiver and physical attractiveness of source as determinants of initial credibility perception. *Western Speech, 38,* 13-17.

Widgery, R. N., & Ruch, R. S. (1981). Beauty and the Machiavellian. *Communication Quarterly, 29,* 297-301.

Wiener, J. L., & Mowen, J. C. (1986). Source credibility: On the independent effects of trust and expertise. *Advances in Consumer Research, 13,* 306-310.

Wilson, E. J., & Sherrell, D. L. (1993). Source effects in communication and persuasion research: A meta-analysis of effect size. *Journal of the Academy of Marketing Science, 21,* 101-112.

Wilson, T. D., Dunn, D. S., Bybee, J. A., Hyman, D. B., & Rotondo, J. A. (1984). Effects of analyzing reasons on attitude-behavior consistency. *Journal of Personality and Social Psychology, 47,* 5-16.

Wilson, T. D., Houston, C. E., & Meyers, J. M. (1998). Choose your poison: Effects of lay beliefs about mental processes on attitude change. *Social Cognition, 16,* 114-132.

Witte, K. (1992). Putting the fear back into fear appeals: The extended parallel process model. *Communication Monographs, 59,* 329-349.

Witte, K. (1994). Fear control and danger control: A test of the extended parallel process model (EPPM). *Communication Monographs, 61,* 113-134.

Witte, K. (1998). Fear as motivator, fear as inhibitor: Using the extended parallel process model to explain fear appeal successes and failures. In P. A. Andersen & L. K. Guerrero (Eds.), *Handbook of communication and emotion: Research, theory, applications, and contexts* (pp. 423-450). San Diego, CA: Academic Press.

Witte, K., & Allen, M. (2000). A meta-analysis of fear appeals: Implications for effective public health campaigns. *Health Education and Behavior, 27,* 591-615.

Witte, K., Berkowitz, J. M., Cameron, K. A., & McKeon, J. K. (1998). Preventing the spread of genital warts: Using fear appeals to promote self-protective behaviors. *Health Education and Behavior, 25,* 571-585.

Witte, K., Givens, V. K., Peterson, T. R., Todd, J. D., Vallabhan, S., Becktold, M. G., Stephenson, M. T., Hyde, M. K., Plugge, C. D., & Jarrett, R. (1993). Preventing tractor-related injuries and deaths in rural populations: Using a persuasive health message framework in formative evaluation research. *International Quarterly of Community Health Education, 13,* 219-251.

Witte, K., & Morrison, K. (1995). Using scare tactics to promote safer sex among juvenile detention and high school youth. *Journal of Applied Communication Research, 23,* 128-142.

Wittenbraker, J., Gibbs, B. L., & Kahle, L. R. (1983). Seat belt attitudes, habits, and behaviors: An adaptive amendment to the Fishbein model. *Journal of Applied Social Psychology, 13,* 406-421.

Woo, T. O., & Castore, C. H. (1980). Expectancy-value and selective exposure as determinants of attitudes toward a nuclear power plant. *Journal of Applied Social Psychology, 10,* 224-234.

Wood, W. (1982). Retrieval of attitude-relevant information from memory: Effects on susceptibility to persuasion and on intrinsic motivation. *Journal of Personality and Social Psychology, 42,* 798-810.

Wood, W., & Eagly, A. H. (1981). Stages in the analysis of persuasive messages: The role of causal attributions and message comprehension. *Journal of Personality and Social Psychology, 40,* 246-259.

Wood, W., & Kallgren, C. A. (1988). Communicator attributes and persuasion: Recipients' access to attitude-relevant information in memory. *Personality and Social Psychology Bulletin, 14,* 172-182.

Wood, W., Kallgren, C. A., & Preisler, R. M. (1985). Access to attitude-relevant information in memory as a determinant of persuasion: The role of message attributes. *Journal of Experimental Social Psychology, 21,* 73-85.

Wood, W., Rhodes, N., & Biek, M. (1995). Working knowledge and attitude strength: An information-processing analysis. In R. E. Petty & J. A. Krosnick (Eds.), *Attitude strength: Antecedents and consequences* (pp. 283-313). Mahwah, NJ: Lawrence Erlbaum.

Woodall, W. G., & Burgoon, J. K. (1983). Talking fast and changing attitudes: A critique and clarification. *Journal of Nonverbal Behavior, 8,* 126-142.

Woodmansee, J. J. (1970). The pupil response as a measure of social attitudes. In G. F. Summers (Ed.), *Attitude measurement* (pp. 514-533). Chicago: Rand McNally.

Woodside, A. G., & Davenport, J. W., Jr. (1974). The effect of salesman similarity and expertise on consumer purchasing behavior. *Journal of Marketing Research, 11,* 198-202.

Worchel, S., Andreoli, V., & Eason, J. (1975). Is the medium the message? A study of the effects of media, communicator, and message characteristics on attitude change. *Journal of Applied Social Psychology, 5,* 157-172.

Worth, L. T., & Mackie, D. M. (1987). Cognitive mediation of positive affect in persuasion. *Social Cognition, 5,* 76-94.

Wyer, R. S., Jr. (1974). *Cognitive organization and change: An information processing approach.* Potomac, MD: Lawrence Erlbaum.

Wyman, M., & Snyder, M. (1997). Attitudes toward "gays in the military": A functional perspective. *Journal of Applied Social Psychology, 27,* 306-329.

Wynn, S. R., Schulenberg, J., Maggs, J. L., & Zucker, R. A. (2000). Preventing alcohol misuse: The impact of refusal skills and norms. *Psychology of Addictive Behaviors, 14,* 36-47.

Ybarra, O., & Trafimow, D. (1998). How priming the private self or collective self affects the relative weights of attitudes and subjective norms. *Personality and Social Psychology Bulletin, 24,* 362-370.

Yoon, C. (1997). Age differences in consumers' processing strategies: An investigation of moderating influences. *Journal of Consumer Research, 24,* 329-342.

Yzer, M. C., Fisher, J. D., Bakker, A. B., Siero, F. W., & Misovich, S. J. (1998). The effects of information about AIDS risk and self-efficacy on women's intentions to engage in AIDS preventive behavior. *Journal of Applied Social Psychology, 28,* 1837-1852.

Zaichkowsky, J. L. (1985). Measuring the involvement construct. *Journal of Consumer Research, 12,* 341-352.

Zanna, M. P., & Cooper, J. (1974). Dissonance and the pill: An attribution approach to studying the arousal properties of dissonance. *Journal of Personality and Social Psychology, 29,* 703-709.

Zanna, M. P., & Cooper, J. (1976). Dissonance and the attribution process. In J. H. Harvey, W. J. Ickes, & R. F. Kidd (Eds.), *New directions in attribution research* (Vol. 1, pp. 199-217). Hillsdale, NJ: Lawrence Erlbaum.

Zanna, M. P., Fazio, R. H., & Ross, M. (1994). The persistence of persuasion. In R. C. Shank & E. Langer (Eds.), *Beliefs, reasoning, and decision making: Psychologic in honor of Bob Abelson* (pp. 347-362). Hillsdale, NJ: Lawrence Erlbaum.

Zanna, M. P., & Rempel, J. K. (1988). Attitudes: A new look at an old concept. In D. Bar-Tal & A. W. Kruglanski (Eds.), *The social psychology of knowledge* (pp. 315-334). Cambridge, UK: Cambridge University Press.

Zhang, Y., & Gelb, B. D. (1996). Matching advertising appeals to culture: The influence of products' use conditions. *Journal of Advertising, 25*(3), 29-46.

Zillmann, D., & Brosius, H.-B. (2000). *Exemplification in communication: The influence of case reports on the perception of issues.* Mahwah, NJ: Lawrence Erlbaum.

Zimbardo, P. G., Weisenberg, M., Firestone, I., & Levy, B. (1965). Communicator effectiveness in producing public conformity and private attitude change. *Journal of Personality, 33,* 233-255.

Zuckerman, M. (1979). *Sensation seeking: Beyond the optimal level of arousal.* Hillsdale, NJ: Lawrence Erlbaum.

Zuckerman, M., Gioioso, C., & Tellini, S. (1988). Control orientation, self-monitoring, and preference for image versus quality approach to advertising. *Journal of Research in Personality, 22,* 89-100.

Zuckerman, M., & Reis, H. T. (1978). Comparison of three models for predicting altruistic behavior. *Journal of Personality and Social Psychology, 36,* 498-510.

Zuwerink, J. R., & Devine, P. G. (1996). Attitude importance and resistance to persuasion: It's not just the thought that counts. *Journal of Personality and Social Psychology, 70,* 931-944.

Author Index

Subject Index

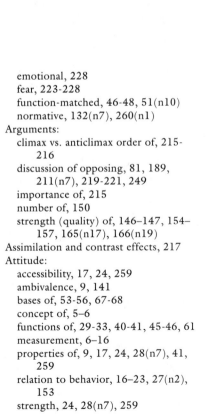

Perceived behavioral control (PBC),
113-115, 116-121, 219
assessment of, 114, 133(n12)
conceptualization of, 113, 119–121,
134(n17)
determinants of, 114–115, 116–117,
133(n14)
influencing, 117–119, 134(n16)
Peripheral cues, 148-150
Peripheral route, 139
Persistence of persuasion, 153, 257–260
Personal (moral) norms, 109, 125-126,
135(n21)
Personal relevance of topic, 141–142,
154, 192, 223, 259
Personality characteristics:
intelligence, 162(n6), 217, 244
need for cognition, 142-143, 154,
162(n5, n6), 258
persuasibility, 28(n8), 241-242
self-esteem, 243
self-monitoring, 17, 34–35, 49(n2),
51(n8), 106, 132(n7), 244,
260(n1)
sensation seeking, 245
Persuasibility:
general, 28(n8), 241–242
sex differences in, 242–243
Persuasion, concept of, 1–5
Persuasive effects:
assessing, 23–26
expected vs. observed, 25–26, 28(n8)
Physical attractiveness, 152, 153, 205–
207
Physiological attitude measures, 13
Planned behavior, theory of (TPB), 113-
127
Planning of behavior, 129
Political campaigns, 258, 263(n18)
Position advocated:
ambiguity in, 218
counterattitudinal vs. proattitudinal,
146, 194, 217, 220, 223,
262(n13)
discrepancy of, 221-223
expected vs. unexpected, 187-190,
210(n5), 221
influence on credibility, 187–190
influence on elaboration valence, 146
Postdecisional spreading of alternatives,
82
Primacy vs. recency effects, 253–254

Prior knowledge, 144-145, 163(n9)
Product trial, 19
Protection motivation theory (PMT),
226–228

Quality (strength) of arguments, 146–
147, 154–157, 165(n17), 166(n19)
Quantity of arguments, 150

Ranking procedure attitude measures, 9
Reasoned action, theory of (TRA), 101-
113
Receiver, 241-253
age, 245
cultural background, 245
familiarity with topic, 220, 253
intelligence, 162(n6), 217, 244
involvement, 142, 162(n4), 212(n14)
knowledge about topic, 144-145,
163(n9)
mood, 141, 147
need for cognition, 142-143, 154,
162(n5, n6), 258
persuasibility, 28(n8), 241-242
self-efficacy, 113-115, 116-121, 219
self-esteem, 243
self-identity, 124-125, 126
self-monitoring, 17, 34–35, 49(n2),
51(n8), 106, 132(n7), 244,
260(n1)
sensation seeking, 245
sex, 242-243
Recency vs. primacy effects, 253-254
Reciprocal concessions, 233
Recommendation specificity, 218–219
Refusal skills training, 251-253
Refutational inoculation treatments, 248
Regret:
anticipated, 22, 122, 123
postdecisional, 83–84
Relevance:
of attitude to behavior, 19–21
of topic to receiver, 141–142, 154,
192, 223, 259
Reporting bias, 183
Resistance to persuasion:
dispositional, 28(n8), 241–242
from different persuasion routes, 153,
258–259
from inoculation, 246–250

About the Author

D aniel J. O'Keefe is Professor in the Department of Speech Communication at the University of Illinois at Urbana-Champaign. He received his Ph.D. from the University of Illinois and has taught at the University of Michigan and Pennsylvania State University. He has received the National Communication Association's Charles Woolbert Research Award and its Golden Anniversary Monograph Award, the American Forensic Association's Outstanding Monograph Award, the International Communication Association's Division 1 John E. Hunter Meta-Analysis Award, the International Society for the Study of Argumentation's Distinguished Scholar Award, and teaching awards from the Central States Communication Association and the University of Illinois.